Stephan,
Thank you for being a part
of my book.

WELCOME TO CULINARY SCHOOL

A CULINARY STUDENT SURVIVAL GUIDE

Daniel Traster, CCC, CCE, CCP

Daniel Traster

Prentice Hall
Upper Saddle River, New Jersey 07458

Library of Congress Cataloging-in-Publication Data

Traster, Daniel
    Welcome to culinary school : a culinary student survival guide/Daniel Traster.—1st ed.
    p. cm.
    Includes bibliographical references and index.
    ISBN-13: 978-0-13-135206-3 (alk. paper)
    ISBN-10: 0-13-135206-7 (alk. paper)
    1. Food service—Vocational guidance.   2. Cooks—Vocational guidance.   3. Cookery—Vocational
guidance.   I. Title.
    TX911.3.V62T73 2010
    647.95'023—dc22

                                                                                            2008050351

Editor in Chief: Vernon R. Anthony
Aquisitions Editor: William Lawrensen
Editorial Assistant: Lara Dimmick
Developmental Editor: Dan Trudden
Project Manager: Renata Butera
Production Coordination: Sadagoban Balaji
Art Director: Jayne Conte

Cover Designer: Bruce Kenselaar
Cover Image: Chad Schaffer/Photodisc/Getty Images, Inc.
Operations Specialist: Deidra Schwartz
Director of Marketing: David Gesell
Campaign Marketing Manager: Leigh Ann Sims
Curriculum Marketing Manager: Thomas Hayward
Marketing Assistant: Les Roberts

This book was set in 10/12 Minion by Integra. It was printed and bound by STP Command Web. The cover was printed by STP Command Web.

Pearson Prentice Hall™ is a trademark of Pearson Education, Inc.
Pearson® is a registered trademark of Pearson plc
Prentice Hall® is a registered trademark of Pearson Education, Inc.

Pearson Education Ltd., London
Pearson Education Singapore, Pte. Ltd.
Pearson Education Canada, Inc.
Pearson Education—Japan
Pearson Education Australia PTY, Limited

Pearson Education North Asia Ltd., Hong Kong
Pearson Educación de Mexico, S.A. de C.V.
Pearson Education Malaysia, Pte. Ltd.
Pearson Education Upper Saddle River,
    New Jersey

Prentice Hall
is an imprint of

www.pearsonhighered.com

10 9 8 7 6 5 4 3 2 1
ISBN 13: 978-0-13-135206-3
ISBN 10:   0-13-135206-7

BRIEF CONTENTS

CONTENTS

PREFACE

HOW TO USE THIS BOOK

Fifty years ago a chef could count on one hand the number of culinary schools training professional chefs in the United States. Today, there are literally hundreds of schools churning out thousands of qualified culinary workers each year. Despite growth in the culinary field, there is simply too much competition for every graduating culinary school student to become an executive chef or culinary celebrity. Moving to the top of the industry today requires far more than just going through the motions to graduate from culinary school.

Foodservice companies today need lots of lower-level employees but far fewer managers, so only the cream of the crop progress easily up the career ladder. To set oneself apart from the sea of graduates entering the workforce each year, a culinary student needs to excel in learning, to possess a substantial quantity of culinary volunteer or work experience, and to pursue ongoing professional development even after graduation. Constant devotion to learning and to self-improvement along with an ever-expanding network of professional contacts can propel a culinary school graduate forward in his career in ways that possession of a culinary degree alone no longer can.

I have visited a large number of culinary schools over the past decade, and my conversations with faculty and students have demonstrated a frightening pattern consistent across most schools: very few students ever do more in college to advance their professional marketability than attend class and go to work. The few students that participate in volunteer activities, study sessions, professional associations, self-directed research projects, and other self-development activities tend to engage in them repeatedly, sometimes on a weekly or daily basis. These exceptional students often earn recognition from their teachers and build contacts with industry professionals to acquire the jobs of their choice at graduation. Many of their classmates settle for less valuable and less rewarding employment, while the weakest students may struggle to find culinary industry work at all. This reality does not need to continue.

Every culinary student has the power to become a strong student, to earn good grades, to build a résumé chock full of culinary experiences, and to become a success in the culinary industry. This book attempts to delineate for culinary students the many ways to achieve such success both in school and in the industry. The book is divided into three parts. The first nine chapters are relevant to all students from the first day of school. This first section begins with two motivational chapters to describe the difference between being a chef and being a cook and to encourage students to focus on learning, not just on earning a degree. The remaining chapters in part one teach students how to get A's, how to study, how to use faculty to maximize one's education, and how to use various library and other resources commonly found at most college campuses. The section also discusses the importance of ethics, professionalism, and work-life balance. Students should begin applying the lessons learned in part one immediately upon entering school to maximize the value of their college experience.

Students will find the next six chapters of the book most appropriate once they have become comfortable with the skills from part one. Part two begins with a motivational chapter on expanding one's education beyond the campus to the larger community. The remaining chapters in part two describe what the industry expects of culinary school graduates, the value of volunteering and of working outside of school, the importance of eating well and of studying one's meals, and the role that professional friendships and networking play on a person's career. Once students have learned to succeed in academics, they should turn their focus to the topics discussed in part two in order to build their knowledge, experience, and professional network even further before graduation. All of these topics apply equally to current students and to graduates, but the sooner current students incorporate these lessons into their lives, the sooner they benefit from them.

The final seven chapters of the book become critically important as a student approaches graduation. Part three opens with a motivational chapter encouraging students to pursue job experiences based on what they teach rather than on what they pay. The following chapters then describe how to utilize a college's support staff during the transition from school to the industry, how to write a résumé, how to interview for a job, how to get promoted on the job, how to get certified (and the many certification options), and how to continue learning even after graduation from college. Students may not find these chapters personally applicable until just before graduation, but the information in part three applies equally well to recent graduates as it does to seasoned culinary professionals. The book concludes with a final motivational chapter to encourage students to stick with the culinary industry and to inspire them to do more and to achieve more throughout their careers.

As you read through this book, you will notice several characteristics intentionally included to direct you down the right path for culinary success. First, unlike most textbooks this book includes motivational chapters alongside solely factual chapters. One of the greatest obstacles that I have found over the years for culinary students is their unrealistic image of the culinary industry. Although the industry is very rewarding, it is also extremely difficult and occasionally frustrating. Knowing that fact upfront often helps students to fight through the periodic challenges to ultimately receive rewards for hard work and persistence. Some students expect a chef's life to be pampered and luxurious; those students tend not to stay with the industry long enough to find satisfaction in the culinary world. Those who possess a realistic picture of the culinary field are more likely to endure periods from the mundane to the overwhelming in order to enjoy the precious, joyous, rewarding times that do exist in the culinary field. The motivational chapters in the book are designed to portray the culinary industry honestly while encouraging readers to engage in extensive self-development and credential-building in school and beyond. A thorough commitment to skill and knowledge growth accelerates the time it takes a young cook to progress up the career ladder while a realistic understanding of the industry helps a recent culinary school graduate to endure and sometimes even to enjoy the time spent in the trenches of the kitchen. Second, this book fluctuates intentionally between third and second person. The third person (he, they, etc.) conveys the universality of many of the lessons included in the text. The English language does not possess a gender neutral pronoun for individuals, so I have chosen to use male pronouns in the odd chapters and female pronouns in the even ones. This is not meant to suggest any gender differentiation on a chapter's subject or in the industry; the book applies equally to men and women. The second person (you) signifies that these lessons apply to you, the reader, and more importantly, that they require you to take action. Many textbooks ask you to read and to recall information. This one needs you to act if it is to be valuable to you. You will learn certain study skills, but if you do not utilize them, your test scores will not improve. You will learn networking techniques, but if you fail to use them, you will not be as effective at networking. If you choose to apply the approaches and techniques described in the book to your own life, you will quickly reap their benefits. Third, whereas some textbooks provide end-of-chapter questions to test what you have retained from the book, I have chosen to include "suggested tasks" instead. The suggested tasks are not designed to test reading retention. (There is no point in memorizing the facts in this book when you can easily refer back to them as long as you own the book.) Rather, the tasks ask you to apply what you have learned to your own life and to gather additional information on the chapter subjects through other resources such as industry professionals and teachers. You need not perform any of these tasks, but the more you attempt, the more you will benefit from the book. Finally, the book includes a multitude of interviews from teachers, industry professionals, recent culinary school graduates, and current students. These interviews add numerous voices to the text, and they show the universal applicability of the book's subjects to culinary schools and to culinary businesses around the country. They are more than just interesting diversions from the primary narrative. These interviews offer a window into the experiences of real people who have succeeded in the industry or in school and who want to share their hard-earned advice with you. Sometimes the interviewees offer alternate suggestions or even direct contradictions to the advice given in the book's main narrative. I have intentionally left many of these alternate viewpoints uncensored to promote class discussion on the topics that vary according to a chef's personal preference. The book recommends an extensive list of behaviors and activities for all culinary students without truly taking into account individual student differences or the many variables that impact students' lives in different ways. To believe that all students will instantly adjust their lives to accommodate all of the suggestions discussed in this book would be naïve. However, a student can benefit greatly from adopting even one or two of the recommendations provided herein. Each suggestion carries merit and value on its own. Over time, the more recommendations a student takes to heart, the greater the benefit to that student.

With the culinary industry becoming more and more competitive, I sincerely hope that this book will help to guide students toward higher achievement and success. Culinary school tuitions continue to climb. A considerable number of students who enroll in culinary school ultimately leave either by choice or at the school's request. Each year a significant number of culinary school graduates fail to find employment commensurate with their education and training. Yet all of these problems are easily overcome by those students who make the most of their time in college. No one wants to take a culinary program twice, even if a second attempt would teach that person everything needed to succeed in the industry. For that reason, it is absolutely essential that students with hopes of someday becoming more than prep cooks gain as much knowledge and skill as possible during their brief time in school. Many students simply do not know how to make their college experience more valuable. This book hopes to provide them that expertise. Most students expect college to propel them toward their goals, but culinary school only starts students down a path that takes years to complete. Those students who make the most of their culinary school education may find that they cover enough distance during school to see their goals just over the horizon; at the very least they graduate with a clear sense of direction and knowledge of how to navigate the road ahead. Those who take little from their college experience often find themselves lost down the wrong path and unable to orient themselves back toward their initial goals. These under-prepared students, unable to turn back to start over again, often wander for years before giving up on their dreams entirely. For those students with lofty dreams and high culinary aspirations, I hope this book will be a road map to lead you through the first stage of your journey, so you may leave college well-prepared to achieve the goals you ultimately seek.

Use this book to change the way you approach education and the culinary industry. Keep it throughout your culinary career, and refer to it often. I hope it will provide you direction and inspiration for years to come.

Daniel Traster

ACKNOWLEDGMENTS

Writing a book is an exercise in patience and determination that tests an author's sanity. I have not only my sanity but a wonderful book, and for that I have several people to thank. Thank you to Barbara Donlon for listening when I told her what colleges really needed for new culinary students. Thanks also to the incredibly supportive team of Bill Lawrensen and Dan Trudden at Prentice-Hall without whom this book would never have made it beyond my own computer and to Sadagoban Balaji for an eagle eye in copyediting. I owe Mike Radis much gratitude for his suggestions on study techniques. I have great appreciation for the folks at the many wonderful culinary associations who assisted me in my quest for accuracy on professional certifications. To my many friends in IACP who provided me support and encouragement in my pursuit of authoring a book, thank you. Thanks to all of the interviewees who consented to interviews and endured my relentless harassment for photos and release forms. I owe much of my personal acumen about culinary education to the faculty and students at Stratford University and the Art Institute of Washington who over eight years provided me with fertile experimental ground and collegial advice to learn how best to help students thrive in school; you straight-A students are my inspiration for this book. My formal training in adult education theory comes from the wonderful faculty of Virginia Tech's Adult Learning program at its Northern Virginia campus. I owe my parents a debt of gratitude and much more for their tolerance of my pursuit of culinary arts after four years of Ivy League education. And most importantly, I am incredibly grateful for my wife and my daughter without whose support and patience I never would have been able to write this book.

ABOUT THE AUTHOR

Daniel Traster, CCC, CCE, CCP, has over eight years in culinary arts education experience, mostly at the program management level. He worked as the Dean of Culinary Arts and Hospitality Management at Stratford University in Falls Church, VA, and as the Academic Director for Culinary Arts at The Art Institute of Washington. Additionally, Traster served two years as the Chair of the Cooking Schools and Teachers section of the International Association of Culinary Professionals after already serving two years as the section's Vice-Chair. Currently consulting for the Metropolitan Cooking and Entertaining Show as their Culinary Director and writing freelance articles for multiple publications, Traster relishes the opportunity to experience firsthand the wide range of career options available in the culinary field. Prior to teaching, Chef Traster cooked in various types of foodservice operations including: Bagels and Donuts in New Jersey, the Four Seasons Hotel in Philadelphia, Provence Restaurant in Washington DC, Occasions Caterers in Washington DC, and as a private chef. Over the past decade he has served on the boards of: the Restaurant Association of Metropolitan Washington and its Education Foundation, the Nation's Capital Chefs Association (a chapter of the American Culinary Federation), the Epicurean Club of Washington, the National Capital chapter of The American Institute of Wine & Food, and the advisory boards for DC Central Kitchen and the Center of Applied Technology North. A strong believer in lifelong education, he holds a B.A in English and Theater from Yale University, an A.O.S. in Culinary Arts from the Culinary Institute of America, and an M.S. in Adult Learning and Human Resource Development from Virginia Tech. Daniel Traster lives with his wife, Katie, and his two-year-old daughter, Abigail in Washington, DC. As *Welcome to Culinary School: A Culinary Student Survival Guide* is the synthesis of advice and ideas from culinary school students, teachers, and industry professionals around the country, Daniel Traster welcomes feedback, comments, and suggestions for future editions. He can be reached via email at WelcometoCulinarySchool@gmail.com

CHAPTER 1

Becoming a Chef Versus Learning to Cook

On television and radio across the country each and every day, hundreds of people talk about food and cooking, and many of them use the title "chef." Restaurant patrons periodically send their "compliments to the chef" under the pretense that the chef personally prepared their food. Yet, across the country there are far more cooks than chefs. The media fawn all over celebrity chefs and help to drive the public's fascination with everything culinary, but the images displayed across television screens and newspapers more often than not depict the chef as the person who cooks. Is there more to being a chef than cooking? Is a really good cook by definition a chef? Can someone become a chef without actually knowing much about cooking? And perhaps most relevant to culinary students, is it ok to aspire to be a cook and not a chef? The answers to these questions typically depend upon whom you ask.

In this chapter, you will learn the various responsibilities of the typical chef and what distinguishes a chef from a cook.

1.1 WHAT IS A CHEF

In the culinary industry anyone becomes a chef when the people who report to that person refer to him or her as "chef." However, the title typically refers to the person who is the chief or manager of the kitchen. In larger operations, there are various types of culinary managers with a range of titles including: executive chef, chef de cuisine, sous chef, pastry chef, catering chef, food and beverage manager, and others. Smaller operations may have one kitchen manager with the simple title of "chef," also known as a "working chef," when he cooks regularly in addition to his other responsibilities.

The primary distinction between a chef and a cook is that the chef oversees a person or team of people in the preparation of food, while the cook's main function is to prepare the food itself. A chef may not work with food at all on a given day, but the cooks always do. When you dine in a restaurant the food is likely not prepared by the person whose name appears on the menu, but in a typical dining room the chef has more influence on your meal than the person who actually cuts, cooks, and plates the food. The menu, recipes, plate presentations, and even the employees' ways of working are the creations of the chef.

The cook has the responsibility of preparing the food according to the instructions of the chef. No dish is added to the menu without the chef's approval. Even the sources of the ingredients in many restaurants are approved by the chef. Cooks may only exercise creativity to the degree that the chef allows. Some chefs allow their cooks to provide a great deal of input into the creation of new menus or specials while other chefs accept no input at all from their staff. No matter how much flexibility is given, the chef always controls the overall operation of the kitchen so that the guests experience the creation of a single person's vision instead of a mishmash of culinary opinions. Just as an architect designs a building that is then created by a construction team according to the blueprints of the architect, the cooks follow the chef's instructions and do not design additions to the chef's blueprints on their own.

1.1.1   The Job of the Chef

That an executive chef may not spend a single minute in the kitchen cooking on any given day begs the question: "What does a chef do all day?" The answer to this question varies greatly with the type and size of the operation, but there are a large number of tasks that are performed by chefs in the majority of foodservice establishments.

As the head manager of the kitchen, the chef typically interviews and makes hiring decisions for kitchen staff. He conducts annual evaluations and determines pay increases and promotions for the staff. He sets up the reporting hierarchy for the kitchen and serves as the primary liaison between the kitchen and other departments in the company. If he does not directly train the cooks, he trains the sous chefs, pastry chefs, and other senior chefs who train the cooks in turn.

The chef also controls the physical resources for the kitchen, such as food and equipment. He often makes budgeting decisions on equipment purchases and repairs and may have input into the kitchen layout and design itself. The chef often selects the food purveyors and the specifications describing the form and quality of the purchased food. He meets with purveyors to review new product options or current product quality; he also screens new purveyors to find ones that meet his delivery time, quality, price, and product needs.

As the person managing multiple resources, the chef typically has some fiscal responsibilities as well. He controls food and labor costs to remain within certain budgeted percentages. Controlling labor costs means scheduling employees, determining pay rates, and writing purchasing specifications that minimize labor; controlling food costs means reducing waste, protecting against theft, and properly calculating sales prices. Clever chefs cross-utilize foods and potential food scraps to reduce some waste, while proper forecasting and purchasing reduces waste from spoilage.

The chef also typically assists in increasing business for the operation. Whether speaking with guests, conducting cooking demonstrations in the community, or pursuing media appearances, the chef is often the face of the restaurant and plays a major role in marketing the company. How the chef categorizes, describes, and prices items on the menu will increase (or decrease) sales. Training the service staff to suggestive sell and the cooks to maintain consistent quality also boosts revenue.

Obeying state and local regulations is another responsibility of the chef. The chef sets and enforces the standard operating procedures for the kitchen to ensure adherence to sanitation guidelines, labor laws, and fire codes. In those organizations where the chef has input into dining room operation, he accepts some responsibility for training servers to follow safe alcohol service procedures.

With varying types of operations the job description of the chef expands. In hospitals, assisted living communities, schools, prisons, and office cafeterias, nutrition plays an important role. In these and other environments with captive audiences the chef personally (or through a colleague) conducts formal or estimated nutritional analyses of menu items to provide healthy options for customers. Catering chefs typically have the responsibility of coordinating preparation, delivery, and service to multiple events to fulfill the timing requirements of each party. Hotel chefs oversee not only restaurants and catered events but also room service deliveries. Personal and private chefs must develop recipes and menus that meet the exact specifications of their clients and provide shopping and cleaning services as well.

As chefs achieve some success, their responsibilities may grow even further. Chefs may need time to prepare for television cooking shows. They may need to write recipes for a cookbook or magazine article. They may make public appearances to endorse certain

Interview with Scott W. Mason, Chef/Owner, Ketchum Grill

What is the difference between being a chef and being a cook?
Knowledge and Responsibility—a chef should accept and have more of both.

What are your typical job responsibilities each day?
I arrive ready to work before the rest of the crew, plan the day's work, direct others, answer the phones, prepare the mise en place, prepare schedules, receive/check-in daily food deliveries, solve just about every imaginable problem that comes along, babysit whining servers, eat, taste, eat again, direct again, finish, and extend inventories for the accountant, promote the restaurant, order food for the coming days, prepare special menus, meet with the floor staff to discuss special menus or nightly specials, cook on the line or expedite plates, answer questions via email, interview with the radio or magazine. Then, I sit down to catch my breath and start again.

Do you get to do a lot of cooking in your position?
Yes, after 16 years in this position as chef and owner, I still cook nearly every day.

In your kitchen what does a cook do each day?
A cook will prepare the food and mise en place for a particular station, prepare specials as directed by the chef, fill orders as they come into the kitchen, communicate problems as they arise to the chef or sous chef, inventory nightly "leftovers," and start a prep list for the coming day.

What advice would you give a young person just starting out in the industry?
A good pair of shoes is almost as important as a good attitude. Work in the best places for the best and most accomplished chefs that you can afford.

product lines or community causes. If they decide to mass market their food, they will need to develop recipes that can endure commercial packaging and shipping.

Of course, some chefs may choose to leave large-scale food production operations to pursue other food-related careers. Recipe developers and testers create or test recipes for clients ranging from authors to periodicals to commercial food production companies. Culinary educators may train everyone from passionate home cooks to future chefs.

The role of a chef obviously goes beyond simply cooking. Expert chefs require skills in math and finance, food science, microbiology, nutrition, writing, public speaking, the visual arts, and human resource management well after they have been promoted out of the role of cook. Today's chef is more likely to use a computer than a knife on any given day. It is a wonder that talented executive chefs ever get the opportunity to cook at all.

1.1.2   Striving to Cook

With the long list of non-cooking activities that a chef performs, you may be rethinking your choice to pursue a career as a chef. What if you really just like to cook? Fortunately, the culinary industry needs a lot more cooks than it does chefs, and no one starts off their culinary career as a chef. The typical chef works for several years as a cook (even if he has gone to culinary school) to gain experience, build speed, and develop his personal style before moving up to a chef position. After years of cooking some people are ready for a change and want to move up to tackle the different challenges that a chef faces; others choose to remain at the "line" where they work with the food firsthand. Unfortunately, some choose to leave the profession for a variety of reasons before they even have the opportunity to become a chef.

The longer you work as a cook under a range of very talented chefs, the better your culinary skills will become. However, many people seek the increase in responsibility, fame, and income that come with a promotion to a chef position. Determining the right balance for you is key. If cooking is what you enjoy, you may elect to remain a cook for many years. Alternatively, you could accept chef jobs only where you have the opportunity to cook regularly, but remember that you will still have to complete all of your management responsibilities in addition to your culinary ones. There is no shame in choosing to cook as there is no shame in leaving the stovetop to manage a kitchen. The only crime is not knowing what you are getting into when that first promotion opportunity arrives.

1.2   WHAT A CHEF IS NOT

Many people have no idea what it means to be a chef when they first decide to pursue it as a career. Some people believe it is equivalent to cooking dinner at home but with greater skill. Some believe that being a chef is saying "bam" in front of a camera for an hour a day while an audience applauds your every move. (Emeril Lagasse worked, and still works, many long hours just to have the opportunity to be on television.) Still others think that being a chef is more about eating than it is about cooking.

Most chefs will tell you that they love food but that they cook so others can eat their food. If your natural response to cooking is to give your food to someone else to watch their (hopefully positive) reaction, then you may have the right mind-set to become a chef. Chefs taste their cooking regularly to ensure that the food going to the guest is properly done, but cooks and chefs get paid to work, not to eat. If you know in your heart that you love eating more than cooking, you may find yourself changing careers before too long.

Being a chef is not an opportunity to make a mess in the kitchen while someone else cleans it up either. Although chefs typically have dishwashers to clean dishes and pots for them, chefs who are slobs never survive in the industry. The best chefs clean almost as much as they cook. Working in a cluttered, dirty area slows down the pace at which a person can cook and plate food, so constant cleaning actually increases the rate at which a chef can serve customers. When the dish machine is backed up or a cook has spilled something on the floor, the best employees jump in to help clean. You do not need to love to mop or scrub dishes, but if you actively try to avoid cleaning activities in the kitchen, you should know now that you may never have a promotion to a chef position offered to you.

Finally, although an executive chef is the "boss" in the kitchen, being a chef does not mean holding oneself to a lower standard than he holds his staff. Executive chefs may have office responsibilities, but more often than not a chef needs to demonstrate to his cooks how to prepare food properly and efficiently, how to employ proper sanitation, and even how to communicate with other employees. Chefs must follow all of the rules that they enforce for others and practice what they preach. A chef who wastes time goofing off, avoiding work, or disobeying his own rules while his line cooks slave away is a chef who will soon struggle with high turnover from his staff. A chef who leads by example, on the other hand, will often have many willing followers in his kitchen.

1.3   THE REALITY AND THE SIMPLE PLEASURES

While the foodservice industry continues to grow, the high-paying chef jobs still require immense talent and hard work to acquire. Most culinary students enter the workforce at entry-level, hourly positions and work their way up if they want to get ahead. There are literally hundreds of culinary programs across the United States training tens of thousands of people to become chefs. What makes the difference between a chef-in-the-making and a permanent prep cook is talent, knowledge, skill, and hard work. The culinary industry is physically and emotionally demanding. Cooks work long, odd hours and chefs work even longer hours. Few people get rich working in a kitchen, and many people quit the industry long before they ever earn an opportunity to take a chef position.

Interview with Andrea Curto-Randazzo, Chef/Owner, Talula, Miami Beach

What is the difference between being a chef and being a cook?
I feel as though I am always a cook, but chefs have responsibilities that set them apart from "cooks." Not only must a chef create menus, manage staff, be able to order properly, maintain acceptable food cost, know ingredients and cooking techniques—the list can go on—but most importantly a chef must be able to teach, motivate, and inspire the young cooks that work in their kitchen to create a solid foundation for these "chefs" of the future.

What do you like most about being a chef?
Aside from just loving food in general, there is great satisfaction in creating a dish, having someone eat it, and seeing the happiness on that person's face.

(continued)

(*continued*)

What are your typical job responsibilities each day?
Well, I am a Chef/Owner, so the job duties are endless. I come in before lunch and make sure everything is running properly. I write the lunch specials and make a soup (which changes daily). I check in product. I butcher fish and discuss with my sous chef the specials for the evening. Different things may happen on different days of the week: meeting with purveyors, checking invoices, writing recipes, general paperwork, writing schedules, payroll, and then just putting out small fires (not literally) that may happen throughout the day in the front and back of the house. For dinner, I expedite. A 10–14 hour shift is pretty regular.

Do you get to do a lot of cooking in your position?
I make specials and do some cooking in the evening; however, I have a staff of line cooks that do the majority of the cooking throughout service. Sometimes I wish all I had to do was cook.

What is a typical cook position like in your kitchen?
My cooks work hard. They are responsible for prepping each dish that comes off their station. Depending on the station, that consists of knife work, sauces, even some butchering. They prep it; they work it and maintain it. I like to train them on all stations so they can be cross-utilized. At the end of their shift, they are responsible for keeping the walk-in clean and scrubbing down the line (top to bottom). This is not a walk in the park job.

What advice would you give a young person just starting out in the industry?
The Food Network is not reality! You are not a rock star; you are a cook. The pay is lousy; you cut yourself; you burn yourself; you work your butt off. But at the end of each day, you come away with a feeling of satisfaction and realize that you are a better cook today than you were yesterday. If you keep on your path, work with passion, dedication, and integrity, and remember that you are doing this for the true love of it, you will experience the rewards of becoming the chef that you dream of.

So why even begin to pursue a career as a chef? The culinary industry offers certain perks that no other industry provides. As a chef, your "office" smells like baking bread and roasted meat. Your creations engage your customers through all five senses. You become a player in making your guests' anniversaries, birthdays, dates, holidays, family gatherings, vacations, and other significant moments special. When your customers' eyes light up and their smiles dance across their faces with each bite of your creation, you smile to yourself and think, "I did that." After you feel the stress of an onslaught of orders that you cannot possibly handle, you experience the accompanying "rush" or "high" that comes after you have successfully handled every order, on time, without a single glitch. You work with a team of people committed to a single vision of putting out great food beyond the expectations of your customers. You bask in the admiration and awe of others who do not understand the first thing about cooking but wish they could cook as well as you cook. Finally, you feel proude that you are part of a long tradition of culinary workers who have developed the industry's high standards and reputation to make chefs the respected and beloved professionals that they are today. Those who yearn for these simple pleasures from a job inevitably find happiness in the culinary industry.

Summary

Although cooks have the responsibility of preparing food for guests, chefs have much greater responsibility and oftentimes a much larger workload. Chefs serve as employee supervisors and resource managers. They maintain fiscal responsibility, market their company, enforce government regulations, and sometimes even cook. Some chefs also play the role of nutritionist, event coordinator, room service manager, housekeeper, media personality, author, food stylist, recipe developer, and teacher. Obviously, chefs are much more than cooks. Some look for jobs that allow them to cook as part of their daily responsibilities, while others find themselves fully occupied with all of the non-cooking activities required of them. Chefs work hard and typically do not have time to spend their day playing the role of media celebrity or sitting around and eating food for hours. Chefs have the ultimate responsibility of making sure that every task needed to keep a restaurant operational gets done; from cutting to cleaning, if no one else can do it, the chef does it personally. Although no person really knows how much he will enjoy working in the culinary industry until he actually does it, people who love to prepare delectable culinary creations for the sole purpose of pleasing a roomful of guests start their careers with the right mind-set for success.

THE MANY HATS OF A CHEF

- Creating the menu, recipes, and plate presentations
- Hiring, training, and managing kitchen employees
- Organizing and maintaining the facility
- Overseeing the food purchasing process
- Controlling food and labor costs
- Marketing the company to increase sales
- Enforcing governmental health, safety, and labor regulations
- Adjusting menus and recipes to meet guests' nutritional needs
- Coordinating with catering salespeople to ensure proper delivery and service of catered parties
- Overseeing hotel room service
- Working with clients to prepare meals to meet their specific needs
- Writing books and articles on culinary arts
- Appearing in the media to discuss cooking
- Designing and styling food for promotional photographs
- Developing and testing recipes for publication or mass production
- Training future chefs

Suggested Tasks

1. Shadow a professional chef for a day. Compare what the chef does with what the other cooks in the operation do.
2. Interview three different chefs who work in very different types of foodservice operations. Compare and contrast their daily responsibilities and required skill sets.
3. Write a self-analysis describing the top five aspects of the culinary industry that most appeal to you and the five common duties of a chef that you find least appealing. Discuss your self-analysis with your instructor to see what type of culinary job is most likely to provide you satisfaction in the future.
4. Compare your current strengths and weaknesses against the skill sets a typical chef needs to succeed. Discuss your weakest areas with your teacher, and ask for suggestions on how to begin developing skills in those weak areas early in your education.

CHAPTER 2

The Degree Versus the Learning

Ask a student why she is going to school and you may hear answers like: "To get my degree," "To get some credentials," or "To help me get a job." In rare cases you may even hear a student say that she is going to school "to learn." You might wonder which is more important: the degree or the learning. Can you get a job without a degree? Does having a degree always help you get ahead of people who have never gone to school? Ideally, everyone in the culinary industry would go to school to learn the core knowledge of the industry, and everyone would graduate with a degree or diploma. It is sadly very possible to get a college degree and learn very little. Only the knowledge and skills earned through education allow a culinary school graduate to excel in the culinary industry.

In this chapter, you will learn the value of a degree and the importance of learning while in school. You will also learn the role grades play and why maximizing your learning is more important than simply doing enough to earn a credential.

2.1 THE VALUE OF THE DEGREE

Two generations ago, many high-level culinary jobs did not require a specific degree. Rather employers looked for people with experience under well-known chefs. Anyone willing to work hard could get an entry-level culinary job. Today, the outlook is somewhat different. Many high-end operations require employees to have some sort of culinary credential just to get an entry-level position, and more and more foodservice companies will not promote cooks to management without a degree or other formal credential. Even though having a degree or diploma does not make a difference in the kind of income you receive during your first few years in the industry, you can very quickly hit a glass ceiling in some companies by bypassing culinary school or dropping out before completion.

While most foodservice workers still do not hold culinary degrees, there is a great benefit to earning a degree early in your career. First, having a degree is becoming a more common requirement for a job or promotion. Many jobs, including executive chef jobs, still only require an associate degree, but more and more companies are looking for people with bachelor degrees to take food and beverage director positions and corporate chef jobs.

Second, a college credential can get you a job interview and eventually your first day on the job over other candidates without diplomas. When two job candidates with similar experience but different credentials apply for a job, the position typically goes to the one with a degree. Some places will not even interview candidates who have not graduated from culinary school.

Many culinary professionals believe that a culinary school graduate should have a command of certain common foundational industry knowledge. Most culinary vocational degree programs teach similar knowledge and skills based on what the average culinary professional will need in the industry. The differences between these culinary schools lie in their approach to teaching rather than in what they teach. All culinary schools provide a compressed learning environment in which students can learn industry-specific skills and knowledge in a shorter time frame than they would be able to learn them on the job. However, in almost every school there is wide variation of student skill mastery. Every college has superstar students, and every college has duds. Only the strong students are in high demand at graduation.

Interview with Michael Symon, Chef/Owner, Lola/Lolita

When looking for employees to hire, how important is it that an applicant have a culinary degree?
I like the foundation that culinary schools give, but I'm looking for the right personality and the right work ethic.

Does having a degree impact the likelihood of a person getting an interview? Does it impact how far a person can progress in your company?
No, it does not. People with degrees are able to move up quicker because of their knowledge, but I always hire whoever is the best person for the job.

Does how much a student learned in school matter to you?
Some people are full of knowledge and have a very good understanding of food, but they can't put their knowledge to use in a high-pressure environment. If someone is very educated and cannot execute what they know, that creates a problem. I look to see that they can execute what they know properly.

Does a student's culinary learning end when school is finished?
They have to continue to learn. If a student comes to my kitchen as if they know it all, they won't get hired (and wouldn't last a week anyway). School gives a tremendous foundation, but the majority of the learning is done after school. Kids who come from culinary school at least made a commitment to the profession. You know they're in it for the long run as long as they're willing to grow.

Does it matter which culinary school a student attends?
There are schools that we prefer because I am familiar with them, but at the end of the day, it is what you put into it during your education that matters. Some kids went to culinary school and must have been in a daze because they know nothing when they come out. Other students go to a school and come out ready to excel.

2.2 THE VALUE OF THE LEARNING

A degree only gets you the first day on the job. Whether or not you get invited to come back to work for a second day, a second week, or a second month depends on your ability to execute what you learned while in school. Students who barely survive school typically struggle during a job interview or hands-on tryout when applying for a job. Students who focus on learning as much as possible in school usually get through job interviews with ease and find themselves with promotion offers in just a year or two.

Consider the impact of learning more than your classmates at school. First, you will command the respect of your teachers and classmates who see your growing skills and capacity to become a superstar. Those teachers will likely provide you stronger recommendations and job referrals than they will for other students. Industry chefs, who see a lot of recent culinary school graduates, will quickly recognize the extent of your knowledge and consider you a stronger candidate for a job and eventually for a promotion. If you were looking to promote someone to management, wouldn't you choose the employee with the greatest skill and knowledge? Students who maximize their learning while in school tend to shorten the length of time that it typically takes to earn a promotion because they require less time on the job to outpace their co-workers. Be careful, however, to distinguish between having a big skill set and having a big ego. Most chefs are far more impressed with a worker who quietly proves her talent in the kitchen than one who merely talks a good game.

Students who excel in school learn certain behaviors that make their future success more likely. First, they develop a love of learning, so they are more likely to pursue higher degrees, certification, or other credentials after graduation. They learn to apply themselves and to work hard for a motivator other than money. Although hard workers often earn pay raises in return for their devotion, people who wait for a promotion and a raise before working harder typically find that the money never comes. They have a passion for the industry that helps drive them ever upward; they never settle for mediocrity. Most importantly, good students develop a strong foundation of skills on which to build, while weaker students spend their first few years in the industry still trying to learn the basics. A degree may get you a job offer, but your ultimate success on the job comes from skills, knowledge, and a strong work ethic, not from any credential.

2.2.1 Why Worry About Grades

With so much future success dependent on what you learn while earning your degree and not on your grades, why worry about grades? Grades are a reflection of how much you have learned. Although others may ask your grades, the person to whom the grades provide the most value is you. If you do not earn an A in a class, then you know you have more to learn on that subject to stay ahead of your classmates. (Earning an A does not mean that you do not have more to learn on the subject; it just means that you have learned most of what the teacher expected you to learn at this stage of your education.) By focusing on learning as much as possible, you will ultimately earn higher grades, and conversely, by doing what it takes to earn an A, you will inevitably learn more from the class than if you aimed for a C.

Interview with Todd Gray, Executive Chef/Co-Owner, Equinox Restaurant

When looking for employees to hire, how important is it that an applicant have a culinary degree?
There are two things I look for when hiring a new employee: a degree and work experience. The degree is not necessarily part of the criteria, but it does help to get someone through the door quicker. Having a degree definitely affects the likelihood of getting an interview.

Does how much a student learned in school matter to you?
I don't have conversations with a student's instructors. I don't pry into their performance in school. But grades are indicative of what and how much was learned, so I do look at that.

Does a student's culinary learning end when school is finished or is it important for a student to continue learning after graduation?
A student should always be learning. I'm still learning even after 20 years.

Does it matter which culinary school a students attends or is there another factor that distinguishes good culinary school graduates from poorer quality graduates?
It's really a matter of what people put in and what they get out. There are probably two or three better schools in the country that lend themselves to instant recognition in terms of the knowledge and talent I look for, but now more than ever, there are lots of great schools out there.

2.2.2   Why Grades aren't Everything

Grades are not everything though. You may have an emergency arise that affects your performance in a class, and you get a low grade as a result. Other times, a teacher may give everyone A's or C's despite huge variations in student learning because of how the grades are calculated. Grades are nothing more than a reflection of a student's performance on graded work in a class. They typically correlate to how much a student has learned in school, but it is the learning, not the grades, that prepare a student for the industry.

2.3   COMPETITION WITH CLASSMATES

The need to learn more than the average student has become a reality for today's chef-hopefuls. The culinary industry has grown rapidly in recent decades, but so has the culinary education industry. Thousands of graduates from hundreds of culinary schools enter the workforce each year. There are plenty of jobs available for these graduates, but only a few of these positions have the potential to propel someone's career to a high level quickly. Although finding work in fast food and mid-level restaurants may be easy, the jobs in high-end establishments are usually the ones that give culinary graduates the experience needed to become future industry leaders. As these high-end jobs are limited, they usually go to the top performers in a culinary class.

If you are aiming for the best jobs to boost your career, you will find yourself competing with students at your school and from other schools for those jobs. Knowing more about culinary arts and having stronger culinary skills than your competition helps you to earn the better job. Competition does not mean backstabbing or sabotaging your classmates. In fact, speaking ill of other students or other schools typically backfires and results in rejection as a job candidate. Chefs recognize talent rather quickly, so the most effective way to compete against others is to show the extent of your knowledge and skills.

The best competition is the kind that makes all competitors stronger. If your classmates seem to outperform you in interviews and in class, ask them for help. Ask how they manage their own learning and improve their skills to become such strong students and job candidates. If they can help you to get ahead, you may be able to return the favor years later in the industry. This form of competition with mutual support and encouragement helps both parties in the long run.

Competition for the best jobs does not end after graduation either. Culinary school graduates will learn a great deal on the job every day, but those who read and study to learn beyond the job will continue to outpace their co-workers. Commit yourself fully to your education and self-development while in school, and you will never lose the desire and ability to learn once you enter the workforce.

Interview with Timothy Tucker, Executive Chef and Culinary Training Instructor, The Salvation Army Culinary Training Program

When you first arrived to culinary school, what did you want to get out of school?
When I was in high school, the chef informed me of the kind of things that I would learn in culinary school. I thought the importance of school was to learn terminology, why chefs do certain things in cooking, food cost, how to run an establishment correctly, management and people skills. I thought it would prepare me for management responsibilities when I became an executive chef.

What did you end up getting out of culinary school?
I got an incredible network. Also, there was an amazing library of cookbooks from which I raked the knowledge to get as much as possible out of them. There are lots of "Jedi knight" chefs who informed me about the great places to work around the country. Don't get me wrong; I did learn food cost, how to make recipes, and how to work with others. I also learned the importance of mopping the floor and keeping a clean kitchen—that never goes away.

What value has your learning provided you?
It helped me to realize where my skill level was and what need to happen for me to continue with my career. I was around professionals and learned how they did things. I remember my second to last quarter in school; my chef was evaluating where our skill levels were. He explained how entry-level and new we still were even though we were strong students. There is just so much stuff to know. That's one of the things that humbled me to encourage me to work under some good chefs.

(continued)

(*continued*)

Did you focus more on grades or on learning?
Definitely the learning part of it. I loved going to the library and learning about new recipes. One of the things that happens in school is that you're surrounded by people who love to cook. I never had that before in my life. School is all about the experience of cooking and talking with people about food. I never really thought it was about a piece of paper. It's about how good your skill levels are; how fast, knowledgeable, and dedicated you are; how willing you are to do pots and pans when needed and to absorb the knowledge of the chef.

What level of competition did you feel between other classmates?
You don't really compete against each other; you compete against yourself. You try to get faster each day. I try not to get too wrapped up in what other people are doing. There will always be "naturals" who are better than you. You may be better than them at other skills which may turn out to be more important in the long run.

2.4   PRIDE IN YOUR SCHOOL

At this point you may be wondering if your culinary school will make you competitive in the job market. You, not the school, will determine just how competitive you are. You hold the power to make your education a wonderful or a disappointing experience. Now you must decide whether you will get as much learning as possible out of your time at school or if you will require the pushing and prodding of the teachers and administration to get you to achieve the bare minimum needed to graduate. When you commit yourself 100 percent to your education, follow the instructions of your teachers, and take advantage of every learning opportunity, you will graduate secure in the knowledge that you are ready to succeed in the industry. Should you choose to view school merely as a financial exchange in which you deposit money and receive a degree in return, rest assured that no school would be able to help you survive the culinary field.

Summary

Although there are benefits to earning a college credential, the value of a degree is only as strong as the learning the student has gained in school. A degree or diploma can give a student an edge in getting a job, but the learning is what helps the student to keep a job, to get promoted, and to earn the respect of her co-workers. Focusing on learning will help a student to earn good grades (as focusing on earning good grades often helps a student to learn more), and increased learning will help a graduate outpace the competition entering the workforce at the same time. Grades are important benchmarks to help a student measure her own performance, but a student must go beyond grades and learn as much as possible to be the best candidate for the prime entry-level industry positions. Passionate devotion to self-edification during and beyond school is the best way to achieve success in the industry, no matter where a student goes to school.

The Value of the Degree	The Value of the Learning
• Meeting a job requirement	• Skills to succeed at a job
• Getting an interview for a job	• Getting through an interview to get hired
• Making the difference between equally experienced job candidates	• Earning a promotion so that an employee search is not needed
• Perception of command of a common foundational industry knowledge	• Actual command of common foundational industry knowledge
• Getting the first day on the job	• Keeping the job beyond the first day

Suggested Tasks

1. Interview two industry chefs. Find out their opinion of the importance of a degree. Ask if they have a degree and how they worked up to their current position. Lastly, ask what they look for when making hiring and promoting decisions.

2. Write a brief essay describing what you hope to gain from going to culinary school. State also what you plan to do to ensure you receive those gains. Discuss your essay with your teacher to see if you need to adjust your plans to meet your desired gains.

3. Research and select three self-development activities to which you can commit weekly to improve your knowledge and skills beyond what is required in your classes. Share your list with a teacher to discuss which of the three would be the most beneficial to your learning and professional growth.

4. Interview a graduating student from your program who is encountering success in job interviews. Ask the student for advice on how to best prepare yourself to be viewed as a desirable job candidate upon graduation. Implement one of the student's recommendations in your life.

CHAPTER 3

Getting Straight A's: The Skills and Qualities You'll Need to Thrive in School

T oo many people believe that they could never be straight-A students. The truth is that anyone can earn an A in a class . . . even you. Straight-A students are not magicians. They have no secret methods for making the grade. They simply apply a few basic techniques for earning the maximum number of points in class. Although these techniques require discipline, time, and effort, anyone can implement them.

In this chapter, you will learn the value of working ahead of schedule, of determining when and how to ask for help, and most importantly, of simply doing everything that the instructor asks of you.

3.1 WORK AHEAD OF SCHEDULE

Imagine that you are given an assignment at work for a very important project that could make or break the company. Your boss gives you a strict deadline and explicit instructions with the promise of a promotion if the project is successful (and a guarantee of termination if you fail in your assignment). What do you do? If you want the promotion, you adjust your schedule to focus as much time as possible on the project, even if it means working long hours for a little while. You work ahead of schedule to leave yourself time for last-minute adjustments to fine-tune the project, and you ask questions of your boss when you are the least bit unsure of what to do on any part of the project. If you do everything your boss has asked (and a little bit more to improve on the instructions), you will likely find yourself with a promotion at the next performance evaluation. However, if you decide to spend the next few weeks getting to work late so that you have less time to work on the project, or worse, if you decide to just throw the project together the day before it is due, you will surely find yourself looking for new employment in the near future. The culinary classroom provides similar opportunities for students to succeed or fail of their own volition.

Since people rarely learn things perfectly from their first exposure to new skills or knowledge, practice is the key to the mastery of learning. In the above example, working ahead of schedule and asking questions provide opportunities to correct mistakes in the final product that will inevitably occur before the project is due. One reason that A students outperform their classmates is that they give themselves more opportunity to practice and correct their learning.

Most students claim to make learning a priority, but only A students make learning their number one priority. A C student, whether by choice or necessity, typically tries to make school fit into his current lifestyle. This student misses class when his job needs him to stay late and is more likely to skip a reading assignment to avoid disappointing friends who have invited him to a party. The A student, on the other hand, arranges his life around school. The A student leaves work, no matter what the circumstances, in order to make it to class on time. He will skip a social event or other minor commitment to complete a homework assignment. In short, he makes sure that earning an A in the course is top priority.

3.1.1 Reading Ahead

Students who procrastinate cheat themselves of the opportunity to learn from their mistakes without hurting their grade. Most students learn early in their college careers (if not in high school) how to make it through a class day without actually doing the reading due that day. This behavior actually requires the student to put in more study time, not less, to get the same learning mastery as the student who keeps up with the reading throughout the course. While procrastinators spend their class time trying to learn new material, the student who reads ahead uses class to practice and refine skills and knowledge, not to learn them for the first time.

Unless you have a photographic memory, you probably do not remember even half of what you read. Most students need to read a chapter multiple times to retain the majority of its content, and even then they may confuse some of the facts they have read. However, you can get away with reading a chapter only once or twice if you read it before the class in which it will be discussed. The teacher's lecture and the class discussion become your second reading while your questions to the teacher on the material substitute for a third reading.

Here's why: During your first reading of the chapter, you retain some of the information in long-term memory in a readily accessible form while the rest of it is either remembered inaccurately or quickly forgotten. When the teacher discusses the chapter's key points, the information you have already learned is reinforced, while the unlearned material has a second chance of making it into long-term memory. Anything that you had learned incorrectly has a chance to be corrected. If there are points discussed by the teacher on which you are still unclear, asking questions becomes a third opportunity for you to learn the material properly.

Although you might think that this process occurs for students who have not read the chapters before class, it does not. When all of the material presented in class is new, the typical student struggles just to keep up with the pace of the knowledge presented. He is trying to learn everything from just a single exposure to the content. Most students in this situation will not ask questions for fear of revealing their lack of preparation, so they also lose the opportunity for instructor clarification of difficult points. Like reading for the first time, most students will remember less than half of the new material presented. Prepared students, on the other hand, have a fighting chance of walking out of the class with a strong command of 80–90 percent of the material covered because they arrive knowing some of the material already. They can focus their mental energy on learning the smaller amount of new material they did not retain from the initial reading.

Next, consider how you will appear to the instructor when you come to class having read the assigned material. You will be able to participate intelligently in class and to answer questions posed to you. Your body language will exude confidence while your unprepared classmates spend most of class trying to avoid eye contact with the instructor. You will be able to complete in-class assignments deftly and quickly, and you will appear to the instructor, in a word, prepared. Not only will the class experience be more enjoyable for you, but you will be well on your way toward earning full credit for any class participation grade that is given for the course.

Interview with Marian Grubor, CCE, Division Chair Business, CIT, Culinary Arts, West Virginia Northern Community College

What behaviors among students have you found help to make someone a straight-A student?
The person who wants straight A's must be very motivated to study the concepts as well as practice the skills. It is not enough to be a great cook; the student must also be a great student in order to get A's in the program. In order to be a great student the learner must master reading comprehension, mathematics, and science. Studying is an integral part of the learning process. As with any subject matter, if students put 100 percent into studying, they will receive A's.

How do you feel about students requesting help from you outside of class on a subject?
I see a student who wants outside help as a highly motivated individual. If the student comes to class, takes notes, and does what is expected, I am honored to offer additional help. However, the student who misses class, does not have a book, and slacks off on studying cannot expect me to waste any more time on him/her than I have already in the classroom.

How do you perceive students who miss a day out of your class?
We are trying to indoctrinate professionalism into the student. In a professional setting if you are scheduled to work, you work. If the student knows ahead of time something is going on, I will try to arrange a convenient time for him to make up the missed time. Our policy is that the student can miss two classes without consequence, as long as they notify us either by phone or email. On the third miss the student is withdrawn. We have made the determination that the student must acquire the goals set out for the class; if three days are missed, it is impossible to acquire the necessary competencies.

Do students have flexibility in deadlines?
One goal is to develop the student to meet deadlines. There is not a restaurant that will let a chef make omelets at their convenience.

Can students earn extra credit in your course?
Extra credit is for high school. Reality is: do the work and earn the grade.

Is there any benefit to the student for assisting in extracurricular activities in which you are involved?
If a student exerts extra effort and volunteers for functions outside the classroom, that student will get: the benefit of grade inflation if the grade is close, free or reduced rate travel to conventions or seminars, nominations to be college ambassadors, or public acknowledgment of excellence.

3.1.2   Submit Early

The practice and refinement of learning can be divided into the two-step process of student performance of learning and teacher feedback on that performance. In the classroom, students have the opportunity to practice their learning through question and answer discussions, ungraded quizzes, and in-class assignments. Large class projects pose a greater challenge to students primarily because students must create their own opportunities to practice their learning. The best and easiest way to practice is to submit early and to ask for feedback.

When you complete your project ahead of schedule, you give yourself a chance to turn it into the instructor as a draft. Some instructors are glad to review the draft and to provide suggestions for improvement prior to your final submission of the project. If an instructor will not critique your work early, a school advisor or tutor usually will.

All students receive feedback on their projects through the grading process. Only the clever ones create ways to get that feedback *before* the project is graded. By getting the feedback early, the student or student group has the opportunity to correct any errors that would have resulted in a lower final grade.

The value of the feedback is so great that it is typically better to submit a partially completed project one or two weeks early to get detailed feedback on that part of the project than it is to turn in a completed project just one day early and get rushed feedback from the instructor with no time to make corrections before the due date. Since logically it should take the same amount of time to complete a project no matter when it is started, beginning as soon as the assignment is given is always to your benefit. You may not be able to complete all parts of the project until certain material is covered in class, but you should do and submit what you can early to leave yourself time for instructor feedback before the due date.

3.2   GETTING HELP AND HELPING YOURSELF

While your instructor can assist you in the learning process, teachers are not mind readers. You must take the initiative to notify the instructor of your specific needs for learning assistance. Ask for help as soon as you realize that you need it. Recognize that an instructor will not re-teach an entire course, so be specific in communicating what you do and do not understand from each lesson. Most instructors will happily devote some time to helping you, but there are a couple of caveats. Do not ask for help unless you have completed the reading for the lesson and attempted all of the homework assignments. Most instructors will not help you unless you have tried to learn the material on your own first. Second, do not ask for or expect much help the day before an exam. Even the best teachers can do very little to help you learn and retain test information at the last minute. Asking for help early not only makes you appear responsible but it also provides you the time to review and master what the instructor teaches you.

Of course, not every difficult concept requires you to request tutoring from the instructor outside of class time. Most questions can easily be answered in class, if you take the initiative to ask them. Clichés aside, there are stupid questions, but a question that helps you better understand the material being studied is never stupid. Always ask questions of your teacher when you do not understand a topic. If he cannot explain it to your satisfaction during class, request some time after class to get the answer. An instructor who sees that you are more interested in learning than you are in leaving campus the moment the class ends will take you more seriously and work with you to help you learn the course material.

Some students refuse to ask questions for fear that it makes them look dumb in front of their classmates. On the contrary, most students who engage in discussions with the instructor appear more intelligent than those who sit quietly in their chairs and never say a word. If the instructor does not have time to answer the question at that moment, he will typically defer the question until after class. The delay is merely a matter of time constraints and practicality; do not take it personally. Simply meet with the instructor after class to follow up on your question. Most instructors appreciate your willingness to respect their needs to move the class forward and meet with them outside of class for a lengthier discussion.

While the instructor can assist you with clarification of confusing material, the retention of information for exams and the mastery of skills to which you have been exposed is your responsibility. Study daily. When you study information each day, you have a better shot at retaining most or all of it than if you leave an entire course's worth of studying for the day before the exam. In fact, the day before an exam should be reserved for quickly skimming all of the material in the course, which by now you should have learned fairly well, merely to keep it top of mind for the exam. As trite as it may sound, the best thing you can do the night before an exam is to get a good night's sleep.

In addition to fact and concept memorization, culinary schools require students to learn the physical skill of cooking. Most schools only expose students to recipes and techniques one or two times at most. The best way to progress from minimal competence to strong proficiency is through practice. Incorporate class recipes and techniques into your cooking at home as much as possible. Most people take years to become proficient in knife cuts, for example, but daily practice reduces the time required to master them. Potatoes are perhaps the most cost-effective, versatile medium for knife cut practice. They can be cut into almost any shape from brunoise to tourné and then roasted, fried, boiled, or simply pureed. When deciding what to make for dinner (if your school does not provide your meals on a given night), purchase ingredients to replicate a recipe learned in class. Pick the dish or skill with which you struggled most, so you have the opportunity to improve upon your performance and learn from your mistakes. Since you need to eat anyway, this form of "studying" should feel more fun and less of an inconvenience than any other kind that you do.

3.2.1 Emergency Setbacks

Despite your best efforts to study daily and to ask for help, you may have an emergency arise that takes priority over school. First, make sure that you are really dealing with an emergency. Severe illness, a death in the family, and a car accident are examples of real emergencies; a mild sniffle, a family vacation, and a car in the shop are not. Missing school for a non-emergency sends the message to the instructor that you are not committed to your education or to learning about the industry, and you will likely be graded accordingly. In the real world, customers expect the chef to make it to work no matter what.

George Southwick, chef/instructor in culinary arts for Ozarks Technical Community College, tells the story of a student who missed his class because his car broke down. The student claimed that it was impossible for him to make it to class. When Chef Southwick asked the student if he would have found a way to make it to school to claim a million-dollar check that would otherwise be given to another person, the student replied,

"Of course I would get there for a million dollars." Chef Southwick then pointed out to the student that it was not a question of ability to make it to school but rather of motivation. When students make school a top priority, they find a way to get to class.

With that said, when a real emergency arises that prevents you from getting to class, notify your instructor immediately of the emergency and of your expected date of return to school. Then ask if there is anything you can do to make up for lost credit or at least to keep up with the material covered in class. Merely asking the question illustrates your commitment to school. Bound by school policies, some instructors may simply advise you to drop the course and retake it another time. Others may offer alternate assignments that allow you to make up some or all of the credit lost during your absence. Either way, you will always receive better treatment and advice by communicating with your instructor immediately than you will by waiting until your final grade is submitted to ask for special consideration. Professionals call out from work when an emergency occurs; employees destined for the unemployment line simply do not show without calling. Make sure that you act like a professional if you want to avoid being treated like a flunky.

Interview with Jonathan A. Zearfoss, Professor in Culinary Arts, The Culinary Institute of America

What behaviors among students have you found help to make someone a straight-A student?
There is something about good students: during lectures they nod while you are talking as a way of paying attention. They are around after class still asking you questions. The topic at hand got them thinking about something else they want to discuss. "Active learner" is a good term for these students. They are the ones thinking ahead. They have a plan. They make you work harder because they want to come in early or stay late to try something they have never tried before.

How often do students approach you to request extra help outside of class?
It depends on the class and the assignments. I get a lot of emails. I worked through a problem with a student by email just yesterday. It took six or seven emails because I don't like to just give them the answer. I like to drag it out of them. It's too easy to just give someone an answer. It's a much stronger educational approach to help them work through the answer themselves. The students learn more from it, and they feel better about themselves afterwards.

Can a student who misses class make up the work to earn back some or all of the points lost for the day?
Yes, but it's grudgingly on my part, and there better be a damned good reason that they missed. Our policy does not allow for that too much, but it's different with a student who has a family emergency versus one who just misses class and wants me to redeliver the lecture to him.

(*continued*)

(*continued*)

How do you perceive a student who arrives late to class?
That drives me crazy. I am absolutely obsessive about detailing tardiness. In my class if you miss a day, you lose five points. If you're late, it's two points the first day, four points the second day, six points the third day. By the third day, I don't want to see you; you would lose fewer points by not coming at all. That is an industry thing for me. If you're not early, you're late.

Do students have flexibility in deadlines?
That's another thing I'm pretty adamant about. I feel very strongly that when the curtain goes up, you have to be ready.

How would you describe your role in grading students?
I document. I am just basically keeping track. I set the parameters and then keep track of how they fall relative to the parameters. I don't play an active role.

3.3 JUST DO WHAT YOU'RE TOLD

Some students might believe that earning an A requires going above and beyond the requirements of the course. Actually, an A comes from simply meeting the requirements for the course consistently rather than erratically. The teacher, primarily through the course syllabus, project assignments, and class lectures, lays out everything that a student needs to do to earn an A. Following the teacher's instructions is the easiest and, in fact, the only way to earn an A in a course.

Although assignments and requirements vary from course to course and school to school, there are some universals in culinary education:

Attend class and arrive on time every single day. Not only do you miss out on the lecture and learning practice opportunities that occur in class, but you lose any participation credit given for that day. Furthermore, it is extremely difficult to change your mind-set and habits overnight. Students who arrive late to school become graduates who arrive late to work, at least until they are fired. Most teachers will not take seriously students who are late or absent even once, as lateness and absenteeism suggest a lackadaisical attitude toward school and education. Once you have missed even a few minutes from a class (except in a real emergency), you have lost any opportunity for special consideration or goodwill that the instructor might have shown you.

Come to class prepared. At the moment the class starts, the A students are already in full uniform, at their desks or in the kitchen, ready to work. Their homework is completed and ready to turn in, and they have all of the tools they will need for class. A student who arrives to class asking to borrow a pencil, a hat, a knife, or a recipe appears disorganized to the instructor, and for better or worse, the instructor's perception of this student's work will be colored by the first impression of disorganization. Even more costly, most culinary schools will not allow a student to participate in class if he is unprepared, which results in a point deduction for the student's participation grade.

Mental mise en place is just as important as physical preparation. When arriving to a lab class to prepare recipes, come with a thorough understanding of the steps in the recipe. Have a game plan for the day, and write out a list of the equipment and foods you will need to gather for the day's production. Plan ahead which recipes you will start first and which

Interview with Aislinn McIntyre, student at Kendall College

What did you do in school that helped you to get straight A's?
Asking lots of questions. If you don't understand something, speak up and get it cleared up. If you are particularly interested in a topic, it can't hurt to ask for more information. Either way, it creates a good impression and tells your instructor that you're there to learn.

How often did you miss class? How often were you late?
Never and never . . . though I did need to leave early once or twice. If you're a good student, most instructors will be flexible with you when your schedule changes suddenly.

Did you ever pursue any extra credit opportunities?
Yes. If there is an opportunity, you should really go for it. Not only will you earn more points, you earn your instructors' respect.

Did you ever get involved in any extracurricular activities in which your instructor was also involved?
I volunteered for pretty much every event that came my way. This can be difficult if you are working a job at the same time you are in school, but if you can, do it. The extra practice alone makes it worthwhile. The networking opportunities aren't too bad either.

will be left for last. With proper planning a culinary student will easily complete all assigned kitchen work in the time allotted for the class, while unprepared students will experience stress and panic in a futile struggle to meet the instructor's production deadline.

Complete all assignments thoroughly. For too many students the course syllabus and project assignment sheets are documents that are read once and never reviewed again. These pieces of paper typically list every requirement for earning an A in the course. Use them as a checklist to verify your satisfactory completion of each project element prior to its submission. If the course requires a 4–5 page research paper on three specific topics with a bibliography citing at least six sources, then a three-page paper citing only four sources has no chance of earning an A. The guidelines are explicit to give the instructor some objective measure for evaluating the project. Just like checking your work in a math problem, check your projects against the written guidelines before submitting them. If you have not met the guidelines, rework your project until you do.

Perhaps most important to the culinary industry, as well as to your success in school, is to *meet all of your deadlines.* In the culinary industry guests will not wait an hour for food that should have been served in ten minutes. Cooks and chefs are expected to make every deadline without fail; schoolwork is no exception. Adjust your social life, your work schedule, even your sleeping patterns, and do whatever it takes to complete your work on time. Electing not to turn in every project complete and on time effectively eliminates any chance you have of earning an A in a course. A students, like professional chefs, find a way to get it done.

3.4   GOING THE EXTRA MILE

With the many ways to improve your retention and understanding of information, your performance on projects and exams, and your participation grades, at some level earning an A is partly a numbers game. Although the following two approaches will not substitute for practicing your learning, they may help nudge you into A territory if your grade ends up on the borderline between A and B.

First, always take advantage of make-up work and extra-credit opportunities. Not many instructors offer these, but those who do are stacking the odds in your favor, if you only accept the challenge. Earning an A requires near-perfect performance on all assignments. Everyone makes mistakes, but occasionally you may make one too many to maintain an A performance. Extra credit and make-up work give you the opportunity to recoup some of your losses. Make-up work typically works like a "do-over" giving you the opportunity to earn back points where you have lost them. Extra credit points are simply free points to give you a buffer whether you are currently underperforming or not. Too often students do not realize that they should have completed the extra credit and make-up work until the course has ended and the final grades have been submitted. Think of these opportunities as car insurance payments. You do them not because you need the benefit now but because you may need it later (and no insurance company pays out after an accident if you were not making payments before you had a claim). Take the time to do the extra work, and the points will be there should you need them at the end of the course.

Although instructors are required to be objective in their grading, there is always some level of subjectivity involved. Like you, teachers are only human. Doing everything you can to ensure that the teacher knows and respects you, in some cases, may help the teacher decide to give you the higher grade in a borderline grade situation. How do you stand out from the crowd? Certainly, making the effort to arrive prepared, on time, everyday is a must, and active participation in class helps as well. However, if there are extracurricular projects with which the teacher is involved, make an effort to get involved in those projects. Once you volunteer, you must follow through on your commitment, but when you do, the one-on-one time that you spend with the teacher will definitely help you to stand out from your classmates. In addition, the conversations you have with the instructor outside of class will help to build your knowledge and skills for school. You may even find that the instructor provides personal counseling and tutoring during the project to help you perform even better in class. Most importantly, the instructor will get to know you as a person who works hard in and out of school. Once you earn this reputation, most teachers will give you the benefit of the doubt in borderline grade cases. If you are still skeptical, take a look around your school to see who volunteers for most extracurricular projects; you will find that most of them are the top students in their classes.

3.5   GOALIES AND SCOREKEEPERS

Unfortunately, despite all of your efforts you may occasionally run into a situation where the A you have been pursuing never arrives. If your natural tendency in this situation is toward anger or frustration, take a deep breath and remember that you came to school for an education, not for a grade. Receiving a grade lower than an A is another opportunity to learn, so treat it as that.

The best way to learn from a disappointing grade is to speak with your instructor for advice. Ask the teacher how you can improve your performance in future courses to help you earn a better grade next time. Request specifics in how your grade was calculated. Sometimes the instructor realizes an error in calculation and can change your final grade. Most importantly though, do not approach the instructor with the goal of forcing him to

Interview with Bethany L.V. Bowan, Pennsylvania Culinary Institute, Le Cordon Bleu, Graduation: December 2007

What did you do in school that helped you to get straight A's?
I knew what I was there for. I worked hard, studied hard, paid attention, and never "took a day off" just because I was stressed out or "didn't feel like it." I had been one of those in high school who skated by and did the bare minimum to pass. "Fake it 'til you make it" is what we used to call it in the Marines. There's rarely been a day gone by since high school that I don't regret my attitude back then. I wasn't going to make the same mistake this time. I went in knowing what was expected of me and realizing what I hadn't in high school: How I did in school was going to affect my entire future. However, although hard work and dedication are key in good grades, they only take you so far. I don't want people to think that it takes no skill or natural talent to succeed in culinary school, or that hard work will be enough. Some natural affinity for the culinary arts has to exist before school if you are to excel.

How often did you miss class? How often were you late?
I missed only two days due to a debilitating stomach virus that made it impossible to stay away from a bathroom for longer than ten minutes. I was late to class three times, and all were due to transportation issues.

Did you ever pursue any extra credit opportunities?
Every chance I got, but not too many of the teachers were keen on giving out extra credit.

Did you ever get involved in any extracurricular activities in which your instructor was also involved?
I was part of student council. I also helped out with the Art Crawl, an event held about once a month in Pittsburgh where the art galleries around our school open up to the public to display their new exhibits. Our school sold soups that our students made in class, hot cocoa, pop, brownies, cookies, etc. to raise money for either student council or, as we did last holiday season, the Children's Hospital.

When you received a grade lower than an A on an exam or project, was the grade usually a fair reflection of your less-than-perfect work or was the teacher generally being unfairly critical?
Well, of course the teacher hated me, right? Just kidding. Actually, I was usually able to see my mistakes and what caused the lower-than-normal grade. It was hard, and I'm not saying that I didn't still feel a bit of resentment toward the teacher, but I was also able to see my failing and where I needed to improve. I may still have fumed as to why they couldn't have been more lenient, but deep down I understood.

change your grade. Argumentative confrontation over a grade is counterproductive and almost never results in a grade change. Instead, you may build a reputation among the faculty as a student who wants a handout rather than to work for a grade. Trust the instructor's professional assessment of your performance, and learn all that you can from his evaluation.

To understand the role the instructor plays in grading is to understand the difference between a goalie and a scorekeeper. In hockey, a goalie actively works to prevent a player from scoring. The goalie sets up obstacles that you, the player, must overcome to earn a point. The scorekeeper, on the other hand, may desperately want you to score, but he can only give you points when you score a goal. Teachers spend most of their time as coaches, training you to succeed, helping you to practice and improve, showing you the tricks to overcome obstacles. However, when your time to perform (on exams, projects, homework, in the kitchen) arrives, the teacher is only a scorekeeper evaluating you objectively against professional standards and grading rubrics. He has no more ability to give you a higher or lower grade for your performance than a hockey scorekeeper has of giving away points. The teacher simply records what you earn.

With that said, a situation may arise where you encounter an instructor who grades you unfairly. In these cases you should still speak with the instructor to first learn how your grade was determined and in which areas you did not meet the expectations for full-credit. Do not discuss any other student's performance or grade, for the teacher cannot discuss another student's grade with you anyway. If, after some serious soul-searching and introspection, you believe that you did meet standards for which you were not given credit or that the standards are inappropriate, speak with the teacher's supervisor, the department director. As the department director has the ability to review the grading rubrics and instructor's notes and grades for all students, the director will be able to determine whether or not your grade is incorrect. If you find that your grade stands (which occurs the majority of the time in student-grade challenges), accept the decision with grace and dignity, and learn from the instructor's feedback. Remember that you are just starting out in the culinary industry and are not in as good a position to determine what constitutes an A performance as the culinary professional teaching your class is.

Summary

Earning an A in a class is much more easily achieved by following a few simple procedures that are easy to understand even if they require real commitment and hard work to implement consistently. Always keep up with reading and homework assignments for all class meetings. Work ahead of schedule on projects and submit them early to the teacher as a draft for feedback; make all of the changes suggested by the teacher prior to final submission. Ask questions in class when you do not understand something, and ask for help from the teacher outside of class when you need assistance understanding more complicated concepts. Study daily, and practice what you have learned in the kitchens whenever possible. Notify your teacher immediately of any emergency that will prevent you from attending class or meeting deadlines, and ask for advice and guidance from the instructor. Arrive to every class on time, in uniform, and physically and mentally prepared for the day's activities. Use the course syllabus and project handouts as checklists to self-monitor your work and class performance. If necessary, make adjustments to your work and performance immediately to ensure you are meeting all grading standards, and never miss a deadline. Take advantage of all extra-credit and make-up work opportunities, and volunteer to work on extracurricular projects in which your teacher is involved. Finally, learning is a difficult and sometimes painful process. When you give your best only to find out that you have a long way to go to achieve mastery of the material, remember that open, honest feedback from the instructor to help you improve and grow is far more valuable to you in the long run than an easy A.

KEYS TO EARNING AN A

- Complete all reading and homework assignments before they are due.
- Submit projects early as a draft for instructor feedback.
- Ask questions in class when you do not understand something.
- Ask for help outside of class when you do not understand complicated concepts.
- Study your notes and books every day.
- Practice the cooking skills and recipes from class whenever possible.
- Notify the teacher immediately if a personal emergency occurs.
- Arrive to class on time every day.
- Arrive to class in full uniform every day.
- Arrive to class with all the tools needed for the day.
- Arrive to class with a written game plan for the day's production.
- Use the course syllabus and project handouts as checklists for your work and performance.
- Never miss a deadline for any reason.
- Take advantage of extra-credit and make-up work opportunities.
- Pursue opportunities to work with the instructor on extracurricular school projects.

Suggested Tasks

1. Meet with one of your current instructors outside of class. Ask for a breakdown of your grade so far, and ask for suggestions to improve your performance in class. Write down those suggestions and implement them immediately. Follow up with the instructor after a few class days to verify that your performance has improved.

2. Write out questions that you would like to discuss in class about a reading assignment due in the next class. Ask them of the teacher during class or hand them to the teacher before class and ask if he can discuss them during or after class.

3. Re-read your course syllabus and determine your weakest area of performance against the course requirements. Write three things you can do to improve your performance in this area and implement those approaches in the next class.

4. In your next kitchen lab class, write out a list of all equipment you will need for the day's production, a step-by-step timeline listing the production activities and the order in which they should be performed, a list of food mise en place to gather and prep, and any questions about the recipes that you have for the instructor. Follow this game plan in class and ask the instructor if there was a noticeable difference in your performance that day.

5. Complete your next written project at least three class periods early. Give it to your instructor and ask for feedback that will help the project score a higher grade. Make the changes recommended by the instructor prior to the final deadline for the project.

6. Speak with three or more faculty members to discover what extracurricular projects in the school still need volunteers. Volunteer to assist on the one project that you can commit to fully, and follow through.

CHAPTER 4

Studying Techniques

Culinary instructors are extremely important in helping students to understand information and to refine their kitchen skills, but the "practice of learning" that results in memorization of facts and concepts and in mastery of culinary skills is the student's responsibility. Studying is as critical in culinary school as it is in any other type of college training.

Most students, unfortunately, believe that studying simply means re-reading the chapters assigned for the class. This form of studying rarely helps a student to prepare effectively for an exam. Consider your day yesterday. Chances are that you remember the events that had significance to you—a fight with a roommate, a special meal you prepared, or a conversation with a significant other. But you probably do not remember the enormous onslaught of information that your eyes and ears observed but your brain decided were not worth remembering, such as the kinds of cars that passed you on the street or the conversations going on at other tables around you at dinner. Your brain would overload on information if it did not have the ability to discriminate between information worth remembering and insignificant data to forget.

Passively reading a text does not help you to separate the interesting stories from the critical concepts. It also does not help you to develop devices that will assist with recall of information during an exam. Most people do not have photographic memories, but just about anyone using the right techniques can sift out the important material to study and find ways to remember that material when exam-time comes.

In this chapter, you will learn several approaches to help you determine what information to study for class, how best to recall that information for an exam, and how to practice your learning to feel confident come exam-time.

4.1 ACTIVE READING AND LISTENING: DECIDING WHAT TO LEARN

Figuring out what is and is not important to know in a chapter or handout is not an automatic subconscious function; it is a deliberate, conscious act that takes time and effort. With the enormous number of responsibilities in the typical college student's life, you may be wondering whether or not the extra time required for active reading is worth the effort. Outlining, designing flash cards, and taking notes all require additional time during the "reading portion" of the course; however, they streamline the "study portion" of the course to make exam preparation quick, fun, and most importantly, effective.

In addition to deciding what to learn, you also need to convert the class information into small data chunks that are easier to learn and to remember. Books and teachers have the responsibility of explaining concepts and procedures in great detail to assist you in fully understanding the knowledge they have to deliver, but once you understand the information, it will be easier to recall later without all of the excess detail that accompanies it. For example, you could memorize all of the primals and subprimals of meat for a cow and the most appropriate cooking techniques associated with each cut, or you could remember simple word pairs, such as "rib-tender; shank-tough." Once you connect these pairs to other learned information, such as "tough = grind, braise, stew," you will know how to cook each cut without having to memorize hundreds of possible combinations of cooking techniques and meat cuts. Active reading approaches help to abbreviate and to simplify the knowledge you have to learn.

4.1.1 Margin Notes and Outlines

In a typical text each paragraph has a single topic or point it is trying to make. One of the easiest ways to simplify a text for ease of studying is to shorten each paragraph to just a few words which capture the essence of what the paragraph is trying to say. Margin notes are brief synopses that you write in the margins alongside the corresponding paragraphs in your text. It is important not to make the notes so brief that you cannot understand them later, but limiting the summary of each paragraph to just a few words will allow you later to study the key points of each page in just a few seconds with a reading of your margin notes.

Many students prefer highlighting or underlining in a book to direct attention to the key points. However, highlighting and underlining pose two potential problems that make them less effective than margin notes. First, since authors must write in complete sentences, just highlighting a topic sentence requires you to read more words later on than you would read if you just wrote key concepts in the margins. The bigger problem, however, is the potential for non-comprehension that comes with highlighting. When a student puts the author's ideas into her own words in the margin, the student must first understand the meaning of the author's words. Simply understanding each word in a paragraph does not automatically result in the understanding of the sentences or the paragraph as a whole. Highlighting does not help a student to understand a paragraph better, but margin notes force a student to wrestle with the author's meaning during the initial reading. If the student has lingering questions on the meaning, she can ask the instructor for assistance in class. However, if the student merely highlights a sentence without understanding it, she will fare no better in understanding it during later study sessions. The act of putting the author's thoughts into your own words automatically enhances your understanding of the text.

Some students take the act of writing margin notes one step further by transferring their notes to a separate page to form an outline. Going this extra step offers two additional benefits. First, the outline for an entire chapter may fit on just a page or two, so the

Interview with David Rashty, The French Culinary Institute, Graduation: May 2008

What study techniques did you use to help you prepare for class and/or for an exam?
Most of the time I created flash cards for each of the lessons. I also copied the recipes (which was required by the school) for each class. I sometimes rewrote the recipes a few times for memorization (more for the tests). While reviewing the class material I would visualize the dishes and the order of the lesson before class. One of the best ways for me was to cook at home. Some of the time I spent at home watching TV I would practice turning cocottes (tournage) which was replaced by sharpening my knives. I also volunteered at God's Love We Deliver and The James Beard House which is not required but helped me become proficient at cutting veggies.

With so many little details in a book, how did you decide what to study?
Vocabulary words/new terminology are always important. The recipes that are covered in each lesson are important because they establish the foundation for everything to come in subsequent levels. The more time that I spent on class preparation, the easier it was for me each class. Some of the classes that I just didn't have the time to properly prep for made things more difficult. I felt like I was trying to learn what we were doing and trying to do the lesson at the same time.

How often did you study?
I studied every day. Taking the Long Island Railroad gave me 45 minutes each way of study/reading time. I would review class material on the way to school, and I would take out books from the school library and read them on the way back home.

Did you study alone or in groups?
Most of the studying I did alone. Sometimes a few of us would meet before class in the library and review before tests. I would have friends quiz me (from the index cards I created) while driving somewhere. I constantly reviewed the information.

student can view in a single glance most or all of the key concepts for the entire chapter, which may shorten the time needed later for studying. Second, the process of organizing the margin notes into an outline form with headings and subheadings helps the student to understand the relationship between bits of information throughout the chapter. Although book chapters may seem like long lists of facts, outlines of those chapters may reveal related themes and larger theories that are not easily recognizable just from margin notes.

4.1.2   Flash Cards and Divided Pages

Many people learn how to use flash cards as early as elementary school, but they often stop using them by college. Flash cards are extremely effective in helping people to learn no matter what their age. Flash cards work simply by putting one portion of a bit of knowledge (a word, a category heading, a cooking technique) on one side of the card and writing on the other side of the card the corresponding piece of knowledge (the word's definition, the category's components, the key steps to the cooking technique).

Like margin notes, flash cards require you to distill key bits of information out of paragraphs and record them in brief, easy-to-recall fragments. However, the format of flash cards makes them perfect for managing the practice of your learning. You can look at one side of the flash card and attempt to recall the corresponding information on the other side of the card. Flipping the card over reveals whether or not you know the information correctly. If you regularly get the information on certain cards correct, you can remove them from your pile of flash cards to focus more on the information with which you struggle. Additionally, the cards can be shuffled, so you can practice learning the information in random order. Finally, the portability of flash cards makes them perfect for brief study opportunities anywhere from lunch breaks to train rides to moments waiting for friends to arrive. Flash cards are extremely effective tools both in distilling information down to key points and in practicing the recollection of those key points.

For students who choose not to spend money purchasing index cards, divided pages may be a good substitute for flash cards. Divided pages are created simply by folding a sheet of paper in half lengthwise. They can be used in one of two ways. One use is to treat them as modified flash cards by putting one piece of information on one side of the page-crease and putting the corresponding information on the other side of the crease. As pages are larger than index cards, multiple flash cards worth of information can be placed on a single page.

The better use for divided pages is to create likely test questions for testing practice prior to the actual exam. You would still divide a sheet of paper lengthwise, but as you read from a text, you would put the key concepts (your margin notes) on the left side of the paper. Once you have finished your reading assignment, you can review your key concepts and guess how the instructor might question you on that concept on an exam. Write your test question on the right-hand side of the paper next to the corresponding key concept. Later, when the page is folded in half, you can read the questions and attempt to come up with the answer. Unfolding the page reveals whether or not you recall the answer correctly. Like flash cards, divided pages allow you to put key concepts into your own catchphrases and to practice remembering these concepts at the prompt of a likely test question.

What ingredients are needed to make chicken stock?	Chicken stock is made from bones, water, mirepoix, sachet d'epices
How long should chicken stock simmer?	Chicken stock simmers 5–6 hours
When do you add the mirepoix when making a stock?	Add mirepoix during final hour of cooking
Name two key steps in the stock-making process.	For all stocks, regularly skim fat and scum and gently simmer, never boil

FIGURE 4.1 Sample Divided Page

4.2 CLASS NOTES

Perhaps the easiest way to figure out what the teacher is likely to put on an exam is to take notes in class. Note taking is an activity that sifts key points out of a lesson and records them in a brief, easy-to-learn format. Typically teachers cover in class the information they believe most important for students to know, so the instructor does the work of selecting for you the information to study. Some teachers may distribute their notes from a PowerPoint presentation or post notes on a Web site, but in class those same teachers will stress certain parts of those notes over others to help direct your studying. (Caveat: taking notes in class does not substitute for active reading of assigned texts. Just because a teacher does not discuss something from an assigned reading does not mean she will not include it on an exam.) Your challenge as the student is to record the instructor's key points in sufficient detail to understand them but not in such depth as to fall behind in the class lecture or discussion.

Like authors, instructors will provide more verbiage than you need to write in your notes, so you should listen to the instructor and condense her points in your notes. Sometimes though, the instructor wants you to remember certain words or phrases exactly as she has stated them; those items should be recorded unabridged in your notes. Clues that instructors often give to identify key points that should be written exactly as stated include writing the key points on the board, repeating a sentence or phrase, and preceding a bit of information with a red-flag statement such as, "This is important" or "Know this for the test." Whether you record the instructor's words exactly or put them in your own words, always make sure that you understand what you have written. If your notes do not make sense to you later, you will not be able to study from them.

For those students who struggle to keep up with the teacher when taking notes, a small tape recorder may be a valuable tool. You can usually tape a lecture (not as a substitute for taking notes) as long as you get permission from the instructor first. You can then listen to the recording later to fill in any gaps in your notes. Not only does this technique help with note taking, but it also provides a second opportunity to listen to the teacher's lecture. Students who learn better aurally than they do visually may also find listening to recorded classes a good study aide when preparing for exams.

Students should not leave information gleaned from class (whether through notes or tape recorder) to languish without review in a bag or desk. Class notes should be converted to flash cards or divided pages to assist with their memorization during later study sessions. Class notes function for a lecture like margin notes do for a text; both need to be studied, not just written.

Interview with Michael Rainforth, M.M., M.A., Certified Sommelier, Dean of Curriculum, Pennsylvania Culinary Institute

What study techniques would you recommend for a student to get straight A's?
First and foremost, you have to be in the right place, with the right tools, at the right time when you study. The "right place" refers to a place that is quiet, comfortable, and without distractions. Turn the lights on, turn your cell phone off, and close the door. The "right tools" are your notes, books, computer, pencil, highlighter, dictionary, etc. Just like preparing your mise en place before

(continued)

(continued)

you begin a recipe, you should have all of your tools at your disposal, so you can avoid interruptions. The "right time" means several things. First, studying should take place every day. You don't have to be in there for hours at a time. At the very least, make time to do your reading or research, and reread your notes on a daily basis. "Right time" also means giving yourself enough time. Study when you have time to study, but also, make time to study.

Are there any tricks that a student can use to help remember what she studies?
Mnemonic devices can be very useful in remembering new information. A mnemonic device is a short rhyme, phrase, or acronym that helps recall information by relating it to something that you're comfortable with. In our mixology lab, we teach our students to set up the bottles in their rails in a consistent order, so they always know where each product is, and which one is missing. The order is: vodka, gin, rum, whiskey, bourbon, scotch, and tequila. To remember that, we give them the sentence: "Very good rum will be sweet tonight." The first letter in every word in that sentence is the first letter of each bottle in the correct order.

How much should a student study to perform well on an exam?
Studying an hour per day is much better than studying for five hours the night before an exam. As you take notes, you are not really retaining any of the information. You're simply transcribing it. If you take the time to reread your notes every day, you are able to actually relate to the information. Another technique I use when I study is to subtext the information. That means to put it in other words. In my hospitality law class, I teach that "the burden of proof is on the accuser rather than the accused." It's not enough to simply write that down. You also must understand what that means. Instead, say to yourself, "If someone sues you, it's their job to prove you're in the wrong. You do not have to prove you're in the right." Now, you actually understand what the passages in your notebook really mean. This takes a lot less time than if you study by rote memorization.

4.3   MNEMONIC DEVICES

When done properly, class notes, flash cards, divided pages, margin notes, and outlines, all become tools to assist in preparing more effectively and efficiently for an exam or even for daily class discussions. However, sometimes long lists of data or complicated rules and theories can be difficult to remember under the stress of an exam. When you find yourself struggling during your studying to recall all the bits of information in a long list or procedure, mnemonic devices may help.

Mnemonics are simple tools that you can use to help you remember facts when other study techniques are not working. Sometimes your brain just needs a little extra memory support beyond basic repetition of information. These tools can make learning much easier and a lot more fun. (Consider how you may struggle for hours to memorize a passage from a text, while you might hear a song on the radio only a few times and know the lyrics by heart.) You can use as many mnemonics as you are willing to invent for yourself, but some classic ones tend to work well for beginners.

4.3.1   Acronyms

Acronyms, using the first letter of a string of words to create a single word (like NATO and NASA), work quite well to help students remember longer lists. Of course, most lists do not easily generate single words, so the more common variation on acronyms is to use the first letters to create a silly sentence whose words also use the same first letters. (Recall, for example, "Please excuse my dear aunt Sally" from elementary school to stand for "parentheses, exponents, multiplication, division, addition, and subtraction.") Students typically have fun generating the silly sentences as reminders for themselves. Generally speaking, the odder or ruder the sentence, the more likely it is you will remember it, but do not spend too much time coming up with the sentence as it is only a tool to help you remember the actual list.

4.3.2 Songs and Poems

For those students who learn lyrics easily from listening to music, writing educational rhyming poems or songs may be just the cure for memory lapses during exams. Poems or songs take longer to write, but once learned, they are hard to forget or to confuse. For example, to remember the wine regions of Burgundy and the corresponding grapes, you could use the poem:

Cotes de Beaunes, Cotes de Nuits
Macon, Chalone, Chablis
These are all in Burgundy.
They use Pinot Noir and Chardonnay
Except for region Beaujolais
Which uses a grape that's called Gamay.

The poem is not going to win any awards on the poetry circuit, but it certainly helps to keep wine regions and grapes straight when taking an exam.

Poems do not need to rhyme either. Alliteration also helps to keep facts straight. For example, in table service you could remember which side of the guest to approach when serving and clearing dishes using the simplistic mnemonic: "Leave left; remove right." Simple phrases like this one make fact memorization faster and far more fun.

4.3.3 Analogies

For difficult concepts analogies may make the material both easier to understand and easier to recall. For example, if you think of pate de campagne as meatloaf and chicken galantine as a chicken hot dog wrapped in chicken skin, they do not seem nearly as complicated or intimidating. The analogies do not have to be exact or even accurate, as long as they help you to remember the material properly.

4.3.4 Common Sense

Although there are many mnemonic devices to help you remember information for an exam, one of the most basic tools that students fail to use under the stress of an exam is common sense. Many of the facts and rules that you learn in a culinary school are common sense if you think about them. For example, you may learn in garde manger that hors d'oeuvres should only be one or two bites and not require a fork and knife. If you envision yourself at a high-end cocktail party, would you prefer to have a lobster tail or a shrimp in your hand while hobnobbing with the governor? If you choose lobster tail, you had better plan on paying for the governor's and your clothes. Shrimp, which can be quickly eaten in one bite to free up your hand to shake hands with the governor, makes a much better choice.

Practical exams are notorious for separating those students who remain calm enough to call upon common sense from those who simply panic. Stop periodically, just for a brief moment, during practical exams to think through what you are doing and to make sure that you are not making any obvious mistakes. Once made, some mistakes cannot be fixed; no amount of sugar, salt, or fat can remove the taste of "burnt" from a dish. However, some errors are easily correctable if you just think rationally. For example, if your hollandaise is as thick as mayonnaise, just add water to thin it out. This may seem obvious now, but in the heat of the moment lots of students will not think of this simple solution. Remaining calm and using common sense may be the best tools you have to help you succeed during an exam.

Interview with Kathryn Gordon, Chef/Instructor, Institute of Culinary Education

What study techniques would you recommend for a student to get straight A's?
Read the curriculum and all recommended textbook areas before class and again immediately after class. Of course, take detailed notes during the lecture and demonstrations. Textbooks have great study questions at the end of each chapter (and some have CD's and other student study guides). Do the extra work. Read more than you're assigned. Review all the pertinent questions. Some students form study groups to review before quizzes and tests. Be careful. I've seen the wrong people in a group. Pick your study mates carefully. Do they take detailed notes? Do they get good grades? Or are they just your friend?

With so much material covered in a class, how does a student know what to study for an exam?
The majority of students these days don't seem to take notes at all. The ones who know how to and reread everything to make study summary note cards—they're the ones to emulate. If this is a competition for the best jobs, get the best training possible out of your tuition investment. Take notes, pay attention, practice at home, and review carefully. Most instructors help tell you what the key points of a lecture are, what topics will be covered in tests. Even with this guidance a lot of your classmates may not be listening. If you study what you're supposed to, you will be able to answer the test questions. Instructors aren't out to trick you. They need you to understand the key points of whatever topic you're learning. Listening is a skill; master it. Stand (sit) near the instructor during lectures and demos. In culinary classes techniques have to be demonstrated throughout the class; not everything you need to learn will occur in the first part of the class. Be prepared to learn continuously; an instructor may be giving the most relevant parts of what you're learning after a formal lecture, during the hands-on demonstration. Keep your eyes open. Learn from what your classmates are doing. You can learn a lot from what goes wrong: Is it possible to fix? Should it be discarded? Why? If you can redo what you learn in class in additional practice sessions, that would be fantastic. It's maybe not realistic for everyone, but whatever skills you can practice will help you really "get" the theory behind what you're trying to learn.

4.4   A NEED-TO-KNOW BASIS

Once you have prepared your study tools, it is time to transfer that knowledge from your paper to your brain. Studying is more than just the reading of your notes; it is the practice of learning and self-testing to verify that you have actually retained what you are supposed to know. Until you know the material well enough to answer any content questions thrown at you, you have not really studied effectively.

Trying to memorize an entire course's content the night before an exam is a near impossibility. Practicing your learning daily makes the study time right before the exam a simple review opportunity to refresh your prior studying. Regular practice also allows you to focus on learning just a few facts at a time instead of hundreds.

If you have not already answered the questions that typically follow the end of a chapter in a textbook (or the questions in a workbook), answer them as part of your studying ritual. If a question stumps you, do not simply skip it. Look back in the text and in your notes to locate the answer. Then, write the question and answer somewhere in your study tools (on a flash card or on a divided page) to practice the learning of that point again before the test. End of chapter and workbook questions are easy sources for instructors looking for potential test questions.

4.4.1   Study Groups

Perhaps the most fun and oftentimes most effective approach to studying is the study group. When students gather together to study in groups, there are some benefits and some potential problems. The best way to maximize the benefits and reduce the risk of problems is to follow a few simple rules for study groups. First, each member of the group should come prepared. Study groups are not opportunities for unprepared students to sponge off of other hard-working students; such students, if allowed to stay in the group, will slow the studying of all group members. At a minimum, coming prepared means bringing potential test questions and their correct answers to test fellow group members. Students may come with specific questions for clarification from classmates, but no one should arrive expecting to be taught the entire course all over again by a classmate. Second, students should plan to work. Although study groups are fun opportunities to socialize, gossiping and eating are not productive study group activities. Lastly, study group members should be supportive, sharing, and honest with their classmates. Group members should help other members through difficult concepts, offer mnemonics, and test each other on potential test questions.

If you have never taken part in a study group before, it is easy enough to form one for your class. Simply ask several students in your class if they would be interested in forming a study group with you. Three to seven students is a good size; too large a group tends to result in socializing and unrelated discussions. Ask each classmate to bring a list of potential test questions and answers at the appointed time and place. Try not to schedule the final meeting on the night before an exam, as getting a good night's sleep really does help in test performance. Plan to study as a group for no more than three hours to avoid mental exhaustion. When everyone arrives, ask each person to test the group with her questions while everyone else tries to answer them correctly. If someone gets a question wrong, the group should try to come up with a mnemonic for the answer. After the questions have all been asked, the remaining time should be devoted to discussing any other potential questions and any areas with which a group member is struggling. Any class notes not yet discussed are a good source for additional questions. A simple session such as this one will typically increase the test scores of every group member significantly.

Since the culinary industry is a hands-on field, a study group can involve some hands-on practice, too. Hands-on sessions should be held separately from theory sessions. Each group member should be assigned a dish or a technique likely to appear on the exam. The group members can share the costs of ingredients or simply bring their own ingredients to the host's kitchen. Once in the kitchen, the group members should work quietly and efficiently under a time constraint, just as in the real exam. At the end of the exam, the group should taste and evaluate each dish honestly and critically. There is little benefit to a student to hear, "It's good." Instead of discussing whether or not a dish is good, ask the question, "What could the student have done to make the dish (or her work habits) better?" Once the student knows how to improve upon the dish, she can practice that change for the practical exam. The cooking and eating process should be fun, but it is important to keep the focus on learning paramount.

Interview with Scott T. Ryan, Cambridge School of Culinary Arts, Graduation: January 2008

What study techniques did you use to help you prepare for class and/or for an exam?
Focus and relax. They may sound like contrary concepts, but I find that they are a perfect match. I spend time in a comfortable place without distraction as best as is available. When I study for a written test, I rewrite my class notes into condensed versions and make association in my mind between food and regions. For practicum/lab tests, I try to remember that I know how to cook, and I'm good at what I do. Otherwise, I wouldn't have started down this road to a culinary degree. I relax, focus and taste, taste, and taste again.

How often did you study?
I try to cook something at home every night that I'm not in class. Not necessarily things that I'm learning in class, but things that will shore up my technique, things that I can be creative with. Book studying is different. I generally wait until two or three days before a test, and then I will completely rewrite my class notes. Usually my original class notes are very cluttered with overlapping ideas and information, so it helps me to organize them along with my drawings in a way that is well-spaced and in order of importance.

Do you study alone or in groups?
You know, when I was younger I would often study along with a study group. Now I find it really distracting. I like to focus on the things that I need to focus on without being distracted by other people's questions or problems.

Do you study or practice for practical exams as well?
There are so many ratios and recipes that must be memorized, but technique is just as important. There are certain things that I know are my strengths, so I spend some time on them to shore up my confidence level. But I primarily cook the things that I have trouble with. I'll execute them over and over until I don't have to think about it in order to get it right.

Summary

Although most students have been "studying" for tests for years, only effective active reading and studying techniques usually result in strong scores on exams. There are a few steps you can take to improve the effectiveness of your studying to get higher scores on exams. Write margin notes or outlines during your initial reading of the material to highlight the key points of the chapter. Use flash cards and divided pages to provide the tools you need to practice your learning and test your knowledge retention. Take notes in class that are clear enough for you to understand key concepts during later study sessions but not so detailed that you fall behind the teacher's pace. Use mnemonic devices, such as acronyms, songs, poems, and analogies to help with the memorization of lengthy lists or difficult material. Get a good night's sleep before the exam, and remain calm during the test. Use common sense whenever you get flustered or confused. Study daily so you will not need to cram all of your studying into the night before the exam. Form a study group that takes studying seriously and whose members come prepared to test each other on possible exam questions. For practical exam practice have the study group cook in a simulated exam situation, and instruct all group members to provide open, honest feedback for improvement on each other's work. With a little practice, these study habits will become second nature. More importantly, you will find that by using these techniques not only will your test scores improve, but you will better remember the information taught well beyond the conclusion of the course.

KEYS TO EFFECTIVE STUDYING

- Take margin notes summarizing key points by paragraph or page.
- For longer, more complex chapters convert margin notes into an outline.
- Create and use flash cards for information memorization.
- Create and use divided pages to practice likely test questions.
- Take notes in every class in enough detail to help you understand the material later.
- Use mnemonic devices such as acronyms, songs, poems, and analogies to help you remember difficult concepts or lengthy lists.
- Remain calm during exams and use common sense.
- Practice your learning (test yourself) daily on the course material and reserve the night before the exam for review.
- Form a study group and participate in it.
- Come prepared to a study group with potential test questions and answers.
- Have study groups practice the recipes or techniques likely to appear on the practical exam, and give classmates honest feedback for improvement.

Suggested Tasks

1. Take margin notes in this book (or another book) for all future chapters. Check the quality of your work against the summary sections to verify that you have included all of the points the author thought were key.

2. For your next exam in a class, prepare flash cards and divided pages to help you study. Compare your test score with your score from a previous exam in that course to see if there was improvement.

3. Show your class notes for a given class day to your instructor. Ask the instructor if your notes are in sufficient detail and if you have captured the key points from the class. Continue with this process until the instructor tells you that your notes are of good quality.

4. For your next exam in any course prepare an educational poem, analogy, or acronym to help you remember the information better. Share the poem with a classmate or the instructor as a potential study tool for other students.

5. Ask 3–5 classmates in your class to form a study group with you. Schedule a meeting time in the next week to begin preparing for the next test. Prior to the meeting have everyone prepare potential test questions and answers. Show the questions and answers to your instructor and ask if there are any glaring omissions in content that the group should also study.

6. Form a study group in one of your lab courses. Schedule a meeting time and place to practice recipes or techniques from class. Give suggestions for improvement to all who attend the practice session.

CHAPTER 5

Making Use of Faculty and Asking Questions

The relationship between student and instructor is too often viewed as tense, dangerous, and full of pitfalls for both parties. Students may perceive a risk to their own grade for "bothering" the instructor, while instructors fear that too close a relationship will be seen as favoritism toward certain students or worse, as harassment or fraternization. Consequently, many students and instructors maintain a safe distance from each other emotionally and intellectually. Many students tend to keep quiet and not draw attention to themselves or to their own inadequacies; they simply listen and follow the teacher's instructions. In turn, teachers follow a standard curriculum and do not delve into students' lives deep enough to learn the students' personal goals, interests, and needs. The relationship is safe but certainly not rewarding for either party. As a result, students learn the minimum required to pass a class, whether or not the information in that class is personally valuable or interesting, and the teacher grinds through lesson plans never knowing what happens to the students after the class ends.

The relationship between teacher and student should never be "friendship." Friends party together, call each other at all hours of the night, and share their innermost thoughts, feelings, and secrets with each other. However, a collegial relationship based on mutual respect between professionals is not only appropriate, but ideal. Students can ask teachers for professional advice, academic assistance, and career development suggestions. With so many students in each teacher's life, the instructor is rarely going to initiate a more-than-minimal relationship with each student. It is instead the student's prerogative to kindle this relationship and to gain from it. With the high cost of tuition at culinary schools, passing on free extra help and advice from instructors simply does not make long-term, financial sense.

In this chapter, you will learn how to get the most value from your relationship with your instructors. You will learn how to develop a professional rapport with an instructor to maximize your opportunities for learning and for professional growth in the time that you have in school.

5.1   THE VALUE OF THE INSTRUCTOR (AND HOW LITTLE OF THAT VALUE IS USED)

Teachers offer students only a small fraction of their potential value through normal curriculum and job requirements. Instructors are not only experts in their course material; they also know about the school's curriculum and about the specializations of fellow faculty members. Teachers typically have a good number of connections in the industry, so they have insider knowledge of real-world opportunities. Finally, they make great guides to help students navigate the intricacies of the college bureaucracy and the challenges of college life.

Teachers are regular people, too. They have personal and professional commitments outside of their jobs, so they usually do not pursue students actively to provide advice beyond the scope of their courses. Students often mistake the nature of this relationship as aloofness or lack of interest on the part of the teacher. On the contrary, teachers want to help their students, but they usually wait for students to make the first move. If you have ever heard a teacher say something like, "Please come see me if you have any questions," the teacher truly hopes that you will use him as a resource. Yet rarely do students ever make the time to speak with their instructors outside of class. Teaching, coaching, and guiding students are an instructor's primary responsibilities, so take advantage of that.

Interview with Christopher Koetke, CEC, CCE, Dean of The School of Culinary Arts, Kendall College

In addition to delivering information to students, what "value" can you provide students?
Modeling is incredibly important. Students recognize genuineness. Ways that educations can model important values include:

- Demonstrating a deep commitment to the individual student's success
- Demonstrating a lifelong commitment to learning and a continual curiosity about all things that interact with food and foodservice.
- Performing acts of service. Chefs are currently in high demand for charity events and have the ability to raise large amounts of money. It is important that our students understand this as it is a responsibility and duty that we have to the greater good of society.

If a student is going to approach you to ask for extra help in class, how should he best ask for help, and how much are you willing to provide outside of class?
At Kendall, we have a philosophy about education that couples very demanding expectations with a caring environment. It is up to the student ultimately to achieve and make it over the bar, and it is

(continued)

(continued)

our duty to help the student as much as possible. We actively encourage students to ask for extra help and attend our tutoring sessions. As for asking for help, all a student needs to do is to alert the instructor and simply let them know that they are having a problem with a particular item. No excuses are necessary. A student should never feel self-conscious or embarrassed about asking. Every professional has also had to grapple with learning skills that were difficult to master. We all have had teachers and mentors.

Do you ever advise/counsel students on matters not related to your own class?
I believe that this is a sign of a healthy learning environment because it speaks to the development of relationships. Many times, students come to our chef-instructors and me to ask many different questions. For instance:

- Advice on a dish they are preparing for a competition.
- Advice on finding the right internship site or job. Many times, alumni ask questions about their career paths or before taking a new job.
- Sometimes students confide in us as to personal or family issues that they may be having.

Do you feel that most students make the most of faculty as a resource?
There are a bunch of students who really do maximize the faculty during their time here on campus. Sadly, I think that many more students could take more advantage of the faculty. In many schools, including Kendall, the faculty is comprised of experts who are here to teach. They are committed to the students. The only thing needed to complete the equation is for the students to engage the faculty. Students should ask plenty of questions about topics relating not only to their current classes. This helps the students grow professionally and taps into the faculty member's vast experience.

5.1.1   The Proper Way and Time to Make Use of the Instructor

Teachers sometimes seem intimidating to students, so many students shy away from any more contact with their instructors than necessary. However, the act of teaching requires instructors to adopt personas, tones, and communication guidelines that they typically do not use outside of class. For example, a teacher may require you to listen quietly, take notes, and raise your hand if you want to speak in class, but outside of class, you will normally find the same teacher more than willing to have a friendly dialogue with you on your terms.

To get the most out of an instructor, you must first ask for the instructor's time and assistance, and there is a proper way to do this. First, wait until a break or after class to ask the instructor for a meeting; do not interrupt the class to make your request. When you ask for a meeting, tell the instructor what you wish to discuss and approximately how much time you will need. Then ask when he might be available to meet. This way the instructor can plan his time to give you his undivided attention and arrive to the meeting better prepared to assist you with your needs. If the instructor suggests a date and time that does not work for you, say so. Ask for an alternate time, or suggest one yourself. Do not agree to a meeting time unless you are certain that you can make the meeting. Missing a meeting that you requested makes it less likely that the instructor will schedule another one for you in the future. Finally, ask the instructor for his contact information in the event of an emergency, so that you can cancel the meeting instead of just not showing.

Once you have your meeting scheduled, arrive on time and come prepared. If you have specific questions that you want answered, write them down ahead of time. If you want to discuss a project, bring with you the work you have completed on the project so far. Always come with a pen and paper to write down information that you want to remember. Lastly, do not forget to thank the instructor for his time. Instructors who know you value and appreciate their efforts are more likely to go out of their way to help you in the future than those who feel taken for granted.

Instructors do not receive extra compensation for meeting with you, so do not make your needs a hardship on the instructor's schedule. If your work and family commitments only leave you with Sundays free to meet with teachers (and school is closed on Sunday), then adjust your schedule to make time for an instructor after class one day. It is worth making time for free advice that you may not be able to get elsewhere in the future.

Finally, despite the willingness of most instructors to spend extra time assisting you, many will not go out of their way to help you unless they feel that you are doing your part to succeed. If you come to class prepared and on time every day, you will find your teacher more willing to help than if you miss several class days and ask the teacher to catch you up on your studies before the final exam. At a minimum, constant presence in class helps the teacher to learn your name and to have a rapport with you before you ask for assistance.

5.2   THE DEPTH OF HELP AVAILABLE

Some students wear blinders that cause them only to see teachers as available to help with course content. Teachers certainly are experts in their own courses and want to work with you to succeed in class, but a teacher can provide assistance well beyond course content. Most instructors willingly provide advice to help you excel in future courses, and they will gladly give you feedback to help you grow personally and professionally. Most importantly, just speaking with an instructor casually to build a rapport can reveal valuable information you did not even know you needed.

5.2.1   Master Course Content

The primary and most common reason that students pursue assistance from an instructor is for help in their current classes. Glenn Walden, Dean of Culinary Arts and Hospitality Management at Stratford University, notes, "Practice doesn't make perfect. Perfect practice makes perfect." A student who works hard at following all of the rules and requirements of a course but never asks for feedback runs the risk of reinforcing mistakes instead of learning proper technique. To ensure that your learning is on track, you should ask for regular feedback from your instructors. In a culinary lab you should always receive a detailed critique of the quality of your work habits as well as of your final products. If your instructor does not give you detailed feedback, ask for it. Harsh criticism is much better for the learning process than is silence. If the teacher tells you that your food is horrible, ask for specifics about what makes it bad. When you are told simply that your food is good, ask if there is anything that you should have done to make it even better. Always strive to improve on your current abilities if you wish to be better tomorrow.

When you struggle to master a skill or concept, ask for help immediately instead of waiting for the final exam review. Small details may require nothing more than an in-class

Interview with Stephan Viau, CCP, Chef Instructor, The Cambridge School of Culinary Arts

If a student is going to approach you to ask for extra help in class, how should he best ask for help, and what should the student do to prepare for a tutoring session?

When I have my class, I tell them "just ask" if you want to meet with me. We can meet either after class or on a day where we don't have class. For those students who need to ask for help but don't speak up, I talk with them and remind them that there is help available for them. To prepare for tutoring I ask them to bring their notes and all of their papers, tests, quizzes, and other information from class. Some students will end up with a pocket notebook and two lessons while other students will have a backpack full of stuff. That's often an indication of commitment. If they're willing to put 100 percent into it, I'm willing to put 110 percent back into it. I don't want to spoon-feed them. I want the students to learn how to learn, how to study, how to do their work without needing tutoring sessions.

Do you ever advise/counsel students on matters not related to your own class?

I do meet with students periodically after they have left my section. Most often, it's helping them to adjust from my style of teaching to another instructor's style of teaching. Employment is also a common request. I first tell them to be aggressive and to talk with the placement office every week. Former students periodically walk back into school, so I also let students know that I can keep them in mind if a job opportunity comes up.

What should a student do to develop a strong relationship with a teacher?

There is definitely a tighter relationship that comes from students who volunteer for different things and work with their teachers outside of class. Students who are willing to stay after class build stronger relationships. I don't want to overlook those students who just come to class and cannot volunteer for everything either, so I try to judge students based on whether or not they are completing their duties. Some students simply write a "thank you" letter at the end of class expressing that they felt a huge connection, but students shouldn't do that unless they really feel the connection.

Do you keep in touch with any of your students after they graduate? Do any ever ask for help from you?

Asking for references happens quite often, usually when students first leave school. There are some graduates with whom I have developed relationships through other organizations and working together on boards or committees. That happens often.

question, but more complex challenges may call for a meeting outside of class time. Do not hesitate to request a meeting with your teacher, and do not stop asking for help until you are comfortable with the material in the class. The amount of time and assistance that you need to learn the course material is irrelevant; the only measure that matters is your mastery of the course competencies at the end of the class. Otherwise, you run the risk of entering the workforce unable to hold down a high-caliber job.

5.2.2   Go Beyond the Course Content

Once you have built up your comfort level with the course content, call on the instructor for advice in other areas. Your teacher observes your performance for an entire course but can only grade you against a predetermined set of standards. Sometimes the instructor recognizes a weakness in your skills that, while irrelevant to your grade, may keep you from excelling in the industry. Ask your instructor for an honest assessment of your overall potential as a cook and future chef. Ask which of your strengths are most likely to help you stand out from the crowd and which of your weaknesses are most likely to keep you from earning promotions. Make sure that the teacher understands that you are not asking for a grade breakdown but rather for his professional opinion as an industry expert. You may be surprised at what you learn, and it may be the most valuable advice you get through your education.

In addition to feedback on your performance, sponge whatever information you possibly can from the teacher to help you succeed in the future. Your instructor will be more than happy to give you advice on sources for personal growth and development both inside and outside of school. Teachers can provide recommendations for other instructors and courses, as well as hints for acing future classes in your program. A good teacher will also relish the opportunity to speak with you on current events and hot topics in the industry. Unlike the information you receive during class time, what you learn from the teacher outside of class only costs you time. A truly inquisitive student may learn more outside of class than during class. Instructors are a resource to which you will have limited access in the future, so using them while in school is your best opportunity to get a jump on classmates who opt not to engage the faculty.

Teachers can also serve as personal advisors for some issues that may not be their area of expertise. For example, instructors have typically observed so many student interactions that your teacher can advise you on how to deal with a difficult classmate even if that teacher does not have any formal training in human relations. Your instructor may be able to advise you on your relationship with your parents, on ways to manage your money or your time, or even on more serious emotional issues. However, do not be alarmed or upset if your teacher directs you to someone else for counseling. Wise teachers may know a lot, but more importantly, they know what they do not know. If your teacher wants to help but does not have the expertise to give you the advice you need, he will likely directly you to someone better able to help you. Teachers often know (or can easily find out) the many school resources available to you.

5.2.3   Learning Spontaneously

One of the greatest benefits that a teacher can provide is to serve as your advocate and mentor, even after your graduation. Once you develop a collegial rapport with your teacher, he will periodically give you spontaneous knowledge or advice you did not even realize you needed. Until you develop this type of relationship with your teachers, you are usually limited only to the answers to questions you know enough to ask. Consequently, earning yourself the opportunity to be mentored by a teacher is potentially the most valuable use of an instructor you can have.

To develop a mentor relationship with a teacher, you first need to find opportunities to interact with that teacher beyond the time constraints of the classroom and the

Interview with Peter Reinhart, Chef on Assignment, Johnson & Wales University In addition to delivering information to students, what "value" can you provide students?

The single greatest value a culinary teacher provides is what I call the mentor/role model relationship. Whether there is ever a formal out-of-class use of this relationship (correspondence, counsel, working on special projects, career advice, etc.), the student derives tremendous value from the experience of "being cared for," that is, of having a person in his or her life who is dedicated to the student's future success. This is much more lasting and influential than even the course material itself, and is delivered in nonverbal as well as reality-based situations.

Is there a benefit to students working with you outside of class on non-class activities?

Absolutely. Students seem to thrive when they partake of these "value added" opportunities. It goes toward deepening the mentor relationship. Of course, the instructor has to be mindful that he or she is always in the role model position, is always being observed, and, to an extent, copied and influenced by the student, so any extracurricular events should be considered by the teacher as a teaching opportunity. Realistically, it's always the same 10–20 percent of students who volunteer, so it's a victory of sorts to get a reticent student to volunteer—it can sometimes change his or her life. I will sometimes offer extra credit just to get them off the dime, with the hopes that they will perceive how much value it is adding to their classroom experience and continue volunteering. But teachers absolutely love students who volunteer without the promise of extra credit. This is a sign of self-motivation and it pays off big time for students in their career advancement. It is exactly the kind of attitude that employers look for, and I tell my students that the classroom is just a dress rehearsal for real life.

Do you keep in touch with any of your students after they graduate? Do any ever ask for help from you?

Yes, but only when they initiate the contact, which happens mainly with the ones who choose a career path in the same discipline I teach. Occasionally, the mentor relationship was influential enough to be helpful in leading a student to a different discipline, yet the mentor relationship continues because it was the "caring" that created the bond, not the skill set. The kind of help asked for is sometimes for referrals, recipes, or how to handle a difficult situation or career decision.

duration of the course. A great way to force interaction is to work with the teacher on extracurricular projects. If the teacher does catering for school activities, offer to help. If he teaches non-credit cooking classes for the community, ask to be his assistant. If your instructor volunteers in the community at soup kitchens or elementary schools, see if there is a way for you to work on those projects as well. In short, the more opportunities you have to work with the instructor, the more likely you are to learn spontaneously from him and to have him agree to be your mentor.

Imagine what you could learn just through casual conversation while working on a culinary project with a teacher. The instructor is more likely to treat you as a peer than as a student. You can get personalized attention for improving your culinary techniques. You may find yourself discussing current events or industry realities that may not be appropriate to share in class. Most importantly, if the instructor enjoys working with you, you may earn an invitation to work with him again on more important and high-profile projects. As chef-instructors have their own reputation to protect, they usually only invite high-caliber students to work on VIP events. If you earn the opportunity to work a VIP event, you will have a great addition for your résumé and may even have the chance to meet the high-profile guests themselves.

Interview with Albert W. A. Schmid, Chef/Instructor, Sullivan University's National Center for Hospitality Studies

If a student is going to approach you to ask for extra help in class, how should he best ask for help, how much are you willing to provide outside of class, and what should the student do first to prepare for a tutoring session with you? The role of an instructor is to help the student succeed. At the same time students need to be proactive in their pursuit of success in the classroom. At Sullivan University we use Fridays as a tutoring day and the students are encouraged to seek out the instructor. I also keep regular office hours and check my email several times a day. I teach both on campus and online, so between the regular office hours and checking my email I am very available to students. To prepare for a tutoring session a student should read the assignment and attempt the homework. By attempting the homework the student gives the instructor a good insight into what successes the student is having with the concepts in class and what the student considers fuzzy.

Is there a benefit to students working with you outside of class on non-class activities?
I think that there is a benefit to chef/instructors working with students on catering (or volunteering) for several reasons. The first, it allows the students to see the instructors in action as a chef, reinforcing what is taught in class. It allows me, the instructor, to access the ability level of my students. I can see where the student can improve. Second, I am allowed to interact with my students in a less formal way. We can see each other work, and we can enjoy working together. Finally, I think working this way builds long-term relationships with students with the hope they will keep in touch with me during their career.

Do you develop stronger professional relationships with some students instead of others? What should a student do to develop a strong relationship with a teacher?
Yes, professional relationships are built on follow-through and showing up. If someone says they will do something the fact that they finish the job speaks volumes. Students who show up every day and complete the work that needs to be done are the ones that I tend to develop strong working relationships with.

Do you feel that most students make the most of faculty as a resource?
Most students don't make the most of faculty as a resource. Students can maximize the use of their faculty by taking advantage of the faculty's availability. The students that do access their faculty tend to gain a better education and many times are better prepared for the job market.

From working with an instructor on extracurricular events, you also get to know a little bit about the instructor personally. You may learn how he began his career and how he ultimately achieved success. His experience may give you ideas on how to build your own career path. You can ask the instructor for recommendations or references to some of the people he has encountered through his culinary career. Those references might open doors that would otherwise be closed to the average culinary school student or graduate. With on-going interaction, the teacher may even feel comfortable inviting you to professional events unrelated to the school, such as professional conferences. You should not expect an invitation to hang out at the teacher's home (and definitely should not accept such an invitation if it were extended), but you may find yourself earning more and more opportunities to interact as your teacher's colleague at professional events. Such learning and networking opportunities are rare for most students, and the few that earn them have an edge over their classmates come graduation.

Once you have developed a professional relationship with an instructor, that person can become a mentor for you well beyond graduation. You may be able to call on him for years to get advice or networking referrals. He may be able to assist you in future projects (such as designing your own restaurant) for little to no cost, while hiring a consultant could become extremely expensive. Most importantly, such a teacher may keep you top of mind as valuable opportunities come up in the future. Obviously, relationships like this are rare and take many hours of volunteerism and months or even years of interaction to bear fruit, but they only grow when students take the first step to work with an instructor outside of class. Giving up your valuable time now to work for free may feel like more than you can give, but the short-term investment is minimal compared with the potential enormous payoff further down the road.

Summary

Instructors have a great deal to offer their students beyond the education they provide in the classroom. Students gain access to the extra perks that teachers can provide only by initiating and building a professional relationship with their teachers. Students can begin building a relationship by interacting with their instructors during and outside of class. By scheduling and attending meetings with teachers outside of class, students can get extra help to master course material as well as additional knowledge and learning beyond the scope of the course. Students can ask teachers for advice on academics and school concerns, personal issues, professional development recommendations, and a range of other topics. Students can also make time to volunteer to work with teachers outside of class on extracurricular activities. As a teacher gets to know a student better, the teacher is more likely to offer networking contacts, recommendations, professional growth opportunities, and personal references to industry acquaintances. If a student continues to remain in contact with an instructor, that student is likely to gain the benefit of the instructor's wisdom and professional connections for years to come. Although many students prefer to minimize their interaction with teachers as they progress from course to course, only those students who nurture relationships with teachers maximize the value they gain from their school's faculty.

KEYS TO GETTING THE MOST OUT OF YOUR TEACHERS

- Schedule meetings with your teachers outside of class time at their convenience.
- Ask questions in and after class to clarify and reinforce your mastery of course content.
- Ask for regular feedback on your performance and skill sets.
- Discuss culinary current events and industry hot topics with your teachers.
- Ask for advice for personal growth and development.
- Ask for help or referrals to someone who can help with personal problems.
- Volunteer to work with a teacher on extracurricular projects outside of class.
- Ask for references and referrals to your teacher's industry contacts.
- Continue working and communicating with your teachers well beyond the conclusion of their courses and your program to gain access to opportunities teachers discover in the future.

Suggested Tasks

1. Schedule a meeting with a current teacher to review your skill sets. Ask for suggestions on how to improve yourself even further to prepare yourself better for the industry.

2. Interview an instructor about his career progression. Ask if he had a mentor and how he used that mentor over the years.

3. Research at least one current topic being debated in the culinary industry. Speak with an instructor about the topic and ask his perspective on the debate. Present your views on the issue and ask him what he thinks of your perspective.

4. Get a copy of your current transcript and program of study. Meet with an instructor and ask for suggestions on teachers or course options. If you already know your next set of courses, ask for suggestions on how to best succeed in those courses.

5. Ask an instructor for a list of community service or volunteer activities in which you could participate. Sign up for at least one of those opportunities if you possibly can.

6. Speak with an instructor about your professional five- and ten-year goals. Ask for suggestions and referrals to industry contacts who can help you meet your goals. Contact at least two of the recommended contacts and introduce yourself. Ask them if there is an opportunity for you to work with them to meet your future goals. Follow through on at least one of the opportunities offered.

CHAPTER 6

Books, Videos, the Library, and the Internet

In higher education research plays a major role in the learning process. Teachers and administrators expect students to learn as much on their own as they do in class. For some students learning on one's own consists primarily of reading the required assignments at home and conducting just enough research to get through the course projects. Taking on additional research projects solely for the sake of self-edification seems like an unnecessary diversion for the student already overwhelmed with work, family, and school.

Self-directed learning, voluntarily pursuing learning on one's own without an external requirement to do so, is all too rare at culinary schools and colleges in general. Few people ever again encounter the vast resources located in college libraries after they have graduated from school, yet many students commonly opt to watch television or to hang out with friends than to conduct optional research. Future chefs who hope someday to become experts in their craft can easily outpace their classmates by devoting a mere two hours per week to study some aspect of the industry not covered in class. The time works out to less than 20 minutes per day, but it adds up to over 100 hours per year. Utilizing the resources available for free at the school, you can easily become a budding authority on the subject of your choice by simply committing yourself to a small amount of daily research.

In this chapter, you will learn how to make the most of the print and video resources available at your school. You will also learn the potential pitfalls that come with using the Internet and how to avoid them.

6.1 KNOWLEDGE IN PRINT

Books and magazines offer incredibly rich sources for information on the culinary arts and foodservice industry. A book with its relatively large number of pages gives the reader an in-depth look into the book's subject matter. Multiple chapters offer an analysis of the many facets that comprise the whole of the book's subject. But books can take well over a year to get into print even after the author has concluded her research. Magazines, on the other hand, offer articles that are relatively short and often narrowly focused, but they discuss information that is timely—often just a few months old. Read in combination, books and magazines allow the reader to build depth and currency of knowledge on one or more subjects.

Unfortunately, there are far too many books and periodicals related to the culinary arts for any one person to read them all. Learning which material to read is just as valuable as the information contained within the pages of the text. Keeping your eyes and ears open for reading recommendations and actively pursuing advice from others will help to direct your "extracurricular" reading.

6.1.1 Getting Reading Recommendations

The first step in becoming an expert on a subject is to read the major works on that topic. You can typically learn the best sources to read from your instructors. When a teacher recommends an "optional" text for the class, buy it. Even if you are unable to read it before the course ends, you will have the resource available when you need it. Teachers know how much reading and written work a typical student can handle during a course, so they may not require all of the reading they think their students should do to master a subject. Optional readings are merely the remainder of the reading assignments the instructor wishes you had time to complete to gain a strong command of the subject matter. Similarly, when a teacher mentions a specific book, magazine, or author in a class, make a note of it and try to locate and purchase that work. Such guidance makes future research and library time much more efficient.

From a cost-saving perspective, never sell back or give away your culinary books when you have finished school. The books you purchase in college represent the instructors' professional opinion of the best work available on the subjects taught. Unless you have a photographic memory, you will likely need to refer to those books in the future. By selling them back early in your career, you handicap yourself against others who have access to that information when they need it. Keep the books and capitalize on their value for a lifetime.

Interview with the Library Staff of the Conrad N. Hilton Library, The Culinary Institute of America

How does a student find the best source for information on a given subject?
First, look in the library catalog. Second, talk with the reference librarian.

What type of assistance does a librarian provide to a typical student and how does a student go about getting such help?
The student gets the help by asking a librarian. The librarian refers the student to the best resources for answering the student's question based on the librarian's knowledge of the collection and other resources.

Is the Internet a good tool for conducting research?
The Internet can be a good tool, but the student has to evaluate the information and its sources that he or she finds. The student should be aware that some Web sites do not present balanced information and some Internet sources may have errors.

Do most students make good use of the library, in your opinion, or is it generally underutilized?
Some do; some don't. Yes, the library is underutilized.

Bibliographies are more than just documentation verifying that the author has done her research in writing a book. A bibliography provides a list of references that anyone can use to learn more about the subject covered in a book. For example, if a person reads a book on barbecue and wants to learn more about the differences between eastern and western North Carolina barbecue, the reader need only look as far as the book's bibliography for a list of sources to consult. By providing a bibliography, the author has done the work of locating additional sources for you.

6.1.2   The Reading Addiction

With so many people going to culinary school and graduating with the same core knowledge, many culinary graduates enter the workforce as "ordinary" employees. They know what their employers expect them to know, but they rarely "wow" other professionals with their depth of knowledge and skill. Imagine the impression that a recent graduate would make if she knew more than just the basics. Simply reading books and magazines to learn everything from current trends to food science and history to cultural dining habits provides a student an expertise to make her stand out from other culinary graduates.

Realistically, most culinary students have little time to devote to non-essential reading, but a minimal time commitment can make a huge difference over the course of a college education. Perhaps the best way for a student to develop the discipline for self-directed learning is to outline a plan for a personal research project. Not as intimidating as it sounds, a personal research project requires only that a student select a subject to research in depth and then conduct that research. Should you wish to pursue a personal research project, the subject you study should have personal significance to you to provide additional motivation for you to learn. For example, if your grandmother emigrated from another country, studying the cuisines of that country might provide personal satisfaction as well as expertise in the country's cuisine. Alternatively, if you only buy organic produce, studying the differences between organics and genetically modified foods might interest you enough to read everything you can find on the subject. What you research is actually less important than how much you research. Do not pick too broad a subject to study. Successful people do not need to be good at everything, but they are usually experts at something.

Once you pick the subject to study, start to locate reading material. In addition to asking instructors for advice you can ask industry professionals, librarians, and even family and friends. A visit to the school library may reveal dozens of books and articles on the subject. There is no need to read everything in a day, so start with one book and move on to the second once you have finished the first. Just do not lose the reading suggestions you have already acquired. Keep the list of books and articles to read in a safe place and check off the texts as you read them.

For many students the actual reading is the hard part. You may believe that you have no time in your day for anything else, especially optional reading. To put it bluntly, make time. Reading just a few pages each night, you would be amazed how quickly you can finish a book. Plus, getting yourself in the habit of daily reading makes lifelong learning an easy goal to achieve in the future. If your goal is fame and fortune, remember that the media and the public only want to hear from experts. Working toward an expertise while in college, you may find the limelight sooner than you think. The time you spend reading now will pay off for years to come.

Interview with Johan Svensson, Executive Chef, Restaurant Aquavit

How often do you research culinary topics to learn new things?
Constantly! That is one thing about our job—it is a constant search for new ideas, techniques, or new ingredients.

What subjects have you researched recently?
Celtuce, the lettuce stem, also called lettuce asparagus—where to try to find it and what to use it for.

Where do you locate your resources for research?
For the above vegetable I used some of my purveyors, Google, and a produce handbook. (I still need to find someone who can sell the item to me.)

How do you know which books to use when conducting research (knowing that there are likely far more on the subject available)?
Reading cookbooks in the store, try to find the ones that contain the subject or talk somewhat about it. I still think the Internet has given us extreme freedom when it comes to doing research; it's easy, accessible, and most of the time pretty fast.

Does it make sense to "read" a recipe book or are those primarily resources for finding recipes?
The more you get exposed to, the better it is to understand different ways of using ingredients. I was exposed early on to cutting fish, for example, and it comes almost naturally these days. It's the same for different cooking techniques and knowledge of different cuts of meat and poultry: the more you learn in school, the easier it will be when it's time to step out into the working world.

6.1.3   A Note on Cookbooks

People often think of cookbooks as recipe collections and nothing more. Many people do not read cookbooks so much as refer to them. However, some cookbooks include introductory sections that discuss equipment, history, ingredients, or techniques specific to the cuisine or subject of the book. These sections are goldmines of information that may be difficult to find elsewhere. So if you purchase your cookbooks solely for a recipe or two, take the time to read the introductory sections in the books that have them. If you do not currently have a large cookbook collection and wish to build one, select books that offer more than just a collection of recipes.

6.2   VIDEOS, NOT TELEVISION

Most culinary schools have a collection of educational videos (on tape or DVD) on a range of culinary subjects. These videos provide a wealth of information in an audiovisual format. Unfortunately, educational videos are expensive, so individuals usually cannot afford to purchase them for home use. Culinary school video libraries offer access to these videos for free, but only to those students passionate enough about learning to make time to view them.

Interview with Philip G. Pinkney, LCGI, CEC, CCE, AAC, Director of Culinary Arts, The Restaurant School at Walnut Hill College

What value is there to a student watching educational videos in the library? Can the same information be found in a book?
There are three ways that we encourage students to learn. Educational videos are good in that you can see what happens. Books are good in that they are often more in detail. And finally, the tactile, physical practice is the third important learning component as students need to practice. You must have all three learning approaches.

Is the Internet a good tool for conducting research?
Yes, the Internet is an excellent tool, but you need to have a fundamental, base knowledge to know what is valuable and what is accurate. It can be overwhelming. It is better if you have some direction first from an instructor or librarian to know where to go as there is so much out there.

How often should a student use the library?
Libraries are fabulous resources, but only the best students seem to use this resource. You pay tuition to be in class and to use the college's resources. It is a waste of money to not use the library. Students who do research just to learn more are wonderful to have in class. They stimulate discussions and engage with the instructors more. I tell my students that if I am teaching a lecture series, without their input the lecture will be boring. Students will waste their time if they don't come into lecture with questions. Researching in advance helps to develop questions. That's why you have a syllabus— to help you know what to prepare for.

Students who watch cooking shows on television to learn about culinary arts would be better off devoting these hours to watching educational videos while in school. The sole purpose of the videos is education; television's goal is entertainment. While some television cooking shows are educational, most dilute or ignore the education to provide entertainment that will encourage a larger audience to watch. (A larger audience means higher-paying advertisers, which means more money for the television station.) Television and the ubiquitous cooking shows will be around long after you have graduated from cooking school. Take advantage of the educational videos while you still have free access to them. If your school does not store videos in the library, ask an instructor if the school owns any videos and if it is possible to watch them outside of class. Chances are that the school will find a way to give you access to them.

Watching educational videos need not be a chore either. Unlike reading a book, you can bring friends with you to watch the videos and to discuss them afterwards. You can also get through most videos in a single sitting. If you miss a video shown in a class, you should make an effort to view the video on your own time. Most importantly, take the videos seriously. While watching them, take notes and watch a section again if you miss its key points. You can keep your notes with you for years even after you no longer have access to the videos.

Although a video typically does not provide the depth of information available in a book, it can provide a visual demonstration of a procedure or process that a book simply cannot. Videos and books offer different benefits to the learner, so ideally a student would use both as part of a self-directed learning strategy. Both offer additional education that you may not get in class. However, neither provides any value unless you take the initiative to access and to use them. Make a habit of watching educational videos and reading books while in school; college is your time to learn as much as possible to prepare yourself effectively for the industry.

6.3 USING THE LIBRARY

Unlike most public libraries, college libraries focus on stocking the books, periodicals, and videos most pertinent to the subjects taught at the school. Schools with culinary programs often have much larger culinary collections than the local public library. Students who wish to gain the most value for their tuition dollar visit the school's library often while in school (and if allowed, after graduation as well).

The library is much more than a building for housing books and magazines. As simplistic as it may seem, the sorting and organization of the books provides two major benefits for the student. First, a search through the library's computers directs you quickly to the right books for information on a given subject. Second, a visit to the shelves holding the books you seek reveals other books on the same or a similar subject nearby on the shelves. A quick walk to find one book will typically result in the discovery of multiple sources for your research.

Interview with Susan Sykes Hendee, PhD, CCE, Dean of Academic Studies, Baltimore International College

What value is there to a student watching educational videos in the library?
Videos support demonstrations, verbal and textbook information. There are multiple intelligences and this method of communication will aid the learning of visual learners with repetition and bodily or kinesthetic learners with movement. When I worked with culinary students in their computer courses, one of the projects was a multiple intelligence survey. I found that a large majority of culinary students scored high in kinesthetic learning.

Can the same information be found in a book?
Books are certainly valuable communication tools. The method of transmission of information, learning and reception by students is varied, and having information represented in various modes only reaches more students. The goal is to reach as many students as possible with all these various modes that best benefit their individual learning styles and intelligences.

Is the Internet a good tool for conducting research?
Yes, with guidance and sound literacy support by a learning resource center (library) the Internet and databases are essential to research by students. Students will best be served by checking with their learning resource center, faculty, and instructors which will qualify their Internet research. Students will want to confirm and check that their research, answers, and proposed solutions come from multiple and reliable resources.

(continued)

(*continued*)

How often should a student use the library?

As often as possible. The library (learning resource center) represents a reliable, informed, and humanistic element to data, information, and knowledge.

Is there a value to visiting the library when a student does not have a class assignment to research?

Yes, there are always other resources and experiences at the library: sitting at a table, being with other people, a comfortable chair, a newspaper, the hardcopy feel of the cover of a book, and the sound of the turning of a page. These are all sensory experiences. We are in the business of providing sensory experiences and cannot lose touch with the power of three-dimensional space, the smell of a book page, seeing another person, talking with someone face-to-face when engaging with a project, problem, or solution. I embrace technology as a tool but not as a replacement for human connections.

Source: Laura Seifert, PR Coordinator, Baltimore International College.

Librarians offer additional support and guidance for students who request it. A librarian can not only help a student locate sources on a given topic but may also know which sources a teacher believes to be the best for completing certain homework or research projects. Unlike the Internet where a student must decide on her own the quality of information on a Web site, a librarian can recommend the best Web pages for given information. You will find librarians can shave hours off of your research time and possibly help you to earn better grades on your projects. Making good use of your school's library and librarians is one of the best ways to squeeze the most value out of your limited research time and your tuition dollars.

6.4   THE INTERNET

Despite the unfettered access to a plethora of free library resources, most students today turn toward the Internet for their research. The Internet provides many benefits, but it also provides pitfalls for students conducting research. The Internet has the benefit of speed. It includes information published on news that occurred within the hour. It also covers almost every subject imaginable and can be filtered and sorted by any number of search engines. However, students should only use credible, reliable sources for their schoolwork and not every Web site meets that standard.

Anyone can create a Web site and post information to it. A disgruntled farmworker could use overblown scare tactics to frighten consumers about the dangers of certain foods grown by his previous employer. A company in the business of selling genetically modified foods will provide information only about the benefits of these foods and ignore any potential concerns, while a pro-organics organization will do the same for organic foods. Books and magazines go through a long approval process overseen by an editor, publisher, and often other industry peers to verify the accuracy of the book's content (which is not to say that a book cannot have errors). Many Web sites, on the other hand, have no oversight, so the information found there may be opinion rather than fact.

Can the Internet be used at all for research?—Of course. There are simply a few tips that you need to keep in mind to help select the best sources. First, look to see who is posting the information on the Web site. If the organization or person is likely to have a biased agenda, take that into account when reading the information on the site. Second, when using potentially biased information, always research the opposing view. For example, if citing the dairy industry for information on the benefits of drinking milk, look up other sites that discuss any possible downsides to drinking milk. Then compare all of the sources to decide which sites are most likely to be accurate. Third, try to rely more on academic journals or reputable news organizations for information rather than on potentially biased organizations or personal blogs which have no oversight. Web sites that cite their sources of information are usually better resources than those that do not cite any research at all. Fourth, when using a search engine, go beyond the sites that are listed first. Companies can sometimes pay to have their sites come up on the first page of a search to help them sell their products. More unbiased, credible sources may not appear until much further down the list of sites related to your subject. Web sites hosted by food magazines, major news organizations, universities, and government agencies (www.usda.gov or www.fda.gov, for example) are excellent places to start.

Interview with Eric Magnani, Executive Chef, Bacchus Food & Spirits

How often do you research culinary topics to learn new things?
I research culinary topics at least twice daily for myself and for the education of my staff. The most recent topic of discussion was the history and hybridization of Asian citron and their influences on the American culinary scene. Another topic was tracing cocoa beans back to their plantation to discern different flavor profiles and how to blend them at the restaurant level to achieve various results.

Where do you locate your resources for research?
The fastest and most time effective approach is to research items via the Internet; however, I spend a great deal of time going through older texts both that I own and at bookstores as well as pulling from my own lifetime of travels.

How do you know which books to use when conducting research (knowing that there are likely far more on the subject available)?
The best method that I have found for researching a subject is to write a checklist of questions that you want answered on the subject and then narrow the search from that point. It may not always be a book where I find my answers. Over the years I have developed a network of friends and acquaintances in the industry, and I have found that most professionals like myself love to talk about subjects that they know well.

Does it make sense to "read" a recipe book or are those primarily resources for finding recipes?
For me, cookbooks represent flavor concepts and visual stimuli, but rarely do I find them technically accurate or historically challenging. So, to answer the question, no, it doesn't make sense to rely on someone else's "interpretation" of recipes that they have collected, altered, or sometimes created anew and treat them as fact.

Is the Internet a good tool for conducting research?
I think that the Internet is a wonderful resource for students to research topics of interest, and they can access it virtually anywhere today. A word of caution on using the Internet: just because it is in print does not necessarily mean that it is accurate. Always, always, always check your facts.

Ideally, you will always use Web sites in conjunction with books, periodicals, and/or journals (even if they are all found electronically online) when you conduct research. The more resources you use, the less likely you are to fall prey to a false agenda promoted by a single person, company, or industry.

Summary

Culinary schools maintain a great deal of resources for their students to use. Students who make use of books, periodicals, videos, and the school library in order to pursue additional education beyond what is taught in the curriculum have an enormous advantage over their classmates. With just a few minutes of reading each day, a student can log over 100 hours of research on one or more subjects over the course of a year. By soliciting help from teachers, librarians, and others to locate the best books and periodicals to read and the best sources for research on a certain subject, a student can easily shave hours off her time spent locating sources for information. The Internet can also be a valuable research tool as long as the student seeks out only credible, reliable Web sites.

KEYS TO SELF-DIRECTED LEARNING WHILE IN SCHOOL

- Use books to gain an in-depth understanding of a subject.
- Use periodicals to get extremely current information focused on a narrow subject.
- Ask teachers and other culinary professionals for reading recommendations.
- Keep all of the books you buy; do not sell them to anyone else.
- Skim through bibliographies of books you like to get other reading recommendations.
- Create a personal research project and read about your selected subject daily for at least 20 minutes.
- Buy cookbooks with large introductory sections, not just a collection of recipes.
- Watch your school's educational videos regularly and take notes on the videos.
- Visit the library regularly and read books that you cannot find elsewhere.
- Ask for help from the librarians when starting research in the library.
- Use the Internet to locate credible, reliable sources online.

Suggested Tasks

1. Interview one of your school's librarians. Find out what types of resources are available in your library and how to use them. If you have an upcoming research project in a class, ask the librarian how to get started on the research for the project.

2. Interview three instructors and ask for their top five recommended books for a culinary student to read that are not

required for school. Compile the list of recommended books and check one of them out of the library. Read that book for 20 minutes daily until you finish it; then check out the next book and repeat the process until the list is complete. Purchase any books you wish to keep for the future.

3. Form a book club at school. Have monthly reading assignments that are not part of class and meet monthly to discuss what has been read. Rotate the meeting host each month and allow the host to determine the next reading assignment.

4. Form a video club. Meet weekly to watch an educational video at the school. Discuss the video after viewing it.

5. Select three potential personal research projects that have meaning to you. Share them with your teacher and discuss which would likely have the most value for you as a future chef. Begin researching the topic you have selected and report back periodically to your teacher with what you have learned.

6. Pick a culinary subject that has information available both on the Internet and in reputable periodicals. Read the information from five Web sites and two periodicals on your selected subject. Compare the similarities and differences in the information you find. Determine how biases from the sources of the information may have influenced the information you found. Discuss the biases and information with your class.

CHAPTER 7

Ethics and Cheating

W ith the pressure of school, work, money, family, friends, and other commitments it is a small miracle that students accomplish much of anything in college. Unfortunately, stress sometimes convinces people that the only solution to the time crunch is to cheat. Cheating is equivalent to using a smallpox-laden bandage to cover a minor cut. While the bandage will fix the immediate problem of covering the wound, it leaves you far worse off than you would have been without any treatment at all. Someone who cheats has a far greater challenge to overcome than completing an assignment.

There are several schools of thought on why students cheat. Perhaps cheaters do not have enough time to get their work done. Perhaps they are ignorant and do not realize that plagiarism is not an acceptable behavior in school. Maybe they are just lazy. More often than not, people who cheat suffer from low self-esteem and from a belief that their own work could not possibly be good enough to pass a course. People who cheat convince themselves that they would have done the work if they just had more time and natural ability.

Chefs never have enough time in their day, and they always strive to push themselves beyond their current abilities and limitations. Students who will someday become successful chefs find a way to get their work done (or they behave like professionals and ask for an extension in the face of truly trying times). Students who give up on themselves so easily that they elect to cheat rather than to endure the stress of completing their work themselves will never survive the culinary industry.

In this chapter, you will learn the importance of remaining ethical in your behavior while in school and the enormous repercussions that result from cheating. Additionally, you will learn what constitutes cheating and unethical behavior in most schools, and you will learn tips to avoid these behaviors.

7.1 WHY ETHICS MATTER

Although you may be a fairly ethical and law-abiding citizen, chances are that you have broken the law multiple times when it comes to obeying the speed limit. Why is that? The police may monitor many of the roads you drive, but they cannot catch and ticket everyone.

As a result, many people drive well over the speed limit multiple times before they get caught (if they ever get caught). The typical driver who speeds may experience positive reinforcement for breaking the law. He reaches his destination faster. He feels the adrenaline "rush" that comes with speeding past others on the road. And if he does get ticketed, he usually just pays a fine—a relatively minor penalty when compared with jail time. What the typical speeding driver does not experience very often is the loss of control, the car accident that results in injuries, or the sense of guilt that comes from causing a fatality. Because the penalties are rare and often minor while the benefits are constantly reinforced, most drivers who speed do so over and over again until a tragic accident occurs.

The truly ethical person is one who does the right thing even when no one is watching. For better or for worse, breaking the rules does not always result in tragedy. As a result, students who cheat may quickly believe that cheating yields positive results. These students mature into professionals who believe that ignoring rules is better than adhering to costly government regulations. While the consequences of cheating at school may seem severe, they are nothing compared to the potential repercussions of ignoring regulations in the industry.

7.1.1 Reputation Rules

Although one might think that restaurants survive or fail based on the *actual* quality of their food and service, it is a restaurant's reputation that keeps it in business. When one person has a great experience at a restaurant, he tells others who may dine there as well. When he has a bad experience, he tells even more people who typically avoid the establishment and never find out if the restaurant was accurately or falsely maligned. Cheating customers, following poor sanitation standards, or breaking the law in general need happen only a few times before a restaurant's reputation drops and its business declines. "Tragic" results from a food-borne illness outbreak to a fatal fire to a lawsuit from a customer or employee can literally put a restaurateur permanently out-of-business. Since a chef never knows which day will bring tragic consequences, it is vitally important that the chef (and all of the company's employees) do the right thing all the time. Building an ethical mind-set early in school is the best way to maintain high ethical standards after graduation.

Interview with Sarah Gorham, MS, CEC, Department Chair—Culinary Arts, Culinary Management, Food and Beverage Management, The International Culinary School at The Art Institute of Atlanta

What are the consequences of violating ethics rules or cheating in your school?
Within the department, it depends on what type of cheating it is. The syllabus spells out what happens if cheating occurs. Depending on what kind of cheating it is a student could fail the assignment or fail the class. If there is more than one instance, the student would be considered for termination from the program. Cheating also includes plagiarism. The faculty member looks at the piece of work to determine if it is the student's work or not. When a student hasn't cited any resources at all, that is a big problem. That is plagiarism. If students collaborate on an individualized project, the students are reprimanded and can end up failing the assignment or the class. Finally, false claims of work submitted by the student fall under Academic Misconduct.

(continued)

(*continued*)

If a student is caught cheating in school, is there an impact on his future in the industry, even if he remains in school?
Yes. I tell students that education is an investment in their future. By cheating, they are cheating themselves. To get a real return on their investment, they need to learn as much as possible in school. If they happen to get by with it in school, they won't get by in the industry. They won't have those competencies in the real world. It could be a kitchen skill set or a costing skill. It will be really evident in the industry that they don't have that competency.

Can cheating that occurs in school damage the reputation of that school for all students?
Absolutely. We have academic credibility. If an institution does not have academic credibility, that word gets out into the industry and effects every student and every graduate. Depending on the student and what they may have cheated on, it effects them not only in the classroom but also in the workplace. Our reputation as an institution is the student's reputation in the industry and vice versa.

How important is a student's reputation to succeeding in the industry after graduation?
What we teach about being professional is an important piece for students to practice before going into the industry to be successful. It is reinforced by the ACF's culinarian's code. We also teach students not to burn bridges in the industry. Their reputation is paramount to their success in the industry.

What should a student do if he observes another student behaving unethically?
Within the classroom, the student should bring it to the attention of the faculty member and then let the instructor determine whether or not the behavior is unethical or not. The student should follow the chain of command. It is not better to ignore the behavior. It is important to retaining academic credibility for the school and the classroom.

7.1.2   Reputation Rules in School, Too

Despite the rapid growth and enormous size of the foodservice and hospitality industry, the industry is still small enough that most chefs typically know each other in their local communities (and sometimes nationally). Cheating your current employees often results in difficulty finding future employees; cheating your employer may make it nearly impossible to find work in the industry again. Culinary school teachers usually remain well-connected in the industry. While instructors can make a student's career by telling their professional connections about the student's exceptional talents, they can also break a student's career by sharing that student's reputation for ethical violations in school. When a student cheats in one class, you can be sure that other instructors will learn about it, and getting any kind of assistance with job placement or recommendations will become extremely difficult for that student.

Cheaters will not find solace in their classmates either. Students who steal from or cheat off of classmates will find their classmates all-too-ready to share that information with co-workers and networking contacts in the community. Your classmates may become your co-workers or potential employers. It is extremely important to deal with them fairly, honestly, and professionally while in school to protect your reputation after graduation.

Perhaps the most dangerous threat to a school with rampant cheating is the diminished value of the degree. As industry professionals learn that many students in a certain school have cheated, they are less likely to hire any students from that school. Professional chefs know that students who cheat in school are more likely to break the rules on the job and to turn to lying and theft at work. Therefore, ethical students who survive on hard work alone have a vested interest in reporting unethical behavior, including cheating, to their teachers. Their own future and reputation depends on eradicating cheating from their school.

7.1.3 Protecting Your Reputation

Most people prefer to work with someone who is a good person than with someone who lies, cheats, and steals to get ahead of others. Although earning A's in school will help with your reputation and future career, getting grades that you have not earned does little to help you learn the skills needed to excel in the culinary industry. Protect your reputation by maintaining high ethical standards all the time, even when you think no one is watching. Even small ethical missteps can have lasting repercussions. By working hard to earn high grades fairly you will become a desired teammate among your classmates and eventually a prized co-worker and employee.

7.2 THE REPERCUSSIONS

There is some variety in the types of punishment doled out for students who cheat, but there are some commonalities across all schools. Typically, a student who cheats in a class fails the course and may be suspended or expelled from school even for a first offense. For those who are expelled there is no way to recover the time, effort, and money already spent at a school they can no longer attend. Such students may attempt to complete a program at another school, but the emotional toll that comes from being expelled is so great that many of these students will not have the strength to complete a college program for years, if ever. Expelled students may never achieve the culinary dreams they had when they entered school.

For those permitted to continue in school despite cheating the penalty goes beyond the extra money and time that it will take to complete the degree. Getting caught cheating usually results in an inability to get recommendations or job referrals from teachers. Classmates, fearing a poor reputation by association, often shun cheaters as well after just a single offense. The student who cheats is ultimately on his own in an industry where having colleagues for support is extremely helpful, if not absolutely necessary, in building a successful career.

7.3 UNETHICAL BEHAVIOR

In the culinary industry, there is great debate as to what constitutes an ethical violation. Some professional associations, such as the International Association of Culinary Professionals and the American Culinary Federation, have written Codes of Ethics to delineate acceptable professional behavior. Although some activities, such as deliberately violating sanitation regulations or not paying employees for hours worked, are clearly unethical, others are borderline ethical at best. Fortunately, what constitutes unethical behavior in a culinary school is fairly clear and easy to avoid.

The Culinarians Code: (Adopted at the 1957 ACF convention, Chicago, IL.)

I pledge my professional knowledge and skill to the advancement of our profession and to pass it on to those who are to follow.

I shall foster a spirit of courteous consideration and fraternal cooperation within our profession.

I shall place honor and the standing of our profession before personal advancement.

I shall not use unfair means to effect professional advancement or to injure the chances of another colleague to secure and hold employment.

I shall be fair, courteous and considerate in my dealings with fellow colleagues.

I shall conduct any necessary comment on, or criticism of, the work of a fellow colleague with careful regard of the good name and dignity of the culinary profession, and will scrupulously refrain from criticism to gain personal advantage.

I shall never expect anyone to subject themselves to risks which I would not be willing to assume myself.

I shall help to protect all members against one another from within our profession.

I shall be just as enthusiastic about the success of others as I am about my own.

I shall be too big for worry, too noble for anger, too strong for fear and too happy to permit pressure of business to hurt anyone, within or without the profession.

FIGURE 7.1   The Culinarians Code
Source: Reprinted with permission of the American Culinary Federation.

7.3.1 Traditional Cheating

Using cheat sheets, copying answers from someone else's homework or exam, and giving someone else your answers during a test are clear examples of cheating and are absolutely unacceptable under any circumstances. Some technology-savvy students "text" answers to each other via mobile phone while others take photos of exam questions to send to classmates taking exams later. These acts constitute cheating as well.

Plagiarism is often misunderstood by students. Although many students have heard the word and associate it with cheating, they do not always know what plagiarism is. Simply put, using someone else's words or ideas without giving credit to the original author of those words is plagiarism and an unacceptable behavior in almost any forum. Prior to the Internet students might have plagiarized by copying whole paragraphs from a book and passing them off as their own work. Today many students simply cut and paste paragraphs or whole articles into their papers without providing proper citation of the source. This is clearly plagiarism and can get you expelled from school. Students may use someone else's words in a paper, but those words should be placed in quotes and the author should be cited in some standardized format (MLA, APA, Chicago, etc.). In fact, you should cite sources when using someone else's ideas even if you paraphrase them into your own words. Students should also avoid using someone else's words for large portions of any paper. One, two, or three sentences copied from another source may be appropriate when cited properly, but there is rarely, if ever, a legitimate reason to copy multiple paragraphs from another source. Putting your research into your own words as much as possible and quoting and citing sections where you use someone else's words or ideas will help you to avoid being accused and found guilty of plagiarism in school.

If you happen to believe you can plagiarize and not get caught, you should realize just how easy it is to identify a plagiarized paper. Every person has a "voice" in writing that typically relates in some way to that person's speech patterns. As you participate in class, your teacher gets a sense of how you speak, of your vocabulary, and of your command of the language. When you copy someone else's words, there is often a glaring mismatch between your voice and the voice in the paper you submit. Any instructor with some teaching experience can easily spot a plagiarized paper on mismatched voice alone. An obvious example would be a student with a thick Southern accent who uses the British spellings of words such as "flavour" and "colour." A subtler example would be a student who uses lots of slang in class but submits a paper with a highly diverse and academic vocabulary. In short, any attempt to present someone else's work as your own is easily identifiable as plagiarism by any teacher who knows you.

Proving that someone has plagiarized has actually become easier rather than harder with modern technology. If a student has pulled wording from the Internet, a teacher need only type a sentence from the paper into a search engine to locate the source. Typically, when a paper seems too perfect, the teacher will simply pick a well-written sentence from the paper and enter it into a search engine. If the original source is found, the teacher can print off the source and use it as evidence against you to have you failed from the course or expelled from school. Teachers look for testing irregularities as well to stop students from copying each other's work. Never assume that you are so good at cheating that you can get away with it. If you have not been caught before, your teachers simply did not care to pursue your violation; in college most teachers will work tirelessly to extricate cheating students from their school. Unlike drivers speeding down the highway, someone is always watching in college.

Interview with Michael J. McGreal, CEC, CCE, CHE, FMP, CHA, MCFE, Department Chair, Culinary Arts/Hospitality, Joliet Junior College, IL; author of *Culinary Arts Principles and Applications,* © American Technical Publishers 2008

If a student is caught cheating in school, is there an impact on his future in the industry, even if he remains in school?
The impact really is that the student will rely on his/her instructors to provide referrals and recommendations for employment as well as the fact that the students rely on their instructors to assist in getting jobs. If the student is found guilty of cheating or unethical behavior, he jeopardizes the relationship and trust of the instructor which could impact opportunities for assistance in securing a great job.

How important is a student's reputation to succeeding in the industry after graduation?
Your reputation is paramount to your success in this industry. A great chef is only as good as his or her reputation and how they are respected by their peers and customers. Once your reputation is damaged, it is next to impossible to get it back to what is used to be.

(continued)

(*continued*)

What types of "cheating" or ethics violations have you seen from students over the years?
The most common are cheating, plagiarism, theft, and degrading behavior to others. We need to respect others as we want to be respected but that is not always the case with some students. I have seen students who turned in papers or projects from students who were turned in a year or two earlier. Also, students have had other students help or do their projects for them to get better grades. We once had a student buy loaves of bread for his bread project from a gourmet bakery.

How often do you encounter plagiarism? Is it easy to spot?
We encounter plagiarism almost every semester, and yes, it is pretty easy to spot. Remember your instructors all started out where you are as a student and we know what level of knowledge and expertise you are capable of. When you turn in a project or paper that is not yours or does not sound like your words, we can usually tell right away.

What types of ethically wrong behavior have you seen from students in the kitchen?
Taking credit for the work of others is the most common. Occasionally, a student's project or recipe doesn't turn out, so they take some from another student and turn it in as their own.

What should a student do if he observes another student behaving unethically?
The instructor usually doesn't have to catch the student since so many students are ethical and believe in what is right. These students will often notify the chef-instructor of the unethical behavior so that the individual and the situation can be dealt with quickly. Remember in a crime, if you see the crime take place but choose not to do anything about it, you are an accessory to the crime. This is the same for unethical behavior; if you witness it and say or do nothing, you have acted in an unethical manner, too.

7.3.2 Culinary Cheating

In addition to the traditional cheat sheets and plagiarism issues, culinary schools have other cheating dilemmas specific to the culinary arts. Stealing someone's mise en place for use in your own cooking is considered unethical and a form of cheating. Similarly, sabotaging someone else's food to make yours seem better in comparison is a violation worthy of expulsion from a course. Simply doing someone else's production may be cause for disciplinary action in testing situations.

Culinary competitions come with their own sets of rules that can result in severe consequences when violated. Ethical competitors will not use unauthorized ingredients in a competition. In the case of edible sculptures, competitors are typically required to use only edible products in the sculpture; using wires or toothpicks for support will disqualify the competitor. Students who cheat in a competition not only bring shame upon their school, but their work is often scrutinized more closely at school afterwards.

7.3.3 Beyond Cheating

In addition to cheating, other behaviors can ruin a student's reputation as an ethical professional. Knowingly violating sanitation regulations is a common ethical violation perpetrated by many culinary students. From not washing hands to serving food from the floor students sometimes skip proper sanitation procedures to cope with stress and time pressure in the kitchen. Although students still in training may forget certain rules in the heat of the moment, deliberately breaking a rule to save time often leads to ingrained poor work habits throughout one's career. There is no excuse for putting the consumer at risk of food-borne illness; eating is never a pleasant experience when the food makes the diner sick. Students should practice good sanitation consistently in school as the time pressure and stress only get worse in the industry.

In culinary schools students often work in teams to complete class production. Students who rely on their teammates to carry them through a course while contributing little to the team garner no respect from their classmates and low grades from their teachers. Attempting to pass a class on the efforts of your classmates is the mark of a poor work ethic and a lack of professionalism. If you are not certain if you fall into this category, ask your teacher and your classmates. They will always tell you honestly if you are not pulling your weight on the team. If you continue to rely on coworkers to cover your work in the industry, you will find yourself regularly unemployed, so develop a strong work ethic early in school.

Other common ethical violations almost always carry severe penalties whether in a school environment or on the job. Theft from classmates or from the school almost always results in expulsion from school and sometimes in criminal charges as well. In the industry theft is a permanent career ender. Working under the influence of drugs or alcohol will result in immediate removal from a class or from a job as doing so puts the safety of the intoxicated student and of his classmates or co-workers at risk. Knives and flame have no mercy for cooks with slowed reflexes. Creating a hostile environment, whether in class or on the job, almost always results in expulsion from school or from work as well. Racism, sexism, and other bigotry is fodder for successful lawsuits and no company or school

Ethical Debates in the Culinary Industry

Whereas some ethical violations have clear-cut legal definitions, such as truth-in-menu laws, others are the source of great debate in the industry currently. Perhaps the greatest conflict revolves around the use of others' recipes both in print and in practice. Legally, a list of ingredients and amounts is not a copyrightable thing. While the introductory story and specific wording on a recipe procedure cannot be reproduced without permission, a person can legally adapt a recipe and print it elsewhere using their own words even if the recipe is essentially someone else's creation. In this case the legal and the ethical constraints diverge. Is it truly ethical to make money off of someone else's recipe? How many ingredients must a person change before he can claim a recipe as his own creation—one, two, three, or more? Is printing someone else's recipe ethical if you give the original author credit in print or must you ask for the author's permission first?

The ethical dilemmas occur not only in printed matter but in actual food creation as well. In an industry where chefs often work at multiple restaurants in their careers can a chef put another restaurant's dish on his current restaurant's menu? Does it make a difference if the restaurants are in the same city or in different cities? Is it acceptable if the presentation is different? Does it matter if the dish is a restaurant's signature item or not?

Although various organizations and professional associations have guidelines that address some of these issues, there are no definitive answers. The only truly ethical way to approach these conundrums is to consult all of the stakeholders involved. If a person asks the original developer or owner of a recipe for permission to use it and discloses how it will be used, he will easily steer clear of otherwise potentially embarrassing and costly ethical violations.

wishing to remain in business permits it to take place. Bribing or threatening teachers or co-workers almost always carries a severe punishment. Even something as simple as spreading rumors and lies about teachers, students, or co-workers can result in disciplinary action. These activities are not acceptable at work or at school, and those students who engage in them have a dismal future ahead of them.

Perhaps you perceive yourself an upstanding person who would never engage in unethical activity yourself. Good! However, being ethical also means not permitting unethical behavior to continue unabated, even if you are not involved in the activity. Report any unethical activity to your teachers or to a school administrator. Permitting unacceptable behaviors to run rampant at your school can make you complicit in them. Speaking up is always difficult, but remember that you did not force the rule breaker to act improperly. In the long run, a school with a reputation for unbridled cheating will reflect poorly on all of its graduates, including you.

7.3.4 Professional Criminals

Unfortunately, crime does take place in the workforce as well. The best approach for any culinary professional is to report illegal activity to a senior supervisor or to notify the appropriate authorities. To do otherwise can subject you to loss of reputation at best and to prosecution and lawsuits in other cases.

Although the list of potential crimes in the culinary industry is vast, some are more common than others. Not paying employees fairly by requiring them to work unpaid hours or by not paying promised wages is sadly more common than one might expect in a professional industry. Although asking employees to work for free can be acceptable, employees should be advised of this arrangement prior to being hired, so the employees can pursue other job opportunities if they wish. Not reporting taxable income to the government is also an all-too-common crime in the culinary industry and should not be tolerated by anyone aware of such behavior. Even misrepresenting the food and beverages served to a guest is a

---

Interview with Alberto S. Tirrito, Chef de Cuisine, The Grill Room, Sleepy Hollow Country Club

How important is it to follow local regulations when operating a foodservice business?
The last thing you want to do is to go against local regulations. When you're in business, you have to realize that you are part of the fiber of the local community, and the last thing you want to do is to irk the town board, board of governors, or the people you're expecting to come in and spend money on your products and ideas. At the least, you could respect the rules they have put into place. Some of them are not easy to follow, but those are the rules you have to play by if you want to be in business there. If you can't follow the rules, they'll tell you they don't want you—plain and simple. They'll close you down or at least make your life miserable perhaps to the point where you are forced to leave.

(continued)

(*continued*)

What would the typical consequences be when a restaurant's reputation is damaged?
There are many consequences resulting from a damaged reputation. First of all, it takes years of practice, lots of money invested in training and advertising, and a lot of hard work to build a reputation. A damaged reputation can erase all of the previously spent time, effort, and money invested trying to build a reputation. Understand that a restaurant's reputation is by far the best form of advertisement, the most dependable tool to attract customers and staff, and can have a huge impact on future events such as contracts with landlords or investors in negotiating future upgrades and renovations, lease extensions, or other ventures such as franchises. When a restaurant's reputation is damaged, you have a shrinking pool of potential employees; your credibility as a business is hurt—which may affect your relationship with your purveyors—and most importantly, your customers lose faith in you and stop frequenting your establishment. It is said that one customer can tell one other of a good experience, but that same customer will tell ten people of a bad experience.

What examples of ethically "wrong" behavior have you encountered among culinary workers over the years?
Well, unfortunately, I've encountered a few dastardly chefs along the way. Aside from the fact that there is a lot of substance abuse in our field, some people act inappropriately, even without the aid of such vile mind and mood-altering chemicals. I once worked for a chef who was so envious of a particular sous chef's work that she stole his entire recipe book. I have also witnessed a kitchen that simultaneously had sexual harassment issues and people falsely accusing others of sexual harassment. Needless to say, trust among those co-workers was dissolved.

crime under truth-in-menu laws. Serving someone a Pepsi when a Coke is ordered may seem like a minor issue, but it can result in a major lawsuit and criminal prosecution against the restaurant and against the employees facilitating such a misrepresentation.

Permitting criminal activity to take place on the premises can cause a company to be shut down by the authorities. Employees should always report crimes such as drug sales or prostitution to keep it from occurring on company property. Similarly, employees should never engage in criminal activity themselves. Serving alcohol to minors or allowing diners to become intoxicated at your establishment can make you personally liable in a lawsuit. No amount of tip money is worth the risk of getting sued for serving alcohol illegally.

7.4 TIPS TO AVOID ETHICAL (AND LEGAL) VIOLATIONS

Despite the dramatic and gloomy portrait painted in this chapter, most people choose not to engage in unethical or illegal activity, and avoiding ethical violations is relatively simple. Your conscience often tells you when you are about to do something inappropriate. Listen to that little voice in your head, and it will rarely steer you wrong. If you are confused by or struggling with the ethics of a given situation, ask for help. A teacher or trusted friend can often provide the support and guidance that you need to avoid making a potentially career-ending misstep.

While you are in school, remain vigilant in adhering to high ethical standards. Trust your own ability to complete your work, since your own work is always better than someone else's submitted under your name. Focus on learning and not on the grades. Cheating teaches nothing, and a cook with a degree but no knowledge typically carries the title "unemployed," not "chef." Always report the cheating and ethics violations you observe in school to protect the reputation of the school for you and for your hardworking class-mates. Rely on your sense of empathy and put yourself in the diner's shoes when you feel pressured to violate sanitation rules. Imagining yourself as the "victim" is often one of the best cures for preventing potential ethics violations.

Finally, in those situations where you truly believe that you can get away with an ethics violation, that no one is watching you, assume that someone will find out eventually. Someone almost always finds out anyway, and you cannot undo a bad behavior once it is done. By doing the right thing even when no one else is watching, you will sleep easier at night and be proud that your achievements are all your own. Over time, your reputation and strong ethical grounding will carry you forward in your career as you earn the support and trust of those around you.

Summary

While the temptation to do the wrong thing may seem appealing at the moment, cheating or otherwise lowering one's own ethical standards is a powerful blow to the character from which it is hard to recover. Ethical violations damage a person's reputation, and reputation is extremely important to any chef's success in the industry. While in school, repercussions range from an inability to gain assistance from teachers and students to failing classes, being suspended, and even getting expelled from school. Although most students know the inappro-priateness of traditional forms of cheating and plagiarism, stealing mise en place and sabotaging someone else's food production is equally abhorrent. Even sanitation violations can have disastrous consequences. To protect themselves, culinary professionals should always report unethical or illegal activity as soon as they become aware of it, and they should never engage in such behavior themselves. Doing the right thing all the time may not seem cool, sexy, or exciting, but it is a necessary quality to flourish in the culinary industry.

PRIMARY REPERCUSSIONS FOR ETHICS VIOLATIONS

- Course failure in school
- Suspension or expulsion from school
- Loss of reputation
- An inability to get recommendations and job referrals
- An inability to get assistance from classmates on school projects and studying
- Dismissal from a culinary competition
- Shame and embarrassment among peers
- Termination from employment
- Lawsuits or criminal prosecution
- Perpetual unemployment
- An inability to locate employees for one's own company
- Loss of customers or complete loss of one's own business

Suggested Tasks

1. Share samples of writing from various classmates, but do not identify the author of the paper. Compare the different "voices" in the writing. See if you can identify the student who wrote each work. As a challenge, also include a sample of writing from a book and one from the Internet. See if you can identify which works came from an author other than a classmate.

2. Discuss the school's standard citation format with your teacher. Purchase a book outlining the official style for that format and use it as a reference for every paper that you write in school.

3. Contact a cookbook author or food writer. Interview the writer and ask about some of the ethical debates going on in the industry currently. Ask what the author considers appropriate use of his writing and what would be considered unethical.

4. Interview a professional chef or human resources director in the industry about ethics. Ask about the disciplinary procedure for employees found stealing, sabotaging co-workers, violating sanitation standards, or engaging in criminal activity on the premises. Ask if any such incidences have occurred in the past year.

5. Speak with an instructor or administrator about setting up a student organization to investigate student ethics violations and to recommend disciplinary action for such violations. If such an organization already exists, ask how to get involved.

6. Write a one-page description of the reputation you would like to have among your classmates. Share your description with a trusted friend and ask how closely this resembles your current reputation. Ask for suggestions on how to create this reputation among your peers and work to build your reputation through your actions.

Bibliography

The Culinarians Code (n.d.). Retrieved May 12, 2008, from http://acfsuncoastcooksand chefs.com.

CHAPTER 8

Professionalism and Image Making

In an industry where maintaining one's reputation is critical, young cooks yearn to prove that they are professionals worthy of promotion and of star status as quickly as possible. They wish to be taken seriously by others and treated as peers rather than as students. Instructors often counsel students that professionalism is key to getting ahead in the industry, but what makes someone a professional is not necessarily clear to many students.

Some students believe that merely pursuing a job in the culinary industry makes them a culinary professional. On the contrary, thousands of high school students work summer kitchen jobs each year and few of them would consider themselves culinary professionals. Some culinary college students pay thousands of dollars in pursuit of a credential, but that act alone does not make someone a professional either.

Imagine two individuals with restaurant jobs. One arrives on time everyday, in full uniform, ready to work. She asks many questions of her supervisor to refine her job performance, and she strives to learn more about other roles in the restaurant to earn a promotion someday. She even offers to help others off the clock to get free cross-training in other positions. The other individual arrives late to work about once per month and misses work as often as two days per month. She does not enjoy criticism as it makes her feel bad about her job performance, so she does not pursue feedback that might help her improve her skills. Although she does her job and earns good money, she refuses to give her valuable time to anyone for free. She would sooner spend her afternoons hanging out with friends than to work extra hours cross-training.

From the brief description of these two individuals most people would label the first person the better employee. The second person may have health or daycare issues that cause the lateness and absences. She may be sufficiently skilled that her supervisor values her, and she has every right to work only when she is getting paid for her time. However, she seems more like someone just doing a job for money than building a career like a culinary professional. Which of these individuals has a college credential seems irrelevant in light of each person's work habits. Their level of professionalism is what distinguishes one from the other.

In this chapter, you will learn what behaviors make someone a professional in the eyes of her peers. You will also learn the image that you portray by engaging in professional versus unprofessional behaviors and the common consequences resulting from each set of behaviors in school and in the industry.

8.1   THE BARE MINIMUM

Thomas Edison is famous for his saying: Genius is "one percent inspiration and ninety-nine percent perspiration." Culinary genius is no exception. Many budding chefs have quite a bit of culinary talent, but they fail to become huge successes because they focus on the inspiration and not on the perspiration. No chef, no matter how talented, is worth even minimum wage if she rarely shows up to work to contribute her know-how. Customers do not care how famous the chef at a restaurant is if their food takes forever to arrive or if the server is inattentive and unkempt. Any person who wishes to be considered a professional in the culinary industry needs first to master some basics.

8.1.1   Daily Attendance

Showing up to work every day is paramount to being viewed as a professional. Although people get sick and sometimes need to miss work, an employee with a larger than average absentee rate is very quickly blacklisted from promotions and good evaluations. Chefs expect to measure the time between their employees' sick days in months not weeks (with the exception of those employees who have a terminal illness). An absent employee throws off the rhythm developed by the kitchen team; others must cover her work in addition to their own while still maintaining company standards for quality and speed. Slower service typically generates more complaints from guests and results in smaller tips for servers. The absence of a single employee can negatively impact the entire staff of a restaurant, so employees are expected to call out only in extreme circumstances.

So what constitutes an extreme circumstance? A person who has a serious cold, meaning with fever, vomiting, or diarrhea, would be expected to call out sick, but headaches, indigestion, cramps, and even exhaustion are not sufficient for an employee to miss work in the culinary field. If you are in doubt, go to work to show that you are making the effort and let your supervisor decide whether or not to send you home. Perhaps you worry that this contradicts proper sanitation code which requires that sick employees not work around food. The purpose for keeping sick employees away from a restaurant is to keep the food supply safe from potential contamination. Stress can cause symptoms such as headaches, indigestion, cramps, and exhaustion without the accompanying fever, vomiting, and diarrhea, but stress is not a communicable disease. Chefs need employees who can deal with stress and not miss work every time they have a difficult day at work or at home.

Other reasons for missing work may be considered legitimate once in a blue moon but not as part of a regular pattern. If a professional's car breaks down, she gets it fixed and finds alternate ways to get to work in the interim. When planning for childcare, a professional always has a backup plan to avoid missing work. When bad weather hits, a professional finds a way to get to work. If the weather is so severe that no one could reasonably be expected to get to work, the restaurant will contact its employees to notify them that it will be closed for business. Until a professional hears from the restaurant, she assumes that she must find a way to work. Deaths in the family are considered legitimate reasons for missing work, but a chef assumes the employee is fabricating excuses when a relative seems to die every month. In all of these situations, an otherwise conscientious employee might be given a "free-pass" for the rare absence, but a person with repeated car or daycare issues is seen simply as disorganized and unprepared for the industry.

There are other situations in which an employee really cannot be at work, but the "emergency" is self-generated. In these situations the employee will be viewed as unprofessional and immature after just a single incident. For example, a person dealing with a hangover will be blamed for drinking too much on a work-night. A person in jail will usually be presumed guilty by her supervisor of doing something wrong to get arrested. The employee who misses work to see the once-in-a-lifetime concert will be viewed as having mixed-up priorities. In short, when a chef gives a job to someone, the chef expects that person to be there if at all possible. When an employee does not meet this expectation, most culinary professionals assume this person does not take her career seriously.

In culinary school the same rules apply. Instructors expect their students in attendance every day unless a real emergency arises. The information taught in class may never be taught again, and the student who misses that information is at a disadvantage in the industry. Chefs will help conscientious students with real emergencies to catch up, but they often dismiss students with habitual attendance problems. Some students claim that their attendance problems will not continue after graduation, but learning to attend "no matter what" takes practice. Students who miss school regularly become employees who miss work regularly. In neither case would a chef consider the person a culinary professional. For a true professional-in-the-making perfect attendance in every course is the goal.

Interview with Nils Noren, Vice President of Culinary Arts, The French Culinary Institute

What are the bare minimum basic behaviors that a student must exhibit in school to be taken seriously as a future culinary professional?
Too many to list all of them, but the most important is having a great attitude and respecting your chef-instructors and classmates. Aside from having basic culinary skills, respecting others and your work environment is one of the most important things that students should take away from their education, and what will help them the most when they start out on their careers.

How important is it that a student be able to work with others on a team?
It's essential for students, or any cook for that matter, to be able to work in teams. I have yet to see a kitchen that is not based on teamwork. Cooking is not a one-man show, and never forget that the front-of-the house is also part of the team.

(*continued*)

(*continued*)

What kind of attitude do successful students typically have in school?
Students that care not only about their own success but also about the success of the class as a whole are the ones that are going to be the most successful. Being eager to learn, asking those extra questions, spending time in the library researching and reading about food, volunteering for events at the school or outside so they start to build a network already when they are in school. What you put in is what you are going to get out.

Is there a benefit to building an image/reputation as a professional while in school?
There is a huge benefit to building a reputation while in school; in the hospitality industry, as well as many other industries, a lot of hiring is done by one chef calling another. If you can build a good reputation while you are still in school, you have a much better chance of getting the position you want at the establishment that you want to work at.

For those students who have earned a poor reputation in school, what generally happens to them?
For the most part they are going to be ok, but they will have a harder time finding the position that they really want. Often chefs call the school for a reference when they hire someone right out of school. We get many calls from chefs asking if we can recommend a student, and obviously we will recommend the students with the best attitude.

8.1.2   Being Present

Showing up to work or school is not the same as being present. Chefs do not want someone who checks in and then mentally or physically checks out for large portions of the day. Professionals are actively contributing from the moment they are scheduled to arrive to work or school and continue participating until the shift officially ends.

Lateness is never considered acceptable. In school a late student disrupts the flow of the class and often requires more attention and assistance from the instructor later in the class, thus pulling the teacher's attention away from those students who made the effort to arrive on time. In this sense, arriving late shows a lack of respect for classmates and for the teacher. Some schools will not allow a student to participate in class if she does not arrive on time. In the workforce a late employee is typically reprimanded (if not tormented) by her supervisor, as late arrival often results in late completion of mise en place and slow service to guests. Employees with repeated late arrivals find themselves replaced with a new employee who may have less skill but more commitment to the job and a stronger work ethic.

The challenge with lateness is in how it is defined by those perpetually accused of arriving late. In the culinary industry a person assigned to arrive to work (or class) at 8:00 is expected to be at her station in full uniform and ready to work at 8:00. A student who just makes it to class at 8:00 and then starts to put on a uniform and to hunt for class materials is late in the eyes of most teachers. If this scenario has a familiar ring to it, you should be sure to arrive five minutes early to class so that you are ready to learn by the time the class begins.

Some people take breaks only when necessary while others view breaks as an entitlement. Students who disappear from class during production or during cleaning show a lack of respect for classmates who must cover the additional workload themselves. Of course, some students never seem to need breaks when there is food to be eaten, but they almost always need that cigarette or bathroom break when the mops come out. Smokers should be able to get through a class without a cigarette break, and all students should be able to keep their bathroom breaks to less than five minutes. In the industry employees may not have time for breaks because of the pace of the kitchen, so employees who take breaks anyway (other than a quick bathroom break here and there) are seen as not pulling their weight. Even a break for a meal is not necessarily provided in all foodservice operations. School, unlike the industry, provides certain times for breaks and for eating, so no student should need to leave class for extended periods of time during production or cleanup. If you are one of those students who elects to leave the room when your classmates need you most, know that your teachers recognize what you are doing and that they are grading you accordingly. This may seem cruel, but it is the reality of the culinary industry.

8.1.3 The Full Uniform

Students often think of a uniform simply as an outfit to be worn in class or on the job, but culinary uniforms serve a purpose. The rules on grooming, footwear, jewelry, hair, and nails as well as on clothing help to keep customers free from food-borne illness and employees safe from injury. Chefs have no respect for people who refuse to wear the assigned uniform as such rebellion shows a ranking of one's individual needs over the needs of the kitchen team. In an industry so based on serving the needs of others, a person unwilling to adjust her own dress and grooming habits to conform to safety and company standards is seen as inappropriate for the culinary industry. In the real world this translates to being sent home or fired; in school it often results in a forced absence from class.

Although the uniforms in schools vary somewhat from college to college, there are some universal standards across all schools. Pants and jackets may vary in style, but how they are worn is fairly standardized. Pant legs should be hemmed short enough that the wearer does not step on the pants while working as this can cause a dangerous fall. At the other end, pants should be pulled up over the hips to hide underwear; exposed underwear in a kitchen is an obvious health concern. Chef jackets should be buttoned fully with the cuffs folded up enough to keep them out of food. Students new to the industry may find it stylish to leave their chef jackets unbuttoned at points, but to do so puts the student at risk. Chef Charles McCormick, General Manager of the Canadian Embassy, relates the story of a former employee at a retirement home. Complaining that the jacket was constricting his movement, the employee refused to button his chef jacket. Only a few weeks into the job, the employee leaned over a range only to have his jacket dangle too closely to a burner and catch fire. The employee suffered severe burns from the incident, endangered co-workers, and earned a trip to the hospital. That week, he lost any hope of being viewed as a professional; he lost his job as well.

Hats and other hair restraints provide protection not only to the guest but to the employee as well. Hair restraints help to keep customers from finding hair in their food. In most cases a diner who finds a hair in her food is going to complain and request a free meal—not a recipe for a successful restaurant. However, employees forget the potential danger to their own safety should their hair get caught in a machine. Positive outcomes to such a situation would be hair ripped from its roots; a bad result would be an employee pulled into a large machine head-first. In such a situation death or brain damage is a real possibility. Hats keep a chef's hair away from moving equipment.

Shoes, too, need to be appropriate for the kitchen. Whereas home cooks may throw dinner together in open-toed, high-heel shoes, professionals would never be permitted to work in a kitchen in such footwear. Professionals wear all-leather, slip-resistant, comfortable shoes. Falls are too common in professional kitchens, and oil or water spills on a kitchen floor can make a kitchen feel like an ice rink to someone wearing smooth-soled shoes. Leather is critical as even the smallest bit of fabric on a shoe allows water to flow easily from the shoe to the foot inside. With so much hot water ever-present in a kitchen a fabric shoe or sneaker allows a simple spill to cause a severe foot burn. Comfort is also necessary as chefs can expect to be on their feet at least eight (if not eighteen) hours per day minimum. Wearing the wrong shoes can turn a day at work into a visit to the doctor or hospital.

Grooming standards are also common across most schools and foodservice establishments. Professionals arrive to work bathed, without jewelry (except perhaps a plain wedding band), and with closely trimmed and polish-free nails. Uniforms should be clean and free of dirt; white chef coats are supposed to remain white, not off-white or cream. Nails and jewelry trap dirt which can make its way into food. Nail polish itself can chip and arrive atop a guest's plate of food. Jewelry can easily fall into food and be served to a guest before the employee notices it is missing. While individuals may highly value certain aspects of their personal appearance (painted nails, earrings, etc.), the kitchen is no place for them. The change to short, plain nails and jewelry-free hands and face may be a difficult one, but it is a required one. A student unwilling to conform to this grooming standard will struggle to keep employment and should consider changing careers before investing time and money in a culinary degree.

8.1.4 Courtesy

Despite the scenarios sometimes portrayed on television reality shows most professional kitchens are relatively free from cursing and harassment. Professionals choose to work with other professionals. While the kitchen environment may be stressful, the most professional kitchens operate with courtesy, efficiency, and clear communication. Employees who resort to foul language and abuse are seen as inappropriate for the management of others, so they remain lower-level employees for extended periods of time. Students who curse and harass classmates are simply removed from class to maintain the integrity of the educational environment.

8.1.5 Verifying the Basics

Although arriving on time, every day, in full uniform, and speaking professionally are not the sole requirements for becoming a culinary professional, failing to do any one of these things prevents someone from being viewed as a professional by her peers. Professionalism may seem like a vague term, but the qualities described above are far from subjective. In fact, these behaviors are so objective that anyone could share them with potential employers as part of a reference check without crossing any legal or ethical lines. Employers may not get more than an opinion by asking about a student's work ethic or talent, but asking how many days a student was late or absent tells more about a student's work ethic than any other question could. You may not think that attendance at school matters as much as it does at work, but students who cannot demonstrate professional behaviors in school may never have the opportunity to demonstrate them out of school. Schools and instructors have their own reputations to

Interview with Ginger Pratt, The Art Institute of Atlanta, Graduation: June 2008

What things do you do that make others take you seriously as a culinary student/future professional?

Acting the part is most important. Believe in who you are and who you want to be and present yourself as that. I am a silly person at times, but in class, it is a different story. I am very serious. I ask questions, open up debates, and study hard so that I can make the best of my student career. I believe the sky is the limit for my success, and because of my devotion and positive attitude, I think others believe the same.

How do you approach working on a team with other people?

I have always been one that felt I could do something better on my own, so I would tend to take charge and do everything myself rather than involving anyone else. I have learned over the years how important it is to work as a team. When working on a team it is important to remember to be humble and flexible. Always listen to your teammates and build on each other's ideas to build yourself as a team. Always remember that one day you will be the manager and you will need to lead a team, but first you must learn to be part of one.

What kind of attitude should a student have to succeed in school?

The typical answer—positive! A positive attitude goes hand in hand with determination. If you are not determined, then this field may not be for you. There are setbacks and challenges that will either cause you to give up or motivate you to try even harder. I never give up, which is why I love this industry so much. It is hard work, and don't let anyone tell you differently, but if you have the passion for cooking, culinary school will only intensify that passion.

Is your reputation in school important to you?

My reputation in school is very important because school is the foundation of your career. How you are viewed there is how you will usually continue to be viewed in the industry. It is very important to be viewed as professional in school because it is your time to practice how you will present yourself in the real world. You must also remember that the faculty in your school will have many outlets to provide you with either during school or at graduation, but they will only want to recommend professional students for the highest regarded positions.

protect and tend not to recommend students with attendance, uniform, or other professionalism "issues" to any but the lowest caliber employers. To give your instructors and future employers the opportunity to see your real talent and genius, put in the "perspiration" now to show that you are capable of being a professional.

8.2 TEAMWORK

Kitchens (and foodservice companies as a whole) work like an orchestra creating music. The executive chef may be conducting operations but without a team of people working in harmony the results fall flat. Consequently, another fairly universal trait among culinary professionals is the valuing of and commitment to teamwork.

Truly team-oriented people put the goals of the team above their own. Most chefs are quick to work the dish machine or to mop floors if such work is needed to keep the kitchen running properly for guests. When a co-worker is struggling to keep up with orders, a professional assists in any way possible to provide customers a quality dining experience. Assisting other employees may add to a person's workload, but that person never knows when she may need the help of a co-worker.

Students should exhibit the same commitment to helping classmates when needed to meet the goals of the class. Although students inevitably have personal differences with some classmates and may prefer to avoid interaction with certain individuals, those wishing to be viewed as professionals need to put aside their differences and to help out wherever they are needed (assuming they can do so without sacrificing their own work). Industry professionals work with a range of personalities, so learning to work with various types of people in school is a valuable exercise to prepare a student for the real world.

Asking for help from others is also a sign of a professional's commitment to teamwork. Despite what many people believe, a person who focuses on the goal of the team and recognizes that she needs help to meet that goal is a better team player than one who stubbornly refuses help and jeopardizes the team's work as a result. Some cooks may feel that asking for assistance from others is a blow to their ego, but most outsiders would view such a cook as exceedingly egocentric and irrational. The scenario is equivalent to a baseball player who asks to play the entire outfield by herself to show that she is truly talented. Everyone knows that covering the entire outfield is too large a job for one person and a ballplayer who refuses teammates in the outfield would be seen as foolish.

Interview with Lance Nitahara, CC, CPC, Culinary Institute of America, Graduation: November 2008

What things do you do that make others take you seriously as a culinary student/future professional?
Besides entering professional competitions, I feel that I try to take every opportunity to participate in any culinary activity that is outside of the CIA's curriculum. Many of those activities have been deemed "not for students" simply because they might require a bit more skill or knowledge that others assume (key word: assume) only chef-instructors and professional chefs possess. This is definitely not the case. I have discovered that, as a student, reaching for things that seem to be out of my reach has made me grow in incredible ways.

How do you approach working on a team with other people?
Being captain of the Hawaii ACF competition team, I discovered the importance of relying on others to help "get the job done." There's a certain amount of trust you have to put in your teammates in order for any kind of working team to succeed. Too many cooks think that they have what it takes to be able to *single-handedly* make their team succeed. This is a problem of ego, one that is so prevalent in our industry today. I know that I'm a pretty solid cook. Yet I have to remember that if I am on a team with my peers, they are most likely to be just as solid, if not more solid, than me in other aspects of the kitchen. Once every member of a team can come to terms with this, the team can begin to move forward without a weak link.

Cooks with more work than one person can successfully handle need to ask for help rather than to allow themselves to fail in their tasks. The guests do not care how many people it takes to get the job done, but they do want their food prepared properly and quickly.

Mentoring is also a behavior exhibited by many culinary professionals. Chefs are often flattered and very willing to mentor young people learning the ropes of the industry. Similarly, students who are strong in a subject area gain respect and gratitude from classmates and even from teachers by mentoring and aiding students in need of help in that subject. The person you mentor today may become a valuable colleague after graduation.

8.3 PRIDE

Some people may confuse pride with egomania. A person with an inflated ego is often unwilling to learn from others or to recognize her own errors. Pride, on the other hand, is the sense of satisfaction that comes as a result of hard work and discipline. Professionals take pride in what they do, and they maintain an unwavering focus on quality and customers. A focus on quality means that proud professionals refuse to take shortcuts that result in poor-quality products. If a customer's request is within their power and within company regulations, professionals do whatever they can to please a guest, no matter how difficult the request.

Professionals also have too much pride to compromise their ethical standards easily. When the stress and fast pace of work become too much to handle, a professional does not simply give up or cheat the customer. Stories abound of foodservice workers with juvenile attitudes who spit in food or send out inedible or unsafe products to customers just to end the stress of a difficult situation or to retaliate against difficult customers. Professionals recognize that chefs are in business to serve customers and to meet their needs no matter how odd they may seem. Students can demonstrate pride in their work simply by making the effort to follow the instructions of their teachers and to do their best no matter what task they are assigned in the kitchen. To cite a cliché, professionals really do believe that any task worth doing is worth doing well.

To improve their ability to provide quality cooking and service to guests, culinary professionals also demonstrate a strong commitment to ongoing self-improvement. Whether through reading, cross-training, classes, research, or just asking questions of others, professionals always strive to improve their performance on the job and their skill sets. By continuously refining their skills, professionals also tend to advance faster in the industry than their co-workers.

Professional development and career advancement does not, however, justify frequent job hopping. In the foodservice industry, employees may change companies often, and it is considered acceptable for an ethical employee to change employers after just a year. However, employees who change jobs every few months appear to have an inability to maintain a job. Job hoppers may have a diverse range of experiences, but they are undesirable employees for operations looking for a stable staff. Although you may need to leave a job after a short period of time, doing so regularly may cause others to view you as unprofessional.

Interview with Charlie Trotter, Executive Chef, Charlie Trotter's, Chicago

What are the bare minimum basic behaviors that a worker must perform to be taken seriously as a professional?
The most used procedure for hiring a potential candidate at most establishments would be the interview, which usually takes place face-to-face across a table. The kitchen at Charlie Trotter's operates somewhat differently than most. We require that a potential employee spend a minimum of two days working with the kitchen brigade for several reasons:

1. We can "size up" a person in the first ten minutes of their arrival. While observing the first task a candidate performs, we are able to observe basic essential behaviors required for one to excel in a fine dining restaurant kitchen. One must be conscious and focused at the task before them. This is easier said than done. One must analyze the situation constantly. One must be able to make decisions on the analysis and act accordingly.
2. One must be aware of one's surroundings at all times. How does one walk down a busy hot line without running into cooks, i.e. reading the play.
3. What is one's demeanor toward one's co-workers; is there a sense of respect and teamwork?
4. One must be passionate about every task put forth. If one must mop the floor, polish copper, or fillet a rare fish from Japan, every task must have the same passion and focus as any other.

If there is a hint of these behaviors, we know we can work with an individual to help him or her realize their full potential with our organization.

How important is teamwork in your operation?
Teamwork is an essential characteristic of any great kitchen. The chef de cuisine of a kitchen is the quarterback of the kitchen, orchestrating how the evening unfolds. Without a strong team to carry out the "plays" nothing of great importance can ever be accomplished.

How do you know when a person is taking pride in her work?
When a cook strives to create cuisine that transcends and exceeds expectations, this is where the magic lies. A young cook must put everything into each and every step in the process from receiving a product to bringing it to the table. This is where pride lies.

What kind of attitude do you want a new culinary hire to have?
New culinary talent should never forget respect, humility, and courage.

Source: Kipling Swehla

8.4 ATTITUDE

Culinary professionals devote their lives to the culinary industry because they love what they do. Of course, most people have occasional bad days and do not love everything they do every day, but a professional maintains a positive attitude even in the face of adversity. Professionals smile and enjoy work rather than complain incessantly about their dissatisfaction with their job. There may be a temptation to bond with co-workers or classmates over negativity through whining or gossiping, but professionals do not complain unless it is to fix a problem. Professionals not only bring complaints to those in a position to correct a problem, but they offer to assist with the solutions to those problems. You can build the proper attitude in school by not gossiping and not participating in conversations designed solely to erode the positive outlook of those involved. People who are truly miserable in a job need to change jobs (or schools) for their own benefit and for the benefit of those around them; those who are always miserable need to change industries.

In addition to having a positive outlook, professionals are typically self-motivated. They know what to do from their training, and they do it without needing to be told to do so. Unprofessional employees put great effort into avoiding work. They may allow a dangerous or inappropriate situation to continue rather than take action to correct it. In school professionals-in-training should accept responsibility assigned to the class as a whole even if it is not assigned to them personally. Whereas some students may take great pains to avoid straining stocks, refrigerating mise en place, or cleaning the kitchen, students who do these things simply because they need to get done will always be seen by their teachers as professionals destined for success.

Finally, professionals look at their job and career as a key part of their lives. They value their work in the kitchen well beyond the income it generates. If you look at foodservice work as just a job and at culinary school as something you fit into the parts of your life that you value more, you may find yourself resenting the tasks and sacrifices asked of you in school and in the industry.

8.5 IMAGE MAKING

Students who adhere to professional behaviors in school earn many rewards. Because teachers view them as hardworking, they are more likely to get strong recommendations from teachers. They usually earn higher grades than their classmates because most teachers have difficulty grading professional students lower than students who behave in an unprofessional manner. Most students want to work with a teammate who seems professional, so the most professional students typically recruit the strongest classmates to work on projects and class production with them. Culinary instructors and administrators often trust students who demonstrate consistent professional behavior with authority and responsibility. When teachers have opportunities to select students to represent the school to the public (often a big honor and great résumé builder), they usually choose the most professional students, for such students are the most likely to represent the school and the teacher well under any circumstances. These students ultimately receive the support and guidance needed to become leaders in school.

In the industry, the most professional people often get promoted fastest. They are likely to be selected as a new-employee trainer. Management and other employees may seek their advice regularly, as they seem competent and exude confidence. Some companies will give their professional employees opportunities for additional learning, from funding for coursework to referrals to other chefs for stages or even for free meals. As a professional employee proves herself, she will also be given the chance to represent the company to the public through cooking demonstrations and interviews, which provides fame, networking opportunities, and a fun change of pace.

One of the best consequences of consistently portraying a professional image is that others believe you to be a professional at the core. When you have a bad day or do the wrong thing, people assume that something external is affecting your behavior to cause you to act out of character. Should you do poorly in class production, teachers assume that they made an error in teaching rather than assume that you did not prepare properly for class. If you really self-destruct in class, teachers will comfort and nurture you under the belief that some personal issue (family problems, illness, etc.) is causing you to perform poorly in class. In the industry any job performance issues will be addressed pleasantly and in a non-threatening manner; for long-time quality employees they may be ignored entirely under the belief that the problems are caused by a temporary external personal stressor. In short, by working hard to show others that you are a professional you earn the right to have a bad day every once in a while without negatively impacting your grade, job performance, or reputation.

Interview with Mitchell Watford, CEC, CCE, Program Coordinator, Stratford University

What are the bare minimum basic behaviors that a student must exhibit in school to be taken seriously as a future culinary professional?
Entering students benefit from having a can-do attitude, a willingness to learn, and an ability to adjust. Having respect for the field, a willingness to accept criticism, infinite adaptability, and a vision to create are also needed. Students must ultimately be resilient.

How important is it that a student is able to work with others on a team?
The focus in the culinary profession is to create a product that is appreciated by the guest. This cannot be accomplished without teamwork. Each participant plays a role in achieving this ultimate goal. The line cooks rely on the wait staff to serve the food and prep cooks to process ingredients for service; the prep cooks rely on the purchasing agent; the purchasing agent relies on the chef for purchasing specifications. Let's not forget one of the most important positions—the dishwashers. The line cooks and servers rely on these personnel to keep the pots/pans, china, glass, and silver clean and flowing. Inside this circle of cooperation are the basic communication and organization skills that keep the interactive staff directed. These directives are initiated by management and passed to the line staff. Ultimately, you are only as good as the staff with which you surround yourself.

What kind of attitude do successful students typically have in school?
Most enter with a clear vision or goal of what they intend to complete. These students are attentive, inquisitive, committed, and goal-oriented.

Is there a benefit to building an image/reputation as a professional while in school?
Culinary school is for some the first introduction into the field. For those in the field it is an introduction to future colleagues. Two expressions come to mind: "It's a small world," and "This is no rehearsal." Those who establish themselves as unreliable will be remembered as so. I have seen

(continued)

(continued)

occasions where poor students have become respected professionals but these occasions are rare. Students will be remembered in the way they have conducted themselves in school. When a fellow student or faculty member has an opportunity to promote or hire a student, reputations are on the line. The student with the best reputation will get the opportunity.

For those students who have earned a poor reputation in school, what generally happens to them?
Occasionally these students experience vertical movement; these instances are rare. For the most part they get stuck in horizontal movement or, due to lack of success, choose another field.

8.5.1 The Wrong Image

Students who fail to earn a reputation as a professional portray an image to others, too, but that image does not serve them well. A student who is seen as unprofessional is often deemed a "slacker" unable to do anything right. Others often believe that such a student cannot handle responsibility and is likely to fail out of the industry or to languish in a dead-end low-paying job. Worst of all, teachers and supervisors will view errors in this student's work as proof that the student is incompetent or simply does not care.

Unprofessional students struggle to get recommendations from anyone, and they rarely get offers to participate in special extracurricular activities to represent the school. While teachers may view poor performance in class by these students as par for the course, teachers will look at a strong performance by an unprofessional student as an anomaly or worse as an incidence of cheating. Once a student earns a reputation for poor professionalism, it is an uphill battle for that student to regain the respect of teachers and classmates in the future.

In the industry an unprofessional employee fares no better. These employees are often micromanaged and regularly criticized by their supervisors. Chefs will often bypass non-professionals for promotions and give them lower pay increases or performance evaluations. Professional employees typically shun their unprofessional co-workers and do not assist them in improving their job performance. If a team project fails, the teammates will likely place the blame on the least professional employee of the group. In fact, employees and supervisors usually assume that an unprofessional worker's poor performance is her own fault even when the worker has legitimate personal emergencies or other problems. When an employee has an image problem, she has difficulty networking and getting references and recommendations. Worst of all, an employee perceived to be unprofessional is likely to be terminated when staffing decisions are evaluated. Whether fair or not, an employee with lots of knowledge and talent will struggle to prove her worth in the culinary field if she cannot conform to the industry standards for professional behavior.

8.6 THE GOOD NEWS

Fortunately, although culinary students and workers cannot get ahead until they first master and exhibit professional behaviors, learning to perform those behaviors is relatively easy. Anyone can adjust her schedule to arrive to school or to work on time every day in full uniform. With practice anyone can learn courtesy and learn how to work in a team environment. As a person learns how to produce a quality culinary creation, she will naturally take pride in her work and develop a positive attitude. The only truly difficult part to adopting professional behaviors is enacting them consistently, as even a few unprofessional incidents invalidate an otherwise positive image.

All employees can point to some days where they arrive on time and in uniform, but only professionals do so every day. Professionals maintain a positive outlook and proper courtesy even in the most stressful situations. They work well in teams even with difficult teammates. You can quickly solidify your reputation as a professional simply by committing yourself to the core professional behaviors no matter what the circumstances. By practicing professionalism daily, you will not only portray a positive image, but you will find the professional behaviors easier to perform consistently in time. Professionalism will become a part of your identity for life.

Summary

Every culinary student and employee has a great deal of control over whether or not others perceive her as a professional. To create an image of professionalism a student or employee should arrive on time every day in full uniform, adhere to proper grooming standards, and speak in a professional, courteous manner. The student or employee should also work as a team player by assisting others and asking for help to make the team's goal, not the internal politics of the group, her focus. Committing to consistent quality and ethical standards, she should take pride in her work and maintain a positive attitude as much as possible. Any individual who demonstrates these behaviors consistently generally becomes a professional in the eyes of teachers, classmates, and co-workers. By earning a reputation for professionalism a culinary student typically receives higher grades, special opportunities to represent the school, and strong recommendations from teachers. Unprofessional students struggle to receive any of these perks. While these basic professional behaviors are prerequisites to success in the industry, none are difficult to master. With continued commitment to professional behavior, every culinary student and employee can earn a reputation as professional others.

KEY BEHAVIORS FOR CULINARY PROFESSIONALS

- Attend school (or work) every day.
- Arrive on time every day and do not take excessive breaks.
- Wear the complete uniform properly and make sure it is clean.
- Adhere to required grooming standards.
- Use proper courtesy when speaking with others and avoid cursing.
- Be a team player and focus on the goal of the team.
- Take pride in your work and maintain a commitment to quality at all times.
- Maintain a positive attitude.

Suggested Tasks

1. Write a list of the professional behaviors and qualities that you exhibit consistently. Then, write a list of your behaviors and qualities that might make others perceive you to be unprofessional. Share the lists with your teacher to ask if your self-analysis is accurate. Finally, come up with a plan for how you will change your unprofessional behaviors to earn your reputation as a professional.

2. Approach one of your culinary lab teachers to discuss your daily performance grades. Ask how well you display professionalism and how it impacts your grade. Request suggestions for how to improve your professional behaviors.

3. Interview three industry professionals to ask them what makes someone a professional. Report your findings to the class.

4. Keep a daily journal for a two-week period. During that time record any unprofessional behaviors that you exhibited and write what you would have done differently to grow your image as a professional. Attempt to correct your behaviors each day so that by the end you have fewer unprofessional behaviors to record. Share your journal with your teacher or with a trusted friend to get an outside opinion on whether or not you have made progress over the two weeks toward becoming a professional.

CHAPTER 9

A Note on Work-Life Balance and Wasted Time

Between attending class, doing homework, using the library, working with faculty, holding down a job, and studying, a student can easily become overextended and burned out quickly. It is important to make time in life for the activities that keep the mind and body refreshed and alert. Sleeping, eating, and maintaining personal hygiene are non-negotiable and must occur for a person to survive the rigor of the culinary school experience. For some students parenting responsibilities and full-time employment cannot be reduced to make school attendance easier.

So how does a student create time for additional learning when there is none to spare? Creating a balance between those activities that are emotionally draining and those that are psychologically restorative helps the typical student to satisfy commitments without sacrificing sanity. What usually undermine a person's ability to carry a heavy workload are time robbers that provide little value to a person's education, health, or happiness.

In this chapter, you will learn to identify what activities add value to your life and which are merely time robbers. You will learn how to create a balance between school and other "life" responsibilities without sacrificing long-term happiness. Finally, you will learn time management techniques to help you complete your goals in the time that you have available.

9.1 ADDING VALUE TO LIFE

Bob arrives to class looking more exhausted than usual. His friend Jim asks if he saw the game last night.

Bob perks up and replies, "It was great. What a finish! Triple overtime and Eddie made a shot from mid-court at the buzzer. I can't believe the game went until 1:30 in the morning. It was awesome."

His friend answers back, "Yeah, I saw that shot on the news this morning. It was incredible. I wish I had seen it last night, but I really needed to study for this test. It took two hours, but I think I finally understand costing. I just passed out at midnight, but I made it here."

"A test today? I totally forgot to study."

The teacher overhears the conversation before class and asks the two students what they plan to do when they graduate. Jim expresses his desire to become a chef.

The teacher turns to Bob and asks, "Are you going to be a sportscaster?"

"No," Bob replied.

"A sports historian? A basketball team manager?"

"No, I'm gonna be a chef, too."

"Too bad," replies the teacher. "The time you spent watching the game on TV last night really would have helped you in a sports career years from now. But by the time you graduate culinary school, you'll probably have forgotten about the game, and you'll really wish that you knew how to cost a recipe."

As this story illustrates, some decisions that seem like good choices in the heat of the moment may appear poorly considered with the wisdom of time. Bob acted on impulse to do what made him happy at that moment. Jim, on the other hand, denied himself the pleasure of watching the game in exchange for learning a skill he needed to achieve his goal of becoming a chef. Bob's happiness is fleeting, while Jim's endures for a lifetime.

When deciding what to do with one's time, a person always has many factors to consider. What has to be done now and what can be put off until tomorrow? What may I choose to do for myself and what responsibilities do I have to others? Most importantly, what will bring me pleasure now and what will provide delayed gratification? Activities that provide long-term happiness (even when they do not provide immediate satisfaction) typically add greater value to a person's life than those which provide only a brief moment of bliss.

When deciding on how to spend one's time, the main question to consider is this: Ten years from now, will I look back at this activity and be glad that I spent time doing it? Although there are an infinite number of activities a person may choose to do at any given moment in time, only certain types of activities usually provide long-term happiness and pride. Successfully overcoming a major obstacle or completing a difficult challenge often yields long-term happiness. Acquiring knowledge or practicing a skill also usually provides a sense of enduring satisfaction. These activities add value to a person's life for years, while other activities simply rob a person of time better spent elsewhere.

Many of the actions performed by a student can be classified as value adders, time robbers, or basic life necessities.

9.1.1 Common Time Robbers

Time robbers often seem like fun activities at the time, but they provide little to no lasting value to the individual. Watching television, playing video games, abusing drugs, and just hanging out with friends can provide some joy, but when the positive feeling ends as soon as the activity does, the activity was nothing more than a time robber. The activities leave you worse off than if you had not done them at all.

Watching television and playing video games are common pastimes among college students. Students may claim that these activities clear their minds and help them to focus on learning later. However, like a drug, television and video games have a high potential for addiction. It may seem easy to turn off the television or a game, but most people have difficulty doing so when they need to spend their time elsewhere. It is nearly impossible to take a ten-minute breather by watching television. Television programming usually lasts for 30 or 60 minutes. Commercial breaks often show promotions for other shows to tease the viewer into watching even more television. By the time a person has had enough diversion to want to turn off the television, he has usually spent more time watching than he had planned, and he finds himself exhausted from the inactivity.

Video games create a similar situation. People tend to play games over and over in an attempt to "win" or to improve upon a previous score. Although the game provides a "rush" for a time, it also drains energy from the gamer while enticing him to play "just one more round" before returning to schoolwork. One game can turn into hours of play before the player realizes he has fallen victim to the addiction. Like drugs, television and video games entice the participant to continue to engage in the activity again and again leaving the participant drained and unmotivated to do anything else afterwards. All that these activities do is to rob the participant of hours (if not years) of life.

Although less addictive, "hanging out" with friends can also be a time robber. Different from building a friendship, "hanging out" suggests a group of two or more people doing nothing together. In reality, it often centers on other time robbers such as watching television or playing video games. While friends can gather together to bond over deep conversation or through a fun event to build their friendship, doing nothing together does little more than waste the time of everyone involved. When your conscience tells you that you have more important things to do, it is time to leave the gathering and get working. You will not be able to pull yourself away from a real bonding experience, but you will have no difficulty leaving when you are just wasting time.

Interview with Jeremy Ryan, Sullivan University, Graduation: 2001

Looking back on your time in school, what things did you do periodically that you would now consider a waste of time?
My third job was a major waste of my time because I was a bouncer at a bar. I was also catering and had a full-time job with a computer company during the week, which made it hard also for school. The catering was good for me because I learned new things. My first job was necessary because at 26 years old, I got a late start. It was a necessity. But the bar job only taught me how to drink and how to throw people out of a bar; it was a waste.

If you could go back and relive those moments, would you still choose to engage in those activities?
I don't think I would do the bar job again. That is time I could have spent working on my classes. I would still have done the catering because I did learn valuable lessons. School is just teaching fundamentals. Real world, hands-on experience is really valuable.

What things did you do in school that added real value to your life (other than going to class)?
I volunteered for certain things in school. I helped Chef Albert with a Russian dinner for the school President, which showed me a whole new style of service. I volunteered to help in the

(continued)

(*continued*)

bakery once with a project that they had going on. Working with Chef Albert was always interesting because he didn't just say, "Do this;" he'd explain the process behind it. When you're in school, it's important to understand the reasons why things have to be done a certain way.

Have you ever found yourself overwhelmed with too many things to do to be able to get them all done on time? If so, how do you deal with this situation?
Prioritize. Figure out what's the most important thing at that time, and work on that. Get it done and get it out of the way. That is the area that I try to work on the most. Put things in perspective, prioritize, and complete the highest priority task before moving on to another one.

9.1.2   Common Value Adders

A value adder, unlike a time robber, is an activity that a person rarely regrets no matter how much time has passed. Typically, a value adder nurtures the self, grows a relationship, or provides a sense of satisfaction from the completion of a goal. Common examples include reading a good book, studying for school, learning something new, building friendships, attending classes, spending quality time with family, and even exercising. Rarely would a person look back a week later and regret spending quality time with family. Students seldom look back at a class and wish they had missed more class days or studied less to get a lower grade. Even the most bookish students rarely wish they had read fewer books over the past year. Unlike time robbers, value adders provide satisfaction long after the activity is complete. A student who studies hard, learns a great deal, and performs well in school will feel proud of that accomplishment years after graduation.

Value adders also often return benefits to a person later in life beyond providing happiness. Those value adders that nurture the self (learning, reading, exercising) can increase your knowledge, skill sets, and physical stamina to help you perform better at work, earn promotions, and increase your income. Those that grow relationships (spending time with family, building friendships) provide long-term emotional support and, in some cases, networking opportunities for career development. Finally, those value adders based on goal completion (schoolwork and ultimately graduating) typically provide credentials and demonstrate a strong work ethic that will help you to get hired for positions of responsibility. In short, more time spent on value adders now returns benefits for years to come.

9.1.3   Necessities

Some activities may not provide the on-going benefits of true value adders, but they must be performed nonetheless. While no one needs to watch television, for example, everyone must sleep and eat as a requirement for living. A person usually does not reflect on his life and feel good or bad about sleeping six hours every night; he simply views it as an activity necessary for functioning in the daytime.

Earning a living is a necessity for most adults who need an income to survive. Commuting or traveling, whether to work or on errands, is a necessary use of time to allow a person to accomplish other important activities. While most people need not work every waking moment, they must factor enough time for work and commuting into their

---

Interview with Benjamin T. Stanley, Kendall College, Chicago, Graduation: Summer 2008

Looking back on your time in school, what things did you do periodically that you would now consider a waste of time?

I consider my biggest waste of time to be not taking more classes when I had the opportunity. Having to go home and wait for another class, instead of sticking around school and helping out a chef or taking an extra class, was a huge waste. Going to culinary school allows you to learn and make mistakes without being under pressure and risking your job.

If you could go back and relive those moments, would you still choose to engage in those activities?

I would have gone back and used all the time I spent sitting around waiting for another class doing something more enriching to my field. Maybe reading a book or even just watching a kitchen in action. Every once in a while I feel I'm entitled to a break, but after school I wouldn't have the opportunity to just go upstairs and pull a book out of a library made up entirely of culinary references.

How do you find a balance in life between work and other activities that enrich your life?

For me, I separate things into levels of importance and things that are needs vs. wants. Work is important, but school is more important. Therefore, I'll put more emphasis on school and tell my boss that I need my schedule reduced. When I first started, I told him my priorities, and he knows that they are important to me. He still chose to hire me. If I want to go to visit some friends, but I need to finish a written practical, then I will do the best I can to finish in a timely manner and give the rest of the time to my friends. Most people are willing to compromise.

schedules to support themselves and their dependents. Those who are fortunate enough not to have to work while in school should recognize and respect the needs of their classmates who have no other choice but to work, and they should use their free time to maximize their learning opportunities.

Maintaining personal health and hygiene is another major necessity for culinary students. Sick people cannot function as well as healthy ones. Students who arrive unkempt to class may not be permitted to participate. Even something as simple as tooth brushing must be attended to daily for students to prevent long-term health issues that could impact their ability to work in foodservice.

Students must include necessities as part of their daily routine if they are to have the ability to complete the value adders and other responsibilities in their lives. Attempting to free up time in one's life by cutting out necessities will not work for more than a day or two, and it does not help students develop long-term strategies for managing their time to create a work-life balance.

9.2   CREATING A BALANCE

In order to develop a sustainable balance in life, one must include necessities, value adders, and short, effective relaxation breaks. Time robbers have no role in the life of a busy student or chef and should only be added to your routine once you have developed a balanced schedule that allows you to complete all of your goals and responsibilities. If you have a television show that you must watch every week, then you are already addicted to a time robber. Eliminate time robbers from your life now before they take over your life.

Relaxation breaks need be nothing more than going for a walk, grabbing a cup of coffee with a friend, or just meditating on nothing for a few minutes. Breaks need not be long as the mind often refreshes rather quickly, but they should be frequent enough to prevent mental and emotional exhaustion. Even changing activities, such as doing house chores as a break from studying, can be enough to allow the mind to recover from a single-minded focus on studying. Television and video games do not work as relaxation breaks as they take a great deal of time, and they usually drain mental and physical energy rather than restore it.

When students find themselves overwhelmed with responsibility, they should look to multitask activities wherever possible. For example, building friendships through participating in a study group allows a student to achieve two goals at once. Studying can be done while commuting on public transportation and while eating as well. Exercising can be done with family or friends to nurture those relationships. For those employed in the foodservice industry, simply going to work provides an opportunity to study culinary information and to practice cooking skills for school. By multitasking you can free up a great deal of time to help you to meet all of your responsibilities.

If you are still overwhelmed after eliminating time robbers from your life and multitasking activities, then you may be allowing others to dictate your priorities for you. Your supervisor at work should not determine whether or not you attend class. If you have notified your boss of your class schedule and have requested not to work during class time (or not to work more than a certain number of hours per week), do not agree to work additional hours that would conflict with class or study time. If your boss threatens to fire you, look for a new job that will allow you to meet all of your goals. Similarly, do not succumb to peer pressure from friends who want to spend the day at the mall when you want to study. Your family may ask you to take a vacation while you are still in class; make sure that you stand firm to your priorities and goals. When you set boundaries for others that allow you to stick to your own priorities, people will respect you for your commitment to school (and to other priorities), and the outside pressure will ease up over time.

Finally, do not sacrifice health to create time. Caffeine does not replace sleep; less sleep merely makes you less productive when you are awake. Illness prevents you from devoting time to much of anything beyond getting well. Even trying to save a few minutes by eating junk food rather than healthy food may cause you to be sluggish and less productive later. A healthy diet based on fruits, vegetables, lean proteins, and complex carbohydrates keeps your mind sharp and your energy level high. Take care of your health, and you will work better and faster in the pursuit of your goals.

Learning to create a balance in life can make you more productive in school, happier in life, and stronger in your academic and culinary abilities. To change your current lifestyle to create better balance in life, start by using a time management approach to direct your schedule.

9.3   TIME MANAGEMENT

Time management is simply a way for people to determine how to make the best use of their time. Too often people do not plan their schedule ahead of time; they are left to make spur-of-the-moment decisions on how to use available time. Unfortunately, many people may sacrifice long-term goals for immediate satisfaction when faced with a free moment in an otherwise frantic day. By creating a schedule for yourself ahead of time, you can prioritize your activities to make time for the most important things first. Most people find that organizing their days and weeks in this manner allows them to accomplish most or all of their goals in the limited time that they have.

To create a time management system, begin by monitoring what you currently do with your time. Keep a log of your daily activities for a week, and record the amount of time that you devote to each activity. Be as accurate as possible; do not merely estimate the time spent on an activity. One problem that some people have is not realizing just how much time they devote to certain activities. By keeping an accurate log you are able to properly analyze your schedule to locate ineffective uses of your time.

Next, label each entry in your log as a necessary activity, a value adder, or a time robber. Label "breaks" as such only if they are brief and surrounded by otherwise productive activities. Be critical and harsh with your analysis. (Was that trip to the ice cream parlor a necessary activity or was it really more of a time robber to avoid studying?) Add to the end of the log a list of any necessary activities and value adders that you wanted to do that week but did not have time to do. Estimate the amount of time that each extra activity would require of you.

After labeling your log, determine which activities could be eliminated (primarily the time robbers) or combined through multitasking to free up more time in your schedule. Also consider which activities could be completed in less time. Do you need to sleep for 12 hours on Saturday morning when you function just fine during the week on six hours of sleep? Could you spend less time with friends and still maintain a quality friendship? By eliminating, multitasking, and even shrinking the time spent on certain activities, you can very quickly free up a great deal of time in your schedule.

Now that you have economized your previous week's schedule, apply what you have learned to write your schedule for the upcoming week. Begin by allotting time for necessary activities. Since school is presumably something you want to make time for, treat class time, homework, and studying as necessary activities and add them into your schedule at this point. If you have required family obligations, treat them as necessary, too. Next, add in

11:00 p.m.–5:30 a.m.	Sleep—Nec.
5:30–6:05 a.m.	Shower, brush teeth, shave, get dressed—Nec.
6:05–6:20 a.m.	Make and eat breakfast—Nec.
6:20–6:55 a.m.	Commute to school—Nec.
6:55–7:00 a.m.	Arrive to class; gather thoughts—Break
7:00 a.m.–2:00 p.m.	Class—V.A.
2:00–2:45 p.m.	Coffee with classmates—V.A.
2:45–3:20 p.m.	Commute home—Nec.
3:20–4:00 p.m.	Computer games—T.R.
4:00–5:00 p.m.	Watch TV—T.R.
5:00–5:50 p.m.	Make and eat dinner—Nec.
5:50–9:20 p.m.	Homework—V.A.

Key: Nec. = Necessity; V.A. = Value Adder; T.R. = Time Robber

FIGURE 9.1   Time Management Log

your value adders. Multitask activities where possible. Finally, be sure to leave at least one hour of free time each day (possibly divided into two or three segments spread throughout the day) to allow for any unforeseen emergencies or for activities that take longer than anticipated, such as homework.

Once you have your schedule filled, create a list of "bonus activities" that you want to add to your schedule if you find yourself with available time. Add them to your day only if time frees up in your schedule. Time may become available if certain activities take less time than expected or if you do not need to use your scheduled free time for emergencies. However, do not treat time robbers as bonus activities; rather, eliminate time robbers from your life while in school. They have a habit of hijacking your schedule and diverting all of your free time away from more productive activities. Since college is one of the few times in life that people have vast resources available for self-development, students should not squander their free time on unproductive time robbers. Only after graduation should you consider allowing time robbers back into your life, and even then you should devote a minimal amount of time to them. Eventually, you may realize that you never needed certain time robbers to find happiness, and you may use your free time to incorporate many value adders into your life.

With your time management schedule in hand, you simply need to keep to your schedule as much as possible. Do not allow others to modify your schedule against your wishes. Use any free time for bonus activities that you had listed or for other value adding opportunities that arise last minute. However, do not create free time by cutting out activities you already planned in your schedule. You can move your study time to another day to make time for friendship-building events, for example, but do not eliminate your allocated study time from your schedule entirely. Continually evaluate your own compliance with the planned schedule and get back on schedule quickly when you get off track.

Interview with Michael Lyons, Chef/Owner, Accessible Gourmet, LLC, author of *A Cook at Heart: A Recipe for Transforming Your Life*

What things did you do in school (other than going to class) that added real value to your life?
Whenever possible, I worked (for free!) with the PCI chefs on any events or programs they were involved with in order to learn even more, and not just about cooking. Things like planning, staffing, cost analysis, and execution are critical components behind the culinary industry that may not be emphasized enough during class time. Not only did I gain experience to support my education during these experiences, but I also managed to begin something very important during one's culinary career—self-marketing. By working hard and demonstrating both solid techniques and work ethic, I was creating a "résumé" that could be communicated in the industry to validate my credentials.

How do you find a balance in life between work and other activities that enrich your life?
My schedule was interesting in that I commuted every day from Cleveland to Pittsburgh to attend PCI, so I could spend time with my family each night. I found that the key to balance was focusing on the activities that were in direct line with my goals. I wanted to ensure that I would

(continued)

(continued)

be a good husband and father during PCI, so I made sure that family time was not forgotten. I wanted to gain the most out of my PCI education, so I made sure that I worked hard during class time and between classes spent my time with the PCI chefs to learn even more. I tried my very best not to stray from the path that I had set for myself. By doing this, I didn't allow for activities that weren't in line with my goals, and thus didn't put pressure on my schedule and threaten the balance of work and life.

What do you do to make the most efficient use of your time?
I literally outlined my goals on a dry erase board before I started PCI. I wanted to excel at school, finish at the top of my class, get the best externship position possible, and not sacrifice my family life. Behind these goals, I would then list the key milestones needed to achieve these goals. By focusing on activities that helped me achieve the milestones, I knew I was on the right path for achieving my goals. With the above structure in place, it was important to focus on the most important time available to any student: free time. Concentrating while in classes or lab is relatively easy. Focusing on what's important while not in a structured environment is the true test of personal fortitude. During my long daily commutes, I would listen to books on tape. During breaks between classes I would either prep for the next class or review notes.

If you find yourself more productive and able to meet your goals as a result of adhering to the schedule, then repeat it weekly. Reserve one hour each week for writing your time management schedule, but know that with time and practice you will be able to create your weekly schedule in just a few minutes. Planning and organizing a schedule usually helps most people to become more productive with their time and to meet more, if not all, of their goals and responsibilities.

Completing school while juggling work, family, and other personal commitments is not meant to be easy, but it should not be impossible. Colleges do not want students to play video games for eight hours per day, but they do not expect students to forego sleep to complete course assignments either. By eliminating time robbers from your life, you will likely find yourself able to excel in school and to get the most out of your education and college experience.

9.3.1 When Nothing Works

Unfortunately, some people realize very quickly when using a time management approach that they really do not have enough time in a week to complete even their necessary activities. Such students may need to consider holding off on college until they are able to devote enough time to school to make it worthwhile and educational. Certain necessary activities arise in life unexpectedly and usurp many hours from a person's day. For example, a student who suddenly needs to care for a sick parent or child may not have the luxury of leaving home to attend classes. A pregnant woman on bed rest is in the same boat. A person who must choose between buying food for the family and giving up hours at work to attend class should also consider whether or not now is the right time to attend college. College may open doors for a person's future, but it only benefits a student with the time to learn and eventually to graduate.

When life's requirements are so great that a student is not likely to succeed in school, he should withdraw from college and return when he is better able to pass his courses. There is no shame in taking time off from school during difficult times to return and complete the program at a later date. However, failing out of school, no matter what the reason, can hamper a student's ability to return to school in the future. If you find yourself overwhelmed and unable to make time for school even after creating a time management plan, speak with a trusted advisor at school about your options. Most schools would rather have you leave and return to graduate later than fail out and never come back.

Summary

Looking back over time, a person might wish he had made different choices in life. Although a person can consider how each action taken today will appear with the wisdom of time, most people rarely go through that process as part of their daily routine. A student who can distinguish time robbers from value adders and necessary activities can consciously decide to engage in activities that add value to life while minimizing time robbing activities that do little more than provide a diversion. The student who employs a time management approach can usually accomplish more in a day than the average student. Such students make better use of their time by not wasting precious minutes on value-less activities, and they build a guide that helps them to prioritize their schedules rather than allowing others to determine their priorities. Using time management to create a personal schedule simply requires logging and analyzing one's current use of time and then planning a schedule to include only necessary activities and value adders. Following a time management system, students often find that they not only handle their many responsibilities better, but they also enjoy better balance and long-term happiness in life.

KEY STEPS IN TIME MANAGEMENT

- Keep a log of daily activities with the amount of time spent on each activity.
- Label each log entry as "necessary," "value adder," "time robber," or "break."
- Identify which activities could be eliminated.
- Consider ways to multitask two activities at once.
- Determine which activities could be completed in less time.
- Create a schedule for the upcoming week, listing activities and time estimates, that incorporates the efficiencies discovered in the log analysis.
- Include at least one free hour of unscheduled time per day in the schedule.
- Do not include time robbers in the schedule.
- Create a list of bonus activities to add to the schedule later if possible.
- Follow the planned schedule as much as possible.

(*continued*)

(*continued*)
- Use any free time for bonus activities.
- Self-assess compliance with the schedule and resulting productivity.
- Repeat the process weekly, if after a few weeks the time management approach is effective in increasing goal completion.

Suggested Tasks

1. Follow the time management approach to analyze your own schedule for a week and then create a new schedule to maximize your productivity. Follow the schedule for the week and analyze the results to determine whether or not you got more accomplished in the week.

2. Select an individual in your life whom you believe to be very organized and capable of accomplishing lots of things each week. The individual should appear generally happy rather than frazzled. Interview this individual to ask how he spends his time on a typical day. Share your results with your class.

3. Write a list of the top five activities that you value most in life and list how much time you spend on each of those activities each week. Next, write a list of the top five activities on which you spend the most time each week. Compare your lists to see how many of your most valued activities command large amounts of your time. Share your lists with a friend or trusted advisor and discuss how you could adjust your time and activities to align better with your values.

4. Hold a meeting with friends and/or family to discuss with them your change in priorities that includes your need to succeed in school. Brainstorm strategies to allow you to meet your responsibilities at school while still maintaining your commitment to loved ones. Follow through on their suggestions and remind your friends and family that they continue to remain a valuable part of your life even as you focus more time on school and self-development.

CHAPTER 10

The Risks and Benefits of Moving Beyond the School Walls Before Graduation

O nce a student has learned how to study, to use the library, and to make use of the faculty, she may find school much easier and more straightforward. Her culinary courses will continue to offer challenges, but the initial difficulty of acclimating to the school environment will have passed by the midpoint of the program. With some time and emotional energy freed up most students will find themselves able to take on additional responsibilities outside of class.

Opportunities abound for students to enhance their résumés and their skills sets with extracurricular activities. The industry expects culinary graduates to be competent, quick, and comfortable in the kitchen; additional kitchen practice beyond the classroom increases the likelihood that a student will meet industry expectations. Volunteer activities, both in school and in the community, offer students a chance to practice their skills, to gain confidence, and to take part in a good cause. Working in the culinary industry while in school also gives students a chance to practice their craft. Even something as simple as cooking for oneself or for friends, if it challenges the student's abilities, can be a great educational experience. Networking while engaged in extracurricular activities may help students find mentors as well.

Obviously, there are benefits to engaging in culinary activities beyond the classroom, but there are also some trade-offs. Time spent volunteering can take away from time needed to study. Students who work in the industry while in school do not yet have the benefit of a college education; their weaker skills may translate to a less than pleasant job experience. Even time spent networking in professional associations can present employment opportunities that may draw a student away from school and thus, away from the ultimate goal of graduating from college. Weighing the risks against the benefits, you can determine which extracurricular opportunities offer the best advantages for your specific situation.

In this chapter, you will learn the risks and benefits of engaging in culinary activities outside of class and school. You will also learn how to determine your readiness to take on additional commitments and how much extracurricular responsibility to accept.

10.1 THE BENEFITS OF DOING MORE THAN JUST "SCHOOL"

Whether a student chooses to work at a job outside of school, to participate in a professional association, or to take part in some form of community service, involvement in the greater local and professional community always returns some reward to the student. The reward may be money, professional contacts, skill development, or résumé-building experiences. Perhaps the benefit is an intangible psychological development, such as building maturity or a sense of community, or maybe it is the sense of satisfaction that comes from helping others. Whatever the gain, students looking to have an edge over their classmates in the industry often look to the world beyond school for opportunities.

Many students eager to apply their newly learned culinary skills to the real world seek kitchen work outside of school. Whether as part of a steady job or through sporadic one-day opportunities, any kitchen work builds on the skills, knowledge, and speed taught in school. Since most culinary schools attempt to teach students a great deal of material in a short period of time, they often do not repeat most lessons in the program. After all, most students enjoy learning new material more than simply reviewing and practicing prior learning. However, the way to refine hands-on skills and to build kitchen speed is through practice. Many industry chefs complain that the one talent most recent culinary graduates lack is speed, so finding opportunities to practice and build speed is an essential component to any student's education.

Kitchen work outside of school can also give a student extra skills and knowledge not yet encountered in that student's program. If a student learns certain culinary skills before they are taught in school, she may outshine her classmates in the corresponding lessons and even earn higher grades as a result. A good learning environment in a kitchen ultimately operates like an outside tutor for the student while in school.

Kitchen environments are not the only places for a student to develop career-enhancing skills. Most jobs, whether paid or volunteer, offer opportunities for a person to work with a mix of people of varying skill sets. The student can learn from some people while training others with weaker skills. Volunteering at a homeless shelter, a church, or a school will provide to the volunteer human relation skills transferable to the culinary field even if the work has nothing to do with food. The student volunteer inevitably learns how to interact and to work with a range of people with varying temperaments and personalities.

People who volunteer outside of school regularly may be seen as leaders by those coordinating and recruiting volunteers. As a result, frequent volunteers often earn more responsibility and leadership opportunities than they otherwise would in class. Practicing leadership builds confidence in oneself and better prepares students for their first job as a manager. Since chefs can usually spot a person with strong leadership and management abilities, learning how to lead while in school may yield faster and better promotions after graduation.

Of course, any opportunity to work, paid or unpaid, allows a student the chance to build a sense of pride in a job well done. Students often join a company or volunteer organization because they believe in its mission or cause. Such passionate students may value the camaraderie

Interview with Janos Wilder, Executive Chef/Owner, Janos Restaurant and J Bar, Consulting Chef, Kai Restaurant, Sheraton Wild Horse Pass

When looking to hire culinary school graduates, how important is it that they have done something other than go to classes while in school (i.e. work, volunteer, etc.)?

Extracurricular activities are very important to us. We want to hire cooks who demonstrate a passion and commitment to their work that goes beyond the classroom. Most culinary schools offer a variety of opportunities for student enrichment including clubs, catering work, pro bono work for charitable events, chances to assist for visiting guests chefs, volunteer work, and a host of other activities. We want the students who avail themselves of the most possible opportunities. It shows us that they care enough to go beyond the expected. Chances are they will do the same when they come to work for us. Beyond that the more exposure a student has the more experience they have when they come to work for us. Everyone wins.

What benefits does a student get from working in the industry while in school? Does volunteer work also provide some of these benefits?

Working in the industry provides many benefits. The most obvious is the opportunity to become familiar with the kitchen routines of working restaurants. These are different than the classroom kitchen or the school restaurants. The demands are greater and the stress is real because the demands come from the guests and the chef. It's not about a grade any more; it's about contributing to working business. In addition, working in the industry provides a chance to routinize the skills students learn in school. In the classroom you learn some knife skills, how to braise, saute, grill, etc. In restaurants you use those skills every day. The exposure you get in the classroom is only the beginning. Good cooks routinize their skills until they become second nature; that comes with repetition and more repetition while working under the demands of a busy kitchen. Volunteer work, depending on the situation, can provide similar experiences. Philanthropic volunteer work also instills a larger ethos—that of the responsibility of the individual to the community. In my restaurants that is very much part of our ethos. The individual is responsible to the smaller community of co-workers and guests and the restaurant and its staff are responsible to the larger community. Working with and providing for the less fortunate brings real meaning to the notion of hospitality and service. Hospitality and service for those who cannot pay truly comes from the heart. It is genuine and brings value both to our lives and to those we have the good fortune to be able to assist.

that comes from working with others toward a common goal. Such emotional and psychological rewards may supplement or even outweigh any financial reward that might be provided.

Working with others in any capacity helps to build a person's professional network. Network-building can occur spontaneously through working with others or deliberately through participation in professional associations. Either way, building connections with others almost always benefits everyone involved in the network. A student with a strong network of professionals may use that network to find a job, to locate a roommate, to gain advice for succeeding at work, to provide a reference in a job search, or even to cross-train on new skills and equipment later in life. Making the time to network now means that you will have others to support you in your career later. Failing to build a network leaves a person with little more than the employment section of the newspaper when looking for work.

As acquiring a quality, post-graduation job is often one of the primary goals of a culinary student, all students should at least consider part-time or full-time culinary work while in school. Working while in school may all but guarantee a student a job after graduation. Many employers look for people with experience, but as the old paradox suggests, it is impossible to get experience if you cannot get a job. Fortunately, most employers are willing to take a gamble on a current student in culinary school, even if that student has no prior experience. The job may pay less than a graduate could earn, but it provides valuable experience to enhance the student's résumé. Many employers hire students as trial runs to see if they would like to retain and even to promote a student after graduation. Getting a job early with a good company is a great way to move up in that organization quickly after graduation. Even if the student wishes to move to another company after graduation, the prior work experience will help the student perform better in the new job. Additionally, students' supervisors can often help them with a job search by calling colleagues or writing reference letters.

Since most culinary schools teach general culinary arts skills, working in a restaurant with a specific cuisine and style also allows students to specialize and to begin to craft their own styles. Students who wish to become caterers should work for a caterer; those hoping to master French cuisine should work in a French restaurant. Even jobs with newspapers or food suppliers are available for those wishing to pursue careers as food writers or purveyors. The experience supplements and enhances the broad scope of most culinary programs.

Finally, any additional activities in which a student engages outside of school suggest to an employer that the student is hardworking and passionate about the industry and/or the community. Employers are interested in workers who love the culinary arts and who do not work solely for money but rather for love of good food and good service. Students with lots of volunteer experience on a résumé exude a passion for the industry or community that goes beyond a basic money-for-work exchange. Students who display a strong work history on their résumés appear battle-tested in the industry and worthy of consideration by choosy employers.

Imagine that you are a chef looking to hire a recent culinary school graduate. One candidate spent her time in school volunteering every other week while holding down a part-time job; her grades are A's and B's. Another candidate with equally strong grades has nothing on her résumé to suggest that she did anything during school other than go to class. Both students have strong grades, but only one seems to love working in the field and in the community. Although it is possible that the other candidate spent all of her spare time caring for aging parents, studying to earn strong grades, or reading to learn more about the industry, one might just as easily assume that she spent her free time playing video games. You might even presume that she has little interest in the field and only attends school (and now, looks for work) because of pressure from family members. No matter what the reason for the second candidate's sparse résumé, most chefs are not willing to take a risk on such an applicant when they have a stronger candidate available. To enhance the chances that you will always be viewed as the stronger candidate, use your time in school to add volunteer and work credits to your credentials. Even a few additional activities make a big difference in how a potential employer perceives your résumé.

Interview with James Mazzio, Executive Chef/Consultant

When looking to hire culinary school graduates, how important is it that they have done something other than go to classes while in school (i.e. work, volunteer, etc.)? Do you like to see such activities on their résumés?

I absolutely want to see those activities on their résumés. I hired a student back after graduation because he worked for me during school. When he came back, he was confident because he had been in the kitchen already. I think all chefs look toward someone who has the wherewithal to get started in the industry while in school. If you're afraid to jump into the industry early, you probably won't succeed. It shows passion and enthusiasm. I love people who show enthusiasm. They get all my attention.

What benefits does a student get from working in the industry while in school? Does volunteer work also provide some of these benefits?

Their confidence level is increased. They improve their skills. There is more pressure in the industry than there is in school. You have to get the food out and it has to be good. They learn how to deal with pressure, stress, heat, the kitchen environment, and other people's stress. People around them also need to get their job done. It is a real test for them. Their skill set gets more developed because of the constant prep time. They may spend three months making one item, so they really bond with the recipes and the techniques they learned in school. Their experience also grows. Volunteer work is usually for a short period of time, so there you gain knowledge and technique. It will help you sharpen your base of what you cook, but it takes 3–6 months to get the repetition. Doing things repetitively is super important.

Do you ever hire current culinary students in your organization? Do you ever make accommodations for them to help them succeed at school?

Sometimes, I do hire current culinary school students. I try to work around their schedule because they have shown enthusiasm and want to be a part of the industry now. I always suggest that they work part-time, just two or three days per week. If there is too much pressure, the students crack. School should be the number-one priority. Working part-time helps to whet their appetite. As confidence rises, they can handle more work. I do make accommodations for students to give them time for tests and schoolwork. Times are changing, so more and more people are taking the culinary field as a serious career alternative.

10.2 THE POTENTIAL PITFALLS OF WORKING OUTSIDE OF SCHOOL

Although there are a great deal of benefits that come from working and volunteering outside of school, shifting time away from studying can present its own challenges and pitfalls. With only 24 hours in a day, every student has a limited amount of time to devote to daily activities. Time allocated to volunteerism or to a job means less time available for studying, engaging with faculty, or taking advantage of the library. There are benefits to reserving some time for extracurricular work, but when a job or other activity prevents you from utilizing the school's resources for your professional growth or even worse, from earning high grades, it is time to readjust your priorities and to refocus your efforts on your studies.

Negatively impacting a student's ability to pass classes is the direst consequence of working too much outside of school, but there are other factors to consider when deciding to take on additional responsibility. Student culinary skills are typically not as strong at the onset of the program as they are closer to graduation. Since a student only gets to make one first impression with each person, starting a job with a desired employer too soon may result in a bad first impression that is difficult to overcome. A student with a "dream" employer in mind may wish to wait until her skills are somewhat more refined before seeking employment with that organization.

Most employers are more lenient and understanding with employees who are just starting school, but they also treat those employees as novices rather than as professionals. There is great value in gaining work experience while in school, but students must recognize that they will likely earn lower wages than their post-graduation counterparts. For young culinary students the experience is more valuable in the long run than the money, but for the student in desperate need of immediate income, a personal budget review may limit the kinds of jobs that student can accept. Furthermore, supervisors may be tough on inexperienced workers to make sure that the newbies do not make or repeat mistakes that result in ruined food or customer complaints. Some managers believe that young students make many mistakes if not closely monitored. Students who cannot psychologically cope with the added pressure of a nitpicking boss may wish to wait until their skills improve somewhat.

Perhaps the worst possible outcome of working outside of school is being lured away from college to pursue full-time employment. Too many students view culinary school only as a vehicle through which to enter the industry. In truth, the goal of culinary school is to maximize each student's potential for prestige, success, and income *long term* in the culinary field. Most students with degrees command higher wages than those students who never finish school, and all employers know it. If your employer believes you to be a hard-working person, eager to learn, and able to follow instructions, she may suggest that you leave school, stop paying tuition, and work for her full time to learn on the job. Do not fall for this ruse. The employer knows that she can pay you less if you do not graduate. Additionally, she knows that you are less marketable in the workforce and thus less able to leave her operation for a better opportunity. Most students who drop out of culinary school find themselves hitting glass ceilings which would not be there if they had only completed their program. The amount of money saved by not paying tuition for unfinished coursework is lost many times over in lower income over a lifetime.

Some students may become overcommitted at work to the detriment of their academic performance. As an employer asks a student to put in more and more hours, possibly under the threat of losing her job, the student may become burned out. She loses interest in studying and may even lose interest in the culinary industry entirely. Some students can over-schedule themselves on volunteer opportunities alone. Although it may be hard to say "no" to an instructor asking you to volunteer, the only thing worse than not volunteering is agreeing to work and then not showing up. Earning a reputation as someone who cannot follow through on promises results in poor references and loss of trust and respect from instructors, peers, and industry professionals. Smart students manage the amount of time they devote to work and to volunteerism so as not to burn out or to ruin their reputations.

Finally, even though working in a kitchen will provide a student with extra opportunities to learn, what is learned may be vastly different from what is taught in school. Different chefs have varying approaches to cooking, different opinions on culinary facts, even widely divergent standards of acceptable sanitation practice. The techniques taught on the job must be followed on the job, but a student must be able to switch to the standards taught at school come exam time. A student who has difficulty applying two

Interview with Nicholas E. Walker, The Art Institute of Atlanta, Graduation: December 2007

What activities have you engaged in outside of school that have helped you in your career preparation?

I guess if you consider work as an activity then that has been the biggest help in preparing me for a career in the foodservice industry. I have had the opportunity to work in many different areas of the industry as I attended school. Each experience, whether it be working as a line cook at a small restaurant to working in a large country club has made the concepts learned in school take on a reality that you need outside of school to be successful.

Were there any risks or trade-offs that you had to navigate by spending time on things other than school? What sacrifices did you make?

When it comes to trade-offs, a lot of it was personal time. You have to be able to manage your time between work and school. Sometimes work could get in the way of school or vice-versa, but when you set out to do something, I feel that it needs to be done right. The risk of working full time while at school is that sometimes you feel that working is more important; when this happens you have to remind yourself that education is just as important. Sometimes sacrifices are necessary for us to reach our goals, and the hardest one for me was being away from my family during the holidays. My family supported me and my goals, so that made things easier.

How did you know when you could handle additional time commitments outside of school?

As school progressed, I felt more comfortable with my abilities. I knew what was expected of me and believed that my employer would not have given the responsibility if they felt that I could not handle it. The cost of education was also a real reason for working, but well worth it.

different approaches to cooking in two different environments may need to consider changing jobs. A trusted teacher can often recommend a foodservice company that shares the school's standards and approaches to cooking. Ultimately, students must always remember that they are paying tuition and taking exams to document that they have learned what the school has to teach, not what someone outside of the school requires.

10.3 KNOWING WHEN YOU ARE READY TO ACCEPT EXTRA WORK

The first step in building your résumé and increasing your marketability is knowing when you are ready to accept more work and responsibility. Every employer would love to have a worker who can juggle a lot of projects and do them all well, but short of that ideal, most people prefer an employee who can do one thing well than one who manages multiple projects and completes none of them properly. By conducting a simple, honest self-evaluation you will be able to determine whether or not now is the time to take on additional work beyond your current academic and personal responsibilities.

Start by assessing the available time in your life. Do you have lots of free time or do you already struggle to get your studying done? Can you create free time by eliminating wasteful activities, or do you spend all of your time performing essential tasks (studying, attending class, caring for your children, etc.)? When you can free up time for volunteer or work activities without shirking any personal responsibilities, then you may be ready to accept more work. However, if volunteering on a project means that you will be unable to study for an exam and may earn a poor grade as a result, you should decline to work on the new project and devote the time to studying instead. Taking on too many projects rarely helps a person perform better on the tasks she already has.

Next, assess your own skill level. A person who struggles with basic addition and subtraction will gain little benefit from a calculus class. Similarly, a culinary student who has not yet learned knife skills might wish to wait before volunteering on a project that requires advanced culinary ability. Students early in their programs should look for volunteer and job prospects that require basic culinary skills, while more advanced students can pursue more challenging opportunities. There is a benefit to pushing yourself to grow beyond your current comfort level, but most people learn best when their goal is just slightly beyond their current skill set and not when it lies impossibly far beyond their reach. In short, be honest about your strengths and weaknesses when volunteering to make sure that you can handle the work. Many companies will train their employees, but organizations looking for one-day volunteers typically will not.

Examine your ability to make a good impression before pursuing any high-profile, public opportunity. If there is an opportunity to represent your school to the public, make sure that you can represent the school well before accepting the challenge. Do you embody a professional, well-dressed, straight-A student, or do you usually appear more slovenly and unprofessional? You never want to be the reason that your school's reputation is damaged in the community. Fortunately, anyone can learn to be a model representative for a culinary school. Ask your teachers if you are ready to represent your school to the community. If they show any hesitation in endorsing you, ask them how you can improve. With a little coaching from your instructors, you will quickly find yourself ready to represent your school with little fear of embarrassment.

Many students struggling financially will not have the luxury of declining paid work opportunities or paying for extracurricular activities. If you must earn money to survive in school, then working a paid position will be a necessity. In this case, you should budget your time to allow for a part-time or full-time job. You still need to look for work that leaves enough time for your studies; ideally, the job will challenge your skills and help you to apply and to reinforce what you have learned in your program. Severe money problems may prevent you from pursuing many professional development opportunities. If you need every dollar you earn to pay for transportation to school or for daycare so that you can attend school, you probably will not be able to pay for membership in a professional association. Fortunately, you may still be able to make time for volunteer opportunities that do not require any additional expense on your part, and you can always join a professional association later in your career. When money is extremely tight, you should be sure that what little you have goes toward facilitating your successful progression through school.

Lastly, examine your comfort level with working or volunteering. You do not need to be comfortable with the job or volunteering itself, but you must be somewhat comfortable in your ability to manage the other responsibilities in your life, such as family, school, and finances. Promising something in an interview and then not following through is a sure-fire way to ruin your reputation and lose your job. Still, as long as your personal responsibilities will not suffer or prevent you from following through after you have agreed to participate, you should strongly consider accepting the challenge. Be honest with your supervisor (and yourself) about your constraints. It is better to lose the opportunity to work than to be fired for misrepresenting yourself, and your supervisor may be able to adjust to your needs if you share them in the interview process. You may wish to try volunteer activities first to build your confidence and to test your ability to handle extra work outside of school.

10.3.1   I'm Overcommitted—Now What?

Although you may have tried to balance all of your responsibilities upfront, sometimes you find yourself overcommitted without a clue as to how you arrived in this predicament. When this happens, you will need to make some tough decisions. You may disappoint some people, but cutting back on some of your responsibilities is better than underperforming on all of your commitments.

With the high cost of tuition and the time commitment you have made to completing school, passing classes should be one of your highest priorities. When academics suffer, you

---

Interview with Charles Reid, Fellow—College of Culinary Arts, Johnson and Wales University, Graduation: May 2008

What activities have you engaged in outside of school that have helped you in your career?
I suppose that my involvement with the Johnson and Wales University Intracollegiate Hot Foods Team has opened the most doors for me thus far along my career path. Not only am I honing both my knife and hot food preparation skills, but I'm continually adding to the foundation that I've built up in classical cuisine.

Were there any risks or trade-offs that you had to navigate by spending time on things other than school? What obstacles did you have to overcome?
Of course there are risks and trade-offs involved with performing any sort of duty or activity not involved with school while you're attending classes during the year. I've encountered numerous situations where I'm forced to prioritize my "to-do" list, and sometimes it's an awfully hard decision to make. Not only are your studies put into jeopardy, but your social life is as well. One thing I've come to realize, however, is that if you devote 115 percent of yourself to your studies during the week, then the weekend is yours to do whatever you'd like with, be it work, socialize with friends, or go on a date. One obstacle that I've had to overcome during my journey through culinary school is staying on campus during certain holidays due to my involvement with extracurricular activities, such as the Hot Foods competition team or my involvement with various clubs in the university. It's difficult receiving calls from friends and loved ones who want to see you at home while the only answer you can choke up is, "I had some things to take care of."

How did you know when you could handle additional time commitments outside of school?
There was really never a point at which I stopped and had some epiphany about being able to juggle multiple priorities at once during my stint at culinary school. It was more a trial-and-error period in my life where I tested the figurative waters, and there were certainly a few times where I almost went under. I believe the period started sometime during sophomore year.

should look to reduce some of your other responsibilities, even if that means asking your boss to cut your hours at work or telling the family that you will not be able to make Aunt Ida's 50th birthday party. Be clear with supervisors, friends, and even family about how much time you have available for them. Friends and family will understand and respect you for your commitment to completing your degree. Supervisors may be less understanding, but you are likely in school to advance beyond your current position anyway. If your employer asks you to stay late at work and it will negatively impact your academic performance, do not hesitate to decline. Rarely does a student ever make enough extra money doing overtime shifts during a semester to cover the cost of repeating a failed class.

10.3.2 Why Risk Getting Overcommitted?

You should always remember that you are in school to invest in your future. Making time now for résumé-building activities or for challenges that build your skills and knowledge provides incredible returns later in life. Whether through better job opportunities, faster promotions, networking connections, or just a greater comfort level at work, volunteering or holding down a job while in school grants a return on investment that is well worth the initial effort.

Do not let the potential pitfalls of accepting additional responsibility scare you away from working or volunteering at all. Awareness of the risks merely allows you to manage them so that you can maximize the benefits while minimizing the potential hazards. No amount of work or volunteerism offsets failing out of school, but recent culinary graduates with strong work histories and records of volunteerism are rare enough as to make them highly desirable to any culinary employer for entry-level and ultimately, for leadership positions. In an industry where many thousands of students graduate from culinary schools each year, remaining highly desirable and marketable is critical to obtaining the best and most prestigious positions in the field.

Summary

Volunteering or working outside of school offers both potential benefits and possible risks to any culinary student. Extra kitchen time outside of class strengthens culinary skills and may even provide additional training not offered in the student's program of study. Extracurricular work also provides opportunities to develop human relation and leadership skills, as well as to grow a sense of pride and confidence in performing a job. Whether through working, volunteering, or participating in a professional association, students gain the opportunity to network with industry professionals by venturing beyond the school walls. Working outside of school also brings in income, a potential post-graduation job opportunity, and a chance to specialize in one aspect of the culinary field. In short, work and volunteerism help to build a student's résumé and to make the student appear more appealing to potential employers.

However, too much time spent on extracurricular activities can take much-needed time away from a student's studies. Taking on too much extra responsibility before a student is ready can disappoint a new employer, negatively impact a student's grades, or result in a difficult work environment. Some students who do find a good job while in school fall prey to the siren call to leave school to learn solely on the job instead; such students rarely reach their full potential in the industry in the long run. Students who work or volunteer too much outside of school risk becoming overwhelmed and burned out, and some employers may train students in ways that are contradictory to what the students learn in school.

To reap the benefits of extracurricular work and volunteerism while avoiding the potential pitfalls, a student must know when she is ready to accept more responsibility and only take on as much as she can handle proficiently. An honest self-evaluation will help a student to determine her readiness to pick up more work outside of school. Those students who do become overwhelmed are better off eliminating some of their extra responsibilities. However, the potential benefit that comes from working in the field or volunteering outside of school is too great for a student to avoid seeking such opportunities for fear of burning out. Extracurricular work and volunteerism really help a student to stand out among today's multitude of culinary school graduates.

THE BENEFITS OF WORKING/VOLUNTEERING OUTSIDE OF SCHOOL

- Improvement of culinary skills and of kitchen speed
- Opportunity to learn material not covered in school
- Development of human relations skills
- Development of leadership skills
- Development of pride in accomplishing tasks successfully
- Growth of self-confidence in one's culinary abilities
- Opportunity to support a cause about which one is passionate
- Opportunity to network with industry professionals
- Ability to earn an income while in school
- Opportunity to "test drive" and possibly to continue in a job after graduation
- Opportunity to specialize in one aspect of the culinary field
- Development of a broad, impressive résumé to increase appeal to potential employers

---

Suggested Tasks

1. Write a self-evaluation of your readiness to take on extracurricular responsibilities. Discuss your self-evaluation with your teacher to determine how much extra work, if any, you should pursue at this point in your program.

2. Research and list at least five volunteer activities available to you either through the school or in the community. Determine which activity would be best suited for you at this stage in your program. If your self-evaluation suggests that now is a good time to pursue a volunteer activity, contact the person in charge of the "best-suited" activity to volunteer.

3. Describe your ideal first "dream" job immediately after graduation. (Be realistic—you will not be ready for an executive chef position for your first job out of school.) Discuss with your teacher what

type of job you should get while in school to best prepare you for your first dream job. Locate at least one job opening that fits the description determined by you and your instructor. If you are ready at this stage in your program, apply for that job.

4. Interview two industry chefs (or other supervisors) for whom you would want to work after graduation. Ask them what kinds of activities they look for on a résumé other than graduation from culinary school. Record the activities they suggest and write out a plan describing when and how you will complete at least half of the activities they suggest.

5. Interview two chef-instructors at your school. Ask them where they went to culinary school and what they feel they learned from school. Discuss with them the pros and cons of earning a culinary degree versus learning on the job in the industry. Write a brief essay describing what you have learned from the interviews and discuss your research with your class.

CHAPTER 11

What the Industry Expects You to Know and to Do

Many students decide to attend culinary school to learn everything there is to know about cooking and running a restaurant. Nearly every culinary school graduate realizes in the first year after graduation that the college's program was merely a foundation rather than an all-encompassing training. Most chefs believe that no one can learn everything there is to know about the culinary arts, for the expanse of knowledge is far too vast.

Culinary school graduates do not need to know how to cook every dish on their station the first day on the job. Chefs need workers who can quickly adapt to their work environment, but the chefs (or other training supervisors) will train new hires in most things needed to succeed on the job. With that said, they will not teach *every* skill the employee needs. Employers in the industry expect culinary school graduates to have some skills, and what they expect is pretty universal across all foodservice operations.

In this chapter, you will learn what skills, knowledge, and work habits industry employers expect you to know as a culinary school graduate. You will also learn the consequences of not demonstrating this knowledge and behavior on the job.

11.1 THE PREREQUISITES OF PROFESSIONALISM AND TEAMWORK

So what does the industry expect of you when they hire you? The company first and foremost expects you to arrive on time, every day, prepared to do your job. There are often allowances for rare exceptions, such as illness or bereavement, but regular professionalism issues with an employee are seldom tolerated for very long. Culinary school graduates are not necessarily better at displaying professional behavior than other employees, but because they are often paid more, the expectations for them are higher.

Similarly, culinary school graduates are not automatically gifted with interpersonal skills as a result of attending culinary school, but employers expect them to be able to work well with others. An employee who cannot get along with his co-workers is likely to hate coming to work each day and to perform poorly on the job as a result. Since most culinary schools force students to work in teams during their program, most employers expect that culinary graduates have learned to work with a variety of personality types. A graduate who still creates friction with co-workers after years of culinary school training is likely to be labeled a difficult employee. Any culinary talent such a graduate displays inevitably will be overshadowed by the conflict he creates with his peers.

11.2 BASIC CULINARY SKILLS AND KNOWLEDGE

There are some culinary basics (beyond professionalism) that chefs will not take the time to teach. These basics impact nearly every recipe, and an employee who cannot perform them proficiently will inevitably struggle in the kitchen. Fortunately, every culinary school teaches and stresses these basics, so they should be part of every culinary school graduate's repertoire.

11.2.1 Knife Skills

Any student learning culinary arts in a quality school has encountered some lesson, if not an entire course, on knife skills. Industry chefs can teach you a thousand preparations for julienne carrots, but they expect you to know how to cut julienne carrots without any training. Although there are a large number of classical knife cuts to learn, the critical ones employers expect you to have mastered are julienne, batonet, dice of various sizes, brunoise, mince, and tournée. While you may not use tournée in many restaurants, the others are quite common in most kitchen operations.

The expectations on knife skills are fairly straightforward. Chefs assume that a culinary school graduate can prepare any of the aforementioned cuts consistently close to, if not exactly, the right size. They also expect graduates to make the cuts quickly and with minimal waste. Although the concept behind making the cuts is simple, most people need years to master them. The best way to master your knife skills by graduation is to practice them daily.

11.2.2 Measurements

As with knife skills, a cook cannot assemble a recipe accurately and consistently without the ability to measure ingredients. For bakers and pastry chefs, an inability to measure accurately makes a culinary school graduate unemployable.

Foodservice employers expect culinary school graduates to measure accurately in three major ways: by weight using a balance beam scale, by weight using a spring or electronic scale, and by volume using cup and spoon measures for solids and liquids. Unlike knife skills which require years of practice, measuring can be learned and mastered in just a day or two. For most supervisors, accuracy and speed are the critical elements of proper measurement.

Of course, chefs also expect culinary school graduates to convert measurement units quickly and easily to increase or reduce the yield on a recipe. This skill often takes much longer for students to master. Practicing mathematical gymnastics daily shortens the time that it takes to learn how to make these conversions quickly in your head. If you are not yet able to multiply a recipe by five (or some other factor) and then convert the units from cups to quarts, teaspoons to cups, or ounces to pounds, then you must continue practicing until you can perform it expertly. Chefs will not train you in how to make these conversions, but they will expect you to do them if you have any aspirations of moving beyond an entry-level position.

11.2.3 Terminology, Identification, and Usage

Culinary employers normally train their employees on the identification and usage of any unusual or specialized equipment and ingredients, but they do expect a culinary school graduate to know some basic factual information about food and equipment. For example, a chef will typically take the time to show you the difference between a pequillo and an ancho chile pepper, but he will be less pleased should you ask him what a red bell pepper looks like. Similarly, you may not be expected to identify a combi-therm steamer/oven, but you ought to be able to tell the difference between a convection and a conventional oven. With both food and equipment there are many products that are so common that not knowing what they are suggests that you know less than the average homemaker. Which of these things should you know and which are rarities for which you get a free pass? Any food item common to most grocery stores and any piece of equipment that can be found in a kitchen supply store is something you must be able to identify, and in the case of equipment, to use.

There are some other pieces of equipment that can be difficult to find in a retail kitchen supply store but are common in professional kitchens. For example, a chef would expect any employee to know the difference between a china cap and a chinois. Fortunately, nearly every culinary school program teaches and uses these pieces of equipment. Paying particular attention to equipment identification and its safe usage in school will save the typical culinary school graduate from a great deal of embarrassment on the job.

Basic culinary terminology is the final core set of knowledge that a chef expects of a culinary school graduate. As with food and equipment, graduates need not know everything there is to know, but defining and executing basic cooking techniques are assumed core skill sets of graduates. Recent graduates need not know the difference between a chutney and a pickle, but they must be able to boil, simmer, or poach a food properly when instructed to do so. In short, if there is a cooking technique that you cannot perform as you approach graduation, make sure that you learn it before you graduate. Waiting until the first day on the job to learn how to grill or how to braise will only create a bad first impression for your co-workers and supervisor that may take you months or years to overcome.

11.3 BASIC WORK HABITS

In addition to what an employee needs to know and to execute, there are certain habits or ways of working that every chef requires of all employees. Most culinary schools teach these habits and reinforce them in every course, but only those students who strive to integrate these behaviors into their every task master them by the time they have graduated from school. Students who fail to assimilate these habits into their work tend to have unpleasant, micromanaged work experiences, and many may struggle to survive for long in the culinary industry.

11.3.1 Food Safety and Sanitation

Nearly every credible professional culinary program teaches food sanitation, and any quality foodservice operation interested in surviving more than a year or two enforces it. While most culinary schools teach the repercussions to the restaurant for ignoring food sanitation principles, not many teach the consequences to the cooks for failure to keep food safe.

Interview with Kevin Rathbun, Owner/Chef, Kevin Rathbun Steak, Rathbun's, Krog Bar

What do you expect from a recent culinary school graduate when they first start on the job?
Before I hire most students, I expect the student to have had one to two years of job history before they go to school to ensure that they have an idea about the stress, hours, and are willing to stomach the pressure of a busy restaurant. When they first start on the job, I usually put them in a garde manger position; after that it is entirely up to them to move up the ladder. In most cases I can see in a short period of time if they have the multitasking skills that they will need to continue on. Their willingness to learn is imperative and their commitment to work and to take direction is of the utmost importance.

What information do you expect them to know?
Having basic skill sets, knife skills, and a passion for the business are the most important things for me. The next most important thing is to have a great ability to get along with peers and a teamwork attitude.

What basic skills do you expect them to be able to perform?
I can teach them to follow my lead if they are willing and if they have a respect for leadership. The most important quality is to have that one- to two-year line cook experience, so they have exposure to multitasking and also what I call the "third gear"—the ability to turn up the pace at any given time and to be proficient in doing so.

What kind of attitude would you like them to have?
Their attitude has to be: quality first, passion for the business, what I call a "sponge" to learn, a willingness to rise to the top, being a great team player and taking direction from peers and subordinates without hesitation, teaching when necessary with an open mind, a willingness to say "I don't know, but I can find out," and admitting faults when things go wrong. Humility is always, in my eyes, the best approach to success; no one likes a know-it-all.

What happens to recent culinary school graduates if they don't have these skills, behaviors, attitude, etc.?
Most problems start and end with a lack of professionalism, teamwork, timeliness, or what I would call "two left feet" where the employee just doesn't have the ability to multitask or have that third gear I spoke of earlier. Some of the poor behaviors employees have are the lack of respect for others, calling in sick for a nose bleed, car problems, hangover, concert they want to go to. This is what leads to an abrupt departure. Not listening to written warnings and constructive criticism about performance and not being honest are my biggest concerns with some.

Most chefs expect their employees to follow food sanitation guidelines, but they do not wish to spend too much time training their employees in these principles. Chefs may have a HACCP system in which all employees are trained, but no chef wants to monitor employees to verify that they wash their hands after using the bathroom. Executive chefs are very busy people, and they do not have the time to confirm that their employees follow proper heating, cooling, and holding procedures every day. (Some culinary operations are changing and encouraging chefs to spend more time focused on food sanitation, but most still provide the chef little time for sanitation oversight.) When a customer contracts a food-borne illness in a restaurant, the chef will likely be blamed by the public and any supervisors. Therefore, those employees who follow sanitation guidelines all the time as part of their normal routine are viewed as valuable workers who protect the reputation of the chef and the restaurant. Those who ignore sanitation rules are less valuable to the company and are rarely promoted.

When a chef observes an employee breaking sanitation guidelines, he may correct and discipline the employee or he may ignore the employee's behavior entirely. Unfortunately, one dirty little secret of the industry is that some chefs willingly ignore sanitation violations if they believe that compliance with sanitation regulations will slow down an employee's performance. However, the moment that a customer sues or that the health department issues a fine for a health violation, the offending cooks are inevitably punished severely. Since changing one's ingrained work habits can be quite difficult to do, many cooks fall back on old habits soon after sanitation training if it is not constantly reinforced. Those who cannot make the change typically cannot remain with the company.

The training environment of school offers the perfect opportunity to practice good sanitation. If a student learns that any dish is incorrect if it is not made in a sanitary manner, then that student will apply proper sanitation in the field as well. Similarly, a student who practices poor sanitation in school is unlikely to change those bad behaviors after graduation or to earn respect as potential management material. A student must know and obey good sanitation practice daily and consistently by graduation to progress beyond entry-level positions in the industry.

11.3.2 Working Smarter, Not Harder

Every chef knows the validity of the old adage "Time is money." An employee who can prepare 50 meals in an hour is far more valuable to the kitchen team than one who can prepare only 10 meals in an hour. Since speed comes in time, most chefs recognize that a brand new culinary school graduate will not have the same agility in knife skills as more experienced workers. However, chefs do expect their hired culinary graduates to work in a clean, efficient, organized manner.

Students who work in messy areas (even if those areas are not unsanitary) tend to work slower. In a cluttered workspace a young cook spends lots of time moving things around to create space to work. People who learn to maintain an organized, clean station end up working much faster in the long run.

Successful professionals also learn to work smarter, not harder. A worker who sweeps the floor before wiping the tables finds himself needing to sweep the floor a second time. A person who carries all of the day's equipment to his station in one trip spends far less time walking across the kitchen than the employee who retrieves equipment one piece at a time. Supervising chefs expect their new hires to work as efficiently as possible to be as productive as possible. Chefs rarely take the time to teach new workers how to economize their efforts, but those employees who find ways to work efficiently always appear more competent and productive than their co-workers. Competent employees earn raises or promotions; less productive employees typically wallow in their jobs indefinitely unable to move to management.

As with sanitation, economy of movement is best learned through practice in school. Students who wish to earn the admiration of their bosses and co-workers after graduation are wise to practice multitasking and working efficiently while in school. You can improve this skill by considering your daily production before arriving to class and then by organizing your day on paper in as efficient a manner as possible. List the ingredients and equipment needed and gather them all at one time. Learn from your mistakes in planning and adjust your approach in future classes. You will be amazed at how quickly you outpace your classmates in the day's production. Whereas school seems fast while you are in class, it is actually a much slower pace than the real world of the professional kitchen. Learning to be efficient early is the only way to keep up with more experienced co-workers on that first post-graduation job.

11.3.3 Following Directions and Consistency

Despite everything that is learned in culinary school, one of the most important skills to possess in the industry is learned by most people as early as kindergarten. Chefs need and expect their employees to follow directions. A worker who cannot follow a recipe has no chance of preparing a dish to the standards of the restaurant. When a chef gives verbal instructions to an employee, he expects them to be followed exactly. A chef does not want cooks to design their own plate presentations if he has given them a photograph to replicate for the plate design. In short, workers are in place to execute the vision of the chef and of the company. An employee who cannot obey the supervisor's instructions cannot work in that company at all.

In a foodservice operation, guests expect to enjoy the same flavors and plate presentations day after day if they continue to order the same food. Many guests have favorite dishes in their regular restaurants, hotels, and cafeterias. When a guest finds a favorite dish to be different (even if it is objectively better), he may be disappointed that his expectations are not met. Therefore, you need to take every care to perform, according to instruction consistently from one day to the next. Should the guest actually enjoy your variation better, he will be sorely disappointed when he returns to the cooking of someone else who does follow the chef's instructions. The only way to meet the expectations of guests is to follow the instructions provided by your supervisor so that the changes in prior procedures are only in response to requests for change from guests.

As seemingly easy as consistency may seem to achieve, it is actually quite difficult in the culinary world. Many ingredients change seasonally, and workers may not have as much time to devote to precise presentation during busy periods as they had during slower service periods. A good cook needs a good sense memory. A chef expects him to make the food taste the same whether the ingredients are coming into season or going out of season. The conscientious cook may need to adjust the salt, sugar, or acidity on a tomato sauce made from in-season tomatoes versus one made from canned tomatoes. (Most chefs would not ever attempt to make the sauce from out-of-season tomatoes.) An ability to replicate flavors and plate presentations from one day to the next is a critical skill for any cook. One might assume that a cook who prepares 99 out of 100 dishes perfectly is performing quite well on the job, but the guest who receives the one flawed dish only experiences the restaurant's food as substandard. Cooks who exemplify consistency in the execution of their work are far more valuable to their employers than those who do not.

Interview with Janis McLean, Executive Chef, Morrison Clark Historic Inn and Restaurant

What basic skills do you expect recent culinary school graduates to be able to perform?
Knife skills and an ability to sharpen a knife, knowing the difference between sweat and sauté, how to read a recipe, and how to set up a station.

What general work habits do you want them to have?
To keep a clean workstation, to do production work in an organized fashion (it is one thing to cut one onion, but to cut twenty requires a different mind-set—peel them all at once, clean off the skins, etc. —to do one at a time is messy and inefficient), to move with a sense of urgency, to multitask (they won't make it if they can't), and to prioritize properly.

What kind of attitude would you like them to have?
Be a team player (it's not a race on the line; all the plates go up at the same time). Watch what's going on around you. Ask questions, but not too many . . . it's a fine line. Don't proceed ahead full steam: do one cut and ask "Chef, is this what you meant?"

11.4   THE RIGHT ATTITUDE

A chef inevitably has a preference for an employee with a specific attitude and philosophy on cooking. Some chefs prefer cooks who think and act like their supervisors. Others only want positive, happy people who love to have fun in the kitchen. Still others want serious, focused workers who do not talk during production except to respond to the chef or expediter. With such variety among chefs, one might assume that there is no "correct" attitude for getting hired and getting ahead at work. However, there are two attitude "elements" that nearly every chef wants from every employee—a willingness to learn and a tendency to take the initiative to solve problems.

11.4.1   Willingness to Learn

Since a chef needs to have control over the operation of the kitchen, he needs to know that his employees will follow his instructions rather than change the status quo of the kitchen. This does not mean that chefs hate change. On the contrary, many chefs enjoy getting ideas and suggestions from their employees, but most prefer that an employee first learn the chef's standard operating procedures before suggesting a change.

Culinary school graduates may feel that they know so much from their education that they are entitled to point out all the errors of their workplace. Attempting to change the standard operation of a kitchen is arrogant and foolish for any new cook to do. A chef may intentionally do things contrary to traditional culinary theory in order to please guests, to save money, or simply to differentiate himself from the competition. If you respect this dynamic and approach the job with humility and with an intention to learn from your chef and co-workers, you will be welcome in every new job. If you attempt to exert your own style on another chef's domain, you are likely to encounter a less than friendly workplace.

To make recommendations for change a graduate must first learn the culture and procedures of the kitchen and then approach the subject of change delicately with the chef. You should meet with the chef privately to pose a logical argument and explain why the change would benefit the restaurant, the chef, or the employees. If the chef is receptive to the idea, he will decide how to implement the change or will explicitly give you permission to make the change. If the chef rejects the idea, then the discussion is over. An attempt to circumvent the chef's authority and to make a change without the chef's approval is considered insubordination and can be cause for termination. Developing a willingness to learn can be difficult, but swallowing your pride and accepting the instruction of your supervisor can mean the difference between a long-term career with a company and a brief footnote of a job experience on a résumé.

11.4.2 Taking Initiative

Although chefs generally prefer employees interested in learning their company's approaches to cooking, most chefs also want their employees to take initiative to complete tasks that need to get done and to fix problems that arise. In order to do this within the guidelines of the company, an employee must first learn what is and is not considered acceptable behavior for a kitchen worker. For example, if the shrimp for the seafood salad does not arrive with the seafood delivery, a cook needs to know if the chef will allow the salad to be prepared without shrimp or if the cook will need to obtain the shrimp from another source. In the spirit of "willingness to learn," the new employee should consult the chef to learn what to do. However, if this problem has been encountered before and the cook knows how the chef normally handles this situation, the cook should take the initiative to solve the problem rather than wait for the chef to discover it.

The alternative to taking initiative is encouraging micromanagement. Most new employees are micromanaged until they learn the ropes. Once they have demonstrated that they can handle a job on their own, they are often given more independence in their workday. As employees gain experience, they often also gain speed which frees up some time in their day. An employee who uses that time to do other valuable work for the team will be viewed as highly responsible and worthy of on-going independence. An employee who squanders the free time by avoiding additional work and not taking the initiative to find out where to help others may quickly find himself micromanaged again. His supervisor may continually push him to work faster and assign him to other tasks as he completes prior ones. In the long run, both types of employees end up doing the same amount of work, but only one earns the respect and the possibility of a promotion from his supervisor.

To best develop a "take-initiative" attitude, you should look for ways to remain productive and to assist your instructor when you find yourself with free time in class. Free time may not occur often during production, but most high-achieving students find themselves ahead of their classmates during cleanup. If you find your classmates in need of assistance during cleanup, take the initiative to assist them without being asked. You will not only speed up the time it takes to clean the kitchen, but you will also earn the respect and appreciation of your instructor, who determines your grade for the day. By the time you start that first job after graduation, you will have developed a mind-se that keeps you productively working and contributing to the team even when you have completed the work assigned to you.

11.5   THE CONSEQUENCES OF NOT MEETING INDUSTRY EXPECTATIONS UPON GRADUATION

Although the industry expects recent culinary school graduates to possess all of the skills, knowledge, and behaviors described above, not every single student will put in the effort to learn them. Some graduates may be able to survive in the industry for quite a while without certain basics, while others may leave the field fairly quickly of their own volition. Of course, some failures are worse than others and certain ones can cause an employee to lose a job just a few days into it.

The most severe consequences come from a lack of professionalism and from an inability to work with others. Obviously unprofessional and unethical behavior, such as stealing, making violent threats, or sabotaging the organization, almost always leads to immediate termination. Other unprofessional behavior such as periodic lateness or absenteeism often results in dismissal as well. Since an employee who cannot work well with others disrupts the team environment, a person who generates conflict with co-workers is often removed from the team and the company.

A lack of basic culinary skills often leads to a loss of one's position in a company but not necessarily to a loss of employment entirely. Line cooks who cannot perform basic culinary tasks are typically reassigned to prep work or even to dishwashing. An employee who can show up on time every day with the right attitude is not typically an employee that a chef wishes to lose, but the restaurant must still fill its positions with people capable of executing their jobs successfully. For someone without basic culinary skills peeling potatoes or washing lettuce is a better match for that person's skill set.

Those workers who lack sanitation, organization, an ability to follow directions, or an ability to create consistent products often receive a great deal of disciplinary action. Disciplinary action can mean anything from retraining to being reprimanded to being micromanaged. Whatever form the discipline takes, co-workers and supervisors will view such employees as incompetent and not appropriate for promotion. Raises and annual evaluations usually remain appropriately low until the employee improves. As a result, these behaviors are best mastered prior to graduation rather than during a culinary school graduate's first year on the job.

People with no passion for learning or with poor initiative have few consequences to their employment and careers at first. Such passionless, lackluster employees typically keep their jobs if they can learn just one station. They may even receive satisfactory annual evaluations and average pay increases. However, these employees will likely be passed over indefinitely for promotions or even for cross-training on other stations. Because these employees show no internal motivation for professional development, foodservice operations usually do not waste their resources trying to develop such workers for higher-caliber positions. Some workers may take the attitude that they will show initiative and learn additional skills when they are paid more. These workers fail to realize that no company wants to take a risk on an unproven employee. Raises and promotions are earned through hard work, personal development, and initiative. Graduates who plan on working beyond the narrow scope of their current job description only after receiving a raise and a promotion often find that they never get the opportunity to do so. Their careers plateau and dead-end all too quickly after graduation.

Summary

Although there are a great many things to learn about the culinary industry, most professional chefs have a finite set of skills, habits, and knowledge that they expect from their culinary school graduate employees. Industry chefs expect culinary graduates to arrive on time, in uniform, prepared to work every day. They also expect them to work well with others in the company. Culinary graduates are expected to perform basic culinary skills deftly such as knife skills, measuring, identifying food and equipment, using basic kitchen equipment, and defining basic culinary terms. Chefs expect these graduates to employ proper sanitation procedures in all that they do and to work in a clean, efficient, and organized manner. These graduates must also be able to follow directions accurately and to replicate their production consistently. Finally, industry professionals expect that culinary school graduates will demonstrate a willingness to learn and show initiative in solving problems and remaining productive. Not possessing and performing these skills and habits can lead to a range of results from losing promotion and pay raise opportunities to losing one's job. Since these skill sets, terms, and work habits are taught in most culinary schools, students need merely to focus on learning and adopting them while in school to facilitate a positive experience on the job after graduation.

THE INDUSTRY EXPECTS CULINARY SCHOOL GRADUATES WILL BE ABLE TO . . .

- Arrive on time, in uniform, prepared to work, every day.
- Work well with co-workers as a team.
- Perform knife skills accurately, quickly, and with little waste.
- Measure accurately by weight and by volume.
- Identify common food ingredients.
- Identify and use basic kitchen equipment.
- Understand basic culinary terms.
- Adhere to sanitation principles in all that they do.
- Work in a clean, efficient, and organized manner.
- Follow directions accurately.
- Display consistency in food preparation and presentation.
- Demonstrate a willingness to learn on the job.
- Take initiative to solve problems and to remain productive.

Suggested Tasks

1. Interview two industry chefs and ask them what they expect culinary school graduates to know and to do when they hire them. Ask if their recent culinary graduate hires possessed these abilities and how these graduates moved ahead (or not) in the company as a result. Share your findings with your class.

2. Review the set of industry expectations discussed in this chapter and evaluate which skills/habits you believe are your weakest. Discuss your self-evaluation with your teacher. Create with your teacher a development plan through which you can best improve these weaker skills. Follow through on the plan completely before graduation.

3. Contact a foodservice company for which you would like to work. Speak with the chef or human resources director to request a job description. Ask what training is provided for the job. Write down an analysis of the difference between what skills and knowledge are taught to perform the job and what abilities are assumed to be held by the employee hired. Submit a report on your findings to your teacher. Discuss with the teacher where in your program you will acquire each of the skills needed. If any necessary skills are not taught in the program, ask the teacher for advice on how to acquire those abilities.

4. Form a "community of practice" study group in which you set a schedule for the group to practice knife skills, measurements and conversions, basic food and equipment identification, and basic culinary terminology. Follow through on the practice sessions at least one a week, if not more. Ensure that each member of the group holds the others accountable for on-going improvement in speed and accuracy. This group can and should practice together regularly until graduation for continual improvement.

5. Pick a week in a lab class and prepare for each class day by writing down a list of necessary ingredients and equipment for the day. Also write a planned schedule of activities with a timeline to organize your day in the most productive manner possible. Be sure to include time for sanitation procedures as well. Implement and follow your list each day. Evaluate your production to see if you are working faster and more efficiently. As you learn approaches to multitask and to work even faster, revise your schedule of activities accordingly. If the planning does help you to work better, faster, and in a more organized manner, continue to use the approach for each class. After a few weeks, try to plan the activity schedule without writing it down to see if you can train your brain to work more efficiently without the aid of a written plan to follow. After the first week, share your paperwork with your teacher and discuss how you could have improved the efficiency and organization of your work.

CHAPTER 12

Volunteering at School and in the Community

People from all walks of life ask culinary professionals to volunteer on community projects. From fund-raisers to cure a childhood disease to large events combating homelessness to something as simple as the opening of a local mall, many chefs encounter more opportunities to donate time and food than they can possibly support. For a chef with a restaurant these charity events offer marketing and public relations gold mines; for a culinary student they provide chances to learn, to network, and to build a résumé. New culinary students may wish to participate in as many volunteer activities as possible, but finding volunteer opportunities may pose challenges to a student who does not know where to look.

Simply agreeing to volunteer does not guarantee that a student will gain much value from the experience either. Volunteer coordinators need and expect their volunteers to show up and to work as directed by their supervisors. Some volunteer activities may be relaxed and fun, while others may be high-pressure and fast-paced. Volunteerism always has the potential to return enormous value to those who participate, but students need to approach each volunteer opportunity properly to make sure that they gain value from the experience and do not waste their time in volunteering.

In this chapter, you will learn where to find volunteer opportunities in school and in the community. You will also learn how to maximize the value that you derive from volunteering to make the experience as worthwhile as possible.

12.1 LOCATING VOLUNTEER OPPORTUNITIES

Students new to volunteerism may find it easier to begin by volunteering at the school. When you volunteer on-campus, you are likely already familiar with the building and with many of the people who will work on the project with you. Word of your good work on the project will surely make it back to your instructors and to others who may help you later in building your career.

However, opportunities off-campus should not be overlooked. By volunteering in the community you will encounter new people whom you might not otherwise meet in the industry. Furthermore, you may learn styles and approaches to cooking not taught in your school.

There are risks to volunteering off-campus, for on-campus teachers may be more tolerant of your learning curve than outsiders who may assume you already have the skills of a seasoned chef. Anyone can benefit from both types of work, but novice students may find their home campus the place to start volunteering before branching out to the community at large.

12.1.1   Opportunities in School

The first and best place to locate volunteer opportunities is through the faculty. Teachers often know the various volunteer recruitment efforts going on at school and can give details about the opportunities available to students (or direct students to a person who can). Additionally, since teachers know their students' skill levels, they are in a good position to guide their students to those opportunities best suited for their culinary abilities. If your teacher does not know of any opportunities now, do not be deterred; simply ask your instructor to notify you when an opportunity does arise. By merely asking for volunteer opportunities you are showing yourself to be a class leader passionate about learning and about the industry.

In addition to speaking with faculty members, students should also contact their department director or dean and their career services or job placement coordinator. These people often have regular contact with industry professionals outside the school and know what volunteer projects the school supports each month. Some of these projects may be coordinated by school faculty and staff, while others are managed by community members who wish to recruit student volunteers. In either case, the culinary and career services department heads typically can provide the necessary information for a student to decide whether or not to pursue a volunteer activity.

Student clubs often coordinate their own on-campus volunteer activities as well. These are great opportunities to volunteer in a low-pressure environment with other students. Students can begin by joining the club and deciding if they like the other club members. As they grow comfortable with their fellow club members and follow the event from its initial planning stages, they can volunteer for the event with full knowledge of the job's requirements and of the personalities of the fellow volunteers. Since clubs often thrive on camaraderie among members, senior students typically assist newer club members at events to ensure that everyone has a great time and looks good. Although club events are student-run, faculty members and others still notice the hard work put in by those students who volunteer, so the chance to impress instructors and guests still exists in many club activities.

In many schools students can learn about a range of events needing volunteers simply by reading bulletin boards and school newsletters. These publicly announced volunteer activities may not be the most prestigious, but they are great starting points for a student new to volunteering. Many postings will not list all of the critical details about the event, but there is no harm in reaching out to the contact person listed to get more information before volunteering. By keeping abreast of the volunteer recruitment postings at your school, you will eventually find the right volunteer opportunity for you.

Finally, the key to getting more (and better) volunteer opportunities is to impress the supervisors on your first few events. By following through on your promise to volunteer and by working hard during the event, you will stand out among your fellow volunteers, some of whom may not even bother to show up. When schools need volunteers to work with VIP or celebrity guests, they need volunteers they can count on—students who will impress the guests and not embarrass the school. Consequently, the staff and faculty coordinating these

Interview with Stacey Boyd, Pastry Cook, Windows Catering Company

What type of extracurricular activities did you volunteer for in school?
As Honor Society President, my extracurricular activities consisted of fund-raising for Hurricane Katrina flood victims, organizing school culinary competitions, coordinating and participating in student cooking demonstrations at a local wine festival, scheduling guest speakers for student body meetings, and assisting an executive chef at one of the embassies in Washington, DC.

Where have you volunteered in the community?
Teaching Sunday school to children, serving food to injured and returning soldiers from Iraq and Afghanistan, Angel Tree Christmas gifts for needy families, cooking for families in need, organizing food drives, cooking demonstrations at NBC4 Your Health and Fitness Expo.

How did you find out about those volunteer activities in which you participated?
At school, through school bulletin boards and chef-instructors' announcements in class. As Honor Society President, I would be provided with opportunities from the Dean. In the community, it was bulletin boards, bulletins at church, flyers, radio commercials, even just finding out someone was in need and acting accordingly.

How did you decide which opportunities to take and which to pass up?
I took opportunities at school that I was passionate and excited about. I especially sought those events that would challenge me and provide a great opportunity for learning. In the community, I always gravitated to opportunities where I knew someone's life would be impacted or changed for the best. I am easily encouraged to participate where I can truly make a difference.

What did you do at these volunteer events to maximize their value for you?
I always kept an open mind that there was something new to learn. I would often talk with others, ask many questions, and gain feedback. The most important thing I do in community volunteering is to put my heart and soul into what I'm doing. I try to maximize the chance to reach out and connect with other people in whatever the event may be.

Did any of the connections you made or things you learned at volunteer events help you in the future with your career?
Definitely! The two most important things I learned from volunteering at school were professionalism and organization. Through planning school culinary competitions and student wine festival cooking demonstrations, I learned that organization is the backbone to success. It has given me an advantage in jobs in the culinary profession thus far.

events often recruit volunteers by invitation only. For many students, being asked to work a VIP event is the ultimate compliment and reward in recognition of their past volunteer efforts. If you volunteer often at school and always work hard at the event, you are more likely than those around you to earn an invitation to volunteer at a VIP event.

12.1.2 Volunteering in the Community

While many students begin volunteering in school, there are a large number of opportunities to volunteer in the community on an incredibly diverse range of projects. One of the most likely places to find culinary volunteer opportunities is through local professional associations such as your local American Culinary Federation chapter or the Restaurant Association for your state. These associations often have Web sites or newsletters promoting their events, and they often need culinary students to volunteer on various projects throughout the year. By simply contacting one of the association's leaders and offering to volunteer on a given event, you will begin the process of networking and meeting accomplished industry professionals. If you can impress these people with your work ethic on a volunteer activity, you may find your name instantly well known by many professionals in the community. Regular volunteerism through culinary associations not only leads to great learning opportunities but often to future job offers from professionals familiar with your work.

Grammar, middle, and high schools also offer great opportunities for volunteer work. Some of these schools offer culinary arts, family and consumer science, or basic home economics courses for their students, but they crave any additional support they can get from culinary college students. Although the school may not have any formal program set up for volunteering, a quick conversation with a public school teacher can generate a range of ideas on how a college student can volunteer with young culinary students. The teacher may suggest regular cooking demonstrations or speeches for the students. Perhaps the students will need a coach to work with them after school to prepare for a high school culinary competition. Whatever their needs, you may be surprised at the confidence and leadership abilities you build after just a few presentations to the students. This is also a great way to add some teaching experience to your résumé should you wish to become a culinary arts teacher someday.

Community centers also offer opportunities for students to volunteer while putting their culinary skills to work. Some community centers, such as the YMCA or YWCA, offer cooking classes for children or for home cooks. While a culinary college student may not yet be experienced enough to teach for money, she can certainly locate opportunities to teach a class on a volunteer basis or to assist another teacher in a class. These classes allow a student to put into practice the skills and knowledge learned in culinary school. Volunteering at community centers, as at high schools, builds communication and leadership abilities beyond what can be learned in the classroom, and these volunteer jobs have the potential to turn into paid part-time positions after graduation.

For those students looking to focus more on cooking than on teaching churches and soup kitchens may be the answer. Soup kitchens often need skilled volunteers to help prepare large quantities of food for the homeless and hungry. Some churches also sponsor culinary events to prepare food for those in need. Soup kitchens and churches may be able to use student volunteers for both one-time and ongoing activities. Finding out how to volunteer is usually as simple as contacting a church official or the local food bank to ask how to participate. These volunteer jobs not only build a student's culinary prowess but they also provide a great service to those in need in the local community.

Culinary students may be able to create their own volunteer activities by contacting a local organization, charitable or not, and pitching an idea. Several culinary schools have prepared food for relief workers assisting with major disasters such as the 9/11 attacks or the Hurricane Katrina flooding. However, a volunteer effort need not come only in the wake of a major disaster. Creative students can find all sorts of ways to support those in need in their community and may even find their culinary schools willing to assist in the effort. For example, students at Stratford University in northern Virginia partnered with a local Ronald McDonald house to provide weekly home-cooked meals for residents and their families. The school donated food for the effort, much of it over-production from classes, while students

Interview with Nathaniel Auchter, Sous Chef, Restaurant Associates, Washington, DC

What type of extracurricular activities did you volunteer for in school?
I was involved in a number of student clubs and activities and in addition worked events and hosted a charity function at the school. I found that the most rewarding for me were activities that gave me a deeper understanding of how the CIA operated, and the real joy came from making connections and getting to know all the great people who worked there.

Where have you volunteered in the community?
In the community I have chosen a worthy charity and donated a large portion of my time and energy in assisting with fund-raising functions for them. Share Our Strength not only has the fantastic goal of stopping childhood hunger, but in addition is composed of a large number of talented and devoted people, who are also volunteers. In addition to SOS, I have also been given opportunities to do various demos at different venues, and for the most part they have been unpaid.

What value have you gained from volunteering in each area?
At school, by taking on big roles in student organizations, I was viewed as a student leader; I was given the respect of many of the different deans and instructors and trust from the men and women who handled all my food orders. In the community I feel it is mainly a networking thing. Even if I only happen to meet a few people, and they aren't the "big name" chefs, these cooks and sous chefs are the next big things, and I have watched many of them rise in the ranks over the past few years. The industry is smaller than one might think.

How did you find out about those activities in which you participated?
Student bulletins, Web searches, and creating them for myself were all ways that I found out about and developed ideas for how to get involved. SOS, the James Beard House, and many others are always looking for volunteers for different events.

Did any of the connections you made or things you learned at volunteer events help you in the future with your career?
Yes. I have maintained the relationships with the chefs and industry leaders that I felt the closest connections to, and these are the first people I can turn to now when I need advice, recommendations, or donations for other events. These people are my network. They know me, my goals, and my ambition, and they also know that I am there for them when they need assistance.

prepared and delivered the meals to the Ronald McDonald house. Through a little creative thinking and ingenuity, a small group of students discovered a way to convert food, which might have gone to waste, into a valuable donation to the local community.

12.1.3 Assisting with Annual Community Events

Not all community service activities need weekly volunteers; in fact, many communities have annual events that operate almost entirely on the efforts of volunteers. Share Our Strength, for example, is an organization that raises funds to fight hunger through an annual culinary event entitled "Taste of the Nation" in cities around the country. A typical event such as this one brings chefs from around a city to a single location to prepare food for paying customers. The proceeds from ticket sales fund the cause. Typically these events need volunteers to assist the chefs in the setup of their booths and in food production and service to guests. Culinary students are a perfect fit for such a fund-raiser. With some knowledge of professional cooking and sanitation regulations, culinary students can provide greater support to the chefs than the average volunteer can, and these students benefit greatly from the access to the local chefs. Students can prove their competence and possibly earn a job opportunity after just one event.

Perhaps the easiest way to volunteer for an annual culinary event is to look in the newspapers and online for advertisements promoting these events. The advertisements often list contact information for advance ticket sales. A quick call or email to the contact person usually can get you in touch with the volunteer coordinator for the event. The coordinator can tell you how to volunteer, but students must contact the coordinator early before all of the volunteer slots are taken.

Another way to get involved with community culinary fund-raisers is to speak with local restaurant chefs. Often the most well-known chefs in the community are the most involved in community activities. A brief conversation with a chef will let her know that you are interested in working with her on any community service activities in which she participates. Most (though not all) chefs will be thrilled to have help on their projects without paying and pulling staff from their restaurants. After the conversation you should leave the chef with your business card or résumé so that she can contact you when an opportunity approaches. Not only will you have the chance to work alongside a well-known chef but you may also earn yourself an unofficial job tryout in the process. These benefits are extremely valuable for such a small time commitment.

12.2   CHOOSING THE RIGHT OPPORTUNITIES

Despite the benefits, a student does not need to volunteer for every activity that comes along. Selecting the right volunteer activity is critical to ensuring that the experience is a positive one for the student and for the other project participants. Deciding which volunteer activities to choose requires a few simple steps.

First, gather as much information as you can upfront before agreeing to volunteer. Find out whether or not the work is a one-time commitment or an ongoing requirement. Ask if you can participate periodically or if you must commit to a regular schedule. You will need to know when and where to arrive, what tools and uniform to bring, and to whom you will report. You should also find out the nature of the work you will be doing as part of your volunteer commitment.

Next, evaluate the time that you have to commit to volunteering. Make sure that the work will not interfere with your studies and other responsibilities. If you normally have many hours to spare each week for volunteering, you may be able to accept an ongoing weekly commitment, but if you can barely spare a minute in your typical week, you should look for one-time opportunities that come during a break from school. Schoolwork must always remain top priority over any volunteer activities, but even the most committed students can usually make time in their schedules once a year for the right volunteer opportunity.

One mistake that some students make is to assume that there are no repercussions for failing to follow through on a volunteer commitment. Volunteer work should always be treated as a job tryout or as a reputation builder. (You never know who is tracking your volunteer work or what that person can offer you in the future.) Arriving late, leaving early, or failing to show up at all can do great damage to a student's reputation and may hamper that student's efforts to network for jobs in the future. If you cannot follow through on your commitment, you should notify the volunteer coordinator immediately. If you cannot participate for the entire event, inform the coordinator of your constraints when you volunteer to be sure that you should participate at all.

Interview with Daniel R. Isaman, Ozarks Technical Community College, Graduation: May 2008

What type of extracurricular activities have you volunteered for in school?
My school has provided me with the opportunity to compete in the national Skills USA Commercial Baking Competition where I have been privileged enough to represent my school and make a name for myself. Also, I have been appointed to the Culinary Arts Advisory Committee, where I have been able to provide a student's perspective and opinion regarding the direction of our program.

Have you volunteered in the community?
I entered the local Taste of Springfield Cake Decorating Competition, where I assembled and decorated a cake for an audience. In addition, I was asked by the local chapter of Phi Theta Kappa to provide the cakes for their induction ceremony this fall.

Is there a difference to volunteering at school versus volunteering in the community?
I would encourage student to participate both in school and in the community. Volunteering at school events has given me the support and guidance that have helped me to succeed. Volunteering in the community has provided me with independence and self-discipline. I believe that both have helped me to gain recognition, both in my school and in the community.

How did you find out about those volunteer activities in which you participated?
The department chairs are very good about posting these opportunities and communicating the details with the students.

How did you decide which opportunities to take and which to pass up?
I decided to pursue those activities that I thought would parallel my career goals. I plan on pursuing a career as a pastry chef, so I tend to accept those opportunities that would help me to hone my baking skills. As I do not have the time to chase every prospect, I have learned to take inventory of my goals and analyze which volunteer opportunities will best help me achieve them.

What did you do at these volunteer events to maximize their value for you?
Volunteer events are not all about performance. It is equally important to learn. I have taken something from every event I participated in. Whether I received constructive criticism from a judge, helpful advice from a mentor, or new ideas from other volunteers, I have challenged myself to always leave knowing more than I did when I arrived.

Source: Pine Street Studio

Select opportunities that stretch your culinary skills and abilities over those that provide minimal challenge. Although you may want to support a cause you believe in no matter what you do, you are better off choosing work that challenges your culinary or service ability over one that has you sharpening pencils at a desk. Culinary-centered volunteer work has a higher likelihood of connecting you with those people in your field who can help you get ahead. Culinary work also provides additional practice and skill development to prepare you for the post-graduation industry. Certainly, you can volunteer on many projects, including those that are not culinary-related at all, but if your time is limited, the culinary activities will provide a greater return on your time investment and will look more impressive on your résumé than the non-culinary ones.

Consider your financial ability to devote time to volunteer work and see if there is a way to convert your volunteer work to dollars. Believe it or not, some students can get paid for their volunteer work. The federal financial aid program allows for students to earn work-study money through a range of jobs, including certain volunteer jobs in the community. Not all students are eligible to earn money through their financial aid package and the work must be pre-approved through financial aid. In reality, a student is generally better off asking a financial aid officer for available work-study job opportunities than she is trying to get a volunteer job approved for pay. However, there are some common volunteer programs set up at colleges around the country that pay students for their volunteer work. Perhaps the most well known of these programs is "America Reads." The America Reads program allows work-study students to earn money for tutoring young children in reading. While not culinary in nature, this tutoring can be exceptionally rewarding and can be done in just a few hours each week, leaving lots of time for other culinary work or volunteer activities. Your financial aid officer can let you know if your school participates in America Reads or in any other community service work-study programs. These programs allow you to add valuable community service activities to your résumé while still earning money for college.

Interview with Tim Recher, CEC, Executive Chef, Hilton Alexandria Mark Center, Finn & Porter Restaurant

Do you participate in community volunteer activities?
Yes, as often as my schedule and budget allows. I do 99 percent locally through different organizations. As a father and chef, I tend to focus on children's events and/or hunger-related issues. This means a lot to me and makes it a personal experience instead of just a business marketing item.

What value do you gain from volunteering?
Well, it is a good opportunity to market your business to people and generate some good press/goodwill in your market, but it is more than that for me. By participating in events that are on a more personal level, it makes me feel good as a human being and helps me to contribute to others in a way that I know how to do.

(*continued*)

(*continued*)

Do you place any extra value on a job applicant who has performed some volunteer work at school?
All things being equal between candidates, it does show the character of the person. Also, on a culinary level, a person who spends his/her personal time working with food and people is demonstrating a passion and dedication that is vital to being a success in the business.

Why should culinary students volunteer at school or in the community?
You should take every chance you can to work with food in any environment. There is so much to learn and much, if not all, of that learning is your responsibility. Every time you cook or talk food with other chefs you will come away a better culinarian. Also, you must never forget that you are cooking for people. You're not manufacturing cars or boxes but cooking something another person will eat to nourish the body and soul. Cooking is a very personal experience whether it is for a friend or 1,000 people you never see. The chefs who truly make an impact in the business and society never lose focus on that.

Do you ever work on volunteer activities where you encounter culinary students also volunteering? Have you networked with them after the event?
Absolutely! As a networking opportunity, it is unparalleled. Chefs and cooks are comfortable and relaxed while they cook. It makes for a great environment to meet and get to know other chefs. They also get a chance to see you operate in a kitchen. Talk to them, ask for a business card, and then follow up with them later. I have a few cooks that came through my kitchens I met at events and was happy to have them on our team. It shows me that a young chef is serious about his career and is dedicated to the hard work needed to become an executive chef.

Once you have gathered the information on a volunteer opportunity and considered its potential impact on your academics, time, skill development, and finances, you can decide whether or not the opportunity works for you. Do not avoid volunteerism entirely simply out of fear or low self-confidence. Volunteering is one of the best and easiest ways to gain confidence and experience in the culinary field. All students should make a point of volunteering at least once during their college career. Those who volunteer early often find the experience so rewarding that they volunteer repeatedly while in school. Although volunteer work does not typically provide a paycheck, the long-term rewards of skill development, résumé building, and networking opportunities provide enormous returns to those who volunteer.

12.3 MAXIMIZING THE VALUE OF VOLUNTEERISM

In order to maximize the value of a volunteer activity, a student must treat the experience like a job tryout. Students who work hard to impress those around them with their strong work ethic and passion for the industry are much more likely to gain the attention of those in positions of importance. Culinary bigwigs sometimes offer young culinary students advice, jobs, or other forms of assistance, but they will not waste their time with someone who does not exhibit the work ethic, talent, and other characteristics needed to excel in the industry. Since you never know for certain whom the most influential people in the room are, you should do whatever it takes to make sure that everyone at the event walks away with a fantastic first impression of you.

Although the occasional bigwig may take the initiative to approach the volunteers, most of the workers at a volunteer event will not provide students unsolicited job offers or other assistance. Consequently, students should make a little time during a volunteer event to network with the other culinary professionals in the room. Students must pick the right time; for example, approaching a celebrity chef in the middle of a plate-up for guests will not yield a positive result. Networking with paying customers at the event is also generally a no-no. However, a student can ask the volunteer coordinator for the best time to take a few minutes to speak with other chefs. You only need a couple of minutes to introduce yourself and to network to build your career.

Networking requires more than merely saying hello to the other volunteers, so students should bring business cards to distribute to other culinary professionals. Business cards need not provide much more than the student's contact information. Local printing companies, such as Kinko's, can make business cards at rates that even college students can afford. Passing out a business card to a person with whom you want to stay in touch is a much classier, more professional approach than writing your information on the back of a napkin.

Students must also get business cards from the people with whom they network. Since culinary big shots may not have the time to follow up with every person who hands them a business card, the student must take the initiative to keep in touch. Follow-up can be a simple as an email or phone call, but with so few people following up on initial network connections a student who does reach out to others is likely to earn an opportunity unavailable to most culinary students.

In addition to the networking opportunities, volunteerism provides chances for students to learn new skills in the culinary arts. Students who only focus on their own work during a volunteer event cheat themselves of the opportunity to learn what others are doing. You can learn from those around you simply by keeping your eyes and ears open. Watch what other chefs create, and observe how they work. See if they have put together a presentation or flavor combination you have never seen before. Ask questions about techniques or ingredients with which you are unfamiliar. In short, use the volunteer event as an opportunity to learn rather than just as an opportunity to add to your résumé.

Finally, to get the most value from volunteering find out if there is an opportunity to work with the same volunteers again to strengthen your relationships with them. To accomplish this goal, a student simply needs to thank the people in charge of the event before leaving and to ask how to work with them again. If there is a particular culinary professional with whom you wish to work, offer to volunteer for any other events on which

John Doe
Culinary Student

123 Cranberry Lane
Washington, DC 20003
Mobile: (202) 555-1111
Email: Doe23@doa.com

FIGURE 12.1 Sample Student Business Card

she works. If you particularly like an event, ask the coordinators how to get on the volunteer list for next year. A student who maintains regular contact with certain culinary professionals by working alongside them at multiple events is likely to remain top-of-mind when one of those professionals needs a trustworthy volunteer or a new employee for her operation. You may find that you not only enjoy volunteering enough to do it regularly but that the benefit you receive from volunteering increases with each event.

Summary

Students can often find a wide variety of volunteer opportunities both in school and in the community simply by asking the right people. Students can locate in-school opportunities through teachers, department directors, job placement coordinators, student clubs, bulletin board postings, and school newsletters. Performing well on a volunteer event is also likely to generate invitations for future volunteer work. In the community students will find chances to volunteer through professional associations, public schools, community centers, churches, and soup kitchens. Students may even be able to create their own volunteer activities in the community. Annual culinary-themed events often advertise contact information for ticket sales in the newspaper or online, and students can usually inquire for volunteer opportunities through the contact person listed or through chefs who participate in those events. Students should make sure that they only volunteer for events when they can commit to the requirements fully. Activities that provide networking and learning opportunities are ideal choices for volunteering. Students can maximize the value they get from volunteering by working diligently to impress others at the event, by networking actively at the event, and by observing other volunteers to learn from their skills and culinary creations. Any student can benefit from volunteering, and all students should make the effort to volunteer at least once during their college career.

KEYS TO SELECTING THE RIGHT VOLUNTEER ACTIVITIES FOR YOU

- Gather as much information as possible about the activity and the requirements for volunteers.
- Evaluate whether or not you have enough free time to devote to this activity.
- Consider whether or not you will be able to give the activity your full commitment and attention.
- Select opportunities that challenge your culinary skills over ones that do not.
- Consider any financial benefits or costs to the activity.
- Agree to volunteer if you can follow through on your commitment without negatively impacting your other responsibilities.

Suggested Tasks

1. Locate at least three volunteer opportunities either in school or in the community. Get as much information as possible on each of these opportunities. Analyze which of these activities, if any, you could volunteer for and which would provide you the most benefit at this stage of your program. If you can commit fully to one of these activities, volunteer for it and follow through on your commitment to volunteer.

2. Interview two senior culinary students approaching graduation. Ask them what volunteer activities, if any, they participated in during their college career. Ask them what benefit they gained from volunteering and what network connections they made as a result. Ask them if they followed up on the network connections and what benefits occurred as a result. Compare the volunteer experiences of the two students and share your findings with your class.

3. Interview a local culinary professional known to participate in at least one community service activity each year. Ask that person why she volunteers and what benefit it provides her. Ask if she values volunteerism on the résumés of job applicants, and find out if she ever assists culinary students who work with her on volunteer projects. Write a report on your interview and submit it to your teacher. If the culinary professional is looking for volunteers to work on a future project, volunteer to work with her, if you are able.

4. Speak with at least two of your teachers to find out if they ever volunteer at school or in the community. Ask them why they continue to volunteer and if students ever work with them on these projects. Find out if previous volunteers have enjoyed the experience of volunteering and benefited from it. If the teachers are seeking volunteers for future projects, gather more information to see if you can volunteer with them. If you are able, follow through and volunteer to work with the teacher.

CHAPTER 13

On-the-Job Experience: Working While in School and Choosing the Right Job

Working while in school can be both a blessing and a hardship. Many students do not have the luxury of focusing entirely on their studies to the exclusion of all else, so a paying job, culinary or not, may be a necessity. A job consumes time that could be otherwise spent on preparing for exams, researching in the library, or volunteering with faculty. Working for money, however, is not entirely without merit. On the contrary, a job allows a student to practice discipline, professional work habits, and interpersonal skills while providing the student the means to pay living expenses and to take fewer college loans. A culinary-related job, either in a kitchen or in a dining room, further provides the student an opportunity to practice his craft and to learn how the real world of the culinary industry sometimes differs from the theories taught in school. Without this real-world industry experience and knowledge on a résumé, a student may be unable to get an interview with certain employers after graduation.

Students may base the number of hours they decide to work, if they work at all, more on personal financial needs than on professional development; that decision rests entirely with the student. No one can or should require a student to forego a rent payment and to risk eviction in order to focus more on classes. However, choosing the right job and setting limits on one's own work schedule can make the student's work experience positive rather than self-destructive. Without limits some students fall into a vicious cycle of working too many hours to pay for tuition only to fail a class and thus increase the amount of tuition they owe. With some self-imposed constraints, a student can reap the benefits of employment without having to delay graduation.

In this chapter, you will learn how to choose the right job for you while in school and how to set boundaries with your employer to keep your job from impeding your academic progression.

13.1   CHOOSING THE RIGHT JOB

Although there are innumerable culinary employers hiring at any given point in time, not all companies are appropriate places to work while in school. Students have a great deal of control over their own lives and schedules (more than they may realize), and choosing the right job upfront can make it easier for a student to maintain that control. To know if you have the right job already or are accepting the right job offer, you need to consider certain questions and variables.

13.1.1   Sticking with the Status Quo

Some students are already gainfully employed before they begin school. These students already know how much money they earn on average each week and if that income can cover their expenses and the additional costs associated with college. They know the nature of their work and whether or not their boss is flexible and supportive of college. They know how often they are asked to work overtime and how often staffing emergencies arise. In short, these students know upfront whether or not the job will make attending college easy or nearly impossible.

The truly difficult question for currently working students is whether or not their current job will allow them to make the most of their time in college. If the job will impede a student's ability to attend classes or to study and to learn, then that student should look for work elsewhere. On the other hand, if the employer is extremely supportive of the student's educational goals and adjusts the student's schedule and job requirements to accommodate classes and study needs, then the student should keep that job as long as possible, even if the job is not related to the culinary field. The student can always leave to find culinary work closer to graduation.

Interview with Peter Tinson, Chef/Owner, Gallery Bistro

How do you manage employees who are currently in school? Are they more difficult to accommodate?
They are a little more difficult to a degree, but generally they compensate for inflexible schedules with their desire to work. A lot need to maintain their job in order to continue going to school. Over the years we learned to accommodate their schedules, and they've responded by trying to accommodate ours.

How do you support current students?
We always ask for their school schedule upfront, and then we put a quilt-work together with our scheduling needs for the restaurant. It's always worked out real well.

Is there ever conflict with students between their work and school responsibilities?
From time to time there is conflict because students can get frantic around final exams and midterms. We work around it because we have enough people who work part-time that we can mix and match to cover other employees. We also have enough people who have worked here before and can fill in for a night. If we treat people well while they're here, they're generally more willing to come back and help out for a temporary gig.

(continued)

(continued)
What is the benefit to students to work for you while in school?
That's an individual issue. However, the benefit to them is that there is nothing they can do for 14–20 hours per week that pays what they can make here front-of-the-house.

What is the benefit to you to employ current students?
Our number one benefit is enthusiasm. They don't come into the establishment with preconceived notions from the past. We get to train them how we like it done. It may sound hackneyed, but we say, "Hire for attitude, train for skill."

13.1.2 Budgeting for Time

Whether starting from scratch or evaluating one's current employment, students must always consider the amount of money they need to survive and the amount of money that a new job might pay. No student should expect to grow rich from a college job, but students should be able to cover their expenses without working 60 hours per week. A job that meets a student's financial needs in just 30 hours per week is far more valuable than one that requires 50 hours per week. Fewer hours at work leaves more time for studying, research, and faculty interaction.

To avoid becoming a slave to the job, a student should begin by creating a budget. An honest budget of a student's current and anticipated expenses will let him know where to cut back to ease his financial burden. Culinary school requires uniforms and students need to budget for their purchase and upkeep. However, college is not the time to build a new wardrobe of leisure outfits. Similarly, college students can survive just fine without daily purchases of five-dollar coffee beverages or weekly movie tickets. Cutting back on some of these optional purchases may allow a student to work fewer hours and thus free up more time for academic endeavors. After creating a fairly accurate and lean budget, a student can safely determine the minimum number of hours he needs to work at the rate a job pays. To build a safety net, the student should budget a little extra money for miscellaneous expenses (or plan to work a couple of extra hours each week), but any extra money should be saved for emergencies rather than used on unnecessary indulgences. A surprise car repair or medical expense will place extreme stress on your budget should you not have an emergency cash reserve.

If part-time work is an option for you and if it can cover all your expenses, strongly consider working less than full-time. Part-time and full-time work both provide similar perks of skill development, résumé-building experience, and networking opportunities. The only real difference at this stage of the game is how much time and money you exchange with the company. There will be plenty of time to earn extra money and to build full-time experience after graduation, but there is only one opportunity to make the most of your college education. Do not overbook your schedule at work if you can survive with fewer hours.

13.1.3 Finding Culinary Work

Students who need to work but do not already have a job that supports their educational goals should look to work in the culinary field. Although industry work is not a requirement, it does provide many benefits that other types of employment do not. Culinary work allows a student to practice kitchen skills outside of school. It provides more impressive experience on a résumé and a greater number of networking connections in the industry. Culinary jobs not only make appropriate post-graduation jobs for students who wish to continue at the same place of employment, but students who have proven their worth while in school can sometimes earn a promotion immediately upon graduation. Foodservice jobs may not pay phenomenally well, but they do offer additional benefits that non-industry work does not.

Of course, not all culinary jobs are appropriate for current students. Some employers expect their employees to put work first over all else. If an employer is not willing to work around a student's class schedule and study needs, that employer should be passed over for a more flexible, supportive one. Too many students allow their supervisors to determine whether or not they make it to class on time, if at all. You cannot permit your job to take precedence over school. Once this happens, you will quickly end up dropped from school for poor attendance or for low grades. Sadly, some employers prefer to have their employees drop out of school, as dropouts have fewer scheduling conflicts than current students and cost less money than graduates. Leaving school to work in any foodservice establishment is extremely short-sighted. The money may seem good at the time, but a student without a degree will inevitably take longer to earn a promotion and large pay increase than a culinary school graduate will.

Finding supportive employers can be difficult, especially for students who have moved to a new city. The easiest way to learn about the best jobs for current students is through faculty and classmates. Instructors generally have connections in the industry and know where the best jobs are for current students. Classmates who already work will know if their company is supportive of student needs; they will also know if any job openings are available. Most importantly, neither classmates nor teachers want to send you somewhere that might poach you away from school. Job placement staff can also be a good resource for job openings, but check with your teachers first to see what they know about the operation. Job placement workers get so many employee requests they may not know the detailed information you want about every operation that contacts them. However, the placement office will know locations to avoid based on feedback from previous students, so a visit to the placement office is worth the time. You should never work for an employer who has a track record of persuading students to leave school to work full-time. Chances are that such an employer will make your life so difficult as to force you to choose between the job and school. There is no point in enduring this stressful environment when you can avoid it.

Interview with Christopher Mosier, student at Anne Arundel Community College

Do you work full-time? How do you budget your time?
I currently work full-time, and I work about 40 hours a week. During the busy season I worked a maximum of 55 hours a week. To budget my time I try to write things down and get what is most pressing or time consuming out of the way first. I know when I will have to work and when I have class. Other than travel and sleep time I just find a way to fit everything in.

How did you find your job?
I found my job when I ran into the head chef of the Maryland Club at the '07 ACF national convention in Florida. I was down there competing in the cold foods salon and my instructors introduced me to him. I had a job offer waiting for me when I got back to Maryland.

(continued)

(*continued*)

Do you set boundaries with your employer to avoid conflicts with school requirements?
Not really. I tell my chef my school schedule, and he respects it. On occasion I have to remind him that I can't work certain times.

How does you employer support you in your college responsibilities?
My employer supports my college responsibilities by respecting my class schedule and by putting me on assignments that will help reinforce what I'm learning in school. He asks me from time to time what I'm currently learning and always keeps me on my toes about general kitchen knowledge.

Have you ever felt pressured to miss class in order to help out at work?
Yes. I have missed class for work once. I had to work extra hard to get caught up at school, and the instructor wasn't very happy but understood the situation. I don't suggest doing it if it is at all possible.

In your opinion, is it ok to miss class to work extra hours?
In the end I don't think it's worth it. It puts extra pressure and work on you, and in the end you get less out of it.

What benefits do you gain from working?
I get a lot of good experience for working. I also gain a lot of knowledge, not only reinforcing what I learn in school, but also giving a completely different perspective on the subjects and experiences I wouldn't get in school. I currently am able to cover my expenses while in school without working, but I choose to work in order to gain more knowledge and experiences in the culinary industry.

Some students look for employers who hire a lot of graduates from the school. This may seem at first like a good approach, but students must recognize that a graduate and a current student have different limitations on their available work time. Some employers recognize this difference and may be great sources for employment; others may not be good options. The best way to know for sure is through a clear, honest conversation with the employer before accepting a job. If the employer seems hesitant about accommodating your academic needs, you should keep looking.

13.1.4 The On-Campus Option

One of the best places to find a job where the supervisors respect educational priorities is right on campus. Although not every on-campus job is culinary-related, all on-campus employers will work with a student's schedule to allow that student to attend class and to study. There are other perks to working on-campus as well. There is very little commute time, so a student will not lose hours of precious study time in a car. On-campus jobs typically offer opportunities to further other student goals as well. For example, some jobs allow students to interact regularly with faculty. Others give students the chance to practice cooking in a kitchen. Even students who work in the library will have the occasional chance to research a culinary topic or to review an educational video as part of their job. On-campus jobs may not seem as glamorous as those in the outside world, but they generally support a student in multiple ways toward academic success.

13.2 SETTING BOUNDARIES

Whether a student already has a great job or is simply interviewing for one, it is imperative that the student set boundaries with the company and direct supervisor. Students must state without any equivocation that they cannot accept a job that requires them to work during class time. They must make clear to the employer that school comes first. Only after setting such boundaries upfront can students agree to work exceptionally hard for an employer with the time that they have available. An employer who agrees to these terms during the interview is much more likely to be supportive of the student's schedule than an employer who is only told of a student's school enrollment weeks after hiring the student. Further, an employer who knows of an employee's constraints in an interview is less likely to view the employee's inability to work overtime as a lack of commitment to the company. Should the employer decide not to hire you because of your constraints, you are better off. You would only find yourself later forced to choose between work and school as your supervisor schedules you for shifts during class time.

During the interview, working students should communicate to the employer the maximum number of hours that they can work each week when school is in session. To determine this maximum number of hours, a student should budget time first for classes, studying, family commitments, and personal "life" needs, such as sleeping, eating, and maintaining personal hygiene. The student should also build a couple of extra hours into each week to account for unknowns ranging from a heavy homework load to a community service opportunity. Whatever hours are left in the week are available for the student to work. Trying to budget other activities around work usually results in shortfalls in primary needs, like studying or sleeping.

Interview with Erika Tucker, French Culinary Institute, Graduation: February 2008

Were you working somewhere before you started school?
Yes, I was a butler at the St. Regis Resort in California. On my days off I would work in the kitchen because I loved it so much. I could have transferred to the St. Regis here in the city; however, I chose not to because I wanted to get the experience of working in a restaurant kitchen as opposed to a hotel kitchen.

Do you set boundaries with your employer to avoid conflicts with school requirements?
My employer understands I am still a student and completely respects that. He is perfectly fine with me coming in after school and gives me days off if I need them to study or to make up classes. However, this isn't exactly common among chefs. I have a friend from school whose chef asks her to come in to work during school hours. Some students do that; I don't recommend it.

Have you ever missed class for work?
Absolutely not. If I ever felt pressured, I would probably quit. School will always come first, no matter what. Consequences of missing class are huge. If you calculate it out, you are paying close to $400 a day to be there. Not only that, but each day is filled with valuable, detailed lessons, and missing only one would make me feel very behind.

(continued)

(*continued*)

If you could cover your expenses while in school without working, would you still work outside of school?
I would absolutely work outside of school even if I didn't need the money. Look at it as an investment. You are investing in your future by attempting to obtain the knowledge and experience necessary for your craft. One of my chefs once said, "Culinary is a craft and we are the craftsmen." It's true. The more you work in the industry, the better educated you are, and the more you will succeed at your craft.

To understand why missing school for work is never the right choice, imagine the typical scenario that causes a staffing emergency. An employee calls out from work last minute and your boss asks you to stay late to cover the shift "just this one time." You know that staying late will result in missing class. Should you help out your supervisor, you will never be able to make up the lost class experience for which you have already paid tuition. Your grade will inevitably suffer, and you will be at a disadvantage in the workforce for the knowledge you failed to learn. Your boss may seem appreciative at the time, but by the following day he will have little concern for the sacrifice that you made to help out at work. In fact, you will have proven to your boss that you are willing to miss class if he begs hard enough. Soon you will find more and more requests for you to work extra hours. The requests will come with increased pressure and frequency until you eventually convince yourself to write off the class you are already failing. At this point, any extra money you earn at work will be funneled to pay for repeating the class you failed. Since college costs hundreds, if not thousands, of dollars per course, you will find that you actually lose money by skipping class to work. To add insult to injury you will never see any benefit from your employer for the extra hours that you worked, for until you graduate (or drop out of school entirely), your supervisor will assume that you do not have the time to accept the greater responsibility of a promotion. Earning a promotion is a fine goal after graduation, but graduating, not taking on more responsibility at work, should be your primary goal while in school. In short, you should feel comfortable maintaining your position that you can only work the previously agreed upon hours.

To make personal constraints as easy as possible for an employer to accommodate, a student worker should notify his supervisor of his course schedule as soon as he receives it. Employers can much more easily adjust a student's schedule with two weeks notice than they can with two days notice. Once the employer accommodates the student's needs, the student should go out of his way to sustain his end of the deal. A relationship of understanding and support from an employer only lasts as long as the student worker does not abuse the relationship. To maintain a good relationship with your employer, you should do everything in your power to work your agreed upon hours and not to call out or to arrive late to work. You keep your promise to work certain hours because you will hold your employer to his agreement not to ask you to work extra hours.

Despite your best efforts to remain candid and professional about your personal constraints, you may encounter a threat, overt or subtle, from your supervisor that not working more hours will cost you your job. Ignore such threats. Chances are that your boss is simply applying a pressure tactic to get you to meet his needs. Managers who want to fire you for your scheduling limitations will not make threats; they will simply fire you. If you do get fired, do not panic. You are better off leaving your current job and finding a new one that allows you to continue your education properly. There are many companies that are happy to support their employees in the pursuit of higher education. Although job-hopping (moving from job to job after relatively brief stints) is generally bad for one's career, most employers understand that it happens regularly to students in school. In the long run, a company that does not value your pursuit of higher education and credentials now will not likely reward your achievements after graduation. You would need to leave such a company soon after graduation anyway to advance your career.

13.2.1   A Real Predicament

What if a student cannot quit his job and the employer is not respectful of his need to attend class? Such a scenario occurs regularly for students whose employers are paying for their education, especially for students who are in the military. Unfortunately, these situations offer no easy answers. If the student changes jobs, he may not be able to afford to go to school. If he keeps his current job, he feels pressure to comply with the company's requests, for it is paying his tuition. However, if the student fails the course, the company rarely pays for the failed class, which leaves the student with a bill he did not anticipate.

Interview with Tony Aiazzi, Executive Chef, Aureole

How do you manage employees who are currently in school?
Most students are on an externship, so they are not currently going to school but are on a kind of break between sessions. The few who are actively enrolled in classes we are very flexible with.

How do you support current students, or is it their responsibility to manage their work and school requirements?
We support them by being flexible with their schedules and providing them with an environment that supports and is conducive to learning the techniques of cooking. Beyond that, the responsibility is theirs. It's also important to note that the financial burden is upon their shoulders as well. Rarely do we pay for part-time help as they are, more time than not, an extra addition to the core staff.

Do you ever employ students part-time? Are you flexible in the number of hours that your students work?
Students are only ever part-time if they are still going to classes. I'll be flexible to a point, but being setup and staffed for service comes first. Part-time in the kitchen is a regular work week in most other fields.

What is the benefit to students to work for you while in school?
Classes at cooking schools are often oversaturated with students. Having a job in a restaurant gives students much more practice than they will ever get in a classroom environment. Cooking is a craft that needs mass amounts of repetition to perfect. They may cook five dishes for a practical exam over four hours in a school, but in a restaurant kitchen there is a practical exam every five minutes.

What is the benefit to you to employ current students?
We are always looking for new talent. Having a good supply of students and relationships with schools gives us a steady supply of cooking willing to work and learn. It's a good opportunity for them and us to see if future employment would be a good fit for all concerned.

When stuck in this predicament, a student should work as closely as possible with his instructors to explain the situation and to prepare for sudden emergencies that may pull him out of class. Constant contact with the instructors will help the student to catch up on missed information to better prepare for exams and class assignments. The student should also continue to stress to his supervisor that he cannot miss class or he risks failing the course. The supervisor may not have much flexibility, but when possible, he will probably help the student to make it to class on time. Most employers and supervisors do understand that they cannot require you miss class regularly if they are not going to pay for repeating the course; they just need to be reminded regularly of your requirement to attend school.

13.3 BITTER REALITY

Most students do not have employers to pay their tuition. With the added cost of tuition, fees, uniforms, commuting, and school supplies, students typically see an increase in their normal monthly expenses upon enrolling in school. Some students pay for these and other expenses through loans and grants; others get support from family members. Still other students have planned and saved for college and pay for school from their own investments. All of these types of students may work part-time or full-time to supplement their current funding for school.

But what about those students who cannot cover their expenses without working well over 40 hours per week? Should they continue to work so many hours while attending school full-time, they may not be able to study enough to pass their exams or their classes. If they cut back on hours at work, they may not be able to afford the books for class, so they end up unable to study, unable to complete their assignments, and unable to pass the class. Students in this predicament need to reconsider their decision to attend school full-time.

Fortunately, there are some options for students in dire financial straits. Students who have no financial safety net and must work far beyond a 40-hour work week should speak with a financial aid officer to discuss any loan options that may be available. Sometimes a student can take out additional personal loans to cover living expenses while in school. Students should also research and pursue any scholarship options they can find to help alleviate some of the need to work large numbers of hours outside of school. If loans and scholarships are not an option, a financially strapped student should speak to a trusted school advisor about part-time school options. Some schools (though not all) allow students to attend part-time. Although this option extends the length of time a student takes to complete a degree, it may be the only way that a student can work enough hours to cover expenses while still attending class and studying for exams.

Unfortunately, if loans and part-time attendance are not possible, students in dire financial straits have to consider withdrawing from school, no matter how difficult that may be to accept. Everyone who can get into college and wants to be in college should be in college eventually, but not everyone is ready to be in college now. Students who try to balance a 60-hour-per-week job and a 30-hour-per-week course schedule with a 2-hour daily commute, a family to raise, and time for studying rarely find themselves successful at school. Whether from lack of sleep or from lack of study time, these students rarely make it all the way through a college program. Such a student would be better off dropping out of school and working even more hours each week to save some money for college. With a financial nest egg of several thousand dollars, a student can usually cover college expenses while cutting back to a mere 40 hours per week at work. The extra money and fewer hours at work allow the student to purchase all of the supplies needed to succeed in class without sacrificing the time required to study and to prepare for class. A financial safety net also keeps students from dropping out of school because of car repairs or utility price hikes. If you believe you are personally in a dire financial situation that is making it impossible to survive college, speak to a college advisor about withdrawing for a time from school. You may only need a few months to build up enough savings to return, but you will find yourself better able to focus and to learn when you do return to school.

Now, before you run off to drop out of school, make sure that you understand the difference between the normal stress of college and a dire situation. Most college students pull the occasional all-nighter. Many find themselves juggling work, school, and family commitments, and inevitably these commitments collide periodically forcing something to give. That is the nature of college. In fact, some people believe that part of the experience of college is learning how to cope with stress and time crunches. There is no need to drop out of school if this is your current experience. If a single sick day means that you must decide between paying your rent and buying your textbook, then you are in a dire situation. If your work and school commitments alone leave you only four hours for sleep every night, then you may wish to withdraw until you can afford to work fewer hours. There is a great deal of truth to the saying "You only get out of school what you put into it." If you have no time to put into studying and learning, you will get very little out of your investment.

Summary

To have the best chance of success at balancing school and work, a student needs to choose the right job while in school. Those students currently working at companies that support their educational goals should remain with their current employers, but students who are not supported at work should look elsewhere for work. While looking for work students must consider how much they need to earn. Creating a budget will let students know where they can cut back on optional expenses and how much money they need to earn monthly to cover their required expenses. A job that pays more is not necessarily better, but students should only consider jobs that pay enough to cover their expenses in 40 hours per week or less. Students should strongly consider part-time work if it covers their expenses to allow more time for school and studying. Employment in the culinary industry should be the first choice for students looking for work while in school. Students should interview their potential employers carefully to ensure that the company and supervisor will support their need to attend class and to spend time studying. Faculty, classmates, and job placement workers can assist in locating such supportive employers. Sometimes the best employer is the school itself; on-campus jobs offer a supportive environment for student workers as well as several other perks. Wherever students work, they must set boundaries with their employers. Students must determine how many hours they have available to work per week without sidetracking their educational goals, and they must notify their employers that they cannot work more than those available hours. Students must also provide their employers with their class schedules as soon as possible to allow an employer to schedule student workers around their course schedules. If employers hold up their end of the bargain

by facilitating students' academic requirements, then students must do their best to
meet the needs of their employers to make
the relationship mutually beneficial. Those
students who cannot leave an unsupportive
job environment must continuously remind
their supervisors of their academic needs to
minimize the number of times that they are
asked to skip school for work. Unfortunately,
some students may be unable to give school
an appropriate time commitment because of
a heavy but necessary work schedule. Those
students should work with financial aid to
locate loans and scholarships and may need
to pursue part-time enrollment in school. If
all other options fail, then these students
should consider withdrawing from school to
return when they are in a more financially
secure situation. Fortunately, most students
who do need to withdraw can usually save
enough money to return to school under
better circumstances in less than a year.

KEYS TO FINDING AND KEEPING THE RIGHT JOB

- Create a budget to determine one's required income.
- Consider remaining with a current employer who is supportive of college requirements.
- Look for work in the foodservice industry to gain field experience.
- Interview employers to ensure they will enable class attendance.
- Consult instructors, classmates, and job placement workers for job recommendations.
- Look for on-campus job opportunities.
- Give the employer a maximum number of available work hours per week.
- Provide the employer a course schedule to ensure that work and class do not conflict.
- Confirm that the terms of employment will not interfere with academic success and do not agree to changes to those terms if such changes will negatively impact college requirements.
- Meet all agreed upon expectations of the employer to maintain continued employment with a supportive employer.

Suggested Tasks

1. Create a budget of your current actual expenses per month. Include both necessary and optional expenses. Write a list of your current sources and amounts of income. Calculate the difference between your monthly expenses and your monthly sources of income. Ask your instructor for the hourly rate that current students typically earn in your area. Calculate the number of hours you need to work at that rate to cover your necessary expenses; then, calculate how many additional hours you would need to work to also cover your optional expenses.

2. Create a spreadsheet recording the number of hours you need to devote to all of the necessary tasks in your life (sleep, eating, class, studying, family, etc.). Include a couple of hours each week for miscellaneous emergencies. Calculate how many hours you have remaining each week for paid employment.

3. Interview one instructor, one schoolmate, and one job placement employee for recommendations of companies to work for while in school. Share your list with your class to create a compiled list of potential employers for current students.
4. Locate five scholarships for which you could apply. Request applications for all five. Apply to at least two.
5. Locate one job opening for a position on-campus. Obtain a copy of the job description and requirements. Write a list of the pros and cons of working at

this particular job. Share the list with your instructor and determine whether or not you should apply for this position.
6. Interview an industry chef who hires current students. Ask the chef how he accommodates students' school needs. Also ask what the benefits are to working in his operation while in school. Find out over the past two years how many of his current student workers have dropped out of school, how many have graduated, and how many have continued to work at the same operation after graduation.

CHAPTER 14

Behaviors that Promote Health and Education

xpert chefs need more than knife skills and cooking know-how to rise to the top of their field. In addition to costing, management, nutrition, and sanitation skills, chefs must know how to combine flavors and to manipulate ingredients to create exciting and delectable taste and texture sensations for their guests. Many of the flavor combinations and recipe ideas that chefs "invent" are actually learned by critically tasting the creations of other chefs.

However, chefs cannot spend every day eating nonstop to maximize their exposure to ingredient combinations, at least not without serious health consequences. For this reason chefs-in-training must make every meal count. Every time a student puts something into her mouth she has the opportunity to learn. Too many meals wasted on gobbling food thoughtlessly results in a limited flavor memory bank. Since a broader variety of dining experiences translates to a greater range of taste memories, a student who makes every meal a learning experience usually becomes a more versatile, talented culinary artist.

In this chapter, you will learn techniques for maximizing the learning value of the foods you eat. You will also learn how maintaining your health and fitness will contribute to your ability to perform and to learn better as a cook, and ultimately, as a chef. Finally, you will learn a few common behaviors that can negatively impact your health and your career.

14.1 NOURISHING THE MIND

Eating is both pleasurable and satiating, but for chefs it is also educational. Restaurants, hotels, catered events, anywhere that serves food is a chef's classroom, and culinary artistry is the subject. A chef who chooses to ignore the educational opportunities available through another person's cooking is equivalent to a writer who does not read; neither stretches the limits of her skills. The more a chef studies food, the more she will improve her ability to create new dishes for her customers.

Simply eating, however, does not necessarily provide an education. For example, a film student may see a film a dozen times, but most of the education occurs in the first couple of viewings. Similarly, a student who subsists on fried chicken and mashed potatoes every day learns little to nothing new about those dishes after the first few meals. Choosing a varied and cosmopolitan diet allows students to gain familiarity with a wider range of ingredients and to garner a large number of ideas to expand their repertoires. There are several simple steps you can implement to maximize your learning from the foods you eat.

First, when eating out, always order ingredients and flavor combinations that are not familiar. If a student has never tasted alligator, she squanders a huge learning opportunity by not ordering it off a menu when she has the chance. Similarly, a dish that pairs black pepper and vanilla bean might seem strange, but a cook may gain inspiration from tasting such a pairing, even if the combination is not pleasing to the palate. Those students who live at McDonald's are training themselves for work at fast-food restaurants. Students who order, eat, and study the foods of higher-end restaurants are educating their palates for more prestigious culinary jobs. If you do not have much money for dining out, do not worry. You can learn a great deal from eating out simply by choosing foods that are unfamiliar. Ethnic restaurants generally provide exotic flavors and ingredients at a reasonable price, and students can usually afford to patronize them every once in a while.

Interview with Nora Pouillon, Chef/Owner, Restaurant Nora

Is it important for culinary students to adjust their eating habits for their careers?
Yes, it is very important that students adjust their eating habits for their careers. First, they should start eating organic, local, and seasonal foods. This will help a student learn about the foods that nature offers at different seasons and what is available locally. This will also educate a student about organic agriculture, its importance on health, and the impact it has on the environment. Second, culinary students should eat out as much as they can afford to expand their knowledge about different cuisines. It is especially important to try various ethnic restaurants to learn about the different cooking techniques, ingredients, and cultures.

Do you keep a journal of things you eat?
I personally collect menus, takes notes on them, and if possible, I take pictures of the food I like.

Is it important for a chef to get regular exercise?
Yes, it's important. Exercise keeps a chef healthy and fit. It is necessary to be fit in order to handle the physical demands placed on them in the work environment. It also helps to reduce stress. Exercise and physical activity helps chefs to be more creative and to understand the importance of a healthy diet.

Have you ever encountered culinary workers with substance or alcohol abuse problems?
Yes, I have encountered culinary workers with substance or alcohol abuse problems, but not that often in my kitchen. I could always help them to seek treatment and for many of them it has worked out. They understood what a setback in their career it was to have those problems.

Is physical injury common in the kitchen?
Luckily, there have not been many accidents in my kitchen. The staff is informed about the possible dangers in the kitchen and instructed on how to properly use various kitchen equipment to avoid accidents.

Another approach to learning about food is to order similar dishes prepared by different restaurants. This technique works especially well for students who know where they want to specialize. For example, a student who wants to specialize in seafood might order clam chowder in several different restaurants to see how the preparations vary from one chef to another. There is still little value in ordering the clam chowder over and over in the same restaurant, but trying variations is educational. You may find the experience of visiting different restaurants fun as well.

Many students avoid foods that they know they do not like. However, a student may have a mind-blowing epiphany by periodically ordering a food she does not enjoy to see if another chef with an alternate preparation can make it more palatable. Take, for example, the student who shuns oysters because she has only had them raw and does not care for their uncooked texture. This student may learn to appreciate and to use oysters in her own cooking if she will only taste them fried or stewed. Even if she still hates oysters, she may learn what about oysters she does not like and perhaps will learn how to prepare them to minimize that characteristic. You should periodically order foods you have not enjoyed in the past to see if you can learn to appreciate them. Without an understanding and appreciation of certain foods, you will find it difficult to prepare them as a cook or to include them on your menu as a chef.

Since chefs must always keep culinary education top-of-mind when eating, they are wise to patronize restaurants that offer smaller portions over those establishments that serve mammoth amounts of food to their customers. Small portions allow a person to order and to taste a wide range of dishes. On the other hand, a person who orders an entrée of an entire chicken is unlikely to have room to sample anything else from the menu. Tasting menus, tapas and mezze restaurants, and smaller portioned entrées have all become trendy. You can take advantage of these trends and find restaurants where you can taste five or more dishes without becoming uncomfortably full. You will find that you can learn as much about an ingredient, flavor combination, or cooking technique in two or three bites as you can in fifty.

If you must go to the same one or two restaurants repeatedly (perhaps because they are the only ones you can walk to from school), then you should try everything on the menu. By trying all of the dishes on the menu, at least you will expose yourself to a wider range of ingredient combinations than you would by ordering the same dish repeatedly. You will only learn the style of the chef at the one restaurant, but you will learn more than just a single recipe.

14.2   ANALYZING FOOD

Eating will not provide education to a culinary professional who does not think critically about the food she consumes. Thinking and analyzing are essential elements to the dining process for a chef. Everyone has moments when eating quickly to stave off hunger is a necessity; time to consider the specific qualities of the meal may just not be available. Perhaps you experience this sense of urgency over breakfast as you prepare for your day, or maybe you feel it as you snack between classes. Moments such as these are part of life, but the more meals you study and analyze, the more you learn about food and cooking in general.

There are many aspects of any dish that you should address to learn as much as possible about the food you eat. First, you should consider your first impressions of appearance,

Interview with Missy L. Monnett, Baltimore International College, Graduation: May 2008

How do you analyze food when you eat it? Do you ever write down thoughts or ideas somewhere to keep a journal?
Well, when I eat new foods or try a new dish, I look at it first to see what physical properties it has. When it comes to analyzing the taste, you take a small bite, taking note of the textures and flavors. This might sound a little crude, but chewing with your mouth slightly open (just enough to allow air into your mouth) helps you to determine flavor profiles better. I don't think about analyzing foods too much unless it's something new that I haven't had before. On the other hand, if it's a new food that I think I could possibly use in a dish or meal, I do try to keep flavor and texture in mind. While I'm trying new things, writing my thoughts and ideas down isn't always easy. I do try to keep odd notes and ideas; they just never make sense to anyone but me.

How often did you exercise in school? Do you exercise now?
Exercising while in school was important, but it was nearly impossible to exercise. There just weren't enough hours in the day to go to school, do homework/papers, and work. Since I've completed school, I have been exercising much more than I had been. Before I started college, I exercised a lot as well as boxed and played soccer. It's important to exercise and take care of your body. You're only given one, and if you don't take care of it, no one else will do it for you.

Is physical safety something you think about often in the kitchen?
I consider safety most when I'm doing something I know could put me or others in danger, like carrying a hot pot of water to the sink or taking a knife to the pan and pan sink to be washed. Those are the things that you should be most concerned with. Worrying about cutting yourself while chopping carrots will make you tenser, and being tense and having a knife in your hand is a bad situation. You prevent injury by using your head. That's how most injuries happen—you weren't using your head.

smell, and taste. Next, you can consider the primary flavor sensations (sweet, sour, salt, bitter, piquant, umami, etc.) followed by subtler aromas and taste perceptions. Think about how each component of the dish tastes on its own as well as how they taste together. Reflect upon the various textures and temperatures of the dish's components. Is the dish straightforward or complex and multi-layered? Is it subtle or overblown? What ingredients and cooking techniques do you suppose were used to create the dish? This analysis may take a few seconds or a few minutes, but you learn a great deal more about cooking and recipe creation through this process than you do by simply wolfing down a meal.

Since every culinary student consumes dozens of meals per month, most students cannot possibly remember all of their eating experiences and analyses from memory. A tasting journal provides a way for you to record your thoughts, experiences, and ideas about food at each meal. A tasting journal is simply a notebook in which a person records each meal that she eats and her analysis of that meal. In addition to the critique of the actual food consumed, you may include ideas for how to improve the dish. Notes for improvement are extremely important for foods which you have cooked yourself to help you adjust your recipes and techniques in the future. You may wish to include additional brainstorming ideas on how to translate a preparation, flavor, or presentation to another dish. For example, you might note that the spice combination used on a chicken dish would apply even better to fish or that the presentation of food in a martini glass would work equally well for an appetizer you prepare. You might choose to draw pictures of presentations or take photos of the food you eat to include in the journal. This recordkeeping might seem tedious, but the journal becomes a resource from which you can pull ideas and gain inspiration in creating future recipes.

Recordkeeping may help with other personal goals as well. Tracking your diet will provide encouragement to try new foods and not to simply rely on the same dishes for each meal. The journal may also help you to determine where you waste calories on junk food that could be used elsewhere or eliminated from your diet entirely should you wish to lose weight. A simple tasting journal can enhance your education in food and improve your health at the same time.

Sometimes the foods you eat in a restaurant may be so foreign to you that you do not know how to begin deconstructing them. You may even have a tendency to avoid ordering these foods entirely. However, these foods provide learning opportunities you should embrace. Rather than trying to guess the answers to questions that may arise in your head, ask the server or the chef about the meal. Many servers can answer your questions quickly, and they may relish the opportunity to share their culture and cuisine with you. Speaking

Interview with Kirk T. Bachmann, CCP, CEC, M.Ed, Vice-President of Education, Corporate Chef, Le Cordon Bleu Schools North America

How should culinary students change their eating habits to help make eating an educational experience?
I think that any change in habit or daily routine has the potential to be educational. I think an easy starting place might involve choosing one new ingredient at the supermarket or trying a new ethnic restaurant. Every time we cook or eat, we have an opportunity to learn something. Once you see the world through food, each experience is valuable in itself.

What value does a tasting journal provide?
A journal is a valuable tool to help students really understand what they eat and cook on a daily basis. Because these activities are so normal, mundane even, it makes sense to record them and then view the findings from a more objective position. It is amazing what you can learn about your own habits and behaviors if you just take a step back.

How important is it for culinary students to exercise?
Exercise is very important. It not only helps if you are in good physical condition in the kitchen, but good mental condition as well. I would encourage students to keep in shape, as one of the "on the job hazards" is overeating.

Have you ever encountered students with substance or alcohol abuse problems? Eating disorders?
I think it's important that any student with substance abuse issues or psychological conditions should seek regular professional counseling. Most of our schools offer support hotlines or in-school counseling services for students with these and other challenges. Many schools have agreements with hospitals and other medical facilities where students can be referred for counseling and other treatment.

with the chef can sometimes result in a tour of the kitchen or a longer discussion on cooking philosophy. You can then record all of this new information in the tasting journal. You may feel shy about speaking with restaurant employees, but you must never leave a restaurant ignorant when you can learn from a novel experience.

Putting a tasting journal to good use is relatively straightforward. A student or chef who needs to create a new dish or menu item can read through her tasting journal for ideas. A previously enjoyed dish may be easily replicated as is or modified according to the suggestions written in the journal. Perhaps a single flavor combination can become the foundation for an entirely new dish. Either way, a tasting journal can help you to move beyond your own natural tendencies to create a broader range of menu items for your repertoire.

The same principles for learning about food apply to beverages, service, and environment as well. A student learns far more from trying new drinks at every meal than from sticking with the same soda standby. Whether sipping wine, beer, juice, or a cocktail, a student can consider the primary and secondary flavors of the drink and how well that beverage complements the food. Since service impacts a guest's experience as much as the food, a culinary student should note what elements of service made the experience enjoyable or unpleasant. Such information will greatly help the future chef who needs to train wait staff to ensure repeat business. The restaurant environment also affects the overall quality of a guest's experience, and a student should record the particulars of the restaurant's ambiance. Lighting, colors, views, aromas, layout, music, noise levels, and even bathroom décor impact a guest's perceptions of a restaurant. You should note these elements for each restaurant to maximize what you learn from each dining experience. You may not need to review this information for years as you will work as a cook for quite a while before becoming a chef, but it becomes extremely valuable when you need to come up with ideas for a restaurant you are building, redesigning, or simply improving.

14.3 HEALTH MATTERS: EXERCISE

Despite the importance of tasting foods regularly, a chef must remain physically fit to move quickly behind the line, to work long hours, and most importantly, to live long enough to enjoy retirement. The constant presence of food in a culinary business can make overeating an unavoidable temptation. Obesity is a job hazard that can ruin a chef's quality of life. If you do gain weight, you will need to put your knowledge of healthy cooking and nutrition to good use to return to your normal weight before it spirals out of control.

Exercise is an important part of anyone's daily routine. For chefs, cooks, and culinary students regular exercise can actually have a positive impact on one's career. Exercise builds stamina and energy, and a student who burns more calories each day can taste more food without gaining weight. More tasting means more taste memory development, and more energy and stamina translates to a greater ability to survive the long, physically demanding hours of the job. Both of these qualities increase the likelihood that you will earn a promotion and succeed in a management role once promoted.

By developing an exercise routine while in school a student is more likely to continue exercising after graduation. Full-time cooks may get plenty of physical activity on the job, but students and executive chefs who spend more time at a desk and less time on their feet will need to exercise regularly to maintain fitness. Starting an exercise regimen is simple. You begin slowly, perhaps exercising lightly for just a few minutes each day, and then gradually increase the length and rigor of the workout until you can maintain an elevated heart rate for at least 20 minutes. A good cardiovascular workout should raise your heart rate to 80 percent of its maximum capacity. (Maximum heart rate is generally calculated as 190 beats per minute minus your age.) Muscle-building routines may not raise your heart rate much; rather, they build your strength through weight training. Both are valuable, but cardiovascular exercise helps more with stamina and energy. Ultimately, you should aim to work out for 20 to 30 minutes per day for at least five days per week. The more calories you burn, the more food you will be able to taste, but keep in mind that you do not want to injure yourself in the process. Jogging a couple of miles each day is better than trying to run a marathon your first day out and spending the rest of the month recovering from an injury. If you have any questions at all about your ability to exercise, check with a doctor first to get advice on how best to begin.

Interview with Mary A. Gehringer, Johnson & Wales University, Charlotte, Graduation: May 2009

Did you change how you ate while in school?
I began to create gourmet meals in my dorm room (well, at the time I thought they were gourmet). Sticking with fruit, granola, oatmeal, yogurt, and healthy snacks, I was able to satisfy my craving for nutritious meals. I tried my hardest to keep my eating habits as regular as possible, but at times I would find myself munching on a midnight apple while getting my homework done. I think the change of eating habit was beneficial. I was able to be more mindful of what I was eating at what times during the day. There are many times I hear other students speaking of the foods that they may have been snacking on at midnight, and I found that my selection was not only more healthy, but much more tasty, too.

How do you analyze food when you eat it? Do you ever write down thoughts or ideas somewhere to keep a journal?
When I eat food, I do pay attention to how it feels or smells. I make sure all my senses are being activated, but I do not keep a written journal of the foods I eat. I am a very visual individual, and I am able to recall smells and tastes very easily. Perhaps that is why I love food as much as I do.

How often did you exercise while in school?
Every day except Sunday. I believe that exercising is very important. Even if it is just taking the stairs to class or walking the long way to school, staying physically active in school is very important. Exercising is beneficial in two ways: it creates an outlet to work out the stress that you encounter throughout your day, and of course, it keeps you fit and healthy.

Is physical safety something you think about often in the kitchen?
Being safe in the kitchen should always be on the mind of a culinary student. Being aware of your surroundings and staying alert will help you in the kitchen. Staying on your toes and being able to read a situation will allow you to be able to prevent a dangerous situation from happening. What I do to prevent injury is to make sure my area of work is clean and organized at all times. If the equipment is where it belongs and I have my area clean, there is less of a chance of me getting hurt or of someone else being injured.

14.4 DANGEROUSLY UNHEALTHY BEHAVIORS

In addition to weight gain, some culinary workers are drawn to other unhealthy behaviors that can damage their careers and ruin their lives. Perhaps due to the stress of the industry, some culinary workers struggle with alcoholism and drug abuse. Unfortunately, substance abusers are common enough in the industry that most culinary students will encounter co-workers (or classmates) who suffer from such an addiction. While some employees may pursue genuine help with their addiction, others may claim to cope and to function just fine with substance abuse. No matter how stressed you may become at work do not turn to alcohol or to drugs for an escape. These substances impair your judgment in an environment where sharp objects and fire are ever-present.

Abusers typically find themselves struggling financially and unhappy in relationships as well. Whatever problems the substance abuse may seem to relieve, they pale in comparison to the vast number of serious problems that the abuse creates. While there is no need ever to take an illegal drug, you will find a need to learn something about alcohol. If you do choose to drink alcohol, a small glass can teach as much as, if not more than, an entire bottle. However, if you elect not to imbibe for any number of reasons, know that you can learn a great deal about alcohol and how to pair it with food simply through reading and study.

Eating disorders also have a tendency on occasion to rear their ugly head in the culinary industry. With the omnipresence of food in the kitchen, some cooks and chefs may find it easier to binge and purge than to watch their intake and to exercise. Bulimia, however, is not a disorder to be taken lightly. Bulimia and anorexia (effectively, self-starvation) result in malnutrition, major health problems, and in too many cases, death. Because these and all eating disorders require psychiatric help to overcome, anyone with an eating disorder should consult a therapist for help. You should not attempt to work through these diseases, either personally or with a friend, without professional help.

Interview with John Ash, Chef and Founder of John Ash & Company Restaurant, James Beard award-winning author, TV and radio host, faculty of the Culinary Institute of America

Is it important for culinary students to adjust their eating habits for their careers?
I think in the beginning it's very important to taste and sample as many different cuisines as they can with an eye (and taste) for identifying those flavors and techniques that define a particular cuisine. That said, it's also important to identify the ways in which those cuisines have promoted healthier eating both in the past and in the present. The Mediterranean Diet is especially noteworthy here.

When you eat someone else's cooking, do you analyze the food?
I constantly analyze other people's food, which I think is one of the great fun things about cooking. I'm interested in all aspects of the food: flavor, texture, use of seasonal and what I call "ethical"

(continued)

(*continued*)

ingredients, presentation, and style. It definitely helps me in my cooking and expands ideas for my food. I think one of the axioms of cooking professionally is that we all "borrow" each other's ideas and blend them with our own.

Have you ever encountered culinary workers with substance or alcohol abuse problems?
Unfortunately, yes. It is endemic to the profession, I'm sad to say. It often is an unhealthy way to relieve tension. I've seen a lot of very talented culinarians burn themselves up with various kinds of alcohol and drug abuse. It's an issue that all new, aspiring culinarians should be aware of, and something that responsible management should have programs to educate, and where necessary, help those who get into trouble.

Is physical injury common in the kitchen?
Injury is fairly common. An ongoing education program can help a lot to ameliorate many unsafe conditions. Like so many activities in life, that commitment and expectation needs to come from both the culinarian and the management. Attitude can make a big difference.

The other major threat to health in the culinary industry is physical injury on the job. Many culinary workers find themselves subject to burns, cuts, muscle strains, and a range of injuries resulting from falls. Although very minor injuries may be inevitable, most major injuries are highly preventable. Unfortunately, many culinary workers take shortcuts on safety either to save time or out of overconfidence in their ability to avoid injury. Whatever the reason, injuries are costly and in some cases can cause a lifetime of pain and hardship. Most companies provide safety equipment, such as gloves or goggles, and expect their employees to wear protective uniforms, including proper shoes, aprons, and hair restraints. You should always place your own safety and the safety of those around you above any other priorities. Simple actions, such as lifting improperly, using a knife recklessly, or cleaning a slicer or band saw without proper safety equipment, can result in weeks out of work or worse, a permanent disability. No amount of time saved, no display of machismo, in fact, no job is worth a lifetime of pain or a physical disfigurement. By putting safety at the top of your priority list in the kitchen, you will be around for many years in the industry to continue to learn your craft, to display your talent, and to increase your speed in the kitchen.

Summary

Chefs, cooks, and students learn about culinary artistry and recipe creation through eating. To maximize the number of learning opportunities, a student should try to taste different ingredients and unfamiliar flavor combinations at each meal rather than relying on the same few foods every day. Analyzing food critically is essential to the learning experience. A student should evaluate the food she eats and document her thoughts in a tasting journal to keep a record for future reference and inspiration. Assessing beverages, service, and a restaurant's environment will provide additional valuable information for a student in the future. Despite the need to eat often a student must work to maintain proper health. Regular exercise helps to burn calories and to prevent obesity even as a student tastes food frequently. Some other threats to a culinarian's health include alcoholism, drug abuse, eating disorders, and physical injury. Students and culinary professionals should avoid these hazards at all costs and should seek professional assistance in overcoming or dealing with them if they fall victim to one of them.

KEY QUESTIONS TO CONSIDER IN ANALYZING YOUR FOOD

- What is the overall first impression in appearance, smell, and taste?
- How is the dish presented and/or served?
- What are the primary flavors?
- What subtle aromas and flavors are present?
- How do the components of the dish taste separately and together?
- Do any variations in texture or temperature enhance or detract from the dish?
- Is the dish straightforward or multi-layered?
- Is the dish subtle or overblown?
- What ingredients and cooking techniques were used to create the dish?
- How could the dish be improved?
- Can anything learned from this dish be applied to another dish elsewhere?

Suggested Tasks

1. Write a tasting journal to analyze all of the foods you eat in a week. Make an effort not to repeat any of the foods in your diet during that week. Be as critical as you can to learn as much as possible about the food you eat.

2. Visit a restaurant (not fast food). Analyze the food, service, and ambiance of the restaurant. Write a critical analysis of your experience and submit the analysis to your instructor.

3. Interview an industry chef about her personal eating habits. Ask her where she eats when not at work and what types of questions she considers when analyzing another chef's work. Ask if she learns a lot or a little from visiting other restaurants. Discuss your findings with your class.

4. Create an exercise regimen that has you exercising at least every other day. Schedule your workouts for the entire month. Share your plan with a friend and ask her to join you during your workouts. Follow through on the exercise regimen so that it becomes routine in your week.

5. Research an unhealthy behavior common in the culinary industry (substance abuse, eating disorders, behaviors resulting in physical injuries, or another behavior). Write a report on your findings. Be sure to discuss the impact on the individual as well as on her co-workers. Share your report with your class and with your instructors.

CHAPTER 15

No One Succeeds Alone: Networking and Professional Associations

Culinary students need education and experience to move up to an executive chef position, but these factors alone are rarely enough to propel a student to the upper echelons of the industry. The top jobs are few in number and cannot accommodate all of the highly talented, qualified people seeking those positions. Sometimes knowing the right person can open a door otherwise closed to most applicants.

In addition to locating job opportunities, professional connections can help with staffing, fund-raising, professional development, and market research among other chef responsibilities. Learning to make friends in the industry (and in related fields) is a skill that pays off in many ways. Not all chefs know how to network and to nurture relationships for both short-term and long-term gain. The most famous culinary professionals are often expert networkers, although some do hire others to network for them. A culinary student can begin networking while in school through professional associations and even through instructors and classmates. While personality does play a role in building a strong network of professional friends, most people can develop the right personal characteristics and skills to foster a broad and valuable network.

In this chapter, you will learn the impact that making friends in the industry can have on your career. You will learn how to network and what personality traits facilitate effective networking. Finally, you will learn the names of several major professional culinary associations and what types of members they attract to determine which association may best meet your needs.

15.1 WHY MAKE FRIENDS

Some chefs choose to believe that they succeed solely on their own merit and talent. The truth is that few, if any, chefs work alone. Aside from those chefs who cook for an audience of less than a dozen people, chefs need help from others. They need employees to cook, clean, and serve their guests, as well as co-workers to handle marketing, accounting, and other management responsibilities. The chef who attempts to perform all of these roles personally usually does not have the time to complete them effectively in any but the smallest of foodservice operations.

Recognizing the need for help, the wise chef is always looking for the best and brightest talent available. Unfortunately, placing a help wanted ad in the newspaper is a gamble. The advertisement may generate many highly qualified applicants, or it may turn up no one appropriate for the position. However, many talented culinary professionals who are not actively job-seeking would consider leaving their current employer for the right offer. The chef who keeps connected with many of the industry's professionals will know who has the qualifications he needs. Then the chef can approach those people discretely to form an extremely powerful, talented kitchen and service team for his operation. If culinary students want to receive an invitation to join such a team, they need to forge professional friendships with a good number of culinary professionals.

Interview with Karen Cathey, President/Founder, Bon Vivant, LLC

Is it important to make professional friends in the industry?
I can't stress how important it is to make professional friends in the industry. Your industry should be viewed as a community, of which you are a member. You will instantly increase your resources when you need to find answers outside of your area of expertise. You'll be able to pull together teams to help you brainstorm, and you will have a support system to reach out to and also to give support when they need it. You'll always have a system within which to network, find jobs, and find employees. You'll be in the pipeline to learn about innovations and trends . . . the list goes on.

What personality characteristics help a person to network better?
Sometimes it can seem really impossible to break into conversations with strangers. Don't be afraid to introduce yourself, and talk about yourself to try to explore things you may have in common with others. It's the standard lesson of etiquette and putting others at ease—ask questions about them and explore their interests.

What associations are you a member of?
I belong to The American Institute of Wine & Food, The International Association of Culinary Professionals, Women Chefs & Restaurateurs, Culinary Historians of Washington, and the James Beard Foundation. I stay involved with each organization because they all help me in some way. That reason could be through providing education, a networking directory, and cutting-edge trend information. They also help me learn what issues are important to others in my industry and what opportunities are available to serve those needs. The individuals who are involved with these organizations may or may not be well known outside of the organization, but they are all leaders within the industry.

How active are you in each association?
I am very active in The American Institute of Wine & Food (AIWF), having been the chapter chairman twice, and the national chairman, as well as serving on many other committees and in other positions. I am still very involved. On the other hand, I'm not as active in the other organizations but still find them valuable. I use the membership directories extensively for research and contact information, and I find their newsletters and other communications extremely insightful and valuable.

(*continued*)

(*continued*)

Should culinary students join associations?

Yes! The benefits vary, but many culinary associations offer opportunities around the country for scholarships and internships that are open to culinary and/or enology students only. The newsletters and other publications are a huge source of knowledge about the industry, especially at the student level where they are just learning about all the industry has to offer. You'll learn who's who, how careers unfold, how you can apply your skills, and what issues are important in the industry outside of your technical skills. Most associations offer cut-rate prices for culinary students and encourage student involvement on the local level, which is a great opportunity for students to get exposed to potential future job opportunities.

Professional friendships differ from personal friendships. Personal friends see each other for meals and parties to relax and to escape their daily job stresses. They gossip. They provide emotional support. They can share with each other their deepest thoughts and feelings. Professional friends may speak regularly and ask each other for favors, but they likely do not hang out at each other's homes weekly or chat much about anything not industry-related. They provide information and help with career development, but they rarely provide extensive emotional support. A chef needs both personal and professional friendships, but not all industry workers fully appreciate the importance of making professional friends.

By building a large network of professional friends, a chef has access to an extensive bank of trusted people to contact for advice and assistance. Friends can ask each other for job leads that may not be advertised to the public. They may request references and recommendations to other chefs to increase their chances of earning an interview for a highly competitive job. Professional friends sometimes ask each other for help recruiting employees as they can refer talented people looking for work, while filtering out interested parties who do not possess the proper qualifications. Friends share advice on marketing approaches and opportunities with each other, and they exchange recipes or cooking techniques to help each other expand their skills. A professional friend can even put a chef in touch with a potential investor to help him fund the opening of his own restaurant. Without a network of professional friends, a chef is forced to scour the newspapers and the Internet for potential contacts and hope that those contacts will respond positively to a cold call. Most people find using a network to be both easier and more effective.

Consider the impact you would have on the industry if your entire class formed a professional network. You would have a team of people working to promote you to employers and researching possible jobs for you. Why would they do this? Inevitably, people run across opportunities that are not right for them but might be perfect for someone they know. If you are right for an opportunity encountered by a professional friend, chances are that the friend will send that opportunity your way. Not everyone you meet in school will become a friend, but the more strong friendships you develop in school, the more people you will have helping your career both before and after graduation. They help you because they assume you will do the same when you have the chance to reciprocate. Most professional networking operates on this assumption.

15.2 HOW TO NETWORK

Networking thrives long term for those who understand how to network because everyone who participates in an effective network benefits. However, too many people begin networking by fixating entirely on themselves and their own needs. The "me, me, me" approach is self-promotion, not networking, and unfortunately, it rarely works very well or for very long. People must feel that they personally benefit in helping someone; otherwise, they are unlikely to befriend that person. No one devotes enormous amounts of energy aiding people just because they meet briefly at an event. As a result, simply meeting lots of people and shaking hands is not an effective way to build an active network. Here is a much more effective procedure for network-building:

- *Meet and Engage People.* Some people may shy away from conversations with strangers, so it is up to you to take the first step. To ensure that you do not lose an opportunity to make a potentially valuable network connection, initiate conversations with others. Put the other person at ease by introducing yourself, shaking hands, making eye contact, and smiling. Learn the person's name and use it during the conversation.

- *Control the Conversation through Questions.* Many people think that the way to control a dialogue is by talking a lot. Beginning a conversation by describing what you do and what you need allows the other person to decide whether or not further interaction would be mutually beneficial. It also gives the other person a chance to ignore you and to walk away. Most importantly, the "me, me, me" approach comes off as selfish, for it assumes that the other person has nothing better to do than to help you. Asking questions, however, puts the control of the conversation in your hands. Your questions force the other person to reveal personal-professional information. As you learn about the other person, you get to decide how the two of you can best work together. Follow-up questions allow you to continue to control the direction of the conversation. By expressing interest in the other person, you also put him at ease and reduce the chance that he will find an excuse to leave quickly. After all, most people enjoy talking about themselves, and they are usually flattered that someone else is interested in listening to them.

- *Listen for Opportunities to Help.* Most people will not usually devote time, money, or energy to helping a stranger, but they almost always accept help for themselves. Asking the right questions will encourage other people to reveal potential challenges they did not even realize they had. For example, if a chef shares that he has a volunteer event coming up, you can ask if getting help from his own staff strains those employees left to run the restaurant that night. Listen to how you can help the other person solve a problem or complete a goal. By helping the other person first, you will be able to form a longer-term relationship and to ask for help more successfully later.

- *Introduce Yourself More Thoroughly and Offer to Help.* Now that you have the information you need about the other person, you can safely introduce yourself. Describe what you do and how you can help the other person. Help can come in many forms. You may offer to work for someone and promise to send that person a résumé. You might learn that the other person is new to the area or to an association, and you can offer to show him around. Upon hearing that someone needs a recipe, you could offer to send one. Even if you cannot help the person directly, you may be able to introduce him to someone else who can. Most people will be thrilled that you offer to help them with their needs rather than asking them to help you with yours.

Interview with Joan Brewster, Executive Director, ACF Colorado Chefs Association

Is it important to make professional friends in the industry?
Professional friends, in your chosen trade, are your best contacts for networking. People who try "to go it alone" miss out on valuable information provided by this important circle of support. Whether you are looking for a vendor, an employee, or even a new position, these friends will be there to help you find all the things for which you are looking. I am always puzzled by people who do not join a trade association. The good ones offer much more than your financial investment; educational seminars, certification, as well as the opportunity to network with leading professionals.

How should a person go about networking?
Volunteer. Every association needs volunteers to help with programs, events, mentoring, etc. By volunteering, the association members will get to know you better. Best advice: Don't volunteer in order to get something out of it. People see what you are doing instantly. Volunteer to help your association become even better than it is. The return will be incredible.

What personality characteristics help a person to network better?
An outgoing personality and friendliness always helps, but even if you are shy about meeting people, just let the association leadership know you are available to assist through the talents you possess. Persistence is also a key to networking. Don't let the current members ignore you. I don't think any association means to overlook a new member wanting to be involved; they just need to be reminded. Association leaders are juggling many things to keep the association going. Keep volunteering. Soon you will be recognized as a valued member.

What associations are you a member of?
I am a member of the American Culinary Federation, the International Wine Guild, and Les Dames d'Escoffier. The benefits include valuable contacts, educational opportunities through seminars and conferences, lifelong friends, up-to-date information pertinent to my industry, and a way of giving back to my community through the associations. All three groups provide educational opportunities for students through scholarships as well as funding for grassroot non-profit organizations in my community.

How active are you in each association?
I am very active in all three of these organizations. I am President of LDEI-Colorado and Executive Director for ACF-Colorado. I feel that you always get more if you are directly involved, but associations should offer something for everyone. Each person needs to find the path with which they are the most comfortable. Some members just enjoy attending educational seminars to help them with their professional growth.

Should current culinary students join associations?
Students are the very ones who should join associations. Trade associations attract the leaders of the culinary industry. Association members are the true believers, movers and shakers. These are the people who will help students on their career path. Members will end up being lifelong mentors for these students.

- **Request a Business Card (or contact information).** Offering someone your business card and hoping that they will call you is a risky proposition. There is a good chance that your card will become fodder for the trash can once the person returns to work. A better approach is to get the other person's card. This gives you the ability to follow up personally on the conversation to develop the relationship further.
- **Write on the Card.** If you are an effective networker, you will meet lots of people at a single networking event. The safest way to ensure that you remember all of the conversations and promises that you have made is to write on the back of each person's business card. It is perfectly acceptable to write on the card even during the conversation. You should first write down what you have promised to do for the other person. You should also write down any information that might help you to remember the person the following day. Such information could include when and where you met, the topic of conversation, or even what the person was wearing. Expert networkers always carry pens with them, and they use them often.
- **Close the Conversation Politely.** Although the conversation may be going rather well, you typically do not want to spend the entire evening networking with a single person. Once you have a person's business card and a reason to contact him again, you are ready to meet someone else. However, you do not want to be rude about leaving either. Shake hands and thank the other person for the conversation. Tell him it was great to meet him and that you will follow through on your promises. If you wish, offer to introduce the person to someone else in the room whom you know. There is nothing wrong with stating that you need to speak with a few more people, if you must give an excuse for ending the conversation.
- **Follow Through on Your Promises.** After the event, contact the other person within a few days. Follow through on your promise, whatever it is. The follow-up phone call or email creates a second conversation with the person, which helps you to stand out from the crowd of other people he meets every day. Helping the other person also makes him feel indebted to you, so he is more likely to help you with your needs later. Following through on your promise shows you to be professional and true to your word. People are more likely to refer opportunities to you and to help you once they know you better and consider you trustworthy. If you do not deliver on your promise, you can almost guarantee that the other person will not assist you with any favors you need.
- **Ask for Help.** Now that you have assisted the other person and had multiple communications with him, you can safely ask him for a favor. Chances are good that the other person will help you out. While some people believe that networking begins with this step, you can imagine the different response you receive when you already have a relationship in place.
- **Maintain Regular Contact.** After the initial exchange of favors, find excuses to keep in touch, so the other person keeps you top-of-mind when opportunities arise. Contact can be as simple as a monthly email or annual holiday card or as complicated as offering to help with another project. Either way, professional friendships need periodic nurturing to remain vibrant; otherwise, they wither and die.

Although networking is important throughout every professional's lifetime, the best time to begin is in school, before you really need immediate help. Since the process requires you to help others first, it is important to start networking early to build your professional friendships before you really need them. Then, when you do need them, they will already be in place.

15.2.1 Personality Matters

Because effective networking requires regular contact with other people, personality inevitably comes into play. People who are shy, self-absorbed, or downright mean struggle to build a network of professional friends. Most professionals avoid contact with people they do not like, so a good networker needs to be likeable. Here are a few of the personality traits that help a person to be a better networker:

FRIENDLINESS A friendly person is easy for others to like. When a friendly person calls, most chefs will pick up the phone to chat. Mean people tend to find that their phone messages are left unreturned and that their conversations with others are inexplicably always cut short.

POLITENESS Although some people may respond positively to crude behavior or to off-color jokes, most will not. The best way to keep a fellow culinary professional in conversation is to remain polite and professional. Rudeness typically ends a conversation prematurely.

EXTROVERSION A person who devotes energy to meeting lots of people inevitably builds a larger network than a shy, introverted person who keeps to himself. Introverts must rely on others to start a conversation, while an extrovert will walk up to a stranger and begin networking.

EMOTIONAL INTELLIGENCE Effective networkers must be able to read the facial expressions and body language of others and adjust their own nonverbal communication in response. Someone who cannot "read" people runs the risk of not recognizing when he offends or upsets others with his words or actions. For example, if a person feels that you are standing too close to him in conversation, he may express his discomfort nonverbally. If you respond quickly, you can salvage the conversation; if not, the other person will likely remember nothing about you other than your close proximity. Whether listening or speaking, a person must constantly monitor his own and the other person's tone and body language. This skill is especially important when networking with people from other cultures with different social norms. People tend to end conversations quickly when they are uncomfortable with the other person's style of communication.

SELFLESSNESS AND SELFISHNESS Both qualities are necessary for a relationship to be mutually beneficial. A completely selfish person does not inconvenience himself to help others, so he inevitably earns a reputation for looking out only for his own self-interests. Most people will not help others when there is no hope of reciprocation in the future. Many people will gladly interact with completely selfless people, but the selfless individuals find themselves feeling used. They get no benefit from the networking relationship, so they tend to stop networking entirely. A good networker makes certain that he and his professional friends all benefit from the relationship.

Interview with Cathy Cochran-Lewis, National Public Relations Coordinator, Whole Foods Market

How should a person go about networking?
First of all, I would have business cards and go to where the connections are. This could be wine and food events in your city or joining professional organizations where you have a core audience of culinary professionals. And, it's not only the "joining" that's important. Utilize your membership in professional associations. Attend events, volunteer to assist in fund-raising or targeted events hosted by the organizations, and be active. Make good use out of your money and your time. There are no secrets in how to network. Do as you would do when engaged in any conversation: make eye contact, listen to the person you are talking to, focus on how you can help them before you focus on how they can help you. Be concise in your conversation and make it "all about them" and not "all about you." Then, follow up. Make notes after your conversation, and then follow up either with an offer to help or a contact they may need. Or even just a "nice to meet you" and "I enjoyed our conversation." I've found that no matter how high profile a professional is in our industry, they are still just individuals who share the same passion that I have, and in that it's a level playing field. Be bold but not aggressive. Offer help before asking for help.

In what association do you hold a leadership role?
I am the incoming president of the International Association of Culinary Professionals, a 4,000-member worldwide association of culinary professionals who are involved in the food and/or wine industry. I have found IACP to be the single-most valuable resource in my culinary career. I turned to IACP initially to learn skills for my new career in non-vocational cooking school management. I was privileged to meet mentors who have worked with me for the last decade in the cooking school field. As my career has moved into public relations and marketing, every facet of my journey can be connected back to those whom I've met through IACP and who have helped me with a referral, an idea, or an inspiration. I am also a member of Les Dames d'Escoffier.

Is there a benefit to current culinary students joining IACP?
We have recently created an "Emerging Professional" category that offers some benefits for discount membership. I would highly recommend any graduating student seek out the opportunities provided by this association.

ORGANIZATION AND FOLLOW-THROUGH A person who does not organize business cards or follow through on phone calls, emails, and promises may meet a lot of people but will not form long-term, mutually beneficial relationships with them afterwards. Meeting people is only the first step in networking. The real work occurs after the initial meeting. Good networkers follow up on all of their promises and their collected business cards, so organization and follow-through are critical.

There are a number of other qualities that tend to help facilitate the networking process. For example, charismatic people often draw others to them, which makes meeting new people even easier. Happy people also attract more people than visibly sad or depressed people. However, learning to be friendly, polite, emotionally intelligent, and organized, as well as balanced in selfishness and selflessness, goes a long way to making someone an effective networker.

15.3   PROFESSIONAL ASSOCIATIONS

The growth of the culinary industry has occurred in tandem with an explosion of culinary associations. Associations may operate locally, nationally, or internationally. Their members may be individuals, companies, or both. Professional culinary associations serve many roles from providing education and certification to their members to representing the interests of their members to the public. Some associations lobby the government and market specific products made by their member companies, while others use collective bargaining tactics to solicit discount rates for their members on a range of products and services. Most importantly, professional associations provide opportunities for their members to network with each other.

Each association has a different mission and a different membership makeup. Knowing the mission and demographics of an association is critical to determining whether or not joining that association will benefit you. For example, a personal chef may want to meet other personal chefs to discuss best practices for storing food for clients, while a food critic will want to meet other food writers and journalists. A restaurant chef may want to meet purveyors who can provide quality ingredients at a low price, or he may want to meet a book agent who can help him sell his concept to a publisher. Each of these individuals has different needs, and each would benefit from joining a different association. Although they might enjoy meeting each other, they probably cannot satisfy each other's needs.

Some culinary professionals join multiple associations in order to encounter a wide variety of people, but cost and time often restrict most industry employees to just one or two associations. Consequently, you must take the time to find out if an association will help you to achieve your goals or if it will merely become a drain on your cash flow. The simplest approach is to determine what type of people you need to meet to help you reach your goals and then to find out which association is most likely to have those people as members. Table 15.1 provides a brief example of how various associations can serve very different roles. A much more extensive list of culinary professional associations can be found in Appendix 1.

Although membership is essential to gaining access to association members, a culinary professional must get actively involved in the association to network effectively. Membership alone does little to benefit the average member. People who volunteer to work on association projects or who run for committee or board positions have a much easier time earning respect and help from their colleagues. Active members are more well known by other association members and thus have an easier time engaging others in conversation. Whereas a person normally needs to help a professional before asking for a favor, a person who works actively to support an association's activities can usually request personal help from other members without assisting each member separately. The active contributor has helped those members already by supporting their organization.

Unfortunately, many people join associations and never make the time to participate in them. The expression "You only get out of it what you put into it" holds true in the case

TABLE 15.1 Sample Professional Associations, Members, and Goals

Association Name	Typical Members	Sample Appropriate Goals
American Culinary Federation	Restaurant, hotel, and country club cooks and chefs as well as culinary educators	Find kitchen job opportunities; Learn new cooking techniques and new ingredients available from purveyors
American Institute of Wine & Food	Restaurant chefs and non-professional "foodies"	Market a restaurant to the public to attract business; Learn about new restaurants opening locally
Foodservice Educators Network International	Educators	Improve teaching skills to become a better educator; Learn about potential teaching positions
International Association of Culinary Professionals	Educators, writers, publishers, television and radio personalities, marketing communicators, entrepreneurs, food historians, nutritionists, test kitchen workers, food photographers and stylists, and restaurant chefs	Find publishers, recipe testers, photographers, and stylists to help with a cookbook; Learn how to market a product to the public; Find work on a television or radio program
United States Personal Chef Association	Personal and private chefs	Learn how to become a personal chef; Exchange recipe ideas with other personal chefs

of associations. Just as paying for a gym membership and not exercising will leave a person overweight, paying for membership in an association and not attending meetings or conferences will leave the person with nothing more than a lighter wallet. Make sure that if you are going to pay the money to join an association, you participate actively to reap the maximum benefit from your membership.

Because a person's career and professional goals change over time, you may need to join additional associations (or to move from one association to another) as your career progresses. For example, a person might enter the industry as a restaurant cook, earn a job as a chef for a country club, open up his own catering company, publish a cookbook, and finish his career as a chef-instructor. In each of these tasks, the individual might benefit from membership in a different association. Associations often help with major career transitions as they provide access to experts in a specific area within the larger culinary community. Since culinary students encounter a major career shift as they transition from

Interview with Zov Karamardian, Executive Chef/President, Zov's Bistro, Inc

What associations are you a member of? What benefit does that provide you?

I am a member of WCR, IACP, AIWF, NAWBO, James Beard Foundation, Les Dames d'Escoffier, and many others. I remain a member because it gives me visibility and reminds people that we do have three restaurants. The benefit that it provides me is that it gives us exposure and inspiration. I am very active in most of the organizations. It is important to give back. The public expects any successful business owner or businesses to truly give back, and the public will give back by frequenting your establishment.

How active are you in each association?

I am very active in any of the organizations I am a member of. I sit on the board. I sit on committees, and I lead some of them. I do it because I love to give back, and I love raising money. By being active, it connects you to people. It makes no different what kind of business you are in, it is all about people. I love people. You must participate in some form or another. You must give something to get something back. That getting back could be on so many levels. It could be emotional satisfaction that you gave something to someone, or financial satisfaction. There is definitely a benefit. It is all up to the individual.

school to the working world, membership in a professional association while in school can help greatly with the first few years after graduation. The American Culinary Federation, The American Institute of Wine & Food, and The International Association of Culinary Professionals are just a few of the associations that offer discounted rates to students or graduates just starting in the industry. You may find the cost of membership difficult to absorb while in school, but if you take part in the association's activities, you will likely find the return well worth the financial investment.

Summary

Many culinary professionals find that they advance their careers and achieve their work goals more easily when they have help from others. Networking creates a group of professional friends available to help each other with tasks or challenges that arise. Building a network requires a person to meet and to assist others in order to forge a relationship beyond the initial meeting. Once a relationship has been secured, both parties will be able to call upon each other for assistance. Because personality plays a role in forming relationships, successful networkers learn to be friendly, polite, extroverted, emotionally intelligent, organized, and balanced in their selfish and selfless impulses. Networking does take some effort, but professional associations facilitate the process by gathering people from specific facets of the field into a single organization to allow them to meet each other more easily. As culinary associations each differ in mission and membership, a person must select the association most aligned with his own goals and participate actively in it to maximize the value of association membership. Making professional friends, networking, and participating in professional associations helps culinary professionals to achieve their goals more quickly and easily than they could otherwise do alone.

KEY STEPS TO EFFECTIVE NETWORKING

- Meet and engage people in conversation.
- Control the conversation through questions.
- Listen for opportunities to help the other person.
- Introduce yourself more thoroughly and offer to help the other person.
- Request a business card.
- Write on the card what you have promised and information to help you remember the other person later.
- Close the conversation politely.
- Contact the other person within a week.
- Follow through on your promises.
- Ask for help to meet your needs.
- Maintain regular contact with the other person.

Suggested Tasks

1. Interview an industry chef. Ask him about the role that networking has played in his career. Find out who his professional friends are and ask how often he keeps in touch with them. Ask if he is a member of any professional associations and ask for his opinion on the association. Finally, ask for suggestions on how you can meet other industry professionals. Follow through on one suggestion for meeting other professionals. Share the results of the interview with your classmates.

2. Create business cards for yourself and get them printed. Attend a networking event; ask your instructor for advice in locating one, if necessary. Network actively with at least five people at the event. Continue networking until you have found at least two people whom you can help in some way. Exchange cards and record your promises to help. Follow through on your promises and maintain regular contact with your network connections, so you can ask for favors of them in the future.

3. Speak with a friend who knows you very well and whom you can trust. Ask the friend to conduct a very honest and blunt assessment of your social and communication skills. Ask for suggestions on how to modify your personality traits to make yourself more appealing to other culinary professionals and to

become a more effective networker. Discuss the suggestions privately with your instructor to get confirmation on their accuracy. Focus for the next three months on adjusting those traits.

4. Research at least three professional culinary associations that you believe might help you to achieve your professional goals. Contact those associations to request a membership application and additional information. Share your goals and the association information with a faculty member to determine which might be the best choice for you. Join the association you believe most likely to help you reach your goals.

5. Interview two faculty members. Ask them what associations they are members of and how often they participate in association activities. Find out how the association benefits them. Ask if they could take you to a local association meeting or event and introduce you to other members. Be sure to follow the steps of networking. If you find the experience valuable and wish to become active in the association, apply for membership.

6. Interview at least three of your friends or classmates in culinary school. Find out their goals and needs, and ask them how you can help them meet their goals. Share your goals and needs with them. Over the next year, share opportunities with them that might help them to meet their goals. In time, they will come to do the same for you.

CHAPTER 16

Choosing the Right Career Track: Experience Versus Money

When asked where they want to work when they graduate, inevitably some students say "whatever pays the most." Jobs provide a great number of benefits beyond money. For recent graduates, job experience and learning opportunities far outweigh wages for their long-term value. A job that does not prepare a student for a higher-level position in the future leads to a dead-end career path and to a flat income. However, a position that allows a student to develop the skills and knowledge needed for her dream job launches that student toward her ultimate goal.

Each job leads down a different path although some may lead nowhere. By setting goals and planning a strong career path, students can plot their progression toward their ideal jobs. As the culinary field contains many different components and tracks, students should consider which direction they wish to head to determine the fastest progression toward that goal. Most goals take years to achieve. No one earns a six-figure salary running a five-star restaurant for her first job out of school. However, with enough time, hard work, and steady progress toward their ultimate objectives, culinary school graduates can obtain the jobs they seek.

In this chapter, you will learn the importance of choosing a job for the experience it provides rather than for what it pays. You will also learn some of the major facets of the culinary industry and some of the potential career paths that lead to high-level positions in that part of the field.

16.1   THE VALUE OF EXPERIENCE

Culinary school teaches students a wide range of skills on topics from basic cooking to advanced management techniques. School generally focuses on the proper, classic method for each recipe and cooking technique. The teachers do not have sufficient time to teach every possible variation for the recipes they cover, and they certainly do not have time to teach every recipe ever written. Students need to build upon their college education on the job.

Work experience exposes students to recipes and cooking styles beyond those taught in school. It helps future managers to learn realistic employee expectations, nuances to the foodservice industry, and upcoming trends that will influence restaurant operations. Experience on the job also introduces students to cooking methods that may not be classic techniques (or even very good ones), but those approaches may work in an emergency when a product is not delivered or when a piece of equipment fails. Managers need to know this sort of information to prepare their employees for the future and to assist them in emergency situations.

Entry-level jobs require no more than a college education, and many do not even require that. However, each job, even an entry-level job, teaches something to an employee new to that role. Jobs that teach you more help you to become a talented, knowledgeable chef faster than jobs that provide fewer new experiences. You should always accept jobs that teach a great deal over ones that give you fewer new skills. After all, you will be unable to acquire and to keep a management job until you possess most or all of the skills needed to succeed in that job.

Most executive chef jobs offer little opportunity for chefs to expand their cooking ability. Executive chefs usually do not have a supervisor capable of improving their culinary ability, and a chef's employees expect to learn from her, not to train her. The highest level chef jobs require a chef to know a great deal about ingredients, cooking, and kitchen equipment, but companies rarely train their top chefs in these areas. Consequently, culinary school graduates are better off spending several years at lower-level jobs learning this information and expanding their culinary abilities prior to moving up to a top position.

The learning curve shifts quickly in the first year that a person works on a job. A recent graduate will learn a great deal in the first few months on a job after which the amount learned will decrease with each subsequent month. Early in their careers, culinary graduates should devote one to two years to a kitchen and to its chef and then move on to work for another individual. Different chefs have different styles, so working for many different chefs provides a broader exposure to various cooking and presentation styles. Operations that allow for cross-training and station rotation are far more valuable than companies that keep their employees in the same role indefinitely, for each new station or position teaches a new set of recipes and skills.

Working under different chefs is also valuable for observing multiple management approaches. Since the top culinary jobs often require a person to focus more on managing others than on cooking, chefs are better prepared for high-level jobs if they have a range of management techniques at their disposal. With each job, you can study and learn from the management style of each chef for whom you work. Consider what practices work best for you, and learn from those approaches.

The quality of the company for which recent graduates work also impacts their career paths. More difficult, challenging jobs at high-end operations often open more doors than easier jobs at lower-end restaurants. For example, McDonald's will gladly hire cooks with experience at the Ritz-Carlton hotel, but the Ritz will not think much of an applicant with only McDonald's experience. The more challenging jobs generally teach more to their employees than the easier ones do. Supervisors and human resource workers usually look for quality experience on a résumé. High quality experience typically leads to even higher quality jobs, while low caliber experience makes moving up the career ladder difficult.

Interview with Robert Danhi, Executive Chef, Chef Danhi & Co., www.chefdanhi.com

What is your current job?
I now lead Chef Danhi & Co. in Los Angeles. They consult with educational organizations, food manufacturers, restaurant chains, and professional associations. I also lead culinary immersion tours for food professionals who seek a better understanding of the cuisines and cultures of Southeast Asia.

Where did you start on your career path toward you current job?
I feel from the very first day I set foot in a restaurant 23 years ago as a dishwasher, I began preparations for this. Effective consultants have a depth of experience from the ground up; much of this useful knowledge is utilized on an unconscious level. Much of what I do right now really started while teaching at the CIA and working with organizations in the food manufacturing world.

For your first job, was money a major factor in your decision to work there?
Money was not a factor. My brother, also a chef, was working there, so it was easy to get in. The environment was exciting, and hard work was rewarding.

What factors should students consider when choosing a first job in the culinary field?
I think one should look at the concepts of several first jobs. Imagine what areas you want to work in, and then get a job in each area of expertise for some time—at least six months. Then, evaluate what you liked and disliked about each situation.

Describe briefly how you progressed through your career.
I worked my way from dishwasher to executive chef over a span of ten years. Then, after restaurants, I taught full-time for seven years; that taught me to communicate effectively on paper. I spent three years as the executive chef of a food manufacturer and really immersed myself in the research and development process for the development of food products for retail and foodservice. Travel, research, and teaching abroad have made me an expert in the cuisines of Asia—thus the culinary immersion tours there. The consulting work I do now is the natural culmination of teaching and culinary experience combined with the expertise in product development and Asian cuisines.

What other types of jobs could people posses in your segment of the culinary industry?
Although independent restaurants are a small sector of the food business (by dollar), they are a good place to start. They enable you the opportunity for repetition, really honing the craft of cooking. Then you can move into other sectors—chain restaurants, food manufacturing, media, test kitchens . . . so many options. Getting a bachelors degree is more valuable than ever, and if you are looking toward R&D down the line, a degree in Culinology © (8 schools have it now) or dual degrees—one in culinary and another in food science—is the best way to prepare.

With that said, students should attempt to work in organizations in line with their professional goals. For example, a student who ultimately wants to manage a hospital foodservice operation should work in hospitals, while a student who wants to own a French restaurant should work in French restaurants. There is crossover in some areas, so a first job in an Italian restaurant does not limit a chef to Italian cuisine for the rest of her life. The skills acquired on the job are the critical element for career progression. A French restaurant generally focuses on food quality first, while a hospital cafeteria usually makes nutrition the top priority. With certain jobs, such as teaching at a culinary school, a broad range of experiences is necessary. In fact, a person would not prepare properly for a chef-instructor position by starting her career at a school; she needs the industry experience first.

Unfortunately, some students jump at the job offer that pays the most without considering what educational value the job provides. Short-term monetary gain without quality experience is not often financially rewarding in the long term. If a job pays well but teaches you nothing, it only qualifies you for the same kind of job you could earn right out of culinary school. However, if a job teaches you a great deal, you continue to train for higher caliber, higher paying jobs just by going to work. After just a few years, you qualify yourself to earn well-paying jobs that are out of the reach of workers who know little more than a recent culinary school graduate. It is not what your first job pays that counts; it is where that job takes you in the future. Higher quality experience and training to advance your culinary skills always pay off in the end.

16.2   COMMON CULINARY CAREER PATHS

Although there are an infinite number of ways for students to progress through their careers to their ultimate goals, some career paths are more common than others. There are a vast number of endpoints as well, so here are just some of the many potential career paths a culinary school graduate might select. (Detailed job descriptions are available in Appendix 2.)

16.2.1   Restaurants

Restaurants of all sorts form the foundation of the culinary industry. Many culinary professionals have worked in at least one restaurant during their careers. The typical entry point for a recent graduate is the line cook position. Line cooks prepare the food served to guests. There are also a number of related positions of equal stature, such as pantry cooks, pastry cooks, bakers, and cooks assigned to specific stations or meal periods (grill cook, fry cook, breakfast cook, etc.). After a few years of experience as a line cook, a graduate would typically move up to a sous chef position; pastry cooks would move up to the pastry chef position. The sous chef oversees the cooks in their production of food and manages the food quality, while the pastry chef manages the pastry cooks and their production quality. Eventually a sous chef will move up to become an executive chef, usually five to ten years after graduation. Pastry chefs can, but do not often, move up to an executive chef position in a restaurant. The executive chef generally has ultimate control of the management of the kitchen, a common goal for many culinary students. When the restaurant is primarily a bakery, the pastry chef controls the kitchen, a typical goal for culinary school students focusing on baking and pastry work.

Larger operations may use other terminology for the executive chef position. On a property with multiple foodservice outlets, a chef de cuisine may oversee a single kitchen, while the executive chef oversees all of the property kitchens. Some large corporations refer to their chefs as kitchen managers. In chain restaurants, an executive chef may have the potential to move up within the company to a corporate chef position. In these companies, the corporate chef may design and develop standardized menus and recipes for all of the outlets to adopt.

Restaurants also have front-of-the-house employees. Servers move up to become assistant dining room managers and eventually dining room managers or maitre d's. Although culinary school attendees do not often pursue dining room positions, such career paths can be quite lucrative and challenging. Service and people skills become far more important than culinary skills for graduates who choose this route. Dining rooms in finer restaurants may also employ sommeliers, who oversee the wine and beverage operations of the restaurant. A sommelier must possess strong wine and beverage knowledge to function effectively. Both front-of-the-house and back-of-the-house employees, including the executive chef, typically report to a general manager or owner, unless the chef is the owner. An executive chef can move up to a general manager position, but such positions are often given to front-of-the-house managers or to people with specialized business and hospitality training.

Interview with Christopher Prosperi, Executive Chef, Metro Bis Restaurant & Prosperi Salad Dressing

What is your current job?
My current job is the chef-owner of Metro Bis—a fine dining, 64 seat restaurant—in Simsbury, Connecticut. I also have a line of salad dressings, a weekly recipe in the Hartford Courant, and I appear bi-weekly on the local NBC affiliate during their "Taste of Today" segment.

Where did you start on your career path?
A busboy position at a seasonal inn in western Connecticut was my first job, and I wouldn't have chosen another. It was there where I learned that the customer is the most important aspect of the restaurant industry. As I progressed to preparing omelets on the Sunday brunch buffet, I continued to see what more a restaurant provides besides food.

For your first job, was money a major factor in your decision to work there?
Compensation has never been a factor for me when searching for jobs, and I have not come from privileged circumstances. I was able to make responsible personal decisions that helped me avoid some of the financial burdens that can quickly change a career path. This allowed me to seek positions in which I was able to learn as much as possible while continuing to work toward my goal of owning my own restaurant.

What factors should students consider when choosing a first job in the culinary field?
Selecting a first job within the culinary industry should be a careful and deliberate process. It is extremely important to discover a position that is a good match as it will determine the direction of the career path. Students should seek a safe and professional experience that is interesting and fun. It is best to find a properly staffed, well-established restaurant where the stress level is low enough to allow for the continuation of education.

Describe briefly how you progressed through your career to your current position.
After omelets on the buffet, I switched to a small restaurant where I worked elbow to elbow with a chef who taught me the value of money to the operation of the business. Then I went on to a high profile, local restaurant where the owners provided an education in public relations and the spin of the press. Later, I chose a nationally renowned restaurant and chef where I honed my culinary skills

(continued)

(continued)

along with a high volume, health-food restaurant where I learned how to flavor without fat. I then chose to work in a restaurant owned by chefs without much business experience. After bounced paychecks I moved on to an establishment where the owner was foolish enough to open all of the books. I learned management, catering, and the financial skills necessary to open my own restaurant. I have no regrets regarding any of the jobs that I have worked (though they weren't exactly in the best order) because I learned something that helped me in my position today.

16.2.2   Hotels and Private Clubs

Hotels and clubs operate in a manner similar to restaurants with line cooks and pastry cooks moving up to sous chef and pastry chef positions before becoming executive chefs. In fact, a graduate with experience in a hotel or club can easily transition to a restaurant (and vice versa) along her career path. Because hotels and clubs often have restaurant, catering, and sometimes room service functions, each of these areas may have its own chef de cuisine who reports to a single executive chef for the property. With so many kitchens these operations typically have a separate purchasing department, so a culinary graduate could transition to a purchasing manager position either by working as a lower-level purchaser first or by gaining experience purchasing as a chef elsewhere. Stewards and the stewarding manager oversee the setup and delivery of equipment to the many function rooms. Culinary graduates do not often pursue stewarding jobs, but they should be able to handle a stewarding position and even move up to stewarding manager after a year or two. Finally, food and beverage managers oversee the executive chef. An executive chef with strong business skills could move up to a food and beverage manager position, but that role involves lots of number crunching and no cooking.

Hotels and clubs also have the same front-of-the-house positions as restaurants with a couple of additions. Catering staff and salespeople oversee events at the hotel or club and sell its services to potential customers. These employees need human interaction skills, sales talent, and project management abilities, but a culinary graduate with these skills should be able to start in either of these positions.

Hotels and clubs also possess a range of other employees from facilities managers to front desk workers. These positions are more appropriate for hotel and hospitality graduates than for culinary school graduates. Although a restaurant general manager could be a culinary school graduate, hotel or club general managers usually require different training and experience to be effective in their roles.

16.2.3   Caterers

The catering field differs somewhat from restaurant work. Although a large catering company will have line cooks, a sous chef, a pastry chef, and an executive chef, an off-premise caterer will also have cooks who travel to an event site to finish and plate the food prepared partway by the workers at a central commissary. The style of cooking with a caterer differs from restaurant work as well, for food is generally prepared in large quantities and served all at once rather than to order. A recent culinary graduate could work as a line cook, pastry cook, or site cook and work her way up through the organization, or she could jump back and forth between catering and restaurant (or hotel or club) work. A restaurant cook may need a few days to adjust when moving to a catering company, whereas a catering cook may need a few weeks to transition to a restaurant, for the pace of a restaurant is typically much faster.

Caterers, like hotels, employ salespeople, who may also function as event managers. Caterers also employ servers and dining room managers or service captains. Other positions, such as truck drivers, may exist for certain catering companies, but culinary students would use little of their training to work as drivers.

Perhaps the biggest difference in career progression for a student wishing to cater is that a culinary school graduate can open her own, small catering company immediately upon graduation. Developing catering clients does take time, so a graduate will likely need to supplement her income in the first year of business. For that first year the graduate would be wise to work for another caterer to experience how large caterers manage multiple parties simultaneously. A student hoping to become a large caterer will definitely benefit from spending a few years working for other chefs to build her repertoire, but for a very limited caterer, this is not necessary.

16.2.4 Corporate Work

With many large businesses looking to provide in-house foodservice for their employees, the corporate foodservice industry is expanding. Corporate foodservice companies operate cafeterias, sometimes with catering capabilities, for businesses in office buildings. Food in such cafeterias can range from very basic to quite extravagant depending on the requirements of the business. Corporate foodservice operations generally work like buffet- or cafeteria-style restaurants, but they often use a cycle menu to keep the options changing for their captive audience. A recent culinary graduate could easily start as a line cook for such an operation, and a strong student could possibly get a sous chef or executive chef position for a small account soon after graduation. Unlike many other foodservice companies, most of these kitchens operate Monday through Friday, and some close after lunch service. Corporate chefs do not commonly move into restaurant work later in their careers, although restaurant chefs can transition easily to corporate work. For some corporate chefs, the end goal is to oversee multiple accounts rather than a single operation. These jobs are usually given as promotions to talented executive chefs within the company.

Interview with Naam Pruitt, Thai Cookbook Author, Naam Pruitt Company

What is your current job?
I am a cookbook author (*Lemongrass and Limes: Thai Flavors with Naam Pruitt*) and a cooking class instructor. I'm based in Independence, Kansas, but work throughout the country.

Where did you start on your career path?
I started very young, watching my mother cook and shop in the local market for the freshest ingredients. I discovered my passion for cooking while entertaining many guests at our home. My first "real" cooking job was at the athletic dining hall at Texas A&M University at College Station, Texas.

(continued)

(*continued*)

What value did that first job experience provide?
I loved my first job and would do it again. I had a great boss who allowed me to be very creative. My task was to make the food presentations attractive. I did fruit, vegetable, and ice carvings. More than the actual work experience, I loved the example my boss set for me and the other employees. She taught me the most effective way to get things done is to work right alongside the employees and not be afraid to get my hands dirty.

For your first job, was money a major factor in your decision to work there?
Money helped since my husband was in grad school, but no, it was not the main factor.

Describe briefly how you progressed through your career to your current position.
Since people have to eat, there is always a market for those of us in the food industry. That has given me a lot of flexibility. We have moved because of my husband's job, and I also have put raising two children as a high priority. I had to be a little creative in keeping active in the field while adapting to these two factors. I worked for a caterer and also had my own catering business for a while. I picked up cake decorating skills at the Wilton School in Chicago, and that was an additional sideline. I've been active in teaching cooking classes, both at professional schools throughout the country and from my home in little Independence.

What other types of jobs could people possess in your segment of the culinary industry?
Well, there will always be a need for cooking professionals. It is such a broad market and with all the different media outlets there are really no limits. I'm a cookbook author and a teacher, and my specialty is Thai food. I recommend finding a niche that sets you apart from general cooking. One could write a column for the local newspaper and try to get syndicated. One could teach a class at the local community college. Try to get on the local television news to establish yourself as an authority. Keep entertaining your friends, so the word will get out that you have talent.

16.2.5 Schools

As with corporate companies, a culinary school graduate could easily find work cooking in a school or college cafeteria and might be able to start at some level of kitchen management. Schools and colleges, like corporate companies, generally provide cafeteria-service meals using cycle menus for a captive audience. They must follow specific health guidelines to ensure that children and young adults meet certain nutrition parameters. Public schools operate only when school is in session, while residential colleges provide food to students and teachers daily. Managing a school kitchen does require some nutrition knowledge, but a nutrition degree is rarely a requirement. A restaurant chef can usually move into a school chef position, but because of the nature of cooking for young people in a school cafeteria, school chefs may have difficulty transitioning into the restaurant industry without first obtaining restaurant line cook experience.

16.2.6 Cruise Ships

Cruises, like corporate operations and schools, provide meals to a captive audience, but the meal service provided on a cruise is generally much more extravagant and upscale. A student wishing to become an executive chef on a cruise ship will need some experience cooking on ships. A good starting point would be to work as a line cook on a ship and then to progress up as in a restaurant over a five- to ten-year period. However, a student could work in restaurants first and then work for less time on a ship before running a maritime kitchen. There are many other jobs on a cruise ship, but most do not seek applicants with culinary training. Cruises, like many restaurants, do require long numbers of hours from their employees, and they operate under the labor laws of the ship's home country. However, cruises can be wonderful opportunities to learn extravagant buffet presentations and to gain experience working with electric, rather than gas, equipment.

16.2.7   Medical Facilities

Whether cooking in hospital cafeterias or working as a private dietician advising patients, a graduate interested in working in the healthcare arena needs to have a strong foundation in nutrition. A culinary school graduate can get a job cooking in a hospital cafeteria but will commonly need to pursue a nutrition-specific college program to earn the ability to manage the kitchen. (In some cases hospitals will allow two employees, a chef and a dietician, to manage a kitchen in tandem, but the chef will need some familiarity with nutritional principles.) People looking to hire someone to give medical nutrition advice usually look for registered dieticians rather than chefs. Consequently, a student with a goal of managing a healthcare operation or providing medical nutritional advice should plan on pursuing a nutrition degree after culinary school.

16.2.8   Supermarkets

With the explosion of upscale supermarkets offering prepared foods in recent years, super-markets are now actively pursuing employees with culinary training. A culinary graduate can begin working in one department and end up managing the department within a year. Supermarkets also provide good employment opportunities for baking graduates when a city has few free-standing bakeries or restaurants (or hotels or clubs) hiring pastry chefs. Restaurant chefs can transition easily into supermarket work, although supermarket employees gain experience that prepares them more for schools, corporate foodservice companies, or caterers than for restaurants.

Interview with Mitch Greene, CPC, Chef-Owner, Another Choice, LLC

What is your current job?
I am currently the owner of Another Choice LLC, a personal chef service business. I work in the Washington, DC area. My work takes me into clients' homes where I prepare meals for them.

Where did you start on your career path toward your current job?
I found the personal chef service industry while in culinary school at the Culinary Institute at Carolina, a part of the University of South Carolina, Columbia.

What value did your first job experience provide?
I was in a market that, at the time, had never heard of a personal chef, and the notion of having someone else cook meals for the family was somewhat countercultural. Most of my clients in SC

(*continued*)

(*continued*)

were transplants from places like DC and New York. I convinced myself that if I could ever turn a profit there, then I could be successful anywhere. My first year was a net operating loss; my second year showed a very small profit. I learned a lot about how to determine which prospective clients were really interested in the service and which ones really didn't need or want a personal chef. I learned where to spend money and where not to spend money. These lessons have served me very well in the DC area as I'm now able to maximize my time and profit while still finding new clients.

What factors should students consider when choosing a first job in the culinary field?
Ask: Do you want to work for someone else while you develop your skills? Do you want only to cook, or do you want to run a business? Do you have the financial resources not to be profitable for five years? Do you have the organizational skills to be successful? Do you have the capital to start a business, or are you willing to go into debt to do so? Do you want to be the next big celebrity chef, or do you want to earn a living cooking?

Describe briefly how you progressed through your career to your current position.
I wanted to own my own business for one overarching reason: I wanted to be in control of my hours, so I could spend time at home with my wife. I began researching the still-fledgling personal chef industry. I became a member of a national association of personal chefs. (There are many now but USPCA was the first.) They offered exactly what I wanted: a fill-in-the-blank business plan, market research, and even tried-and-true recipes that worked in the freezer. All I had to do was get a client. That was it. I was instantly a personal chef. After two years of experience with long-term clients and after taking a comprehensive test, plus meeting a variety of other standards, I became a Certified Personal Chef—a federally recognized certification.

16.2.9   Personal and Private Chefs

The growth in the number of personal and private chefs in recent years is astounding. Personal chefs prepare and store food for multiple families, while a private chef works for a single family. Both work in the family's home kitchen, so the chef does not need special permits for the facility. Unlike most other culinary jobs, private and personal chefs often work alone. A culinary school graduate could obtain a personal or private chef job immediately upon graduation or at any point in her career. The skills needed to succeed in this job will vary greatly depending on one's clients. Some clients want extremely high-end foods, while others want foods to meet their dietary needs. The requirements of the job may vary as well, but most include shopping and cleaning as part of the responsibilities. With the ability to work independently and the potential for large incomes, many culinary students are choosing this line of work. However, because of the pace and quantity of personal and private chef cooking, these chefs will transition easier to supermarkets, schools, caterers, and corporate foodservice jobs than they will to restaurant work.

16.2.10   Food Writers

In the world of books, magazines, and newspapers, there are many people who work to write recipes and stories about food either in book or periodical format. A culinary school graduate can write a cookbook at any point in her career, but getting that book published is difficult. Publishers only print books that have mass appeal and potential for huge sales. Consequently, famous authors get books published much more easily than unknown chefs.

Unless a culinary graduate has an incredibly original book idea, she may wish to build her reputation and résumé before pitching the concept to publishers.

Periodical writers may work for a company, but many work freelance, pitching their articles to a number of publications. These writers may benefit from some culinary training, but writing skill far outweighs a food writer's need to cook well. Students who wish to become food writers or restaurant critics should take a class or two in writing or journalism to prepare for this type of work. Although graduates can write on the side while maintaining another culinary job full-time, writing alone does not prepare a writer for kitchen work.

16.2.11   Research Chefs and Product Developers

Students with a strong interest in food science and recipe development can become research chefs. Research chefs work for companies to develop convenience or prepared items for large-scale production. The job may resemble kitchen work, such as developing a boxed cake mix, or laboratory work, such as inventing a processed, bagged chip. The lab-type work often requires employees to have a science degree rather than a culinary degree, but culinary graduates could pursue a product development job of the boxed cake mix variety at anytime in their careers, including right out of culinary school. These types of jobs require patience and meticulous note taking, but because of their pace, they do not prepare employees to return to major food production jobs.

16.2.12   Recipe Developers and Testers

Recipe development and testing involves skills similar to research chef work, but little food science knowledge is required. A culinary graduate could obtain this type of job right out of school or at any point in her career. Recipe developers create recipes for food companies to help them sell their products. Every recipe printed on the back of a box, bottle, or bag of food has been written by a recipe developer to encourage consumers to use that product in a recipe. Recipe testers may test the recipes of recipe developers to confirm their accuracy. Some recipe testers work for magazines, newspapers, and publishers to test recipes written by an author for publication. This line of work may prepare someone to write a cookbook or to work as a research chef, but it usually does not help a person to obtain a major food production job.

16.2.13   Food Stylists and Photographers

Whether in magazines, books, television shows, movies, or product labels, images of food that will be published on a large scale are almost always created by a team of a food stylist and a food photographer. The stylist prepares the food and arranges the background to create a certain look for the shot, and the photographer captures the image on film. Photographers need photography experience, not culinary training, but food stylists benefit from a culinary education. However, because food styling sometimes uses cooking techniques not generally seen in a restaurant kitchen, a student needs to apprentice for an experienced stylist after graduation to learn the specialized tricks of the trade. A stylist must have a strong visual artistic ability as well as culinary skill. Because of the nature of the work, food styling does not prepare a person to work other culinary jobs. Similarly, other culinary work does not help someone to become a stylist. A student wishing to become a food stylist should begin working for another stylist immediately upon graduation to develop the specialized visual skills a stylist needs.

Interview with Mary Ellen Rose, Food Stylist, Self-Employed

What is your current job?
I am a freelance food stylist. I make food look beautiful, appetizing, and mouthwateringly scrumptious, so a photo may be taken to entice the viewer to smell the food and want to lick the page . . . and of course, sell the "product." The jobs vary—still photography and commercials. Primarily I work in a studio, but sometimes on location at a restaurant or any location decided upon by the production company. A food stylist can be hired by: a client directly, a photographer, a production company, or an advertising agency.

Where did you start on your career path toward your current job?
Art and drawing classes. Food styling is not about how the food tastes, only how it looks. A strong background in art, painting, and drawing is vital. Science, biology, and chemistry is also important; you must understand what happens to things when you cook, and how to "fake" things for an effect. Then add in how differently things look in a camera: light, color, texture, composition, angle, and how it will look when it is reproduced . . . it is a whole new world!

What factors should students consider when choosing a first job in the culinary field?
Ask: How well do you work with others? Do you have a collaborative mind? Are you ok with change? Can you work quickly? Do you have good communication skills? Can you draw? How well do you visualize? How do you deal with pressure on the job? How well do you network? Can you deal with no one ever tasting your food? Can you check your ego at the door?

If a student were looking for a career in your segment of the industry, where should she start?
Be an assistant food stylist. Find someone and learn from them. A good assistant is hard to find and train. Be flexible and open to learn new things. School is a controlled "ideal" environment. Working in advertising requires a calm, quick, flexible mind and a great deal of skill in art composition. When you are ready, your "lead" stylist will turn you loose in the world to be on your own.

Source: Mark Langford Photography, Inc.

16.2.14 Purveyors

While someone interested in purchasing can work in a restaurant, hotel, caterer, or other foodservice operation, a graduate interested in selling food to foodservice companies will ultimately work for a purveyor. Purveyors come in all sizes and specialties. Some companies sell very limited product lines, while others provide thousands of products to their clients. A culinary graduate can work for a purveyor at any point in her career. Culinary knowledge, such as that acquired in school or on the job, is extremely valuable to salespeople, as it helps them to make suggestions to a chef for how to use a certain product. However, salesmanship and people skills are equally, if not more, important. Selling food will help a chef to gain familiarity with certain products and thus prepare her for some culinary jobs, but without the ongoing kitchen practice, a chef will struggle to return to a large food production job after years with a purveyor.

16.2.15 Food Marketing and Public Relations

Whereas a purveyor sells entire product lines to purchasers, food marketers create marketing campaigns to encourage chefs and home cooks to purchase specific products. Marketers may benefit from some culinary knowledge, but marketing, not cooking, skills are essential for someone to become a food marketer. A culinary school graduate interested in food marketing should take marketing courses and begin working for a food marketing company soon after graduation.

Public relations, a means of publicizing a brand through avenues other than paid advertisements, relates as much to chefs as to food in the culinary industry. Some chefs hire public relations specialists to promote themselves and their restaurants to the public. A culinary school graduate needs strong public relations skills to succeed in this line of work, so working for a PR company immediately after graduation is essential. Culinary abilities play almost no role in working as a successful public relations person.

Neither of these jobs prepares a graduate to work in other facets of the culinary industry.

16.2.16 Sanitation Inspectors

Although sanitation inspectors deal with chefs almost every day, their background is rarely in culinary arts. Sanitation inspectors typically must have an education in science to understand the role bacteria play in making people sick. Although a culinary arts degree does not prevent a person from becoming a sanitation inspector, without a science degree a chef will have difficulty finding work as an inspector. The nature of the work is such that it does not prepare inspectors to work in other parts of the culinary industry with the possible exception of science-based product development jobs.

16.2.17 Television and Radio

The prevalence of television and radio shows today might suggest that there is plenty of work available for graduates interested in working in the media. Media outlets do hire culinary professionals to conduct food research and to prepare mise en place for their stars, but most of the work on a show is done by people with television or radio training, not culinary education. As the demand to work with celebrities is high, the best way for a graduate to obtain a job on television or radio is through networking. The training a person receives in culinary school is usually sufficient to work behind the scenes on a show, but without the network connection, a graduate may have difficulty getting an interview.

So how does one become the culinary celebrity in front of the microphone? Unfortunately, whereas culinary ability is a prerequisite, other skills and qualities are equally important. For mass media, physical appearance and voice quality play a role as does personality. Current fame also helps a chef become a media star. A chef such as Emeril Lagasse can get a television show because he is already famous for his many New Orleans restaurants. The media experts know that they have a built-in audience for their shows if they depict someone famous, but putting a "nobody" on the air is risky for ratings. To increase her chances for becoming a celebrity, a chef should take every opportunity to get on television or radio, even if only on the local news or on a public access channel. Those experiences expose a chef to how a TV or radio program works. Media training classes and coaches can also help a chef learn to perform for a mass audience. Then, the chef should put together a demo tape and cover letter to send to multiple media outlets. If she has a network connection she can use to get someone to review the tape, she should use it. Otherwise, the tape may be thrown out before it is even watched by a producer. Ultimately, most celebrities are famous for something other than their media work, so the best way to become a media celebrity is to focus on becoming a success elsewhere in the culinary field. Once famous, not only radio and television shows, but product endorsement opportunities, too, will fall into a chef's lap.

16.2.18 Teaching

Becoming a culinary arts instructor requires a person to possess both teaching skills and expertise in one or more facets of the culinary field. A culinary school graduate might be able to get a teaching position at a middle or high school right out of college, but a college teaching job takes years to acquire. Colleges require their faculty to have certain credentials (degrees, certification, or both) and a minimum number of years of quality experience. Students expect their teachers to be subject-matter experts, so ten years of food styling experience might qualify a chef to teach food styling but not breakfast cookery. Culinary graduates hoping to become chef-instructors some day can best prepare themselves for teaching by working in high-end food production operations at an executive chef level. This experience alone may take years to achieve, but for many schools it is a prerequisite to getting a job interview.

While most culinary schools require culinary experience, they do not necessarily require teaching experience. However, teaching does take practice to execute effectively, so a future teacher should pursue opportunities to teach whenever they arise. A chef can practice teaching through public chef demonstrations as well as through the teaching of home cooks at a range of recreational teaching facilities around the country. Pursuing higher degrees in education will help a graduate to acquire a teaching position, but such a degree may not be necessary as long as the graduate can teach well enough to pass a teaching tryout at the school.

Most schools, both college and high school level, provide professional development training to their teachers to help them improve their teaching skills. Some require the instructors to pursue teaching credentials at their own cost. Because of the training investment required, a student or graduate interested in becoming a chef-instructor should pursue opportunities to interview and to observe current instructors at a school. Seeing firsthand what it is like to teach may help a graduate decide if she wishes to invest the time and money to prepare to become a teacher. Although teaching does not always pay well, teaching experience on a résumé is generally considered prestigious and often helps a chef-instructor to pursue other paid opportunities in various parts of the culinary field. For most teachers the opportunity to learn and to help others as they begin their culinary careers is the main reason to pursue and to retain a teaching position.

Summary

Although culinary school provides a foundation for students going into the culinary field, experience helps to develop skills further and to allow graduates to specialize in a specific culinary arena. The value of experience, sometimes underestimated by students, has a major impact on a graduate's career path and long-term earning potential. Students with lofty career goals should not attempt to skip or to rush through the critical entry-level years, as those years provide a great deal of experience and training to prepare students for their future leadership roles. Entry-level jobs in restaurants, hotels, clubs, catering, and cruise ships (in quality operations) all provide extensive cooking practice that can propel a culinary graduate in any number of career directions. Jobs in corporate foodservice, schools, medical facilities, and supermarkets provide quantity cooking experience that may be slightly limiting in the direction it can send graduates, although each of those industry threads can become a rewarding career path unto itself. Personal and private chefs, research chefs, product developers, recipe developers, recipe testers, and purvey-ors benefit from culinary education, but their work tends to make returning to a quantity food production environment somewhat difficult. Food writers, food stylists, food photographers, food marketers, public relations specialists, and sanitation inspectors work in culinary-related jobs, but they need specialized training beyond the scope of most culinary programs. Finally, celebrities and teachers tend to acquire their jobs as a culmination or an addition to another successful career path. There are a great many possible career paths, but by planning a potential path early in one's career, a culinary school graduate increases the chances that she ultimately will achieve her goal.

KEY CONTRIBUTIONS THAT QUALITY EXPERIENCE PROVIDES TO CAREER DEVELOPMENT

- Real-world variations on the theories taught in school
- Access to a wide range of recipes and cooking techniques
- Awareness of upcoming trends
- Additional cooking practice to refine skills
- Exposure to the cooking styles of various chefs
- Exposure to various management styles
- A strong résumé to help acquire further high-caliber work
- Opportunities to specialize in one area of the culinary field

Suggested Tasks

1. Interview an industry chef who has a job similar to the one you would like to have in ten years. Ask her to describe her career path, including where she started, how she progressed, and how long she stayed at each job. If she is willing to share, ask how much she earned on her first job. Ask which jobs were the most valuable and which the least valuable in helping her to reach her current job and why. Compile the results of your interview into a report and share the report with your class.

2. Locate five entry-level culinary jobs in need of applicants. Use the newspaper, Internet, or any other source you wish. Contact the companies to find out the job title, approximate job description, and salary range. Bring your research to

class and discuss the results with your classmates and instructor. Discuss where each job experience would lead in one to two years, and decide which would likely lead to the highest-paid position in five to ten years. Compare the results to each job's current wage rate to see if there is any relation to the salary to which it might lead.

3. Determine three career goals that you have. Write out a possible career path for each goal. Share the paths with an instructor to determine their viability and approximate length of time to achieve. Begin researching possible job openings that match the first job listed on each career path.

4. Identify three areas of the culinary industry in which you would enjoy working. Interview a culinary professional who works in each of those areas. Ask each person to describe her typical day, her job responsibilities, and her work environment. Also ask what she loves most about her job and why she chose this line of work.

CHAPTER 17

Making Use of the Support Staff at the School

After going through months of classes, homework, and extracurricular activities some students finally feel ready to take on the world all by themselves. Other students feel some anxiety and trepidation about leaving the safety net of school. Fortunately, most colleges do not simply toss students out of school after graduation to sink or swim. There are support systems in place at most colleges; the problem is that too few students utilize them.

Prior to graduation every student should visit his school's career services or job placement (or other similarly named) office to prepare for the job search. Students who leave school carrying debt should also pay a visit to the financial aid office to learn about the many options for working with loan companies in the event of a financial emergency. Student services (or similar) offices can help to provide counseling to those students experiencing elevated levels of anxiety about entering the workforce. Finally, although students may not officially become alumni until after graduation, a quick trip to the alumni office to learn about the services that it provides is well worth the time. Each office that a student visits before graduation helps to ease the transition to the post-graduation world and sets up some safety-net systems for that student for the future.

In this chapter, you will learn about some commonly available support services that help a student to transition into the real world. You will also learn how to use those services to your own advantage.

17.1 CAREER SERVICES/JOB PLACEMENT

Whether your school calls it "career services," "job placement," or something else, chances are that your college has an office dedicated to helping you locate employment. Many students, if they visit this office at all, go solely to get printouts of job openings around the country. However, the placement office in most colleges is a great resource to help prepare for getting job offers, not just job leads.

Most career counselors have the ability and experience to read and to critique a résumé. Students who have never written a résumé before may have difficulty getting started, or they may put together good résumés in need of just a few tweaks. Either way, a career counselor can help anyone to generate a better résumé than that person could prepare independently. Counselors can help with writing cover letters as well. Since a student must write a cover letter for each job, even those students who already have polished résumés can benefit from meeting with a career counselor. Just having the counselor check for spelling errors is well worth a ten-minute visit to the office.

Like résumé writing, interviewing can be challenging even for people who have interviewed for work dozens of times. Since graduates only have one chance to make a good first impression on an employer, they should not treat their first few interviews as practice rounds. They should practice interviewing before they meet with the first potential employer. Most career counselors will gladly work with students to practice interviewing either in general or for a specific job. Counselors can correct everything from clothing faux pas to weak handshakes to poor eye contact. Simple errors such as these can cause a student to lose job opportunity after job opportunity. Role playing with a career counselor will not only build your confidence, but it will help to make you a strong interviewee as soon as your first interview.

Once students have put together their résumés and developed interviewing skills, they should still visit the placement office regularly to get leads on jobs. Most colleges get calls, letters, and faxes every day looking for graduates to fill open positions. Not all leads will be desirable, but some gems do arrive periodically. Since new leads arrive all the time, students should visit the placement office weekly until they have gotten a job offer they want. Career counselors can often assist not only with providing leads but also with contacting them. If the lead requests a phone call rather than a fax or mailing, you should role-play the call with the counselor first to make sure that you come across as professional on the phone. Some employers may state that the position is filled (even when it is not) if the caller sounds unprofessional on the phone. Practicing with the counselor will help you to avoid major blunders when speaking with potential employers.

Career counselors can also teach students how to find lucrative job offers on their own. A typical job search encompasses the pursuit of job leads from at least four different sources: help wanted ads in newspapers or magazines (or their corresponding Web sites), personal networking connections, job search Web sites, and the school's placement office. While some people prefer to network or to check the local newspaper for job leads, a career counselor can introduce students to those Web sites that provide job postings for culinary graduates. Although Web addresses can change and new companies pop up all the time, some of the current Web sites for locating culinary jobs are: starchefsjobfinder.com, culinarycult.com, chefjobs.com, chefsemployment.com, chefjobsnetwork.com, foodindustryjobs.com, hcareers.com, careerbuilder.com, hotjobs.yahoo.com, monster.com, and craigslist.org. Simply learning the addresses of these and other job source Web sites and learning how to use them can help a student find gainful employment for decades.

Before graduation students should find out how much access to the placement office they get after graduation. Some schools only provide assistance to students for a few months after graduation; others work with their alumni for life. You should learn how to receive job postings after you have graduated from school. Many students do not realize that their alma mater will help them with job placement years after graduation. With some employers approaching colleges for executive chef candidates, graduates with a few years of experience could discover a treasure trove of potential job offers simply by staying in touch with their

Interview with Philipp Denfeld, Externship Coordinator, Le Cordon Bleu College of Culinary Arts, Miami

What services do you provide to your students?
I assist students in obtaining an externship site for their final class of externship. I mentor students on the needs of the industry and what employers are looking for both specifically and generally. I do my best to frame all information in a real-time scenario: that is, in season demands, what will make a student more marketable to any employer (attitude). I help students realize that they should use their moth in proportion to their ears, and the two words that will get you the best result in any kitchen are "Yes, Chef." I also explain the importance of having a well thought out career objective, an accurate and professional résumé, and a professional portfolio. I instruct students to have at least three qualified professional references on them at all times, preferably five. I make students realize that the human resources department or recruitment director will have the ultimate say in whether they are eligible to be hired.

What kinds of help do students usually request from you?
Some students want me to call employers for them; I tell them that we are of the thinking of teaching a man to fish and not feeding a man a fish.

school's placement office. Since executive chef jobs are not appropriate for recent graduates, these job leads often go nowhere unless alumni contact the school. Staying in touch with your school will allow you to take advantage of those lucrative job opportunities.

17.2 PAPERWORK

Sometimes students need a copy of their transcript either as proof of graduation or for their professional portfolio. Getting a transcript before classes are complete and grades are entered will not provide evidence of program completion. Students should request a copy of their transcripts for their records as soon as possible after graduation. Transcripts can take weeks to mail, but the registrar's office may be able to process a request the same day for students who visit the office in person. So before leaving the campus for good, visit the registrar's office and request a copy of your transcript.

Just as you may need paperwork from the school, your college likely needs paperwork from you. Nearly all colleges require employment verification documentation from their students. If the placement or registrar's office requests this information from you, complete and return it as quickly as possible. Most colleges are required to document this information to maintain their accreditation status. Even if you have decided not to work in the culinary field or are not proud of your current job, let the school know where you work. If you are not employed, you can notify the school of that fact and, if desired, ask for help in finding employment. Since the school's reputation impacts the value of your degree or diploma for years to come, you harm your own credentials by putting the school's accreditation status at risk.

17.3   FINANCIAL AID

As soon as students graduate, many of them begin laying out money to relocate, to pay for rent and security deposits on an apartment, and to purchase new furniture and living supplies as part of the transition from dorm life to independent living. Making payments on student loans may be a financial hardship that a graduate simply cannot afford right out of school. Fortunately, your financial aid office can help.

Many students do not know all of the rules and regulations that surround their student loans. Most federal loans do not require any repayment until six months after the student graduates, and those payments can be deferred even longer for students pursuing further college education. In some instances, the financial aid office may also be able to adjust the length of time over which a loan is repaid. A longer time frame for repayment means smaller payments but more money repaid overall. As a graduate's income goes up over the years, he could always put extra money toward the principle of the loan each month to reduce the total amount of interest paid and to shorten the length of time to pay off the loan. Since entry-level culinary jobs do not usually pay very well, smaller payments may help students get through the lean years until they have earned promotions and larger salaries. Some students may avoid interaction with the financial aid office, but simple counseling from a financial aid officer can often help students to manage their cash flow after graduation.

Interview with Lynn M. Robinson, Director of Student Financial Services, Johnson & Wales University

What services do you provide to your students?
JWU Student Financial Services (SFS) consists of three departments: Financial Aid, Financial Planning, and Billing & Collections. These three departments provide a variety of services to JWU students. The Financial Planning department has a team of financial planners who assist students with the process of applying for financial aid, getting referrals for outside scholarships, and determining payment options for tuition and fees. The planners are the customer service department of SFS and reach out to students to make financing a higher education more affordable. The Financial Aid staff determines eligibility for federal, state, and institutional aid for students who apply for financial aid as well as processes all student loans. The Billing & Collections department provides students with term invoices, maintains the student's accounts, and collects all payments from students on Federal Perkins Loans.

What kinds of help do students usually request from you?
Students are always looking for ways to make education more affordable. They need assistance in the financial aid process as well as ways to pay their tuition balance after financial aid. They are often overwhelmed by the process and need guidance.

(continued)

(continued)

What other things do you wish more students asked from you to better help them?
Some families have difficulty completing the application for financial aid (FAFSA); the SFS staff would be more than happy to assist them. If families need assistance in determining the best alternative payment option, we want to encourage them to contact the Financial Planning department.

What advice would you give students to help them maximize the value they get from your department?
The number one thing a student can do to maximize the value they get from SFS is to remain connected. Communication is essential to the student's success. Students need to read all correspondence sent to them via email, mail, or telephone messaging. If students have financial difficulty, they should meet with their planner. Students need to be aware of the timeline and remain up to date with all payment plans to avoid holds.

Source: Johnson & Wales University

Graduating students should also speak with the financial aid office to learn how to contact their loan companies in case of an emergency in the future. Most loan companies will work with you as long as you stay in touch with them. You can ask to defer or to skip a payment should you become unemployed for a time or suffer from financial hardship. The loan companies understand that emergencies do occur, and they generally work with their clients to get through difficult times. However, when a graduate does not communicate with the loan companies and simply stops paying on his loans, he ruins his credit and find the loan companies unsympathetic to his plight. If you stop repaying your loans and fall off your creditor's radar screen, you destroy your ability to get a loan for a car, house, or personal business from any lending institution indefinitely. In short, make sure that you know how to reach the loan companies in case you find yourself unable to make payments in the future.

17.4   PERSONAL COUNSELING

Many college students find themselves struggling with fear and anxiety over the future. Although some students encounter these emotions upon starting school, others face them for the first time as graduation approaches. It is natural to experience some nervousness about leaving college. Students should speak with friends, family, faculty, administrators, or even co-workers about their feelings to help alleviate some of their fears. Some classmates may have years of experience living independently and can offer advice to students who have only known dorm life outside of their parents' home. Despite the many unknowns most college graduates survive just fine after graduation.

However, if your anxiety is more than just basic nervousness, you may need more substantial help. Night terrors, insomnia, major weight change, or an inability to continue with normal daily activities may be signs of clinical anxiety or depression. Most schools either provide counseling or refer students in need to a professional counselor. A student services worker or a department dean can usually refer you confidentially to a mental health professional. Social workers and psychologists can speak with you to see if your fears need professional attention. Because some therapy takes weeks to show results, you should request

Interview with Ann Stapleton, Dean of Student Affairs, The Art Institute of Washington

What is your title and where do you work?
Dean of Student Affairs, The Art Institute of Washington

What services do you provide to your students?
At The Art Institutes, which house The International Culinary Schools, the Departments of Student Affairs consist of several functional areas. We provide school-sponsored housing, counseling services, disability testing and assistance, student activities, student leadership programs, and student development programs; in some of our schools academic advising and registration is conducted through Student Affairs. We provide information and services related to independent housing; we prepare and present the federally required Jeanne Clearly crime report. We also distribute information regarding available health insurance. Student Affairs organizes orientations for new students, and assists the Career Services department with job fairs, portfolio shows, and graduations. We are always looking for ways to meet the students where they are and help them move along their educational path.

What kinds of help do students usually request from you?
Students come to Student Affairs for all kinds of assistance. We handle everything from lost cell phones and umbrellas to emergency housing and medical crisis intervention. We assist students with developing as professionals and lifelong learners throughout their educational career through specifically designed programs and events that introduce students to social, educational, and psychological developmental activities. We provide assistance to any and every request presented, and if the particular situation calls for intervention from another department, we facilitate the dialogue so that the student gets the assistance that he or she needs.

What other things do you wish more students asked from you?
We could do much more to help students if they came to us with their situations, whatever they may be, when they first begin to arise and before they are out of control. Ask for let; let people know what is going on with you. Don't think you need to do this alone. The Student Affairs staff can offer advice, guidance, support, information, and most importantly, a person you can rely on who really wants you to succeed in reaching your educational goals, and we will do all that we can in our power to help you reach those goals.

What advice would you give students to help them maximize the value they get from your department?
Make yourself known. Get involved. Introduce yourself to faculty and staff on your very first day. Ask questions about things you are not sure about. Read the materials you are given and reference them often, especially your catalog and student handbook. Attend the seminars offered; attend the social activities; join the organizations that interest you; start a new organization. However you do it, become a leader on your campus. Campus events help you develop skills even if you don't realize it.

referrals from the school and set up a session with the recommended professional before graduation. Getting professional help while in school can ease the transition into the working world. Waiting until you are out of school to begin to address mental health issues will only make the post-graduation transition more difficult. Since clinical anxiety or depression will not go away on its own, the sooner you start treating it, the sooner you will feel comfortable in your new role as a working professional and as a culinary school graduate.

17.5   ALUMNI ASSOCIATIONS

Although students do not technically become alumni until after graduation, they should find out before leaving campus what services the school provides alumni. Some alumni associations offer job postings just for alumni. A student should learn how to access this information as soon as possible to benefit from it immediately upon graduation. Students should also find out about alumni gatherings and reunions. Registering to get notices of reunions will help graduates stay connected with faculty and classmates for future networking. Most schools communicate with alumni through email or newsletters to keep them informed of changes at the school, so learn how to get on the mailing list. Since changes at the college impact the school's reputation and by extension your own, you should keep informed about any major changes to your alma mater.

Some schools begin asking for donations to an alumni fund almost immediately after graduation (if not before). Your decision to contribute to the school is a personal one. Do not feel bad if you cannot afford it or choose not to donate at this point in time. However, do not write off donations forever. You may find later in life that you wish to give back to

---

Interview with Steve Swofford, Executive Director of Alumni Relations, The Culinary Institute of America, Hyde Park, New York

What service do you provide to your students?
The alumni office is here to help students network with our alumni, trustees, and industry leaders. There is a wonderful way for students at the CIA to be connected personally, educationally, and professionally, and this is by requesting an alumni mentor. The alumni mentor can help bridge the gap between what a student learns in class and what they will encounter in the industry. The alumni mentor can assist students with identifying externship goals and the sites that meet them. A mentor will also guide a student in setting professional and personal goals and help develop action plans to attain them. The alumni office can also run lists of alumni in certain areas of the country or various industries. So as students are preparing for graduation and may be moving to a certain part of the country to start jobs, they have some possible contacts they can reach out to for advice.

What kinds of help do students usually request from you?
I tend to get quite a few students wanting assistance in guiding them on their career path.

What advice would you give students to help them maximize the value they get from your department?
I wish students would stop by our office more often to talk about their career paths earlier in their education. We see many employment opportunities come through our office, and when we know students, we are able to make quick referrals. Get involved, get involved, get involved. Our office is involved in many events both off and on campus where we like to take students, so they can network with industry leaders. It's by interacting and forming bonds with faculty and staff that students earn these opportunities. Offer to volunteer or work your college's development office's annual phone-a-thon. Assist in the annual meeting of trustees. Join a student alumni club or student foundation/service club.

your alma mater. Donations can help to grow the school and to build its reputation which helps all alumni, including you. Your donation may also financially help a student who would otherwise be unable to afford college. If you were able to attend college due to the generosity of an alumnus, this may be an important motivator for you to give back in the future. Remember that your income will continue to increase over your lifetime, and your donation will help to nurture the next culinary generation.

Finally, ask someone in the alumni office about ways to stay involved with the college after graduation. Some schools ask alumni to speak with current students about the realities of the industry. Others call upon powerful alumni to hire graduating students. Your college may even use alumni to recruit or to interview potential incoming students. Whatever role you can play, do your best to stay involved with your alma mater. You will find the networking benefits well worth the effort.

17.6   EXIT INTERVIEWS

Among the many students who complete a college program, some love their college experience while others have less than stellar opinions of their alma mater. No matter what your experience, you should find out how your school collects critical feedback from graduates and participate in that process. Some schools collect information through forms while others conduct in-person interviews. If there is no mechanism in place, find out whom to approach and share your feedback with that school official. Any problem that you encountered in school will likely arise for other students. Voicing your concerns and making suggestions for improvement gives the school a chance to change for the better. Even if future change will not resolve the problem for you, any adjustment that improves the school experience for others and enhances the school's reputation ultimately increases the value of your degree as an alumnus.

Summary

There are a great many benefits that a school provides to its graduating students if they merely take the time to utilize the school's services. Prior to graduation students should meet with an official from the job placement or career services office to review and to revise their résumés and cover letters. Students should request meetings with placement officials to role-play job interviews and to get leads on job opportunities. Students should make sure that they know how to find job opportunities on their own, but they should also learn how graduates can access job opportunities sent to the school. Graduating students should request copies of their transcripts and complete any job placement documentation forms. They should speak with a financial aid officer to learn about repayment options and to make sure they know how to contact their loan companies in the event of an emergency. If a student is suffering from severe anxiety or depression, that student should ask a school official for a referral to a professional counselor and should schedule an appointment with that counselor prior to graduation. Students should also visit the alumni services office or the person who manages alumni to learn how to stay in touch and to stay involved. Alumni benefit from getting on the school's mailing list, attending alumni gatherings, and staying informed of changes to the school. Alumni may also wish to stay involved with the school by speaking at the school, hiring other graduates, or assisting with school recruitment efforts. Finally, students should complete all exit interview requirements and share their critical feedback on their school experience with a school official.

IMPORTANT TASKS TO ACCOMPLISH PRIOR TO GRADUATION

- Get résumé and cover letter help from the placement office.
- Practice interviewing with a placement professional.
- Get a list of job leads from the school.
- Learn how to find job leads in the future.
- Get a transcript from the registrar.
- Complete job placement documentation forms.
- Speak with financial aid to learn about all repayment options and borrower rights.
- Request a referral to a professional counselor to deal with severe anxiety or depression.
- Contact the alumni office to learn about their services and about how to stay informed about the school.
- Find out how to stay involved with the school as an alumnus.
- Learn how critical feedback from graduates is collected and schedule an exit interview with the appropriate school official to share major concerns and recommendations.

Suggested Tasks

1. Write a first draft of your résumé. Bring it to the placement office and have an employee in that office review it critically for you. Make the suggested changes and share it with the employee again for a final review.

2. Get a list of current job opportunities from the placement office. Write a draft cover letter for at least five different jobs in which you are interested. Share those cover letters with a placement office employee for feedback and critique. Make any changes suggested, and send out the cover letters with your résumé to each of the job opportunities.

3. Meet with a job placement employee and ask him to show you at least three ways to locate job opportunities. Find out how to get access to the school's job opportunities once you are no longer on campus. Ask the employee for a business card to keep in touch with the school.

4. Meet with a financial aid agent at the school. Ask him to share with you all of your rights as a borrower and your options, if any, in adjusting the length of your loans. Find out how to contact your loan companies in the event of an emergency and store that information in a safe place.

5. Visit the registrar's office and request a copy of your transcript after your final grades have been entered. Store the transcript in a safe place or insert it into your professional portfolio.

6. Meet with an alumni coordinator. Find out how the school communicates with alumni. Get on the alumni mailing list and ask how you will be informed of reunions and alumni gatherings. Ask if the school ever uses alumni for guest speakers or for new-student recruitment. If you have the time available, volunteer to assist the school in one of these functions.

7. Write a list of your school's top five strengths and top five weaknesses. List several changes that you would recommend to the school president to improve your experience at the school. Share the list with the appropriate school official (department dean or a senior campus manager). Provide your contact information in case the individual would like to speak with you further about your suggestions.

CHAPTER 18

Résumé Writing

The first introduction that most people have to a potential employer is through a résumé. A résumé has the distinct challenge of summing up a person's entire career, skills set, and credentials in a single page or two while motivating a potential employer to contact the applicant for an interview. Understandably, writing an effective résumé can be difficult for college students (and for many experienced graduates, too). Since most employers will not interview a job applicant for a high-caliber position without a résumé, students must learn how to write good résumés to advance their careers.

In addition to a résumé each mailing to a potential employer also requires a cover letter. A well-written cover letter and résumé can convince an employer that a candidate is worth contacting for an interview; however, if either is poorly written, most employers will not hesitate to throw the application into the trash. There are many ways to write a résumé and a cover letter, but certain approaches often get better results than others.

In this chapter, you will learn how to write an effective résumé and cover letter. You will also learn realistic expectations for responses to your applications.

18.1 THE RÉSUMÉ

Although a résumé is not necessary for every job in the culinary field, the more desirable positions generally require that the applicant have a professional, quality résumé. A résumé must sound impressive and must present a person's qualifications in as strong a manner as possible, but it must also leave the reader wanting to know more about the applicant and how she achieved her accomplishments. The goal of the résumé is not to get a job; it is to get an interview.

Résumés are generally written in one of two styles: experience-based (typically called a chronological résumé) and skills-based (typically called a functional résumé). The more common experience-based résumé highlights a person's job experience and suggests a person's skill sets through the tasks performed at previous jobs. This style of résumé is appropriate for young students beginning a career or for people with some experience in their field. The skills-based résumé highlights a person's skills separately from their work history. The skills-based résumé works better for people who are changing careers or for individuals who have spent substantial time out of the workforce (to raise children full-time, for example). Since the skills that a person learns in a different field or through parenting may not appear obvious from a simple work history, the writer has to spell out the skills for the reader to show their relevance to the culinary field.

18.1.1   Category Headings

Nearly all résumés are divided into sections with specific headings. Although an individual can list any heading she wishes, there are some standard headings that most employers expect to see.

NAME AND CONTACT INFORMATION   Not generally listed with a heading or title, the writer always places her name and contact information at the top of the page. The name should be written in a larger font size than everything else on the résumé to help the reader to remember the person's name. If the writer has a certification, it should be listed as initials immediately following her name. The contact information should include a mailing address, phone number, and email address. The mailing address should be a permanent one. If you will be changing addresses less than three months after you send out your résumé, you must take care to have the post office forward all of your mail to the new address. The phone number should lead to a voicemail box or answering machine that allows a caller to leave a message, and you must check messages daily. Emails require similar attention. Too many applicants provide an email address that they never check or that they plan on changing in a few weeks. If the employer sends an email that gets no response, or if she calls and cannot leave a message, she will not waste her energy trying to reach you a second time. Make certain that you do not change your phone or email information within three months of sending out résumés, or you are likely to miss potential interview opportunities.

Just as a résumé must look professional to generate interviews, any display of immaturity can discourage an employer from hiring you, thus ending the job search process as soon as it begins. To provide a professional first impression, your voicemail or answering machine must have a professional message during your job search. An employer who hears, "The Smith family is not home at this time; please leave a message after the beep" will likely leave a message. Someone who hears any style of music or a highly "creative" message may decide to hang up and offer the interview to someone else. Email addresses, too, have the ability to portray you either as a serious candidate or as a teenager playing grown-up. A good email address would involve your name, initials, or possibly something related to food or cooking. An address, such as "partygirl," "boozeman," or any reference to sexual activity @whatever.com can send your résumé to the trash can. If you do not have a professional-sounding email address currently, get one before writing your résumé, and use it for all communication with potential employers.

OBJECTIVE   Some people forget to put an "objective" or "goal" heading on a résumé, but a person's objective succinctly tells the employer whether or not the applicant is applying for the right job. For example, if an applicant states that her objective is "to own a restaurant," she will probably be rejected for a line cook position. However, an objective discussing a person's inter-est in "cooking and training under a talented chef" will usually get that résumé to the top of the pile for a line cook job. For students applying for entry-level positions, which often do not require much industry experience, a well-written objective can make the difference between one candidate and all of the other recent culinary school graduates. An objective simply states the type of job, work experience, and/or company the applicant seeks. The more closely aligned the objective is with a job opportunity, the more likely the interviewer is to read the résumé.

An objective need not be a full sentence, and it should not run more than two lines. Examples of good objectives for recent culinary school graduates are:

1. To practice high caliber, from-scratch cooking in a high-end restaurant
2. To prepare breads, pastries, and other baked goods while refining my baking and pastry expertise under a well-respected pastry chef
3. To serve as a personal chef for a family interested in culinary experimentation and modern fusion cuisine
4. To teach culinary arts skills to students in an environment that promotes learning, professionalism, and continual self-improvement for students and teachers alike.

Each of these objectives is appropriate for a different kind of culinary job. However, each gives a concise and specific depiction of the interests of the applicant. A student with the first objective might get several interviews at five-star restaurants or hotels, but her résumé would never make it past the first round for a teaching position. Similarly, the fourth objective would work for a teacher, but not for a line cook. If you are applying to vastly different types of culinary jobs, you may need to create different objectives (and multiple résumés) for each of the positions to which you apply.

EDUCATION Although some highly experienced professionals may put the "education" heading near the end of a résumé, a recent culinary school graduate should place it immediately following the objective. Information listed under education should include: name of each school attended, city and state where the school is located, date or anticipated date of graduation, and major and degree (or other credential) earned, if any. Students with GPA's over 3.0 should list their GPA. If the GPA will round up to the nearest tenth, then list it to one decimal point (e.g., write a GPA of 3.17 as 3.2). If the GPA will round down to the nearest tenth, then write it to two decimals points (e.g., write a GPA of 3.14 as 3.14). If a person has attended multiple schools, even if she has not graduated from them, she should provide information for all of them beginning with the most recent school and working backwards in time. Students who graduated from a culinary-focused high school program or who had extremely high GPA's in high school may decide to list their high school; otherwise, high school education need not be listed.

Students who have little to no prior work experience in the culinary field may also wish to list subjects studied for their culinary degrees. Listing of subjects studied should not be a list of classes but rather five to ten major subjects mastered during the student's program. For example, a subject list could include hot food production, cold food production, breakfast cookery, garde manger, nutrition, sanitation, kitchen management, and table service. However, students should not list a specific subject unless they feel fairly competent in the material, for the interviewer may decide to ask questions about that subject during an interview. The purpose of a subject list is to suggest to the employer that the breadth of knowledge attained by the student during her program makes up for the lack of multiple culinary work experiences. Students with three or more quality culinary work experiences need not include a list of subjects studied.

Interview with Matthew Jansen, Executive Chef, Radda Trattoria and Mateo Restaurant Provencal

What do you look for in a résumé when deciding to offer someone an interview?
It's nice when it's a professional résumé. It doesn't always help to have a whole list of places of employment where they've stayed for only a short period of time. It's better to see that they stayed for a year. Culinary school is great on résumés even if they don't have a lot of practical experience. It is nice to get fresh starts with people who haven't picked up any habits yet—good or bad. The most important thing is to have that great, professional-looking résumé to get invited to an interview: no spelling errors and professional presentation.

What do you expect to see in a cover letter?
We receive so many. The catchiest ones are just very professional and do not come across like they're doing the business a favor by considering employment with us. A more humble approach is really nice. We get a lot of people who are moving to the area for the first time, so they set up interviews to visit before they move. That's a nice way to go about it and to show interest in the job.

Are there any major turn-offs in a résumé or cover letter that would cause you to toss aside the application?
The humble résumés always get a second look. Egotistical writing styles are easy to pass over.

How do you prefer to receive résumés?
We get them via email, which is really convenient and by mail as well. Email allows us to request a convenient time to talk. That's a great way to get your foot in the door. The most important thing is to follow up with the correspondence. It's nice to have someone follow up to confirm we received the résumé. If they don't hear from us, a second call is welcome. A turn-off would be people who stop by the restaurant in the middle of lunch or dinner service. It shows a lack of forethought.

How do you feel about applicants contacting you to check on the status of their application?
Regular contact is a great thing. It suggests the applicant is serious and interested in gaining employment. Brief, professional conversation is always welcome.

EXPERIENCE/WORK HISTORY For an experience-based résumé, this section is typically the longest on the résumé. Each entry under this heading will list the job title, company name, city and state of employment, and dates of employment. The entries should be listed in reverse chronological order starting with the most recent. Under each entry, the writer should consider including bullet points describing specific accomplishments or job duties. Recent positions should have more bullet points, while older or less impressive positions should have fewer bullets, if any. Each bullet point should use an action verb describing what the person does or did. The description should also be specific and measurable or observable. For example, "managed seven cooks in food production" is a well-written bullet point, while "was responsible for entire kitchen" is not. The writer should trumpet her accomplishments, but no job should have more than five or six bullet points. Each bullet point should fit on a single line with few exceptions. Finally, although people should take credit for their achievements, they must be careful about providing misleading information. When a line cook writes "increased sales by 15 percent over six months," she must be able to describe to an interviewer how she personally increased sales by 15 percent. If she does not have a strong answer, she will be better off writing "cooked on kitchen team during six-month 15% sales increase." Should an interviewer suspect that items on a résumé are exaggerated or inaccurate, she may discount the entire document. Some companies have policies that call for the termination of employees who provide false information on their résumés, so you should take extreme care to ensure that your résumé is accurate.

SKILLS Skills-based résumés will effectively divide the "experience" section into two headings: "skills" and "work history." "Skills" should come first, immediately following "education" for recent college graduates. The skills section may be written in paragraph form, bullet points, or most commonly, a combination of the two. The combination begins with a description of the skills that a person possesses. It may include how the skills were obtained, such as "My experience increasing the family's net worth on a fixed income enhanced my budgeting and fiscal management skills." Alternatively, the paragraph could describe briefly the person's experience in a prior career and provide bullets of the skills mastered during that career. However the section is written it should only focus on the skills relevant to the type of job sought. An employer will stop reading a résumé as soon as she senses that a person cannot differentiate between pertinent and irrelevant job skills.

Unlike the experience-based résumé, the "work history" section of a skills-based résumé is solely a listing in reverse chronological order of previous jobs held. It should include job title, company name and location, and dates of employment, but it should not provide bullet points for any of the jobs. The skills section replaces the need for bullet points by describing in a summary format the transferable skills learned over the person's career or lifetime.

An "additional work experience" section would be appropriate in an experience-based résumé for individuals with significant culinary experience and significant experience in another career. This situation occurs often in the military where an individual has both a military career and a civilian career. In such a situation, the person would record her culinary work experience with bullet points immediately after the education section, and then place a simple, non-bulleted work history of non-culinary jobs under the heading "additional work experience."

AWARDS/HONORS Although some people may eliminate this section, those individuals with at least one award to their credit should share that recognition with potential employers. An award or honor could include anything from a culinary competition medal to an "employee of the month" award at work to an invitation to speak before a professional organization. Awards should be listed in reverse chronological order with the name of the award or honor and the date received.

EXTRACURRICULARS/COMMUNITY SERVICE/ASSOCIATIONS The exact title used for this section will vary from one résumé to another. Its purpose is to show a person's initiative and passion for the field and for the community. An actively involved person suggests a strong work ethic, while someone with no extracurricular activity (or work experience while in school) may come across as lazy on paper. This section should include school club or professional association membership; if the person was a committee chair or club leader, she should also list her title. The section should also list any community service and extracurricular activities. Any activities, whether elementary reading tutor or intramural soccer player, provide a sense that the writer does something productive with her non-class time.

The activities listed need not be culinary-related, although culinary activities will hold more weight with some employers than non-culinary ones. Each entry in this section should list the activity name and dates of involvement.

SKILLS This section is truly optional and should be used only when a person has a specialized skill relevant to the job in question. For example, a person might list "fluency in Spanish" and "CPR certified," as these are sufficiently rare and valuable enough to merit ink. However, "computer literate," though relevant, is not uncommon enough to be included here, and "certified scuba trainer" is not normally pertinent to the culinary field. Items which are directly culinary-related and obvious from a person's work history, such as an expertise in sugar sculpture, are better included earlier in the bullet points under work experience.

18.1.2   Items Not to Include

Whereas some applicants want to share everything with their interviewers in the spirit of complete candor, some information should not be included in a résumé. Personal information, such as race, religion, sex, marital status, sexual preference, having children and childcare arrangements, medical conditions, and age should not be mentioned on a résumé. A person may choose to allude to one or more of these topics as part of a "skills" section (in a skills-based résumé) to illustrate how certain abilities were acquired, but such information is shared at one's own risk. By law, employers are not supposed to consider many of these items in their hiring decisions, but some bias does exist with certain individuals who may influence hiring decisions. Many of these biases rest in stereotypes. An employer may think that a Jewish candidate will never work a Saturday shift, that a woman will never meet the physical demands of a kitchen, or that a parent will call out sick weekly to care for her child. Most of these stereotypes are disproved quickly when an applicant shares her passion, work ethic, and commitment to the job during an interview. But listing such personal information on a résumé may prevent an applicant from getting an interview at all.

In addition to very personal information a résumé should also not list references. A person has the option of: including references on a separate page, stating "references available upon request," or simply not acknowledging references at all on the résumé. Although an applicant will likely need to provide references later, they are an unnecessary consumer of space on a résumé. Most employers will not read them or need them until the interview phase, so there is no benefit to providing them early (unless you list a famous industry person or a professional friend of the interviewer). You are better off using the space for information that will get you an interview.

18.1.3   Stylistic Issues

Because reviewers and readers of résumés typically give each résumé only a few seconds, the style and appearance of a résumé can be as important as its content in impressing the reader. Some young people believe that a two-page résumé is automatically more impressive than a one-pager. On the contrary, a one-page résumé that is packed with information is far more impressive and likely to gain the reviewer's attention than a two-page document with lots of empty space. Many employers will not even read the second page, so critical information must be included on the first page. In almost all cases, a student in culinary school does not have sufficient culinary experience to merit a two-page résumé. Those students with prior

123 Promotion Run
Philadelphia, PA 62626
Phone: (215) 555-7483
Email: John.Doe@resume.com

John Doe, CC

Objective	To prepare high quality appetizers and entrées in an upscale restaurant environment under the tutelage of a talented chef
Education	Colonial Culinary College; Philadelphia, PA *Associate of Applied Science, Culinary Arts* – 1/09; G.P.A. 3.84 Subjects studied: *food safety and sanitation; savory hot and cold food production including soups, appetizers, salads, and entrées; a la carte station mise en place and execution; nutrition; basic bakery production*
Experience 12/07–1/09	**Colonial Cafeteria**; Philadelphia, PA *Line Cook* • Prepared all hot sandwiches with specified accompaniments to order • Designed and prepared daily hot entrée special within budget guidelines • Set up and broke down hot station at beginning and end of shift • Contributed to 2.4% increase in food sales from 2007 to 2008
9/05–6/07	**Bill's Cheese Steaks**; Philadelphia, PA *Prep Cook* • Sliced and par-cooked all onions and bell peppers for sandwiches • Sliced and portioned meat for cheese steak station • Assisted with cheese steak cooking and assembly during busy periods
1/04–8/05	**Pie in the Sky**; Camden, NJ *Pizza Cook* Topped, cooked, and portioned frozen pizzas to order for evening take-out
Awards	Colonial Academic Achievement Award—1/22/09 Employee of the Month, Bill's Cheese Steaks—2/06, 8/06
Extracurriculars	Taste of the Nation, *volunteer*—4/08 Elysian Hospital Health Fair, *cooking demonstrator*—1/08 Colonial Gourmand Club, *Secretary*—2008 Brotherly Love Elementary School, *reading tutor*—9/07–12/08
Skills	Proficient in spoken and written Spanish ServSafe Certified

FIGURE 18.1   Sample Experience-based Résumé

careers should still keep to one page as providing multiple pages of non-culinary experience does not generally impress most culinary employers.

To get a résumé down to a single page, a person must be succinct and selective. What generally drives up the page count is the number and length of bullet points in the experience or skills section. People with long work histories should limit bullet points to the most recent two or three jobs. Keeping each bullet to a single line helps to limit the length of the résumé. If a résumé still goes over a page, the writer should consider eliminating some of the older and briefer job experiences and extracurricular activities. Jobs held in high school are rarely relevant to a person over 40 years of age. A job held for less than three months may portray the applicant as a job hopper; such jobs are best left unlisted unless they can fit on a single page résumé.

---

789 Rocky Road
Manhattan, KS 38720
Cell: (270) 555-0156
Email: Jsdoe@resume.com

Jane Doe

Objective   To obtain entry-level employment preparing food and to continue my culinary education under a talented restaurant chef

Education   Wheatfield Culinary University; Manhattan, KS
Associate of Applied Science, Culinary Arts (anticipated 5/10); G.P.A. 3.9
Subjects studied: *culinary sanitation; a la carte and large scale food production; personnel management; garde manger; breakfast cookery; catering*

Mid-Atlantic Business Academy, Washington, DC
Bachelor of Arts, Business—5/98; G.P.A. 2.7

Skills   My decade of experience in the business world has provided me with strong time management and organization skills. I have learned to work quickly, professionally, and according to the instructions of my supervisor. Knowing the importance of supporting the team, I make arriving to work on time, every day a priority. Most importantly, my passion for food and cooking could not be stronger. Additional skills relevant to food preparation that I possess include:
- Attention to detail
- Attention to workplace cleanliness
- Understanding of inventory control
- Customer-satisfaction mind-set
- Strong financial management ability
- Ability to learn quickly

Work History
8/08–present   Mickey's Diner. Manhattan, KS. Prep Cook
6/04–7/08   Belli & Belli Financial Consultants. Montgomery, AL. Financial Advisor.
6/00–5/04   New Dominion Power and Electric. Richmond, VA. Financial Manager.
9/98–3/00   Berman Brothers. New York, NY. Investment Banker.
5/96–5/98   Knickers. Leesburg, VA. Assistant Manager.
12/95–5/96   Knickers. Leesburg, VA. Retail Customer Associate

Recognitions   Student Government, Vice-President—12/08–present
Dean's List—12/08, 5/09, 12/09
One of only three students invited to assist Chef Carol Moss during her school visit and cooking demonstration for the student body—2/09

Community Service   Wheatfield Culinary University, student math tutor—1/09–present
Helping Hearts Soup Kitchen, weekly volunteer—1/09–present
Shepherd's Church Coats for the Cold, volunteer—11/08–12/08
Kansas Beer Festival, cooking booth volunteer—10/08
Manhattan Fall Harvest Fundraiser, pie service volunteer—9/08

FIGURE 18.2   Sample Skills-based Résumé

By condensing information to a single page a person can also fill her résumé page with text, leaving little white space on the page. As bullet points keep to a single line and do not roll over to a second half line, the page appears fuller. A full page subliminally suggests that a person has so much experience to share she can hardly keep it to one page, whereas a relatively empty page (or worse, two empty pages) implies that a person has to stretch out very little experience to make it appear more substantial than it actually is. Since many reviewers will hardly glance at a second page, a single, densely packed page generally gets better results than a lightly filled two-page résumé. The most densely packed résumé should still appear clean and readable to the eye. Too many fonts make a page look cluttered, so never use more than three fonts including the one you use for your name. Instead, use bold and italic functions to help key information stand out on the page. Assume that the reader will only take the time to skim the bold words; she should still get a strong picture of your qualifications and credentials. Generally, bold the most important information, such as colleges attended, places of employment, and/or job titles to create an easily skimmed version of your résumé.

Choice and size of font should be selected for readability. Fonts should be simple and easy to read. Script or Gothic, for example, do not lend themselves well to a quick glance-over from a reviewer. Rather than slow down to read them, most résumé reviewers will simply toss them out. The font size should be large enough for people to read but not so large that you appear to be compensating for lack of content. Ten to twelve point fonts generally work best although your name should be written in a much larger size. To make your name easy to find when flipping through a stack of résumés, put it to the right or in the center of the page. Americans typically flip through a stack of pages with their right hand, so a left-aligned name is likely to be missed.

Margins, too, contribute to the readability of a résumé. When text runs too close to the edge, it tends to be hidden under the fingers of the person holding and skimming the page. However, margins set too wide make the page seem empty and short on content. Margins set to approximately one inch on all sides of the paper work well although that measurement could be adjusted slightly if it helps to keep the résumé to one page.

Paper quality also sends a subliminal message to the reader. Use white or off-white shades of heavyweight paper for résumés. Other colors come across as whimsical and fun, but not professional. Heavier weight (thickness) in paper also makes the résumé seem more substantial in the reader's hand. A lighter weight paper gets bent, torn, or crumpled more easily. A thicker, stronger paper subliminally suggests that the résumé is worth keeping around. Professional printers, such as Kinko's or Staples, can provide high quality printings of your résumé. Order at least 50 copies to start, as you will send out lots of them during an aggressive job search.

18.1.4 Avoiding Mistakes

The worst problem that a résumé can have is a spelling or format error. A single error can send an otherwise great résumé directly into the trash. Small errors show carelessness and lack of attention to detail—qualities that no employer wants in an employee. Major errors project full-blown incompetence. You should share your résumé with at least one other person to look for spelling or spacing errors before you pay for quality copies. Résumés with errors must be thrown out and redone; they are worthless as a tool to get job interviews.

Résumés can have content errors as well. Unless the writer intentionally lies on the résumé, which can generate long-term problems in maintaining employment, most errors occur when a person forgets to update her résumé with changes to her career. The best way to avoid such oversights is to update your résumé at every job change and after every new award receipt. If you notice that your quality printings are inaccurate, print new copies of an updated résumé and send those instead. By having a current résumé available you will be able to respond to wonderful, but fleeting, job opportunities on a day's notice.

Sometimes a graduating culinary student does not yet know which direction she would like her career to take. Perhaps she wants to work two very different jobs simultaneously, or maybe she just wants to leave the choice to fate. Either way, she may need two different résumés. For example, a graduating student may choose to apply for full-time line cook positions and for part-time restaurant critic jobs. One job requires a focus on culinary skills, while the other needs to highlight writing ability. The work experience will likely be the same, but the bullet points and objectives may differ. The differences between the two may be slight, but a résumé that does not appear appropriate for the type of job sought rarely gets the applicant an interview.

18.2   COVER LETTERS

Cover letters, unlike résumés, are unique to a particular job. They are designed to direct an employer to the applicant's skills most relevant to the available position. Since people do not usually include on their résumés every possible skill they possess, a good cover letter may mention some skills that are missing from the résumé. A cover letter also demonstrates to the reader that the applicant has done some research on the company and on the job. By showing the reader some awareness of the company's philosophy, applicants have greater credibility when they say that they believe themselves qualified for the position.

Interview with Lisa Schroeder, Executive Chef/Owner, Mother's Bistro & Bar & Mamma Mia Trattoria

What do you look for in a résumé when deciding to offer someone an interview?
It should first of all look good: nice paper, good formatting, not a copy of a copy. Try not to use the pre-existing formats that come with every word processing program. Otherwise, your résumé looks like everyone else's. There should absolutely be no misspellings or typographical errors. I would never consider hiring somebody for a sous chef position who could not spell it.

What do you expect to see in a cover letter?
It should be short, well-written (résumé rules apply here, too), and point out what aspects of your experience make you uniquely qualified for the position for which you are applying. Do not repeat all the information in the résumé. No one has time to read things twice. Use the cover letter to sell yourself and why you believe you are the right candidate for the job.

(continued)

(*continued*)

Are there any major turn-offs in a résumé or cover letter that would cause you to toss aside the application?
Shabby presentation, little attention to detail, and misspellings are big turn-offs. Also, I absolutely refuse to consider any applicant who has only spent months at any job. If I don't see tenure at previous positions (at least a year), I do not consider the candidate.

How do you prefer to receive résumés?
I love email because I can look at it on my time, but really prefer that the résumé be included in the body of the email. The problem with that is that it usually messes with the applicant's formatting, but I am always willing to forsake their formatting for convenient reading. Anyone who takes the time to come down to my restaurant with a résumé is always considered above all others. If one is willing to take the time to show up in person, even if only dropping off a résumé, I always try to make the time to talk to them, and give their application extra attention.

How do you feel about applicants contacting you to check on the status of their application?
If someone wants a job badly enough, they should follow up and check back. That keeps them top of mind. I truly believe that it's the squeaky wheel that gets oiled, and it's the vocal candidate who gets hired. Regular (but not annoying) contact is a great thing.

As with résumés a cover letter must be accurate and straightforward. A letter that possesses misleading or outright false information will get the applicant in trouble during the job application process. Because you must write a new cover letter for each position, you must double-check each one to make sure that you have not mistakenly included information from another company or job. A small error such as this will send your résumé right to the trash can. Fortunately, although it does take time to write a cover letter for each application, cover letters generally follow the same format each time. To make the letter writing process faster, you can set up a basic template with some stock language and then insert the specifics for each job. Although the sections do not include headings, like a résumé does, a cover letter generally has the following elements:

WRITER'S ADDRESS AND DATE   The letter, like all formal business letters, begins by listing the sender's mailing address and the date that the letter is written. Both are tabbed over far to the right of the page. Whether the applicant is submitting a résumé by mail, fax, email, or in person, this information should always be included in the cover letter.

ADDRESSEE'S INFORMATION   The name and address of the person to whom the letter is sent is listed next. This information is aligned with the left of the page. It begins with the full name and title of the addressee on one line and that person's mailing address on the following lines. In the event that the address or name of the letter's recipient is not known this section may be omitted.

SALUTATION   This simple greeting is generally in the form of "Dear Mr./Mrs. (last name of recipient)." If the person's name is not known, the letter may be addressed "Dear Sir or Madam" or "To whom it may concern." All salutations in a professional letter end with a colon.

OPENING PARAGRAPH The first paragraph of the body of the letter generally states the name of the specific job for which the applicant is applying. Many companies have multiple job openings at one time, so a letter that does not specifically mention a job may go to the wrong department. If the letter does not get to the proper reader, the applicant will not be given an interview. This paragraph should also mention how the sender learned of the position. The writer could state that she saw an ad in the newspaper or online. Alternatively, she could mention the name of the professional friend who recommended she apply for the position, if that friend has a connection to the company.

MAIN PARAGRAPH The second paragraph of the letter should describe what the applicant knows about the company and the job and why the applicant is qualified for the job. To sound knowledgeable about the position the writer should do some research about the company. The more informed she appears, the more impressed the reader will be. The writer may also wish to mention why she is looking for work at this time. However, the applicant should only mention this information if she has a good reason for looking. Good reasons include personal growth, relocation, or graduation from school. Better hours, more money, or current unemployment are not reasons that should be mentioned in the letter.

CLOSING PARAGRAPH The final paragraph should state the applicant's interest in getting an interview to speak further about the job. The writer should also state how best to contact her and the best time to reach her.

Ms. Agatha Halline
742 Big Sky Road
Ranch, MT 73402
January 11, 2009

Chef Melinda Money
Garden State Catering
3 Cliffside Way
Trenton, NJ 08950

Dear Chef Money:

    I am writing to apply for the line cook position that was advertised in the January 8th issue of the *Trenton Tribune*.

    I will complete my culinary associate degree from Herdsman Culinary College in March, and I am looking to move to the East Coast for my first industry position. I have researched your company, and your reputation for high quality cuisine using local ingredients appeals to me greatly. As a recent culinary school graduate, I have a strong foundation in foodservice sanitation and basic culinary skills. However, I know that I have a lot to learn, and I would like to continue to learn under your tutelage. Although I am just entering the industry, I believe you will find me passionate about cooking, catering, and the importance of supporting local farmers. I am also a hard worker and a fast learner as my 3.84 G.P.A. suggests.

    I have enclosed my résumé for your review, and I hope that you will consider granting me an interview. You can best reach me by email at ahalline@hccmt.edu, but you are welcome to contact me by phone at 909-555-0012 as well. I look forward to hearing from you soon.

Respectfully,
Agatha Halline

FIGURE 18.3 Sample Cover Letter

CLOSING AND SIGNATURE The letter should close with a professional, not personal, closing. "Sincerely" and "Respectfully" work well; "Fondly" and "Yours Truly" do not. The letter should end with the writer's name and signature. The applicant should leave several spaces between the closing and her printed full name for the signature. The signature always comes above the writer's printed name. Cover letters are usually fairly formal, so the letter should look like a page from a book rather than a work of art. The letter should be written in a single 12 or 14 point font. If at all possible, the letter should be kept to one page. Because cover letters, unlike résumés, are rewritten for every job application, they may be printed on a home printer using plain, white paper.

18.3 SENDING THE COMMUNIQUÉ

How the cover letter and résumé are sent is also important in portraying a professional image. If the papers are sent in the mail, you should type or neatly print the address on the envelope; typing is generally better. If you are faxing the papers, always use a fax cover sheet. The cover sheet should include the name or department to which the fax is going. Such information is often included in a help wanted ad. The fax cover sheet should name the position for which the person is applying in case the receiver is collecting résumés for multiple job openings (and not reading the cover letters). Emails follow similar protocol. The text of the email should include the job title for which the person is applying. The cover letter may be sent either as the body of the email or as an attachment, but the résumé should always be sent as an attachment to the email. To be sure that your résumé is easy for the recipient to locate after she downloads it onto her computer always name the attachment "(your name) résumé."

When sending a cover letter and résumé always use the form of submission requested by the company. If the advertisement requests a fax, then send a fax; if it states mail, then mail a letter. Do not hand-deliver a résumé, unless the ad states that applications must be completed in person. Dropping in unannounced on a manager and requesting to speak with her in person when a fax submission has been specifically requested is rude and often annoying to the manager. Employers want to see that you can follow directions during the application process, and ignoring their specific directions will get your résumé thrown out without a review.

18.4 NORMAL EXPECTATIONS

Although everyone who enters a job search would love to get an offer from every résumé sent, such a response is entirely unrealistic. A typical job search in an average market requires an individual to send out 100 résumés to get ten interviews yielding one or two job offers. Stronger résumés and candidates may do better. Higher caliber positions and high paying jobs are generally more difficult to get, but fortunately, students usually apply for entry-level positions, which are much easier for culinary school graduates to obtain. By refining your writing skills, building lots of volunteer experience, getting good grades, and aiming for appropriate caliber jobs based on experience rather than on money, you will get a much higher percentage of responses than the average student.

Recognize that the job search process does take time. Job searches can take three to six months in some cases, although some entry-level culinary jobs can often be acquired in a matter of days or weeks. Do not get frustrated if you receive few or no responses to your résumé in the first couple of weeks; however, do look critically at your résumé if no one calls after a couple of months. You may need to get assistance adjusting the résumé to get a better response, or you may need to aim for a different caliber job at this point in your career.

To give yourself the best chance of gaining employment prior to graduation, start applying for work at least three months before your last day of school. This advance planning should give you sufficient time to go through the interview process with several companies. If an employer likes your résumé but does not have a position open months in advance, stay in touch with that employer during your final three months of school. See if you can interview with that company anyway to prove your qualifications. Then, check back with the employer as graduation approaches. Because the culinary industry has a high turnover rate, many companies find that they need to hire new employees nearly every month. With proper planning, a quality résumé, and a well-written cover letter a culinary student will earn several job offers well before that final day of school.

Summary

A résumé is a snapshot of a person's skills and experience, and its purpose is to get an individual an interview for a job. Résumés have many possible sections, but the most common are: name and contact information, objective, education, experience/work history, skills, additional work experience, awards/honors, extracurriculars/community service/associations, and skills. A résumé should not include private, personal information or references. To appear professional and substantial, a résumé should be a full page with little blank space, bold in places to direct the reader's eye, and printed on heavyweight white or off-white paper. Cover letters are written for a specific job application and accompany a résumé. They generally state how an applicant learned of a job opening, what she knows about the job, and why she believes she is qualified. It should close with a request for an interview. Résumés and cover letters should be sent according to the instructions requested by the hiring company. Students should plan for a job search to last at least three months, and they should expect to send out as many as 100 résumés to get sufficient job offers. With proper planning and quality résumés and cover letters a typical student can expect to leave school with a job offer.

KEY SECTIONS TO INCLUDE IN A RÉSUMÉ

- Name and Contact Information
- Objective
- Education
- Experience or Work History (experience-based résumé)
- Skills and Work History (skills-based résumé)
- Additional Work Experience
- Awards or Honors
- Extracurriculars or Community Service or Associations
- Skills

Suggested Tasks

1. Ask friends, colleagues, and industry professionals for copies of their résumés. You should gather at least ten different ones. Analyze each of them to decide what you like best and what you like least. Write down your own information to include in a résumé. Put that information into a format that incorporates your favorite elements from the collected résumés. Share your first draft with a job placement advisor for critique. Make the changes she suggests.

2. Locate two jobs openings in the culinary field. Research each of the companies and the specific jobs. Write out at least five key points about the company and five key points about the job. Select three points from the pool of ten that align with your skill set and/or personal interests. Write a draft cover letter to each of the companies highlighting the connection between you and the job. Share the cover letter with your instructor.

3. Interview a culinary professional who might review résumés and applications for your ideal first job after graduation. Ask her what she looks for in a résumé when deciding whether or not to interview someone. Ask how much style and format play into her decision. Share the results of your interview with your classmates.

4. Interview a graduating student or a recent culinary graduate about her job search. Ask where she looked for job openings, how many résumés she sent out, and how many interview offers she received. Find out where she located the job she ultimately took. Also ask how long it took her to create her résumé and how long the job search lasted. Share the results of your interview with your classmates.

CHAPTER 19

Interviewing Skills

The interview phase of a job search is much more competitive than the résumé phase, for the other interviewees have already outlasted most of the initial applicants. To select the best candidate for a job, a skilled interviewer typically evaluates the applicant's skill sets, passion for and knowledge about the position, and interpersonal skills. An interviewer generally asks about the candidate's work experience and may ask the applicant to answer several hypothetical questions. Ideally, an interviewer also shares with the applicant a good amount of information about the company and about the job to help entice the individual to accept the position if offered.

To differentiate between equally qualified candidates an interviewer may turn toward seemingly insignificant particulars of an applicant's interview, so every detail matters in the interview process. A candidate needs to come armed with information about the company and to practice answers to likely questions. The interviewee should dress professionally and pay close attention to body language and personal speech. Sometimes a friendly smile and a strong handshake make the difference between winning an offer and getting rejected. High caliber companies will assess every interaction with an applicant from phone calls prior to the interview to follow-up conversations afterwards. Knowing how to interview well increases the chances that a person will receive a job offer from a competitive company.

In this chapter, you will learn how to communicate with potential employers prior to an interview and how to prepare for an interview. You will learn what approaches work best in an interview. You will also learn how to follow up professionally with the interviewer after the interview is over. Finally, you will learn how to handle a job offer if one is extended to you.

19.1 PRE-INTERVIEW COMMUNICATION

Because interviewers evaluate every interaction that they have with an applicant, a person must portray professionalism and enthusiasm in every phone call, letter, and email. The applicant should speak politely, clearly, and respectfully to everyone in the company. A secretary who is belittled by a job applicant will surely share his disapproval with the interviewer. For a highly competitive job, a poor "phone" impression will all but guarantee that the job goes to someone else. Emails should possess a professional tone with no spelling errors. They should also be written as letters and not as text messages. Writing "thx" or "c u l8r" in an email comes across as childish and immature rather than as professional.

Sometimes the applicant will contact the company to follow up on a résumé. Following up on a résumé is a great way to make sure that a résumé gets reviewed, but the applicant must avoid harassing the employer and leaving him with a bad impression. To check on the status of his résumé, the applicant should call or email the employer two to three days after the résumé's anticipated arrival. The applicant should merely ask for verification that the résumé has arrived and that it has gotten to the proper reviewer. The candidate may also ask when the company anticipates contacting the finalists for interviews and if he should call or write back at that time. If the interviewer grants permission to call again, then the applicant may call back on the date given. This repeated contact helps the interviewer to remember the applicant's name and to perceive him as an interested go-getter who really wants the job. If the interviewer asks the applicant not to call back, then the applicant should respect that request. Ignoring requests from the company does not leave a positive impression with the interviewer. For companies that grant permission to contact them about the status of the interview process, applicants may call back as often as once per week until the job has been filled. Calling back any more frequently will annoy the interviewer and come across more as desperation rather than as interest and enthusiasm.

Eventually an interviewer will call the finalists to schedule interviews. When that person calls you, you should agree to a date and time that you can make without fail. If you arrive late or not at all, you will not get the job. Should you have an emergency that will cause you to miss the interview, contact the interviewer immediately to see if you can reschedule; however, recognize that some employers will not accommodate you and may simply eliminate you from the running. When you receive an opportunity to interview with a company, be sure to ask for the location and contact person for the interview. Some companies have multiple buildings with many offices, so you will need to ask for directions to the interviewer's office. You will likely not need to communicate with the company again before the interview, but you should call one to two days in advance to confirm the interview, location, and contact person. If you are unfamiliar with the area and need directions, you should ask for them at

---

Interview with Matthew Camp, Executive Sous Chef, The International Golf Club, The Culinary Institute of America, Graduation: AOS 2002, BPS 2004

What advanced preparation did you do to prepare for job interviews?
I would always look in advance through the Web site the company has set up and for any kind of background on the people I'm interviewing with, like the chef. I will call my colleagues, too, to see if they have any information.

How did you decide whom to include in a list of references?
I always come with a list of six—three I give upfront, and three I use as backup. The first of the core three would have to be a person directly involved with my career, either a past employer or chef-instructor. The second person is a past professor or

(continued)

(continued)

colleague I know who is in the business I'd like to get into, but not necessarily an employer. The third person is a friend, but not family, who can explain or describe my personal characteristics. The other three references are the same breakdown but as backups.

When interviewing, what things do you do to perform well in the interview?
Dress to impress is my number one rule. Also, I always do a virtual run-through of the interview the night before to help me sleep a little better because I've worked out potential kinks in the interviewing process. It gives me a game plan and organizes my mental mise en place. On the day of the interview, I read over the information one more time to feel confident and to be prepared.

What follow-up did you do after the interviews?
I usually let it go for 2–3 days. Then I touch base back to see how they're feeling, unless they contact me first. I take everyone individually to determine how quick to do a follow-up, but no sooner than two days. I'll send either an email or a thank you note, especially when looking at a sought-after position where I may be one of 7–10 candidates.

Have you ever negotiated for higher wages, benefits, etc.? What did you do?
What I do is to make a pro and con list of what the job offer entails and what pros and cons the job provides. If it all weighs out, I look at potential living arrangements and if that wage will work for me personally. If all the answers point to "yes," there's no negotiation. When I do negotiate for higher wages, I come back with a "little extra" list. I go in-depth on things I may not have brought up in the interview and then end the discussion with a new offer of what is right for me. For new students, the early jobs are stepping stones to start a career, so a new graduate may have to humble himself and take a little less. I took a job once worth $20,000 more than I got, but it opened doors to upper-management positions just two years later.

this time. It is better to request help than to drive around lost for hours only to arrive late to the interview. Finally, during the confirmation call, ask how many people will speak with you during the day of the interview. Knowing how many interviewers to expect often helps a person to remain calm in the event of a group interview. By asking for information professionally and politely, you will not only appear confident and organized to the interviewer but you will gain some idea of what to expect when you arrive.

19.2   ADVANCE PREPARATION

To prepare thoroughly for the interview, the applicant should research the company and the open position as much as possible. By knowing the company's values, brand, mission, and products/services the applicant can adjust his answers to show off those skills and attributes most valuable to the company. When an interviewee displays little knowledge about an organization, that person appears interested solely in locating an income. Most employers know that a person who is passionate about work beyond the income it provides will perform better on the job and not leave for another position elsewhere simply because it pays more money. Applicants who demonstrate strong knowledge of the organization appear enthusiastic and committed to the work and to the company's values. Since no supervisor can train "passion," such employees are extremely valuable and desirable in any organization.

In addition to conducting research, you should arrange your personal life around the interview so that no conflicts or emergencies arise. If you have children, you should confirm babysitting arrangements. If you have car trouble, you should arrange alternate transportation. Interviewers will not care why you miss an interview opportunity; they will merely assume that you do not have sufficient control over your life to get to an interview (and by extension, to the job) on time every day. Creating such a perception effectively kills your chances of getting that job.

Applicants should use the days prior to the interview to practice their answers to probable questions. Most interviewers ask applicants about their work history and about the skills that are most relevant to the position. By comparing your own skills and work history to what you know about a company, you can prepare answers that show off the skills most likely to be important to the interviewer. Interviewers also tend to ask why an applicant wants to work for an organization. For graduates right out of college, expressing a desire to learn and to grow generally impresses interviewers; stating that you need to work for the money does not usually endear you to the interviewer. You can practice role playing the interview with a teacher, placement counselor, or even a friend to help you feel more at ease when the actual interview finally arrives.

In addition to mental preparation, there are some concrete items every interviewee must gather in advance of an interview. You must acquire proper clothing for the interview if you do not already own professional dress. Applicants should wear business attire to an interview; chef uniforms should be reserved for cooking tryouts only. You should make enough extra copies of your résumé and cover letter to provide a copy to everyone attending the interview. You should prepare and bring a list of references in case the interviewer requests it, and you should bring your professional portfolio if you have one. Gathering these items in advance will keep you from racing frantically to gather them on interview day, a day when your mental energy is better spent focused on your answers and on remaining calm.

19.2.1 The Reference List

Preparing a list of references is fairly simple, but an error in the process can cost you a job. Begin by thinking of five to ten people who have worked with you in the past and who can attest to your job skills and to your work ethic. Do not include relatives. Co-workers are appropriate, but teachers and supervisors are much better references. Once you have your list, contact these potential references to confirm their contact information and to ask if you can use them for a reference. If anyone provides even the slightest hesitation, do not include that person on the list. Some people agree to serve as references even though they may provide only a mediocre depiction of your skills, so make sure that your references are enthusiastic and positive about you. Once you have your confirmations, whittle down the list to the three to five individuals most likely to give you a glowing reference. Your list must include one supervisor or teacher though, for an absence of supervisors suggests that your bosses do not think highly of you. Prepare a single reference page that lists your final choices. Each reference should include the person's name, title, company/employer, phone, email, and mailing address. The page heading should state "References for (your name)," and it should appear neat and professional. Optimally, the references should fit on a single page.

```
┌─────────────────────────────────────────┐
│                                           │
│             References                    │
│            For Jane Doe                   │
│                                           │
│        Katherine Alabaster                │
│        Chef-Instructor                    │
│        Milliner Culinary Academy          │
│        9 Icicle Lane                      │
│        Bear, AK 99887                     │
│        (907) 555-0987                     │
│        K.Alabaster@milliner.edu           │
│                                           │
│        Leslie Moore                       │
│        Sous Chef                          │
│        The Snowshoe Inn                   │
│        1922 Main Street                   │
│        Juneau, AK 99801                   │
│        (907) 555-1984                     │
│        lesismoore@aka.com                 │
│                                           │
│        Steven Woods                       │
│        Teacher                            │
│        Bear High School                   │
│        16 Mountain Road                   │
│        Bear, AK 99887                     │
│        (907) 555-1556                     │
│        stevenwoods@bear.k12.ak.us         │
│                                           │
└─────────────────────────────────────────┘
```

FIGURE 19.1   Sample Reference Page

19.2.2   The Professional Portfolio

Although not all culinary professionals possess a portfolio, presenting one to a potential employer provides concrete evidence of one's talents and abilities in a visual manner. To create a portfolio you should take or collect photographs representative of your best culinary work. You should also gather any certificates, awards, letters of recognition, and a copy of your résumé. Most professionals use transparent sleeves that can be inserted into a three-ring binder to hold their documentation. Pages are inserted into the sleeves to protect the information inside while allowing the reader to see what is included in the sleeve. Multiple photographs can be taped or glued to a page (if they are not electronically printed on the page) with simple captions written underneath describing the food, event, and/or date of the work in the photo. Photos should only depict work prepared in part or entirely by the portfolio's owner; presenting someone else's work as one's own is not only unethical but dangerous. Chef Ian Ale, now retired, tells of an applicant who presented a portfolio showing photos of work that Chef Ale recognized as that of professional colleagues. Not only did the applicant not get the job, but the stories that spread within the culinary community of his attempted misrepresentation made it difficult for the applicant to find work anywhere in the area.

A portfolio shows not only a person's past accomplishments but also his ability to compile and to present his work in a professional manner. Appearance is important. A good portfolio looks clean and organized. Using a three-ring binder allows you to add to your portfolio as your achievements increase and to change the photos as your skills improve.

Recent culinary school graduates will have shorter portfolios than seasoned professionals. A few pages of high quality work are much more effective in impressing employers than many pages of lower quality work. If you do not have many photographs of high-caliber culinary work that you have prepared, do not present a portfolio at an interview. A portfolio is not necessary to acquire most entry-level jobs, but a bad portfolio can keep you from getting a job. There is always time to put together a portfolio in your first year after graduation as long as you retain all of your certificates and documentation of awards and recognitions. You can begin taking photographs of your culinary work at any point to include in a portfolio, but realize that a portfolio can take months to compile. You should start to put together a portfolio before you begin your next job search, not after you are invited to interview for a position.

Interview with Ris Lacoste, Chef, Washington, DC

During an interview, what do you look for from a potential applicant?
Bring a copy of a résumé. Some chefs do not file well and most will have no idea where your résumé is. In an advanced interview, the places you have worked, the pedigree you are establishing, and the length of time you have held your jobs will be of the most importance. In a rookie interview, I look more for presentation of the résumé, attention to detail, education, etc. It tells me about the person, but then I go to personality and enthusiasm to make my decision.

- Timeliness is huge. Be on time for the interview.
- Any efforts at grooming, dressing well, caring for self, putting in the effort to make a good impression are always welcome.
- Honesty—don't be more than you are. If you are green, you are green. Say what you know; don't try to over-impress.
- Openness—be excited but let yourself be nervous. Interviewing is tough; it never gets easier.
- Passion—we love passion. You have to have it; show it.
- Preparedness—do your homework; be ready for the interview. Know about the restaurant, the chef, yourself, and what you want. Be ready to talk about yourself. Ask questions about the process, the service, the dining room, the kitchen, everything.
- Availability—you can work any time!
- Willingness to do whatever it takes to get in the door and learn all day every day.

Does having a professional portfolio increase an applicant's chances of getting a job?
Hiring from the school level, a portfolio is certainly not necessary. I don't discourage creating one to start a journal of one's career, but it is certainly not necessary for an interview. Cooks need to cook.

What kind of follow-up do you like from job applicants after the interview?
Generally, I have made my decision by the end of the interview. I get a pulse of the applicant's feelings and usually give a day or two of mutual time to think about it, unless we decide right then and there that we are suited for each other. I do follow up on references. If I do ask the applicant to call me, I expect a call, whether or not they are interested. Other than that, just follow whatever instructions I may give. They should make sure to ask any questions of things expected of them that are not clear. No questions are stupid.

(continued)

(*continued*)

Do you ever negotiate wages with job applicants?
Most chefs have an established range of pay for each level of applicant. Consideration is taken for experience, of course. The applicant should be prepared to offer a wage request. It is then up to the chef to consider the value you bring, the need he has for you, and the budget available. Each situation will be different.

19.3   THE INTERVIEW ITSELF

On the day of the interview you should arrive early to the location. You should enter the building about 15 minutes early to use the restroom, to check your appearance, and to locate the interviewer. In addition to copies of your résumé, cover letter, reference list, and possibly portfolio, you should bring a pen and paper on which to write notes during the interview. The interviewer may provide critical information about the job or about the application process that you want to remember. Having something to write on allows you to focus on your continued performance in the interview instead of on the information you wish to recall later.

When you first meet the interviewer, you should stand, shake hands firmly, and smile. You should display quiet confidence and enthusiasm in your body language and in your tone of voice. You should sit only when invited to do so by the interviewer, and if offered a beverage, you should either politely decline or request water. Drinking during an interview can become a distraction to you and to the interviewer, and you run the risk of spilling something on your clothes. Finally, you should offer the interviewer a copy of your résumé and cover letter. He may decline, but the offer shows that you have considered his needs in your preparation for the interview—a positive quality for anyone working in the hospitality industry.

During the interview the interviewer will ask a range of questions both to hear your qualifications and to observe how you communicate. You should answer questions completely, directly, and honestly. Many interviewers can tell when you are lying, so do not do it. You should speak at a normal pace and tone, and you should avoid babbling or talking for too long on any single question. Most questions can be answered fully in just a couple of minutes; a five-minute answer is a long one. Talking too much communicates nervousness or lack of conviction in your answers. However, you will need to give more than a one-word answer to most questions to avoid appearing shallow or uncomfortable with human interaction.

So how should you portray yourself right out of school when your work experience is obviously limited? First, show your knowledge of the company in your answers. Simply showing that you have done your research will catch the attention of the interviewer. Next, accept that everyone knows that recent culinary graduates have much to learn. If you dwell on your exceptional culinary prowess, the interviewer may presume you an egocentric with no concept of your industry greenness. However, if you acknowledge that you have a strong foundation but much to learn, the interviewer will find you credible and honest. You should stress those qualities which have little to do with experience but everything to do with success on the job. Discuss your work ethic, attention to detail, ability to follow directions, and desire to learn. Most chefs prefer someone who wants to learn and to adapt to a kitchen's unique culture over an applicant who purports to know everything. You should highlight the strong foundation you have received from your education and from any prior work experience, but you should never claim it as more than a foundation on which you hope to build.

Most interviewers give applicants the opportunity to ask questions themselves. Some people believe that there are taboo interview questions or that you must ask some questions of the employer when given the opportunity. Asking questions simply to ask something comes across as insincere and awkward. Although it is not necessary to ask questions, you should be sure to get whatever information you need to make your decision should you receive a job offer. You should leave with all of your questions answered, and you should not worry about how asking a question that is important to you makes you appear to the interviewer. (The only "taboo" question that you can safely avoid is pay rate; you will learn the answer to this question when you get an offer.) For example, if you know that you can never work overtime because of your childcare arrangement, you should feel comfortable asking whether or not overtime will ever be required for a job. If the question makes you appear less desirable in the employer's eyes, so be it. You would not be able to succeed on a job that required overtime given this scenario. The interview process is as much for you to decide if you want to work for a company as it is for the company to decide if it wants to hire you.

To close your questions you may wish to ask, "What is the next step?" You should continue to converse with the interviewer under the assumption that you are still a contender for the job (even if the interview has been a disaster). Most interviewers will not give you a job offer on the spot, so asking what to expect next is appropriate. Some companies will require another round of interviews or a hands-on tryout while others will simply contact you later to make an offer. Once the interviewer has briefed you on the next step, you should offer to leave a copy of your references with him if you have not done so already. If you have a portfolio with you, you should offer to show it to the interviewer before you leave.

Interview with Holly Smith, Chef/Owner, Café Juanita

What communication do you expect to have with an interviewee prior to an interview?
I expect a résumé and cover letter sent, and ideally the cover letter is specifically addressed to me and shows an interest and understanding of my restaurant. Knowledge is key, and preparation shows that you are genuinely interested in working for me, not just in getting a job. Homework lets me know you care. Asking for the hiring manager or chef, and having no idea of who that person is, is a turn-off.

What advance preparation do you expect applicants to do prior to interviewing with you?
Read the menu. Read reviews or articles, and research what we do. This should be a two-way street. You need to know what you are interviewing for as best as you can to ensure success all the way around.

During an interview, what do you look for from an applicant?
A firm handshake is a must; this is an immediate turn-off for me if it is weak or a half shake. Eye contact and communication skills are a must. You can certainly be nervous, but you need to be connected and active in the interview.

(continued)

(continued)

Do you require hands-on tryouts of applicants?
Yes, we will bring a candidate back in for a "trail" be it a cook, server, or busser. They are not allowed to do much in my kitchen or floor. Basic prep: picking herbs, peeling onions, and cleaning shallots, are standard. The test in my kitchen is perfect shallots; knife skills and speed can be easily assessed. We hope you will show us how you are physically in a kitchen and that everyone gets a chance to get to know you somewhat. Ideally, the "trailer" also finds the right moments to watch the food, see the pace of my line, and again get a sense if they will fit into my kitchen.

What kind of follow-up do you like from job applicants after the interview?
I like a person who follows up after an interview, be it by email or phone. I try to set a reasonable expectation for a call back from me. If we interviewed but had no job at that moment, following up monthly is great.

Do you ever negotiate wages with applicants?
I do not negotiate the hiring wage, but I do set parameters for raises and a timeline for those raises. The candidate needs to agree to our terms. This would be different, I assume, for hiring in a manager, but I believe in paying well, giving raises regularly, and promoting from within.

As the interviewer has invited you to the interview, he will let you know when it has concluded. Wait to stand and to leave until the interviewer has stood up or has stated that the interview is over. You should smile and shake hands firmly with the interviewer before leaving no matter how well (or poorly) the interview has gone. You should also thank the interviewer for his time, for his time gives you an opportunity to earn a job. Most interviews only take an hour, but you should leave several hours free in your schedule just in case it runs long. Ending an interview prematurely may not provide the interviewer the time and information he needs to make a decision. If you have prepared properly and shown interest, competence, and confidence without too much egoism, you will have a good shot at getting a job offer.

19.3.1 Multiple Interviews

Some companies require a series of interviews with multiple people. A human resources director may want you to meet with the chef; the chef may want you to speak with the food and beverage director. Although the same guidelines for interviewing still apply, there are a few extra bits of information to know. First, remember that each person with whom you speak has not met you before, so you should treat each interview as if it is your first with that company. You will likely repeat much of what you said in a prior interview, but if you appear bored or frustrated with repeating yourself, you will come across as a potentially unpleasant employee. Second, after the interviews are complete the multiple interviewers will consult with each other about you. Therefore, your answers should remain consistent from one interview to the next. You need not repeat your answers word for word, but you should not contradict things that you said with a previous interviewer. Contradictions leave interviewers confused about your true beliefs on a subject. Finally, maintain patience with the process. Some companies take months to hire people. Taking out your frustration with the long process on the interviewers always backfires.

19.3.2 Hands-on Tryouts

Some kitchens require a practical exam or a day of working in the kitchen as part of the interview process. This approach allows the chef and the other kitchen staff to observe your sanitation, speed, organization, skills, accuracy, ability to follow directions, and ability to work with others. A hands-on tryout is generally more accurate than a sit-down interview in evaluating a person's culinary ability, so more and more kitchens are employing this approach to hiring. When working in a kitchen, keep in mind that everyone around you is evaluating you. Show kindness and courtesy to everyone from dishwashers and servers to the other cooks; they all have the ability to sabotage your employment if they find you unpleasant. When potential co-workers genuinely like and respect you, they often put in a good word for you to the chef.

Some chefs notify their applicants of what to expect during a tryout, while others cloak the process in secrecy. If you know in advance what you will be doing, practice those skills repeatedly before the tryout. However, in many cases you will know nothing about the tryout. In these instances just relax. Get a good night's sleep before the tryout, and try to remain calm and focused in the kitchen. Arrive in full uniform with your knife kit, and make sure that your knives are sharp before you get there. If you perform your best in the kitchen, you can leave with your head held high whether or not you receive a job offer.

19.4 POST-INTERVIEW FOLLOW-UP

After an interview many applicants simply return home and wait for a call from the employer. To stand out from the crowd and to demonstrate continued interest in the job, send a thank you note to the interviewer. An email is acceptable for saying "thank you," but a handwritten note is much better. The note can be brief, simply thanking the interviewer for his time and expressing your continued interest in the job. (If you have decided not to pursue the position any further, you should let the interviewer know immediately.) A thank you note not only shows class and professionalism, but it also helps an applicant to stand out from others who fail to send a note.

Most job applicants leave their final interview knowing when the company expects to make a hiring decision. If the company does not contact you by the "decision" date, you may call or email the interviewer to see if a decision on the job has been made. One call shows your continued interest in the job; you should never call daily or pressure the interviewer to rush a decision. Appearing desperate by calling repeatedly does not make you more desirable in the eyes of the interviewer.

Because job seekers often interview with multiple companies simultaneously, sometimes an applicant accepts a position with one company before hearing back from another one. In this situation you should notify the companies still in the decision process immediately. This simple courtesy shows professionalism and respect for the interviewer. It may also help you should you apply to that company in the future. You should always remain professional and courteous with all interactions with an organization even if you do not intend to work there, for you never know when you may need to apply for a job with that company again.

Interview with Sherry Klein, Director—Graduate Employment Services, Sullivan University

How do you work with students to help them prepare a professional portfolio?
That is done from day one in orientation. I instruct students to take pictures from the beginning of their program at each step of the process in a dish, especially for visual things like decorating a cake. Put your name in the photo to show that it is yours, not someone else's. If you make up a signature recipe, include that. Make sure the portfolio looks professional, neat, and precise. Include a résumé and letter of introduction. Pictures should have captions to describe them. Never leave the portfolio as it might get damaged or lost. Don't include recipes that are not your own.

What tips do you recommend for students to help them perform well in an interview?
Wear clean chef jacket, black dress pants, and clean shoes. Come clean-shaven with an ironed, pressed uniform and groomed hair and nails. Bring a résumé on clean résumé paper. Make sure that the contact information on the résumé is up-to-date. I recommend a mock interview to prepare. I go over what the employer is looking for to make sure the student can do that work. In the interview discuss only the information that is relevant; don't go into personal information that isn't professional. If a student has never worked before, then they need to get a part-time job while in school. It is difficult to get a job with no work experience at all. Finally, never ask a "me" question (for example, "What are you going to give me?"). If the employer is interested in you, they will tell you all of that information—salary, perks, etc.—or it will come up with the job offer later. If the employer brings it up and you don't understand, then you can ask questions to clarify. Always think about what you (the interviewee) can do for them to stand out above all other applicants.

What advice would you give a student about wage negotiations?
I tell students to do a Web search first and look at the city in which they are interviewing (on salary.com) to see what that position should be paying. See what the going rate is. You don't need to go backward in salary, only forward. If offered a salary range that the student cannot live with, then the student needs to be honest about their comfort level with the salary. Ask the employer if the salary is negotiable. If the employer stands firm, do not cave in. Nine times out of ten, if they really want you, they will find a way to come up with your salary needs. Hand the employer a list of all the things you can do or have done in a previous job to show why you should command a higher salary. Sometimes they need to see the list rather than just hearing you say it.

19.5 GETTING THE OFFER

After many rounds of interviews, tryouts, and job applications you will eventually get a job offer from someone. If you have asked appropriate questions during the interview, you will already know the parameters of the job. If you have any constraints or requirements regarding the position, you must state them upfront prior to accepting the offer. For example, if you have a week-long vacation planned in three months, get your employer to agree to grant you the time off as part of the conditions of employment. If your childcare arrangement prevents you from arriving to work before 8:30 a.m., then share that constraint with the employer, and do not accept a job starting at 8:00 a.m. until the company has agreed to change the job hours. Once you have accepted a job offer, you have no leverage to negotiate any changes to the parameters of the job. Should the company not agree to a change in job terms, you still have the ability to accept or decline the offer, but you should not take a job whose requirements you cannot meet. To do so almost always results in rapid termination from the company and in a return to the job market.

Most entry-level positions have hourly wages that are not negotiable; however, there is no downside to countering a job offer from an employer to get higher wages. If you really want to work for a certain chef but cannot live off of the wage offered, reply that you cannot accept the position unless it pays (insert your amount) dollars. A company that cannot increase the offer will let you know and will still give you a chance to accept or to decline the job at the lower rate. However, if the company agrees to your terms, you must accept the offer immediately. To attempt to negotiate an even better deal at this point will likely cause you to lose the job offer entirely.

In a negotiation the side with the most information is generally in the best position to win the better deal. Employers who ask for your income requirements do so to gain the advantage in negotiating. For example, if you state that you must earn $20/hour to accept a job and the company would have gone as high as $25/hour, the company saves $5/hour on your wages. (If you state $30/hour, the company will still only offer you $25/hour.) When asked for your income requirements, always reply that they are "negotiable." The company will offer a low-ball wage, but you can counter to negotiate a higher offer. To negotiate professionally without sounding negative, simply state "I'll take the job if you can bring the salary to [insert your counter-offer]." The offer should not be substantially different (double, for example), but a slightly higher counteroffer is both professional and effective. Most companies will increase the rate a little if they can afford it, although they do not always increase it to the level you request. You can continue to make counteroffers until the company stops increasing its offer. At that point you need either to accept or to decline the offer as it stands.

Some people worry that countering an offer may cost them the job entirely. Remember that the company offers the position to the applicant it finds most qualified and will continue to offer that position to the best candidate until that person declines the company's final offer. Rarely, if ever, does a company hang up the phone and make an offer to a second-choice candidate simply because the better candidate makes a counteroffer. So feel comfortable making a counteroffer when you receive your initial job offer; you will be unable to negotiate your wages up once you accept the position.

When negotiating, recognize that the process takes time. People who panic over a two-day delay in a return phone call generally end up accepting a position at a lower rate than what they could have negotiated. A company needs time to review its budget to decide if it can offer you more money or not. You may request a day or two to think about a company's job offer to decide whether or not you are willing to work at that rate. You may need to start work desperately, but accepting an offer simply to avoid another week of negotiations may result in a lower salary for you. Those people who fear negotiations often work for less than they could earn. Although the wages of most entry-level positions are not negotiated, almost all high-level salaried positions are negotiated upfront, so there is value in learning how to negotiate.

Once the negotiations are complete and you have accepted an offer, you may wish to request a written offer letter. Having the terms of employment in writing avoids any possible confusion in the future. Some companies may offer extensive perks and benefits as part of the negotiation that are not commonly given to employees, so putting them in writing ensures that those benefits do not suddenly disappear should the interviewer leave the company. An offer letter states the job title, requirements and compensation package for the employee, and it has the signatures of both the employer and the employee to show that both agreed to the terms of the letter upfront. Although most chefs and foodservice managers are ethical people, the industry does have its fair share of "employee abusers" who make an offer and then pay less money once the employee has started work. Even more common is for a chef to offer a wage or salary for 40 hours per week and then require their employees to work 60 or more hours per week at no additional compensation. Outlining the job requirements and the job offer in writing keeps an employer from taking advantage of a well-intentioned employee who puts his trust in the word of the interviewer.

19.5.1 Learning from Failure

If a person interviews for work often enough, he will eventually get rejected by an employer. To learn how to improve your interviewing skills you should speak with the interviewer after the rejection to ask how to perform better in future interviews. Some interviewers will elect not to share such feedback, but those that do provide rare insight that few industry workers ever receive. When you ask an interviewer for advice, state upfront that you want candid, honest feedback for self-improvement. Let the interviewer know that he will not hurt your feelings by being truthful. Listen intently to what the interviewer says, and do not interrupt or get defensive, which may cause the interviewer to end the conversation abruptly. Take notes during the conversation to help you remember the suggestions. Thank the interviewer for his honesty and for his time. Then carefully review your notes to see how you can improve in future interviews. Most people do not want anything to do with an interviewer who rejects them, but getting feedback from an interviewer is the only way to avoid making the same mistakes over and over again in job interviews.

Summary

To provide a company with the best impression possible, a job applicant should remain professional and polite in all of his communication with the company. An applicant should call to follow up on a submitted résumé but should not contact the employer more than once per week to check on the status of his application. When given an interview opportunity, he should make sure to select a time free of conflicts that would cause him to arrive late or not at all. To prepare for the interview the applicant should research the company and the job. He should role-play the interview to practice his answers to likely questions, and he should gather professional attire, copies of his résumé and cover letter, a list of references, and if possible, his portfolio to bring to the interview. The applicant should arrive at least 15 minutes early to the interview site. When greeting the interviewer he should shake hands and smile. The candidate should answer questions completely, honestly, directly, and concisely. Recent culinary school graduates should focus on those skills not related to experience and should express a strong desire to learn from the company. Interviewees should ask questions to get the information they need to make a decision on accepting a possible job offer. The applicant should leave the interview knowing the next step in the process as some companies require a series of interviews or a hands-on tryout. After the interview the candidate should send a thank-you note to the interviewer to express continued interest in the job. If the applicant gets a job offer, he should make sure to confirm acceptance of all of his constraints before accepting the offer. He may also present a counteroffer to negotiate a higher wage. Once the applicant and employer have agreed on the terms of employment, the applicant may request a written offer letter to avoid any future confusion or abuse by either party. In the event that the applicant does not receive a job offer, he should consider contacting the interviewer to request feedback for improvement. Learning to interview well takes practice, but all people have the capacity to learn this vital professional skill.

KEYS TO SUCCESSFUL INTERVIEWING

- Display professionalism and enthusiasm in all communication with the employer.
- Research information about the company and the job.
- Clear all personal commitments for the day and time of the interview.
- Obtain proper business attire for the interview.
- Bring one's cover letter, résumé, reference list, and, if available, portfolio to the interview; also bring a pen and paper for taking notes.
- Arrive early to the interview.
- Greet the interviewer with a firm handshake and a smile.
- Answer questions honestly, completely, directly, and concisely.
- Express a desire to learn while highlighting one's culinary school foundation.
- Ask any questions needed to make a decision on a future job offer.
- Find out the next step in the interview process.
- Close with a firm handshake and a smile.
- Follow up with a "thank you" note to the interviewer.

Suggested Tasks

1. Research a company for which you would like to work. Determine an entry-level position in that company for which you would be qualified. Write out ten likely questions you would expect an interviewer to ask you in an interview for that job. Write your answers to those questions highlighting your compatibility with the company based on your research. Share your questions and answers with your instructor.
2. Set up a meeting with a job placement counselor to role play an interview. Come in professional attire with copies of your

résumé. Tell the counselor the type of job you would most like to get after graduation and pretend to interview for that position. After the role play, ask the counselor to evaluate your preparedness for interviewing. If the counselor suggests that you need more preparation, schedule another practice session.

3. Interview a culinary professional in the industry who hires employees as part of his duties. Ask him what questions he typically asks applicants during an interview and what kinds of responses he looks for from a candidate. Ask if there are any responses to the questions that will cause the applicant to instantly lose the job opportunity. Share the results of your interview with your class.

4. Partner with a classmate to practice negotiating terms for a job. One of you should play the employer while the other plays the applicant. You should agree on the job title and basic job requirements in advance. Then, the applicant should secretly write down the minimum wage for which he is willing to work while the employer secretly writes down the maximum wage he is willing to pay. The job of the applicant is to negotiate as high a rate as possible while the employer must try to negotiate as low a rate as possible. Ask a third person to observe the negotiations to see if there is anything that the applicant could do differently to improve his negotiating skills. Switch roles periodically to give all parties an opportunity to negotiate as the applicant.

CHAPTER 20

The Basic Steps to Getting Promoted

No matter how fulfilling, a graduate's first job out of school should not be the endpoint of her culinary career. New culinary students enter school with dreams of becoming chefs, restaurateurs, business owners, and possibly even the head of a culinary empire. The student's first job in the industry is only the initial step in a long journey toward those goals.

Although some culinary professionals find higher-level positions in other companies, others acquire management opportunities through a promotion within their current company. Earning a promotion requires patience and hard work, but culinary graduates who remain focused and determined can achieve their management dreams. For some individuals the path toward a promotion takes decades, but by following a few simple steps a student should be able to earn some type of culinary management position in five years or less.

In this chapter, you will learn some basic steps to take to earn a promotion in your company. You will also learn how to pursue a management position in another company if your current employer does not have one available.

20.1 THE PROMOTION QUEST

When considering employees to promote to management, most organizations skip over the complacent workers and turn instead to the go-getters. Although a go-getter may wish to take a management position as soon as possible, there are some benefits to spending a few years in the trenches as a frontline worker. The employee must first understand the nature of entry-level work to effectively manage people in those positions. She must also prove herself to her co-workers and to her supervisors to earn credibility as a strong, respectable worker. Culinary go-getters often take a common path on their way to management. Making a deliberate effort to follow along this path often results in arriving at a management position early in one's career and, more importantly, prepared to succeed.

20.1.1 Master the Entry-Level Work First

The first step in getting promoted is to demonstrate competence in one's current position. Rarely are people promoted to a higher position when they are incompetent in their current roles. The foundations learned in college apply even more so to the industry. A future manager must arrive to work in uniform, on time, every day. Employees with attendance problems or with an inability to follow company regulations effectively remove themselves from consideration for any promotion within that company. Businesses need managers who can enforce company policies, and a worker who cannot follow the rules has no chance at motivating others to obey them.

To master a job as quickly as possible, treat it like a class at school. Bring a pad and a pen to work each day and take notes of everything you must do. Diagram station set-ups and record mise en place quantities. Write down recipes and draw pictures of the plate presentations for each dish. Then, study your notes each day at home until you have them memorized. The sooner you learn the details of a station, the sooner you can focus on building speed and efficiency on the station.

Your chef or supervisor will pressure you to maintain the kitchen's standards and to increase your production speed, but she will not be able to watch you at every moment. You must self-monitor your work and try to get faster, more organized, and more consistent in your production. You have not mastered a station until you can complete your mise en place fully and accurately well ahead of the first customer's arrival. You must also learn to handle every guest's order quickly and consistently even on the busiest days before attempting to move beyond your current station. By mastering an entry-level job first you prove your competence in kitchen skills and your ability to learn new tasks quickly.

20.1.2 Move Beyond One's Station

Once you have mastered your current station and job responsibilities, you should continue on-the-job training and development by learning from those around you. As you get faster and more efficient in setting up your station, use the extra time to assist co-workers (if they are willing) in their production. This simple act not only builds rapport with colleagues but also helps you to learn a kitchen station other than your own.

If learning from others during the workday is not an option, shadowing co-workers on a day off usually is. You should treat cross-training as part of your education. Some culinary professionals view working for free outside of one's assigned shift as inherently unfair, for they believe that the company should pay for that extra labor. However, culinary graduates should recall that they paid a college for the benefit of education; cross-training for free provides additional education at no charge. Although some companies will not permit their employees to work off-the-clock, many sincerely appreciate the time that an employee devotes to her own training. Training costs foodservice operations a substantial amount of money, so an employee who trains for free saves that expense for the company. Further, when a kitchen needs to staff an open position, most chefs will turn toward an already trained employee rather than pay for a new person to go through the training process. If you put in the time to cross-train on a station before or after your shift or on a day off, the chef will look to you when an opportunity on that station arises.

Interview with Frank Stitt, Chef/Restaurateur, Highlands Bar and Grill, Bottega and Chez Fonfon

What do you look for in a current employee when deciding to promote that employee?
Enthusiasm, respect, honesty, not making excuses, pursuit of excellence/quality.

What things could an employee do to prove herself worthy of a promotion?
Go beyond minimum expectations; have a passion for providing great service/food.

What things would you encourage an employee to do to prepare herself for a promotion to management?
Pursue interest in the success of the business, reducing waste, improving efficiency, creativity.

What skills must an employee have to succeed in management?
Professionalism, making decisions based on logic, performance not emotion, patience, and a positive outlook.

Do you have a management training program in your company?
We have no program per se. Managers get training working hands-on with the top managers, observing the leaders, and emulating their actions.

How receptive are you to allowing employees to shadow you to learn about your job?
Very receptive.

Is there an application process for promotions?
Simply ask!

How important is it for a manager to continue to learn, knowing that she has already learned enough to have earned a promotion?
We are always learning and can never rest or coast.

If a person is ready for a promotion, but no spots will be available in the company, would you help that person pursue a promotion elsewhere?
Yes. I would check with other businesses for openings.

How long should a student work after graduation before pursuing a management position?
There is no "set" number of years, but three years is typical.

In the event that your company does not allow you to cross-train on your own, you should speak to your supervisor to request a transfer to a different workstation to continue to learn and to grow. A good rule of thumb for restaurants that do not change their menu is to change stations every three months. For a restaurant that changes its menu often a person may work longer on a single station as the work shifts dramatically with each menu change. Some managers may hesitate to move workers from one station to another, but you should insist upon new challenges over remaining with an already mastered assignment. Languishing on a single station for too long will slow any serious culinary professional's career advancement.

Go-getters should look beyond cooking to enhance their knowledge base in a wide range of areas. A cook can learn a great deal about purchasing and receiving merely by helping with the process. Helping to receive and to store product provides knowledge on standard case sizes and product quality control. Assisting with inventory-taking reveals an operation's typical usage and in some cases opportunities to reduce waste and spoilage. You can volunteer to work on your employer's community events, if the company gets involved in local fund-raisers or street festivals. Some companies have committees staffed with employees to address certain business challenges; taking an active role in a committee not only teaches numerous non-cooking skills but also demonstrates a desire to lead and to problem-solve. Simply showing up to work and doing your job is not good enough to earn a promotion in today's competitive workplace. By taking the initiative to learn other stations and to get involved in multiple facets of a company, you gain the wider perspective on the organization that every manager needs, and you prove your work ethic and drive to those who make decisions on promotions.

20.1.3 Demonstrate People Skills

Strong interpersonal skills are essential for anyone to be considered for a position managing people. While working in the trenches you can demonstrate strong people skills by making an effort to get along with everyone in the organization. By displaying fair, ethical, and considerate treatment to all people while maintaining a strong work ethic, you can earn the respect of co-workers and supervisors. This respect is a prerequisite to a management position, for a boss cannot effectively manage people who do not respect her. Senior managers often look for workers who have their colleagues' respect when deciding whom to promote.

Navigating a company's culture to maintain cordial relations with all co-workers can be exceedingly difficult in some organizations. Some people thrive on gossip about colleagues, while others wallow in constant negativity by complaining about bosses and co-workers. These unprofessional practices usually result in tension or conflict between co-workers which negatively reflects upon their perceived ability to manage. The best way to avoid developing a poor reputation is not to get involved in these practices at all. Shun company politics; simply pretend they do not exist when you need to interact with others. Approaching people directly and honestly appears far more professional than playing politics to achieve your goals. Do not badmouth co-workers, management, or the company itself, even in private discussions with colleagues. Most people do not keep secrets for very long, so assume that anything you say will circulate through the company. If you speak ill of another person in your organization, chances are that you will have difficulty ever developing an amiable relationship with that individual. Office gossip is particularly harmful to relationships, so do not participate in work gossip or pass on any rumors heard through the grapevine. Do not become part of a clique either. Cliques are exclusive groups of people who form strong ties with each other often by shunning those who are not part of the clique. Inclusion in a clique may seem to strengthen relationships with some co-workers, but it does so at the expense of relationships with other co-workers. Simple behaviors, such as smiling and greeting others every day or complimenting co-workers on their work, go a long way toward forming strong, professional relationships with all colleagues. By fostering such relationships, you will gain a reputation among the managers as someone who works well with others and who should be considered for a promotion to management.

20.1.4 Show Problem-Solving and Leadership Abilities

Almost every company has at least one employee who does nothing but complain all day. Such an employee will rarely, if ever, earn a promotion to management. Managers are problem-solvers, not whiners. When you recognize a problem in an organization, you should identify an effective solution. You should present that solution to your supervisor, and then volunteer to take part in its implementation to demonstrate your support for the solution. By doing so, you demonstrate both problem-solving ability and leadership skills.

To further portray yourself as a leader, you should offer suggestions for business growth and workplace improvement to your supervisor. Not all ideas may be feasible, so you should not take it personally if your suggestion is rejected. However, if the recommendation is adopted, you should offer to assist in implementing the change. Posing a suggestion for others without volunteering to help with the additional work is a passive-aggressive form of complaining; it simply points out what others should be doing to fix the company's problems. By joining the effort to solve the problem you become a problem-solver and prove yourself to be management material.

A true leader often leads by example. Someone hoping to become a manager someday must never settle for low-quality work from herself. You must keep your standards as high as or higher than those of your co-workers. When working on a team project, you must motivate your teammates to keep their standards high as well. In some situations this requires you to help out others with their production. If a co-worker finds herself in the weeds, a would-be manager jumps in and helps her out. Similarly, you should not shy away from asking others for help. A worker always looks better sending out a quality product with help than she does creating a sub-par product on her own. If given the opportunity to manage a project, you should enlist the help of co-workers not just to lighten your workload but also to foster a team to lead. By leading a team that effects a change successfully, you demonstrate your strong leadership abilities and your worth as a future manager.

20.1.5 Ask to Train for Management

Although demonstrating work ethic, drive, leadership, and problem-solving skills is critical, a manager-in-the-making must eventually learn the specific tasks required of managers. Rarely would an entry-level employee learn or refine such abilities as part of her daily job, so she must request management training from her supervisors. Management training sometimes comes in the form of dedicated classes delivered by the company. If your company offers management training, simply asking for permission to enroll in the training may be sufficient to gain access to it. These formal classes often substitute for your normal workday, and you receive compensation for attending class. However, most small foodservice companies do not provide special classes to train managers. In such circumstances you must take matters into your own hands.

To design your own informal management training begin by asking a manager whom you trust and respect for an opportunity to shadow or to assist her on slow days or on your days off. You can learn a great deal about management simply working alongside a current manager. Offer to perform some of the manager's tasks under her supervision until you have gained competence in those tasks. Each skill acquired now is one less skill to learn before

Interview with Adrian Hoffman, Group Chef of the Lark Creek Restaurant Group

What do you look for in a current employee when deciding to promote that employee?

It's all about attitude. The employee needs the right frame of mind to be worthy of promotion. They need to be hungry for it and willing to work hard to get it. They need experience in the kitchen, but it is really a balance. I'd prefer to promote someone who has the right attitude over someone with more experience.

What things could an employee do to prove herself worthy of a promotion?

Learn the job without being asked. The easier a transition would be from a cook to a sous chef, the more likely a chef is to make the promotion. If the cook can go out of her way to learn some of the ropes, or at least be an expert on all stations, they become an obvious choice for promotion.

What things would you encourage an employee to do to prepare herself for a promotion to management?

Honestly, they need to distance themselves from the rest of the hourly staff. The other cooks, if too close, might have a difficult time answering to their drinking buddy.

What skills must an employee have to succeed in management?

Something I learned early in management is that everyone needs to be managed differently. We're managing a diverse group of individuals, each one with different needs and motivation. So a good degree of open-mindedness is an important skill for a manager-to-be.

Do you have a management training program in your company?

We have an MIT program that is the transition from all hourly to management staff. Basically, it outlines all the standard procedures in our kitchen, and the manager in training needs to prove they are proficient at all of them before we'll make the move to full-on management.

If a person is ready for a promotion but no spots will be available in the company in the near future, what should the employee do?

Either stick it out until something opens up, or I'd be happy to find a good spot in another restaurant for someone I thought deserved it. If someone was really that valuable, maybe we'd go out of our way to create a position for them.

How long should a student work after graduation before pursuing a management position?

It depends on their goals. The student should not work toward anything besides being the very best they can be in the position they are in. If they are on salad station, they should work at being the best salad cook the restaurant has ever seen. They shouldn't worry; if they work hard and excel, they will get promoted to a different station soon enough. If a cook works hard enough and excels at her job, the chef will notice. There is no hard and fast rule as far as time is concerned.

becoming a competent manager. By gaining skills in management on your own time, you prepare yourself to be the most qualified candidate for a promotion when a management position becomes available.

As lower-level employees do not generally have a bird's-eye view of their company, you may not possess the perspective that a manager needs. A major part of your personally developed management training should be to ask multiple managers about company policies and procedures beyond those directly related to your day-to-day job. For example, asking the company's process for purchasing and receiving will help you to understand how food arrives to your kitchen. Inquiring about the company's food and beverage management procedures will help you to understand how decisions on food cost and sales prices are made. Asking questions allows you to learn as much about the company as the managers are willing to share; however, recognize that a manager may not be able to tell you everything she knows. Some company information is confidential and cannot be shared with all employees. Other procedures and policies may simply be beyond the scope of knowledge of the person whom you ask. The manager you approach may not have the time to answer all of your questions either, so be sure to ask your questions at an appropriately slow time. Volunteering to do some of your boss's work as part of your own training may persuade her to devote time to your questions, but even then a manager may not have the time to spare during a very busy day. Respect the boundaries and work requirements of your supervisors, and they will be more willing to assist you in your personalized management training.

As your supervisors become accustomed to your steady self-preparation for management, express your interest in applying for a management position someday. Ask your supervisors for their advice on what it takes to become an effective manager. Unlike the factually based information about policies and procedures, a manager's opinion on good management should be taken as a suggestion rather than as scripture. Approach several managers to get each one's perspective, and consider which ideas might work best for you and for your developing style of management. These discussions with managers not only provide training for your management future, but they also build rapport between you and the management team. As your company's leaders begin to understand your commitment to becoming a manager, they are more likely to recommend you for hire when a management opportunity arises.

20.1.6   A Note on Sucking Up

No discussion on volunteering to do the boss's work would be complete without a mention of the stigma of "sucking up." Many people fear that any attempt to provide unsolicited assistance to a manager will cost them the respect of their co-workers, who might view the action as a veiled request for favoritism. First, all employees should recognize the difference between professional and personal boundaries. Offering to pick up the boss's dry cleaning or to babysit her children could legitimately be construed as sucking up in exchange for preferential treatment. However, volunteering to perform a work task in order to learn how to execute that job properly is nothing more than self-development.

The problem with "sucking up" lies in its inherent unfairness to co-workers who wish to be evaluated solely on their job performance. A go-getter who masters her own station should be rewarded for that work, but a person's efforts in assisting the boss with an employee schedule, for instance, should not supplant an otherwise poor performance of primary duties. A go-getter's devotion to management skill development should not play a role in determining her pay increase or work schedule; however, it most definitely should factor into a promotion decision. After all, the best candidate for a job is the one with the strongest skills, and a person who has devoted many hours to that skill development should be selected over someone who has no training in management. If your co-workers refer to you as a "suck up" for doing extra work for free, encourage them to do the same to expand their culinary skill sets. Let them know that you are merely training for a management position someday and that unless they want to spend their entire career in an hourly position they should devote some time toward preparing for management as well.

20.1.7 Apply for a Promotion

No matter how much you have discussed your interest in becoming a manager, you must still apply for a promotion when the opportunity arises. Do not assume that a promotion will be given to you, for most supervisors want to receive an application verifying your interest before approaching you. If you are not confident and forward enough to apply for the job, they will not give it to you.

When applying for a promotion, treat the application process as a formal one no matter how comfortable and friendly you are with those doing the hiring. Update your résumé and submit it with a cover letter through the proper channels. Prepare for an interview as you would for any other company. However, unlike an entry-level interview where you should stress your interest in learning, in an interview for a promotion you should point to evidence from your current job performance that demonstrates your ability to learn, to work hard, and to get along with others. If you have devoted time to gaining management skills, say so. Describe what you have learned and from whom you have learned it. Hard evidence of your skills, passion, and commitment to self-development is far more effective in obtaining a management position than is a promise to learn on the job. Of course, if you have not taken the time to master your station, to learn from others, and to pursue management training, then you will not show well in an interview; in fact, such unprepared candidates should not waste their time applying for a promotion they have no chance of earning.

Like any other job application process, the candidate who gets the job offer still has the ability to negotiate the salary. If you get a promotion to a management position, you should feel comfortable making a counteroffer. However, unlike negotiating an entry-level wage, there are far more variables on the table at the management level. You may become eligible for a salary and benefits; you may also have the ability to earn bonuses based upon job performance. A safe way to negotiate a higher income, especially when a company will not consider a higher salary, is to pose incentives for achieving certain benchmarks. For example, you might request a bonus for lowering the food cost or labor cost below a certain percent, or you could ask for a bonus corresponding to an increase in sales. Such bonus structures are appealing to companies who take a chance on an unproven manager. If you do not achieve the goal, the company does not pay out the bonus; if you do, the company still ends up saving or earning more money than it pays you. For an entry-level worker cutting her teeth on her first management job an incentive-based bonus structure may be the easiest route to negotiating a higher income.

Interview with Adam M. Greiner, Director of Banquets, Nemacolin Woodlands Resort

What things did you do to earn your first promotion?
The key to getting promoted is your internal desire to grow and develop. You can only get back what you are willing to put in. Concentration, dedication, and finishing what you started is a good place to begin.

What extra things did you do besides just doing your basic job requirements to prepare yourself for a promotion?
You have to show the big decision makers that your ideas and goals not only match the direction of the company but add an unmatchable value to future growth. Stay fresh; stay current, and be ready, willing, and able to accept critics.

What skills should a manager have to succeed in her job?
A manager needs to have a very basic set of "skills" to make it in the industry. It is your personality and concern for both your internal and external clients as well as your drive to assist others' growth that will give you the edge.

Have you ever shadowed another manager in her position?
I have never had the opportunity or time to do so. I have always kept an eye open to what other successful managers are doing and how they handle themselves and others. Building relationships with these successful people, however, may prove to be more important than shadowing them for a short time.

Do you ever work with other employees to let them shadow you?
I often take on interns and give them the opportunity to shadow. I am more interested to have them experience the joys and heartaches that are involved in a single workday and to give them firsthand experience in coping strategies than to learn what I do day-to-day. I don't want other managers to be like me. I want them to think for themselves, create their own path to success, and learn from their own mistakes. It is the only way to grow.

Was there a formal application process to get a promotion?
I graduated in 2003 from the Pennsylvania Institute of Culinary Arts. In the last five years, I have experienced six promotions. I have yet to apply for a promotion.

What do you do to continue to learn and to develop your skills and knowledge?
Read leadership development books. Read current industry specific periodicals. Reflect back on your success and your failure. Who can you outdo next?

20.1.8   Continue to Learn and to Move Up

Just as a person's entry-level position should not be the final stop on her progression up the career ladder, a culinary graduate should continue to prepare herself for promotion even after moving into her first management position. Most people do not become executive chefs for their first management job. Titles of sous chef, pastry chef, assistant manager, or department manager are far more common for a first foray into management. To continue on the path toward executive chef, food and beverage director, or general manager, first-tier managers should continue to learn from their supervisors to improve their current performance and to prepare for the next promotion.

Managers do not always receive the ongoing feedback that entry-level workers get. Some people assume that managers already know how to perform their jobs well, but the work that managers do often differs greatly from the work that they mastered prior to the promotion. Consequently, managers should request regular feedback and advice from their supervisors. Feedback once a year during an annual evaluation is simply not enough for new managers to master their work in an efficient manner.

Managers are ultimately responsible for their own learning if their supervisors do not provide periodic training. Since a break from learning and growing translates to a halt in career advancement, every manager at every level should continue to pursue professional development. In addition to requesting coaching and training from one's supervisors, a manager should locate management training courses available in the community. Most local colleges offer some form of management training, and professional training organizations may deliver management seminars in the community. A quick scan through the Internet and through college and community center publications will turn up opportunities for ongoing management training. Such training often comes at a price, but the cost is an investment in one's future that often results in a faster progression to a higher position and to a higher salary.

20.2   WHEN MOVING UP MEANS MOVING OUT

Despite a go-getter's best efforts to do everything right for a promotion, sometimes there is just no place to move up within a company. Perhaps the only manager is the owner, who has no intention of turning over the reins to anyone else. Maybe the executive chef of the kitchen is so wonderful that employee turnover is almost nonexistent. Sometimes several extremely talented line cooks with management skills are all waiting to apply for the next available promotion within the company. In these circumstances a young cook has the option of remaining with the organization at a lower-level position or of looking elsewhere for a management position.

When faced with a glass ceiling, if you have a strong relationship with your supervisors or with senior management, you should speak to them about your desire to become a manager. Ask for a referral to a professional friend who has an available management position. Sometimes a referral from one chef to a colleague moves a job applicant to the top of the interview pile. You should not hesitate to use your co-workers to help you find a position elsewhere either.

You should also use your network of professional connections to locate available management positions elsewhere. If you find yourself rejected repeatedly after interviewing with multiple companies, you should ask the interviewers for feedback. They may be able to help you prepare better for other companies, or they may reveal that you are not yet ready for a management position in the industry. To learn that you need more experience and preparation for management is not a major setback; rather, you should take that feedback merely as advice to continue your pursuit of professional development and to earn additional experience in frontline positions.

If you choose to remain at your lower-level position in your current company, you should still discuss your management goals with your supervisors. Request an opportunity to go through management training or to shadow some managers despite the dearth of advancement possibilities in the company. If a management position has still not opened up by the time you finish your training, you will at least have the skills needed to succeed in management elsewhere.

20.3 THE RUSH TO ADVANCE

Although most culinary school graduates want to advance as quickly as possible through the industry, every graduate should recognize that most people are not ready to manage until they have held several lower-level jobs first (either in the same or in multiple companies). Without sufficient experience even the most skilled applicant will be bypassed for a more experienced managerial candidate. Rarely will a culinary school graduate earn a management position at any level with less than two years of post-graduation industry experience. Most graduates need at least three to five years to prepare themselves to take on a management role.

To gain sufficiently diverse experience to refine your kitchen skills and to develop your own culinary style, you should devote one to two years to a kitchen and then move on to another chef to learn a different menu and style of cooking. A cook learns a great deal in her first year in a position, less in the second year, and very little after that unless she is promoted to management. If you have made an effort to learn a new station every three month, you have probably will have rotated through all of a kitchen's stations in two years. To avoid being labeled a job-hopper you should stay with each company for at least a year, but you should move to a new kitchen to learn new skills before the end of your second year in an organization. You should always try to work for the highest quality place possible, for it is easier to move to management from a high quality company than it is to move from a lower-quality establishment. After five years of training under several talented chefs and of building skills in management (either formally or on your own) you should be prepared to apply for a management position successfully.

Summary

A culinary school graduate should treat each job as a training ground for a higher position. First, the graduate should master the entry-level work at her own station to demonstrate her ability to learn and to perform well on the job. Next, she should learn other stations in the kitchen. She can assist co-workers or cross-train with them during slow periods or on her days off. An employee can also request from her supervisor a transfer to another station. The manager wannabe should demonstrate interpersonal skills by working well with others and by earning their respect. Involvement in gossip, cliques, and office politics hampers a person's ability to work well with all people. The would-be manager should present to her boss solutions to company problems and should offer to participate in those solutions. She should ask permission to enroll in the company's management training program or create her own informal self-development program. By shadowing current managers, asking them questions about company policies and procedures, and volunteering to complete management tasks under their supervision a lower-level worker can learn a great number of the skills needed for management. The worker will need to apply formally for a management position and outperform her fellow applicants, so she should take the application process seriously. However, her training efforts and strong job performance will offer powerful evidence of her ability to thrive as a manager. Once in a management position a manager should continue to learn and to refine her skills to prepare herself for a promotion to the next level of management. She should ask for feedback from her supervisor and should pursue management training courses within the company or in the local community. In the event that a management position will not be available for some time a go-getter may consider changing companies. She should approach her supervisors with her intentions and solicit help from them and from her own network to locate a management position elsewhere and to obtain a professional reference to the hiring chef. Most culinary school graduates need three to five years of training under a variety of chefs to earn enough experience and skill to succeed as a culinary manager, but with hard work and with a commitment to skill development a graduate should be able to obtain a management position just a few years after college.

KEY STEPS TO EARNING A PROMOTION

- Master one's own station first.
- Move beyond one's station to learn other stations in the kitchen.
- Demonstrate people skills and try to get along with everyone equally.
- Demonstrate problem-solving and leadership abilities.
- Ask one's supervisor for an opportunity to train in management skills or to shadow a manager.
- Apply for a promotion when one becomes available.
- Continue to learn the skills for the next job in the career ladder to prepare oneself for a promotion to a higher position.
- Use one's network and the help of managers and co-workers to locate management opportunities in other foodservice operations if no promotion opportunity exists in the current company.

Suggested Tasks

1. Interview an executive chef in the industry. Ask her how many managers work in the kitchen and what their titles are. Ask how many of those managers have been promoted from within the company. Find out what the chef looks for from an employee when deciding to promote her to management. Compile your findings into a report and share that report with the class.

2. Interview a culinary school graduate (ideally from your own school) who is now in a management position. Ask her what she did to prepare for management

and how she earned her current position. Find out how long it took for her to become a manager after culinary school and what jobs she held after graduation.

3. If you are currently working in the industry, evaluate your behaviors on the job (if not, consider your performance in your current kitchen classes), to see if you are properly preparing for a promotion to management. Do you push yourself each day to improve your speed and organization on your station? Have you devoted time outside of your work schedule to learn other stations (spoken with classmates to learn their assignments)? Do you work well with all of your co-workers (classmates)? Have you shadowed managers to learn how to do their jobs (spoken with teachers to learn how to manage a kitchen)? Consider these and other factors, and determine what more you could do to better prepare yourself for a management position. Share your self-assessment with a trusted colleague (or your teacher). Ask for further suggestions on how to prepare better for a management position, and implement at least one of those suggestions.

4. Research management class opportunities in your community. Locate at least three options and compare their costs and their time commitment. When you are ready to apply for a management position (this will come several years after graduation), enroll in one of those courses to refine your management skills.

5. Identify a problem at your company or in your school. Come up with a solution to the problem. Present your solution to your supervisor or teacher, and include a description of your role in the proposed solution. If your supervisor or teacher (or higher school official) approves the plan, follow through on your involvement to demonstrate your problem-solving and leadership abilities.

CHAPTER 21

Getting Certified

The decision to pursue certification from a professional culinary association is a difficult one for many people. Certification requires time, money, and effort. Not everyone who attempts to earn a certification passes, so many people worry whether their efforts may be for naught. Other people fear that a failed attempt to acquire certification will ruin their reputation in the community. Still others do not see the value in investing in a certification. But despite the many reasons not to pursue certification, many culinary professionals seek one or more certifications for themselves.

Certification offers some benefits. It validates a person's qualifications and skill sets. Some organizations require certain employees to hold a certification, while others pay higher salaries to certified workers. A certification behind a person's name conveys a sense of status and achievement to the public. It may also help with networking in some associations. The benefits of certification, for some people, make the challenge of earning it worth the effort.

In this chapter, you will learn how to decide whether or not certification is right for you. You will also learn some of the many types of certifications available through a range of professional organizations. Finally, you will learn some best practices for completing certification applications and for preparing for certification exams.

21.1 THE DECISION TO GET CERTIFIED

Not everyone needs to get certified, but many people do benefit from earning a professional certification. You must first ask yourself whether or not you need a certification to thrive in the industry. You must then consider the likelihood that you can earn the certification you want. For example, you might benefit greatly from becoming a certified master chef, but there is no point in pursuing that certification if you are not sufficiently experienced and prepared to pass the lengthy exam. You might conduct a self-analysis only to find that you are borderline-ready to earn a certification; when this happens, you must decide whether to pursue the certification now or to wait until you are better prepared. All of these issues must be considered to make a thoughtful, proper decision on pursuing a certification.

21.1.1 Who Needs Certification

There are some people for whom the decision to get certified is simple. If a person needs a certification to keep or to obtain a desirable job, then that person needs to get certified. If a person earns a higher salary for earning a certification, he, too, should attempt certification. However, for other people the decision is not quite so simple.

When certification is not a job requirement or a salary booster, then a culinary professional must honestly assess his culinary prowess and fame. Someone with strong skills who is not well known as an expert in his market will generally benefit from certification and should pursue it. In this case, a "market" is the audience a person needs to impress. For some chefs that market is a customer base while supervisors and potential employers constitute the market for other chefs. If a chef's market already knows and respects him, a certification is not necessary. For example, Emeril Lagasse does not need certification as his customer base, potential employers, and the media already view him as an expert in Cajun and Creole cuisine. A certification would not add to his reputation although a failed certification attempt might detract from it. However, an unknown chef in a low-profile job or one recently relocated to a new city would benefit greatly from the stamp of approval of national certifying body. In short, if you are not a local celebrity in your market, you will likely benefit from certification.

Interview with Leslie Bilderback, CMB, Author, *Complete Idiot's Guide to Success as a Chef* (Alpha Books, 2007), *Complete Idiot's Guide to Comfort Foods* (Alpha Books, 2007), *Complete Idiot's Guide to Spices and Herbs* (Alpha Books, 2007), *Complete Idiot's Guide to Good Food from the Good Book* (Alpha Books, 2008), *Complete Idiot's Guide to Snack Cakes* (Alpha Books, 2008), *Complete Idiot's Guide to Sensational Salads* (Alpha Books, 2009), *Everything Guide to Family Nutrition* (Adams Media, 2009), Chef Instructor, LAUSD Nutrition Network, US Navy Adopt-a-Chef Program

What is your certification?
Certified Master Baker

When did you first get certified and at what level?
I began the process in 1998 or 1999, and completed it in 2000. I was a culinary instructor and wanted to move up the ladder in education. The CMB was closest in subject to the classes I was teaching at the time, and frankly, it was the cheapest one I could find. When the company is not paying, or only paying for part of the process, the money plays a big part. Young chefs are not rich, you know.

What was the process like for getting certified?
It was fun, actually. I had to pass a written exam first, for which I was given a study guide, so that was easy. Then, after passing that, I took a practical two-day exam at what was then the National Baking

(continued)

(continued)

Institute in Minneapolis. There were seven or eight of us taking the test that weekend, and I was the only instructor. The rest were bakers for large companies, like Pillsbury, and small family-owned shops. I had to prepare tons of stuff: laminated doughs like Danish, sweet rolls, artisan breads, loaf breads, cookies, and a couple of cakes, which I had seven minutes to decorate . . . or some crazy time limit. The judges were all big-time bakers, and they scrutinized the product like I had never seen before. I learned a lot about how to evaluate students that day (and how not to). I passed all but one of the breads, which had too dense a crumb. I got to retake that portion, which I passed later that year.

How did you prepare for certification?
The hardest part was learning to bake by formula, something they seldom teach in culinary schools. The rest was just review, as I was a teacher at the time and knew most of it inside-out.

What value has being certified provided you in your career?
It has opened several doors and legitimized everything else I do. I get noticed with the letter after my name, even though people don't know what they stand for. I am taken much more seriously than if I were just a baker or just a chef. For those of us who are not celebrity chefs, a certification is the best way to call attention to the work you do.

21.1.2 Are You Certifiable

Fortunately, only the local (or national) celebrities run any risk of encountering ba publicity for failing a certification attempt, but the average, unknown chef still faces th costs of lost time and money from a certification attempt that ends badly. You should beg the process fairly certain that you can meet the certification criteria. So how do you know you are likely to make it through the process?

First, you should locate the requirements for certification on the certifying body's W site or speak with an already certified professional about the assumed body of knowledge f a given certification. Nearly every organization providing a certification tests applicants their knowledge of certain subjects. Finding out the subjects tested allows chefs to deci whether they possess sufficient knowledge to pass the exam. If a person does not know least 70 percent of the body of knowledge tested, that candidate is unlikely to pass the exa For example, if a test covers the topics of cooking, baking, and table service equally, an person knows nothing about baking and table service, that person is probably not ready test for this certification.

Next, request sample tests from the certifying body. Most certifying organizatio have sample exams or descriptions of exams to give people a sense of what to expect. R through the sample test to learn in which subject areas you most need remediation. may find that you know almost every question on the sample exam, in which case you probably find the actual exam easy. However, if the practice test seems exceedingly diffic you may wish to study diligently before taking the exam.

Finally, ask for recommended reading lists or other resources to strengthen y skills for the test. If there is a major benefit to becoming certified, a person should not up on certification solely because of a difficult practice exam. Even those chefs with br knowledge bases often find that they benefit from reviewing recommended books, so e preparation should be taken seriously by all applicants.

21.1.3 The Borderline Cases

Some certification candidates conduct an in-depth self-analysis only to discover that they are borderline-ready to pass a certification exam. What should you do in such a situation? On the one hand, there is some value to taking the exam even if you fail it. Failing gives you a better sense of what to expect next time on the exam. It will let you know how to prepare better for your second attempt or perhaps make obvious that you are not an appropriate candidate for that particular certification. On the other hand, attempting an exam, whether successfully or unsuccessfully, costs time and money. You might decide to wait until you feel better prepared for the exam to risk your investment. Still, you should not put off certification indefinitely. Too many people give up before even trying to pass the exam, and the earlier you earn a certification, the sooner you begin to reap its benefits. Usually a year of serious study and practice is more than enough time to convert a borderline case into a strong candidate for certification.

21.2 TYPES OF CERTIFICATION

There are many types of licenses and certifications that a cook or chef can obtain. Knowing the particular focus of each license and certification helps people to determine whether or not a given credential is appropriate for them. This section includes a list of various organizations and the credentials they provide. The list is not meant to be comprehensive; these are merely the certifications most commonly seen in the culinary industry.

21.2.1 Food Handler's License

The food handler's license is probably the most commonly held culinary credential in the foodservice industry. Based on the USDA's Food Safety and Inspection Service requirements for foodservice establishments, this license certifies that a culinary worker understands the principles of safe food handling. The license is generally administered by a local jurisdiction (county or conglomeration of counties), so some of the food safety regulations may vary slightly from one locality to another. However, a student who has performed well in a culinary school's food safety and sanitation course will likely have little difficulty in acquiring the food handler's license.

   Most jurisdictions require that at least one person with a food handler's license be present at a foodservice operation while it is open. This requirement means that having a food handler's license can help a person to obtain and keep a job over people without the license. Therefore, this license is one that all culinary students should pursue as soon as possible after graduation, if not sooner. Culinary professionals generally obtain the license in one of two ways. Either they take an exam through their local health department (or its proxy) or they take a national exam, such as the National Restaurant Association's ServSafe exam, and present their scores to the local jurisdiction. Note, however, that the exam results do expire, so be sure to pursue the license within a year of taking the exam.

   More and more jurisdictions are requiring that culinary workers also document completion of a food safety course, not just a passing score on a test, to earn the food handler's license. A food safety course in culinary school generally suffices although health departments may refer foodservice workers to local programs offering food safety courses.

These courses may not be necessary if you did well in your college food safety course, but many people find them a good study aide prior to taking the exam.

Requirements for renewal of the license vary greatly from one jurisdiction to the next. Some simply require that the license holder pays the fee to renew the license before it expires. (In many cases, a person who does not renew before the license expires is treated as a first-time applicant.) Other jurisdictions mandate that license holders take a refresher course as part of the renewal process. A review of your health department's Web site or a quick phone call to a health inspector will provide you the requirements for application and for renewal in your local area.

Interview with Peter Timmins, CMC, Executive Chef, The Greenbrier Resort

What is your certification?
Certified Master Chef

When did you first get certified and at what level? Why?
CMC was my first certification. I came to the US when I was 36 and did other certifications in Europe. I got the certification because someone else out there had it. There are other people out there who claim to be better, so a chef tests himself constantly to be better or at least as good as other chefs. Since others had a CMC, I wondered if I was that good.

What was the process like for getting certified?
The CMC exam was a culmination of life's experiences. The knowledge and experience required is quite vast. I was doing things for the exam that I hadn't done in years. It comes back to you like riding a bicycle, but if you don't know how to do those things, you cannot learn them by studying the night before the test.

How did you prepare for certification?
To prepare for certification, from the day you begin school or apprenticeship, find out what your mission is and use every day to brush up or find answers on information that will be included on that certification. When you go to school, nobody teaches you anything. They provide you an environment in which you can learn. You need to know what you really want to figure out. Then you have to take the initiative to learn it on your own time using the resources available. Potential is only as good as the effort you're willing to put into it.

What value has being certified provided you in your career?
Noel Cullen used to say that coming to the ACF for a Master Chef is to get a rubber stamp approving what you know and are. You should be one when taking the test, not trying to become one. The certification was only proof that I was a CMC. Other people think more about it than I do and throw opportunities my way because of it. It has opened a lot of doors, but it is very personal for me. There are other people in the country who are as good as I am, but without the certification they are not given the same opportunities.

When in their careers should culinary school students apply for certification?
Students should be certified before they leave culinary college at any level they can achieve. They should also understand the next level and begin pursuing that next level immediately.

21.2.2　American Culinary Federation Certifications

The American Culinary Federation (ACF) is one of the oldest culinary associations in the country to award certifications for chefs. The ACF system offers 14 different types of certifications to meet the needs of culinary professionals at various stages in their careers. The ACF measures a person's educational and work experience to determine for which level a candidate qualifies. Although the requirements for each certification vary, all candidates are required to document education in sanitation, nutrition, and management.

In addition to educational and work experience requirements, all ACF certification levels require written and practical exams. The questions on the written exam vary by certification level and become more challenging at the higher levels. The practical exam requirements, too, correspond to the level of certification pursued and the requirements do change periodically. However, assessment for the exams generally covers four areas: food safety and sanitation, organization, cooking skills and culinary techniques, and taste and presentation. An example of a typical certified culinarian practical exam would be: to prepare julienne and batonnet carrots, fine chopped parsley, and standard mirepoix; to fabricate a chicken and to use the carcass to begin a chicken stock; and to prepare a sautéed chicken breast entrée with appropriate vegetable and starch accompaniments in a two and one-half hour window. The American Culinary Federation Web site (www.acfchefs.org) provides detailed information on the requirements for each certification level as well as a listing of practical exam site locations.

Although the certifications vary greatly, the ACF certifications are most appropriate to people working in a foodservice establishment either as "food-preparers," as managers of food-preparers, or as instructors teaching in culinary programs. The type of food prepared (savory or baked goods), the type of work (cooking, personal chef work, or management), and the specific job responsibilities and number of people supervised determine which certification is most appropriate for each applicant. The ACF offers certifications specifically for culinary educators at the high school and the college level; these certifications require both culinary and instruction expertise. The certified culinarian and certified pastry culinarian are appropriate credentials for recent culinary school graduates. (*Note:* The ACF is currently in the process of revising its certification system. Any changes and updates can be located at www.acfchefs.org)

21.2.3　American Hotel & Lodging Association Educational Institute Certifications

The American Hotel & Lodging Association Educational Institute (AHLAEI) offers a wide range of professional certifications as well as certificates of knowledge. Although their list of certification options is extensive for workers of all sorts across the hospitality industry, there are two certification levels most appropriate for chefs: the Certified Food and Beverage Executive (CFBE) and the Certified Hospitality Educator (CHE). The CFBE relates most directly to industry chefs, while the CHE is designed for teachers. CFBE candidates must document at least six months of experience in their current job as an executive level manager (executive chef counts!) and must pass a written exam. CHE applicants, who must possess both teaching and industry management experience, must attend a CHE workshop, pass a written exam, and submit a videotape illustrating their teaching proficiency. A full list of certification options is available through the AHLAEI Web site at www.ei-ahla.org/certification.asp.

TABLE 21.1 American Culinary Federation Certification Requirements

Certification	Education	Experience	Additional
CC **CPC**	High School diploma or GED *or* 100 hours of Continuing Ed	2 years (FT) as a cook/baker	Written Exam Practical Exam
	1-year certificate from culinary arts program	1 year (FT) as a cook/baker	Written Exam Practical Exam
	Associate's degree *or* ACF Apprenticeship program	No experience necessary	Written Exam Practical Exam
CSC **CWPC**	High School diploma/GED *plus* 50 hours of Continuing Ed	5 years (FT) as a cook/baker	
	150 hours of Continuing Ed	5 years (FT) as a cook/baker	Written Exam Practical Exam
	Associate's Degree	3 years (FT) as a cook/baker	
	ACF Apprenticeship program	4000 hours On-the-Job Training	
CCC	High School diploma/GED *plus* 100 hours of Continuing Ed	3 years (FT) as a Sous Chef	
	200 hours of Continuing Ed	3 years (FT) as a Sous Chef	Written Exam Practical Exam
	Associate's Degree or ACF Apprenticeship program	3 years (FT) as a Sous Chef	
CEC **CEPC**	High School diploma/GED *plus* 150 hours of Continuing Ed	3 years (FT) as Chef de Cuisine or Executive Sous Chef	
	250 hours of Continuing Ed	3 years (FT) as Chef de Cuisine or Executive Sous Chef	Written Exam Practical Exam
	Associate's Degree or ACF Apprenticeship program *plus* 50 hours of Continuing Ed	3 years (FT) as Chef de Cuisine or Executive Sous Chef	
CMC **CMPC**	High School diploma/GED *plus* 150 hours of Continuing Ed	Minimum 1 year as an Executive Chef	*See CMC/CMPC manual
	250 hours of Continuing Ed		
	Associate's Degree *or* ACF Apprenticeship program *plus*		

	Education	Experience	Exams
PCC	Same as CSC	4 years (FT) as a cook *plus* 1 year (FT) as a Personal Chef	Written Exam Practical Exam
PCEC	Same as CEC	3 years (FT) as a Personal Chef	Written Exam Practical Exam
CCA	Same as CEC	3 Years (FT) as an Executive Chef	Written Exam for CCA *and* CEC/CEPC Narrative Paper
CSCE*	Bachelor's Degree	1200 contact hours (FT or PT) 120 hours in Education Development	Written Exam Classroom Video Practical Exam for CCC or CWPC
	Associate's Degree *plus* a State-issued teaching certificate	1200 contact hours (FT or PT) 120 hours in Education Development	
CCE	Bachelor's Degree	2 years (FT) as a Chef de Cuisine or Working Pastry Chef 1200 contact hours (FT or PT) 120 hours in Education Development	Written Exam Classroom Video Practical Exam for CCC or CWPC
	Associate's Degree *plus* a State-issued teaching certificate	2 years (FT) as a Chef de Cuisine or Working Pastry Chef 1200 contact hours (FT or PT) 120 hours in Education Development	

All levels require three 30-hour courses: Nutrition, Sanitation, Supervisory Management. Above information is valid as of March 2008 and is subject to change.

*CSCE also requires a 30-hour course in Basic Food Preparation.

Source: Reprinted with permission of the American Culinary Federation.

21.2.4 International Association of Culinary Professionals Certification

The International Association of Culinary Professionals offers one comprehensive certification—the Certified Culinary Professional (CCP). The CCP requires extensive achievement in a wide range of areas in the culinary industry. Applicants earn points for formal education, professional development courses, conferences, professional association leadership, community service, professional presentations, work experience, published writing, competition judging, and receipt of honors or awards. Although the required level of achievement and involvement in the industry is high, the application parameters are broad enough to accommodate professionals in a wide range of culinary-related jobs, not just chefs. The CCP is appropriate not only for chefs and bakers, but also for culinary writers, nutritionists, food scientists, food marketers, and a range of other culinary professionals accomplished in their industry niche.

To verify expertise in the culinary field, the CCP requires a written exam. The exam covers a wide range of topics including food safety and sanitation, food chemistry, nutrition, baking, food identification, wine/beer/spirits, and a range of cuisines including the foods of France, Italy, Asia, and the Americas. The exam also requires completion of multiple essay questions to verify analytical ability in addition to factual knowledge. Although the exam content is broad, it covers information that most well-versed chefs will find familiar. More information on the CCP certification can be found at www.iacp.com.

Interview with Robin Kline, MS, RD, CCP, Principal, Savvy Food Communications

What is your certification?
Certified Culinary Professional through the International Association of Culinary Professionals.

What was the process like for getting certified?
The application is most rigorous. There are requirements of professional experience that must be fulfilled, for example, and the application process attempts to attract candidates with a rather broad experience in the culinary world.

What were you feeling during the process?
Frankly, intimidated! Full disclosure: It took me about 2–3 years before I dove in and filled out the application. However, I want to underscore what a great discipline completing the application is. The exercise helped me, a culinary professional, outline and document the many professional experiences that have molded me.

How did you prepare for certification?
Review, study, review, study, review, and study. The CCP committee within IACP maintains excellent, current bibliographies for texts that help the applicant review germane bodies of knowledge: cuisines of the world, nutrition, food safety and microbiology, classic preparations

(continued)

(*continued*)

techniques, ingredients, food service. I approached taking the exam as seriously as I did for my certification for the American Dietetic Association; I studied rigorously and prepared thoroughly.

What value has being certified provided you in your career?
I feel as though I've got a solid base of culinary knowledge and experience which is reflected in this certification. As a registered dietitian, a master's degree in nutrition, an undergraduate degree in food science, and this culinary certification are my credentials for being an expert in cuisine, food preparation, flavor trends, and so forth. I bring "added value" to the writing and consulting projects I take on. The CCP has been invaluable.

When in their careers should culinary school students apply for certification?
The certified culinary professional needs to have at least a few years of professional experience before taking this exam, but it's good for a student to have the CCP on their professional radar for the future.

What advice would you give a student about certification?
When in culinary school, pay attention to and do your best in all coursework, as it's the well-rounded professional who is qualified to take this exam. The certification indicates that you have "met the bar" of many disciplines within the culinary world.

21.2.5 International Food Service Executives Association Certifications

The International Food Service Executives Association (IFSEA) offers three tiers of certification: the Certified Food Manager (CFM), the Certified Food Executive (CFE), and the Master Certified Food Executive (MCFE). Unlike most other certifications, the IFSEA certifications require content knowledge verified through an exam rather than a lengthy application documenting industry involvement. An applicant can simply call the association and schedule to take the exam with no preparation, but most benefit from utilizing IFSEA's study materials or preparatory classes first.

The IFSEA certifications do require industry involvement for renewal and CFM's must upgrade to the CFE level after a certain number of years. The goal is to encourage professional development and knowledge expansion to move individuals through the certification levels ultimately to the MCFE. Once the MCFE is attained, no additional recertification process is required. Topics on the CFE and MCFE exams include menu design and analysis, kitchen management and food production, service management, purchasing and inventory control, accounting and financial management, marketing, beverage management, and human resource management. The CFM, the beginning level of certification, is appropriate for recent culinary school graduates willing to study to prepare for the exam. The CFE and MCFE become more appropriate as a person moves into a management position in the foodservice industry. More information on the IFSEA certifications can be found at www.ifsea.com.

21.2.6 National Restaurant Association Education Foundation Certification

The National Restaurant Association Education Foundation (NRAEF) offers a single certification—the Foodservice Management Professional (FMP). The FMP requires supervisory work experience and completion of a food protection management exam, such as the NRA's ServSafe exam. Consequently, most culinary professionals with experience in foodservice management will find the FMP easy to acquire.

The NRAEF also provides single-topic certificates verifying content knowledge on a range of subjects through its ManageFirst program. Individuals can use ManageFirst study guides to prepare for each exam and can earn certificates by taking exams even while still in school. Although a single certificate documenting subject proficiency is valuable to an employer, the NRAEF allows people to earn an even higher credential by demonstrating certain work experience and passing five exams in specific topic areas. While the FMP certification is appropriate for foodservice managers, ManageFirst certificates are highly appropriate credentials for recent culinary school graduates. More information on the NRAEF certificates and the FMP can be found at www.nraef.org.

21.2.7   Research Chefs Association Certifications

The Research Chefs Association (RCA) offers two certifications: the Certified Research Chef (CRC) and the Certified Culinary Scientist (CCS). The CRC is appropriate for people with culinary arts education, while the CCS is designed for individuals with a food science or related degree. Both certifications require education and work experience in the foodservice industry and in culinary research and development; both also require a written exam that tests food science and culinary arts knowledge. While these certifications are not appropriate for all chefs, they are highly valuable for chefs working in product development divisions for food companies. More information on the RCA certifications can be found at www.culinology.com.

21.2.8   Retail Bakers of America Certifications

The Retail Bakers of America (RBA) association offers four different certifications, all appropriate for bakers and pastry chefs. The Certified Journey Baker (CJB) can be acquired by recent culinary school graduates through bakery work experience and a written exam. The other levels of certification require more substantial work experience (four years for Certified Baker and Certified Decorator; eight years for Certified Master Baker), a practical exam, and verification of food safety and sanitation knowledge through an exam such as the NRA's ServSafe test. The Certified Master Baker credential also has additional education and professional development requirements not needed for the other certification levels. Although not designed for line cooks, the RBA certifications are appropriate for all culinary school graduates who devote their careers to working in commercial bakeries. For more information on the RBA certifications, visit www.rbanet.com.

21.2.9   United States Personal Chef Association Certification

The United States Personal Chef Association (USPCA) offers a single certification—the Certified Personal Chef (CPC). This certification requires two years of work experience as a personal chef, education (including degrees, other related work experience, continuing education courses, association participation, and/or conference attendance), completion of a home study course, a ServSafe certificate, and completion of the USPCA written exam. Although the work performed by a personal chef takes place in a kitchen, preparing food for clients in their homes for possible storage and future reheating differs significantly from the work typically

TABLE 21.2 Retail Bakers of America Certifications

Certified Journey Baker (CJB)	• A baker at this level assists in the preparation and production of pies, cookies, cakes, breads, rolls, desserts, or other baked goods for a commercial bakery. Duties may include stocking ingredients, preparing and cleaning equipment; measuring ingredients, mixing, scaling, forming, proofing, oven tending, and product finishing. He/she must demonstrate a basic knowledge about the principles of sanitation.
Certified Baker (CB)	• A Certified Baker prepares and produces baked goods while assisting with general commercial bakery operations. He/she has considerable responsibility and autonomy and participates in a broad range of both complex and routine work activities, including supervision of other staff and allocation of resources. He/she must demonstrate a basic knowledge of bakery sanitation, management, retail sales/merchandising and staff training.
Certified Decorator (CD)	• A decorator at this level and for this designation prepares and finishes sweet baked goods for a commercial bakery. Duties include preparing icings, decorating a variety of cakes using various techniques, seasonal displays and specialty designs, and working with customers. He/she demonstrates a basic knowledge about sanitation.
Certified Master Baker (CMB)	• A baker at this level and for this designation participates in a broad range of complex, technical or professional work activities, performed in a wide variety of contexts with a substantial degree of personal responsibility and autonomy. Responsibility for the work of others and allocation of resources is present. He/she must have the technical and administrative skills necessary to operate and manage the production area of a full-line independent or in-store commercial bakery. He/she must produce high quality bakery foods, and demonstrate a basic knowledge about the principles of sanitation, management, retail sales/merchandising and training.

Source: Reprinted with permission of Retail Bakers of America © 2005.

performed by chefs in a restaurant. Therefore, the certification is solely appropriate for people working as personal or private chefs who wish to demonstrate professional credentials to potential clients. Possession of this credential by personal and private chefs can make a significant difference in acquiring clients who require a verifiable level of professional skill and knowledge. For more information on the USPCA certification, visit www.uspca.com.

21.3 PREPARING THE APPLICATION

No matter which certification you pursue, there is a basic process that makes applying for certification simpler. First, obtain the application form from the certifying body. Most allow individuals to download the application from a Web site. Next, photocopy the blank application to have a scratch copy for notes and a clean copy for final completion. Using the scratch copy, fill in as much information as you can recall off the top of your head.

Once you have your scratch application outlined, locate documentation to verify the information you have listed. If you are missing needed documents, contact those people who can provide them to you. For example, if you need verification of past employment, contact your old employer or supervisor; if you need a transcript from school, speak with your college registrar. During this process you may locate or recall other activities to add to your application.

Once you have gathered enough documented points (most certification applications use a point system) to meet the minimum requirements for a certification, complete the clean copy of the application with all of the pertinent information followed by your gathered documentation. The certifying body generally provides instructions on how to assemble the completed application (binder with tabs, simply stapled, etc.), so be sure to follow its instructions before mailing the application. Because you are applying for a professional credential, a professional-looking, easy-to-navigate application may make the difference between a smooth application process and a quick rejection.

If the first draft and the documentation-gathering process reveal that you do not have enough verifiable points to meet the certification criteria, do not throw out the application. Instead, make a concerted effort over the next year or two to perform tasks that earn points. Enter a competition. Engage in some community service, or pursue additional education. Gather corroborating documentation as you complete each activity and store it with your application. When you have finally gained enough points to meet the minimum standards of the certification, complete and submit the final application. Using this process will help you to pursue certification in a direct, efficient manner without overwhelming you along the way.

Interview with Glenn Walden, CEC, CCE, CHE, Dean of Culinary Arts and Hospitality Management, Stratford University

What is your certification?
Certified Executive Chef, Certified Culinary Educator, Certified Hospitality Educator

What made you decide to get a certification?
I did not actually seek advanced certification until 1995. I was working at ATI Career Institute as the senior instructor teaching culinary arts courses. The director pushed me to get certified to boost the reputation of the school, so I applied for and received the Certified Chef de Cuisine level in 1996.

What was the process like for getting certified?
Hours of paperwork, tracking down past employment verification, and studying for the exam.

(continued)

(continued)

What were you feeling during the process?
I was thinking: Wow! I really have been around a long time; I wish I had kept better records; I hope I know all the answers on the exam; where is the study guide. When all is said and done, the hardest part was organizing the documentation and tracking down signatures from past employers. The exam was comprehensive and since I was teaching, most of the information was fresh.

How did you prepare for certification?
Each level of certification was slightly more challenging. My first level, Certified Culinarian, was earned after completing a two-year culinary degree. The CCC was more work due to the employment verification and refresher courses in sanitation, management, and nutrition. The CEC required more studying and documentation. The CCE took the most effort due to the college education required in curriculum planning and design, evaluation and testing, teaching methodology, and educational psychology. My last certification, Certified Hospitality Educator, was the most condensed and challenging: 20 hours of classroom lessons, a two-hour exam, and a one-hour video of me demonstrating (in a real classroom) mastery of the techniques learned in the class. I felt this was the best lesson and validation of teaching skills.

What value has being certified provided you in your career?
The certification process is a way for me to be recognized by peers in the industry for achieving a milestone. No other person from outside really knows and may not even care what it takes to be certified. Certification is for us in the field to be recognized and allows us to recognize others. When I review résumés, certification gets you a second look.

When in their careers should culinary school students apply for certification?
Start gathering documentation immediately. When you complete your externship, get your supervisor to sign the employment verification and make a copy.

What advice would you give a student about certification?
Certification is a way to show your commitment to your craft. Certification is not mandatory, and only the most committed will do the extra work necessary to be certified. Certification is an industry recognition to put on your wall to show you are a professional who cares.

21.4 PREPARING FOR THE EXAM

As most certifying organizations require some type of exam, completion of the written application is only the first step in the process. Once you have submitted the application, contact the association's certification division and request a reading list. Most associations recommend certain books and resources from which their test questions are taken. Study those texts for several months. Take notes; make flash cards. Generally prepare for the exam as you would any major exam in college. You may wish to work with a person who has already been through the certification exam to get a better sense of what to expect and to help direct your studying.

For practical exams get the guidelines for the exam from the association administering it. Most of these exams will be exceedingly difficult without some practice prior to the actual test, so practice regularly until you can consistently complete the exam at a high standard within the time frame. If you know of someone else taking the exam in the weeks or months before your testing date, observe that person's practical and learn from his successes and mistakes. If possible, ask a certified person to observe and evaluate your practice sessions to provide suggestions for improvement prior to your exam. Always practice under similar conditions to those expected during the exam. For example, if you will only have one oven and one prep table during the exam, do not use two ovens and two tables during your practice rounds. With a practical exam, most people perform about as well during the exam as they did during their practice sessions, so be sure to practice often until you can "pass" the exam consistently during practice.

The certification process is difficult for most people. If it were so easy that anyone could do it, the certification would have little value. However, a devotion to study, practice, and self-improvement greatly increases a person's chances of acquiring a certification.

Summary

Although not everyone needs a professional certification in the culinary industry, culinary professionals who are not well known in their market can benefit from earning a certification credential from a nationally known organization. For most certifying bodies, the process for certification requires the completion of an application with accompanying documentation, a written exam, and in some cases, a practical exam. An applicant can often determine his self-preparedness for a certification examination by reviewing sample exams and recommended reading lists provided by the certifying organization. There are a wide range of certifying bodies, each offering varying levels of certification, so culinary workers interested in acquiring certification should research their options to determine which certification suits them best. Once the appropriate certification is determined, the applicant should gather documentation to complete the application and then study thoroughly for the exams. In the event that an applicant is just short of meeting the experience requirements for a certification level, that person should make an effort to work toward the completion of those requirements and to gather documentation of his achievements along the way for inclusion in the application. With sufficient preparation and study, culinary professionals have a strong chance of earning a certification to verify their skill sets and experience.

KEYS TO APPLYING FOR A CERTIFICATION

- Research various certification options to determine the most appropriate certification.
- Complete a first draft of the application and collect the supporting documentation.
- Contact the necessary parties to obtain any missing documentation needed for the application.
- Make a concerted effort to complete the necessary activities to earn enough points for that certification level if one has insufficient points for a certification.
- Complete a final draft of the application, including only those activities with accompanying documentation, and submit the application.

(continued)

(*continued*)

- Obtain a recommended reading list and guidelines for exam preparation.
- Study actively for written exams.
- Practice for practical exams repeatedly.
- Complete the process by taking all required exams.

Suggested Tasks

1. Determine what certification would be most appropriate for your current skill set and experience. Obtain a copy of that certification application and complete it to see if you are eligible to test for that certification. Request a study guide and/or practice exam for that certification and evaluate your familiarity with the required knowledge base. If a certification is something you desire, submit your application and take the test(s) to get certified.

2. Interview an industry chef with a certification. Ask him what value the certification provides him and why he chose to get the certification in the first place. Ask him how he prepared for the certification application and how difficult it was. Ask what topics were covered on the exam. Find out what additional certifications, if

any, the chef has an interest in pursuing. Compile the findings from your interview and share the results with your class.

3. Contact an employer for whom you wish to work in the future. Ask him what role certification plays in the employment process. Is it a requirement? Does it translate to more money? Does it make an applicant more desirable? Find out which certifications the employer most desires from his applicants. Share the results of your interview with your class.

4. Contact your local health department. Find out where and how to obtain a food handler's license. If you currently possess an exam certificate, such as the ServSafe certificate, ask if that certificate can be converted into a license. Follow through on the instructions you have learned and get a food handler's license within 30 days.

Bibliography

ACF Certification Requirements 2008. Retrieved May 12, 2008, from http://www.acfchefs.org/download/documents/certify/Certification_Requirements.pdf.

AHLAEI certifications. (n.d.). Retrieved May 12, 2008, from http://www.ei-ahla.org/certification.asp.

CCP certification information. (n.d.). Retrieved May 12, 2008, from http://www.iacp.com/associations/7870/files/ccpapp.pdf.

IFSEA certifications. (n.d.). Retrieved May 12, 2008, from http://www.ifsea.com/professional_inside.cfm?itemid=16465&catid=2326.

NRAEF's FMP certification. (n.d.) Retrieved May 12, 2008, from http://www.nraef.org/fmp/fmp_about.asp?level1_id=2&level2_id=3.

NRAEF's ManageFirst certificates. (n.d.). Retrieved May 12, 2008, from http://www.nraef.org/managefirst/.

RBA certifications. (n.d.). Retrieved May 12, 2008, from http://www.rbanet.com/Educators/educators.html.

RCA certifications. (n.d.). Retrieved May 12, 2008, from http://www.culinology.org/certification/index.cfm?Fuseaction=CCRC&newlevel=2&topparentid=30.

USPCA's CPC certification. (n.d.). Retrieved May 12, 2008, from http://www.uspca.com/membership/certification.html.

CHAPTER 22

Lifelong Learning: Research, Travel, Stages, and Higher Degrees

Despite the many hours devoted to study and to self-development, a recent college graduate has only reached the starting point of her journey toward becoming a professional chef (or some other type of culinary professional). With ongoing advancement in technology and changes to culinary trends, there is always more for a culinary professional to learn. College provides a structured environment in which learning opportunities abound, but after graduation learners must locate educational activities on their own. No matter how successful they are today, culinary professionals must continue learning throughout their lifetimes if they are to avoid becoming outdated, has-beens in the future.

In this chapter, you will learn how to plan a self-directed learning activity and several common approaches that culinary professionals take to continue learning throughout their careers. You will also learn the importance of investing in continuing education.

22.1 DEFINING AND PLANNING SELF-DIRECTED LEARNING

For young students who have transitioned right from high school to college the term "self-directed" learning may be unfamiliar. Unlike the education provided at many colleges where teachers determine the what, when, and how of the students' educational experiences, self-directed learners seek, plan, and direct their own learning activities. Self-directed learning usually requires four steps.

1. *Analysis.* The learner conducts a self-analysis to determine her learning needs. Although some people enjoy learning for its own sake, many people prefer to focus on learning those subjects which will provide them the greatest immediate benefit in their lives. For example, a chef who has just been given the responsibility of developing a restaurant's profit and loss statement has a greater learning need for basic accounting than she does for an unrelated subject, such as beekeeping.
2. *Planning.* Once a learner determines her learning needs, she often creates a goal for her learning projects. Then, she sets benchmarks to know when the objective has been achieved, and she locates teachers or resources to help her meet that goal. In the

aforementioned example, an appropriate goal for the chef would be to learn how to create an accurate, professional profit and loss statement. She could reach out to co-workers or networking contacts for training, or she could look for courses or books to teach her that skill.

3. *Instruction.* At this point, the learner simply needs to follow through on her planning. If she needs training from other people, she should meet with them regularly. If she prefers to work from a book or through a computer program, she must open and use it until she accomplishes her goal.

4. *Evaluation.* At the end of the learning activity, the learner generally assesses her growth and development against her preset goal. If she has not reached the goal, she typically seeks additional activities to move her closer to the goal and then repeats the planning, instruction, and evaluation steps again. Continuing with the above example, after her training the chef verifies that she can complete an accurate, professional profit and loss statement. If she cannot, she may look into other courses, books, or friends to teach her more about P/L statement creation.

For many people the planning process is the most difficult step. Locating the right resources and learning activities to meet one's learning needs is not always as easy as it was in college. Once a person no longer has a team of qualified faculty on hand, finding appropriate teachers and resources takes a great deal of research. However, people with substantial networking contacts can often ask their professional friends for ways to meet their learning goals.

There are vast numbers of ways in which a person can learn, but certain learning activities are more common among culinary professionals than others. Some people prefer to learn on their own, while others do better learning in a group setting. Both of these learning styles can be accommodated in a number of ways. The following sections describe several common learning activities for each style preference.

22.2 COMMON SELF-DIRECTED LEARNING ACTIVITIES FOR INDIVIDUALS

22.2.1 Research Projects

Learners who wish to become subject-matter experts on a single topic at their own pace benefit greatly from conducting a research project. To conduct a research project, you merely select a subject you wish to learn and then study it in-depth until you reach the level of expertise you desire. The subject can be small, such as learning to make a single recipe, or expansive, such as understanding the history and cultural issues surrounding genetic modification.

Research can be pursued through various resources. Learners can read books and articles, speak with experts on a subject, and test their learning and knowledge with others. Because research projects (for graduates, at least) originate typically from within and not from an outside "teacher," some learners struggle to maintain their motivation and planned progression through a long research project. To overcome this obstacle you can formalize your study goals on paper and then share them with a friend or mentor who holds you accountable. Friends and mentors can serve as excellent motivators simply by checking-in regularly and asking about any progress made on the project.

At the conclusion of a research project, you may opt to take your information gathering one step further and present your research to others formally. Professional presentations allow you to synthesize your learning while earning respect, admiration, and sometimes even compensation, from others in the process. Presentation of research can take the form of a written article for publication, a speech given to colleagues at a conference or meeting, or even a course taught on the subject studied. Whether you choose to present your research or not, a research project that is well-planned and executed can greatly enhance your expertise on the subject of your choice.

Interview with Ming Tsai, Chef/Owner of Blue Ginger, Host/Executive Producer of "Simply Ming"

What forms of lifelong learning have you engaged in over the years?
The art of eating: enjoying food, traveling to under-the-radar spots like street food stalls. Most people can easily go to a fine dining restaurant and enjoy their meal, but to really learn about a culture and get in touch with the culture, you've got to eat what the people there eat. The only thing better than street food is eating at someone's home, though the challenge there is getting invited. Also, learning from my elders: everyone should spend as much time as possible with their elders.

What learning experience has been your most enjoyable?
Working abroad was the most fun and enjoyable. Living in Paris, working for Pierre Herme, living in Osaka and working for sushi master Kobayashi. Japanese was (and is), for me, so different than any other cuisine; it was amazing to have the opportunity to be there.

What learning experience has been your most valuable?
The most valuable is definitely everything my parents and grandparents taught me. I learned classic technique and recipes, as well as their own little tips and tricks for things. It taught me to respect the basics but also not to be afraid to experiment. I also recently went to China twice this past year, which was amazing. Seeing Peking duck made when you're actually in Beijing is the best lesson there is. To see a dish made in its native land, being made the same way it's been done for centuries, is priceless. The dumplings there are being made the same way they've been made for centuries.

How do you support lifelong learning in others?
Our staff is given ServSafe training; we do wine tastings every week. I take chefs and cooks to various events throughout the year, so they learn not only from me but from other chefs, and they learn not only restaurant, on-the-line cooking, but large-scale events, tasting events, etc. More than half of them are for charity, actually, so it's good to expose them to that, too. It's important to learn to give back. For my TV show, "Simply Ming," we have volunteer culinary interns who can learn not only East-West cuisine but also what goes into making a TV show. There's a real sense of accomplishment when a show is completed. They know they were a part of something.

(*continued*)

(*continued*)

What advice would you provide a recent culinary school graduate about lifelong learning?
Keep your ears and eyes open. Even though the books say to do it one way, there may be an easier (or a harder) way to do something; as long as it yields you better results, don't be afraid to do your own thing. Spend time with your grandparents and other elders. I spent every Friday afternoon growing up in Dayton, Ohio, with my grandparents, and I wish it had been seven days a week.

22.2.2 Travel

Some culinary professionals enjoy learning about other cultures and cuisines. One of the best ways to experience another culture firsthand is to travel. Educational travel to other cities or countries differs from vacation travel in several important ways. Whereas vacations allow you to relax and to escape responsibility, a learning excursion requires that you engage in educational activities on your trip. Chefs without copious amounts of vacation time can reserve a day or two from their "getaway" vacation for learning activities if they wish both to relax and to learn on the same trip.

To maximize learning opportunities when traveling, a person must plan ahead. You can research the best or most authentic restaurants in the area and reserve time to dine at them. If possible, you may wish to set up appointments to speak with local chefs during your trip. You should not forget about locally produced foods either; a visit to a local producer, such as a cheese maker, a beer brewer, or an olive grower, can provide a chef a deeper understanding of those ingredients. If a culinary school operates in the area, you may wish to register for a class on the local cuisine.

Such localized learning experiences can provide a wealth of knowledge, but poor planning will make a potentially wonderful education fall short. Many working adults and organizations can only accommodate tourists at specific times. By contacting the places you wish to visit in advance, you can find out if and when they allow visitors. Then, you can arrange your travel plans to arrive when a local contact has time to speak with you, or even better you can schedule an appointment with your contact. A tour of a cheese factory, for example, is far more educational when it includes an interview with the cheese maker. Taking the time to make local contacts, appointments, and an efficient travel schedule will greatly enhance the educational value of your trip.

22.2.3 Stages

A stage (with the "a" pronounced "ah" as in "father") is a short time period spent working in a chef's kitchen, usually for free, to learn that chef's menu and style of cooking. Similar to learning in an apprenticeship, in a stage you learn simply by watching and imitating what you see going on around you in the kitchen. A stage can last for a few days or for several weeks, but some people incorporate many brief stages into their careers between jobs, on vacations, or during scheduled days off from work. A stage not only expands your culinary repertoire by teaching you new recipes, but it also exposes you to new flavor combinations and cooking techniques. Because some of the most innovative work done in today's kitchens may take months or years to make its way into print, a stage in a very progressive restaurant can help you stay cutting edge.

Choosing the right chef under whom to study in a stage is critical to making it valuable. Select a chef and a kitchen where you will learn the kinds of skills you most want to learn. For example, if you want to add Thai flavors to your repertoire, work for an authentic Thai restaurant rather than for an upscale place that incorporates some Thai flavors into another cuisine. If you work hard to learn from your temporary boss and co-workers, you may find them willing not only to teach you on site but also to network and to help you once you return back home.

To set up a stage simply contact a chef to see if she is willing to let you work for free in her kitchen. Most chefs are grateful to have the free labor, but a few either cannot accommodate an extra person in their kitchen or simply do not have the time to train an extra person. Occasionally, a large company will forbid non-employees from working to limit injury liability lawsuits. If a chef allows you to volunteer in her kitchen, all you need to do is to show up prepared and work hard. You should pay attention to what other cooks are doing, but you must complete your own responsibilities, too. Your work is your payment for the education, but the education is usually worth the extra effort.

22.2.4 Educational Technologies

Students can learn independently by purchasing electronic format education modules. Some colleges and educational organizations, such as the Culinary Institute of America, the American Hotel & Lodging Educational Institute, and the American Culinary Federation, produce and sell educational videos and DVD's that anyone can purchase to watch and learn about a particular topic. Some companies, which produce and sell technologies used in restaurants, such as point of sales systems, offer training software for people to learn how to use their technologies.

Some educational organizations offer self-paced learning opportunities online. Different from typical synchronous online classes where students meet deadlines and complete assignments according to the guidelines of an instructor, asynchronous or self-paced online education allows students to progress through learning modules on their own schedule. The "courses" may be available entirely online, or students may need to purchase CD's to complete the courses on their own computers. Such learning experiences do not always provide college credit, but they may be useful in meeting continuing education requirements for certification. A quick search through the Internet will turn up a range of educational culinary resources open to individuals who just want to learn and improve their skills.

22.3 LEARNING WITH OTHERS

22.3.1 Higher Degrees

For those people who prefer to have compatriots learning alongside them, formal education is one of the most traditional and widespread options available. Many colleges offer bachelors degrees in culinary arts or in related topics such as hospitality management, food science, food marketing, and even business degrees designed for hospitality employees. Some schools offer masters and PhD degrees, too, although degrees at these higher levels rarely focus on culinary arts. Hospitality and food science advanced degrees have existed for many years, but a few food studies or gastronomy graduate programs have popped up around the world in the past decade. These food-related programs often connect cultural culinary issues and science to encompass such fields as culinary cultural anthropology, food history, nutrition, and food politics. Despite the higher emphasis on reading and research and minimal hands-on cooking, the formal education setting will seem somewhat familiar to those who have been through culinary school already.

A major perk to learning through formal education is that you earn a substantial credential in the process; however, the degree does not come easily. The workload and focus is determined by the instructor and can be significant. Degrees require tuition payments as well.

To pursue lifelong learning through formal education first research school options to find the one that best suits your needs. Choose a school because it aligns most with your learning needs, not because it is cheaper or easier. If relocation is an option, look beyond local schools. Next, discuss your new commitments with your family and with your employer to make sure that you can schedule enough time to complete your program successfully. A degree program holds little value if you never make it to class. Finally, apply for admission to the school. The application process for higher degrees can be challenging and not everyone who applies is accepted. However, do not allow your own insecurities to prevent you from applying; the only way to know if you can get into a program is to apply.

Interview with Matthew Raiford, Executive Chef, Galaxy Diner, Gaylord National Resort & Convention Center on the Potomac

How big a believer are you in lifelong learning?
Huge! I am a staunch advocate of lifelong learning. There is always something for you to learn. Especially in the culinary industry, there are so many growing facets, tools, and styles/types of foods/dishes. There are chefs breaking down the molecular structure of food to create the "perfect" taste. Culinary is more than cooking; there is the science, history, culture, and growth of foods behind it.

How do you make time for learning in your busy schedule?
People make time for what they want. It is easy to say, "I do not have time to learn something new" and fill your day with other things and/or get distracted by life. Managing staff, vendors, budgets, and family is quite time consuming. The same energy I put into my operations and family I put into learning. A successful business is contingent on one staying on top of the trends and innovative things in the industry. It is about balance. I take at least 15 minutes a day to read the food section or a food-related article. I attend wine tastings, food tastings, and travel. Some say they do the exact same things, but my challenge is: Are you doing it to learn or to say you heard about it? Some are reading the food section to gossip or contend with ratings rather than to read about a fresh idea or spin on an old one. I also take the time to research food items and dishes and share that information with my staff.

What has been the benefit to you for continuing to pursue lifelong learning?
The ability to teach and share with others, to expand their minds on what, to many, seems ordinary.

(continued)

(*continued*)

How do you support lifelong learning in others?
I teach and mentor students and staff. I always encourage them to look past what they already know and to be open to what they already know. You may know how to sauté, but can you create what the chef is looking for?

What advice would you provide a recent culinary school graduate about lifelong learning?
Lifelong learning can be done with little or no money. Read and keep reading. Volunteer for culinary events in and outside of the state or country. Start small and think big. Keep your eyes open. Read the local paper. Hang out at the bookstore in the cookbook section. Budget and dine at a restaurant once a month. Participate in professional associations or volunteer organizations that will introduce you to new things.

22.3.2 Short Culinary Courses

Although you may be more familiar with the comprehensive vocational training program at your college, many schools also offer one-day or one-week, non-credit courses for professionals. These courses require a much smaller time commitment than a full degree program, but they can convey a lot of information on a single subject in a short period of time. They are also easy to locate. Generally, an Internet search will turn up dozens of schools around the world (including close to home) that offer courses for culinary professionals. These courses rarely require any application process, so you can enroll simply by selecting a course and paying the registration fee. Because there is still some time commitment, you may need to adjust your work schedule, but scheduling time off to attend a one-day or one-week course is much easier than accommodating an entire degree program.

22.3.3 Conferences and Workshops

To learn about recent changes and trends in the industry many culinary professionals seek out conferences, workshops, and trade shows. These learning experiences often require a financial investment for registration, travel, and lodging, but they offer a condensed learning experience over just a few days. The culinary industry boasts enough conferences that a professional could attend one nearly every week of the year. To choose the ones that are best for you, research the topics discussed at the conference and the reputation that the conference (or workshop or trade show) has among people who have attended it in years past. Some conferences are of higher quality than others, and the topics vary greatly from one show to the next. Conferences also create great networking opportunities, so find out if the typical attendees are the kinds of people whom you would like to meet. A little research will help you to find the right conference for your needs.

Once you have selected your conference, workshop, or trade show, speak with your supervisor to request time off from work. Some companies provide funding for their employees to attend such activities, so ask about that as well. Register for the program early. Many conferences offer a discount for early registration, and some workshops sell out well in advance. Make your travel plans early, too, as airfare and hotel prices often go up closer to the departure date. Once you have done your advance planning, you just need to attend. Take notes during sessions as you would during a class to help you remember important facts once you return home. Network actively, too, to help make your experience valuable beyond the education you receive.

22.3.4 Professional Association Meetings

Although some professional associations do not meet regularly, others meet often and include educational programming as part of their meetings. Locating the right association for your learning goals will require some research, but professional contacts can point you in the right direction. Beware, however, that associations do change over time. The topics presented at each meeting may not fit your exact goals, and the quality of education may vary greatly each time. Still, attending an association meeting is a good way to learn new things while networking with colleagues. The cost is typically minimal beyond the association membership, and the time commitment is rarely more than a few hours per month. To take advantage of this learning opportunity, you need only to join an association and to commit to attending the meetings.

22.3.5 Communities of Learning

A community of learning could be described as a cross between a professional association and a book club. In a community of learning, individuals join together and schedule regular activities or meetings to enhance each other's skills and knowledge. Communities of learning often require members to teach new skills to each other, so everyone contributes and everyone learns. The topics typically depend on the interests and skills of the members. Meetings may be formal with practical demonstrations, but an informal sharing of knowledge over dinner can sometimes be just as effective.

Perhaps the most appealing quality of a community of learning is the ease in which it can be created. Colleagues can form a community without membership costs and simply schedule meetings at each other's homes or businesses. Time is often the only cost to a member. You can form a community of learning by speaking with other professionals, maybe even classmates, and asking them to meet regularly to share newly learned skills with each other. Working together an active community of learners can greatly accelerate the speed at which community members learn new skills and knowledge.

Interview with Mark Miller, Culinary Consultant

What forms of lifelong learning have you engaged in over the years?
The three are: books (I have over 6,000 and buy them continually), real-life experiences of going to restaurants in a native environment and to big cities, and travel to other countries (chefs are too influenced by food television and fooled to think that a two-day course compares with a trip through the many regions of China). I used to go through the back roads of Guatemala for a month. I'd go on a bus, visit the churches, see the tortillas sold by the women there. You can't understand tortillas if you only have a couple of commercially made ones. You can't understand bread if you've only bought it at Whole Foods. Learning from other chefs is also important. When I go to El Bulli, it increases my culinary knowledge of what's possible.

What learning experience has been your most valuable?
Travel. Up and down the markets of China in the 80's. My last passport had 89 stamps to Thailand. I have not been to NYC in 18 months, but I've been to Tokyo 6 times in a year.

(continued)

(*continued*)

What has been the benefit to you for continuing to pursue lifelong learning?
The ability to have a long-term culinary career that is not attached to a restaurant. I continue to practice making available my knowledge, skill, and perceptual level. I can aid people conceptually and do strategic thinking. I also evaluate concepts for people. I lecture on sense of place and talk to companies about that, too. Food touches on our lives in many different ways. It is about our identity, our consciousness, our belief system. So continue to learn additional skill sets. Think about being a food professional, not just a chef. You can learn the business applications.

What advice would you provide a recent culinary school graduate about lifelong learning?
Get a job from the best chef. Plan to learn over a given period of time. The best student I ever had was someone who rotated stations every four weeks to learn more in six months than anyone else ever had. He had a plan of action to accomplish a set of goals. You have to evaluate your skill set and then have a plan of action. Limit yourself to work somewhere only as long as you're learning. Align yourself with your own internal culinary clock, and do what you do best using your individual skill set. Think of your career in three stages. The first ten years require intense learning. In the next 20 years you practice and refine your skills. In the final 30 years, sell that knowledge and talent back to capitalize on it; work as a consultant. Students should not ever think of their careers just as being chefs in kitchens. It is too limiting and doesn't prepare them for their careers—learning, practice and selling their experience/skills.

22.4   WHY LIFELONG LEARNING IS SO IMPORTANT

Human beings have the capacity to learn throughout most of their lifetime, yet too many people believe that there is no need to learn after "schooling" has been completed. In addition to the mental stimulation and the self-satisfaction that comes from learning something new, a culinary professional encounters many benefits from continuing to learn over a lifetime.

Imagine a culinary school graduate who begins her career in the 1960s as a talented, well-respected chef. She excels in all of the classic dishes of the 1960s and her food reflects the style of the times—large, heavy center-of-the-plate items with rich sauces, vegetable custards, even large roasts carved tableside for guests. But by the time she reaches retirement age she attracts few customers; most people view her cooking as old, tired, and passé. Her cooking is the same as it always was, but by the year 2000, society had changed. This chef never adjusted to the trends over the years in which people requested healthier, lower-fat meals, vegetables in more natural preparations, and fancier plate presentations from the kitchen not simpler ones assembled tableside. Had the chef continued to learn and to adapt through her lifetime, she could have retired wealthy and successful. Instead, she quickly cooked her way into obscurity.

Learning about new kitchen technologies, changing culinary trends, and modern eating habits you avoid getting stuck in a rut, and you stay current with your customers' needs. With new culinary school graduates entering the workforce each year, chefs who do not evolve lose customers to the more recent graduates who know more about modern cooking than they do. Even management styles change, so a chef who sticks with an old-world style may lose employees to younger, more progressive managers.

Lifelong learning offers benefits to entry-level employees and to first-tier managers as well. Cooks who expand their skill sets to perform better at work will likely earn promotions and pay increases faster than their co-workers. Newly learned skills can help cooks with moves to other companies or even with a new career focus, such as shifting from food preparation to food writing or food television.

One of the most common stumbling blocks with lifelong learning is the loss of momentum after college graduation. Students begin learning in school and then fail to incorporate learning into their lives after graduation. By the time they need to learn new skills they have forgotten how to study, how to make time for learning, even how to motivate themselves to engage in learning activities. Most culinary school students come to school because they find value in learning. That value does not diminish as a person ages.

You probably already feel some personal satisfaction from learning new things. Continuing to learn after graduation allows you to sustain that sense of satisfaction and to build upon the foundation you have gained in culinary school. Everyone who completes culinary school enters the workforce with a similar culinary foundation, but only those who continue to learn stand out in the constantly evolving culinary industry. Make education a lifelong pursuit, not just a youthful diversion, and you will continue to flourish in the culinary profession.

Summary

Self-directed learners recognize a learning need within themselves, plan a learning activity to satisfy that need, engage in that activity, and assess its success in satisfying the learning need. Self-directed learners may engage in learning throughout their lifetimes in a number of ways. Learners who prefer individualized learning activities may plan research projects, schedule educational travel experiences, set up stages, or complete electronic learning modules. People who prefer to learn alongside others may pursue higher degrees, take brief non-credit courses, register for professional conferences or workshops, attend professional association meetings, or create a community of learning.

Culinary professionals who continue to learn throughout their lifetimes generally advance beyond those who stop learning after college. Lifelong learning helps a culinary professional to keep up with changing trends and to avoid being outshined by recent culinary school graduates with more current information and modern skills. Cooks and chefs may pursue lifelong learning to earn a promotion or simply to experience the pride that comes from acquiring new knowledge and skills. Now matter why a person chooses to continue to learn, lifelong learning always gives a culinary professional an edge over those colleagues who opt to stop learning at some point in their careers.

COMMON WAYS TO ENGAGE IN LIFELONG LEARNING

- Conduct a research project on a subject of interest.
- Arrange travel plans to make trips as educational as possible.
- Set up stages to learn the cooking styles and recipes of other chefs.
- Enroll in a degree program in a college or university.
- Register for non-credit courses to learn new skills.
- Attend conferences, workshops, or trade shows to keep up with industry trends.
- Attend professional association meetings when education is included in the program.
- Set up a community of learning to teach and to learn from others.

Suggested Tasks

1. Research several lifelong learning approaches that you find interesting. Select the one that you believe will be the most valuable for your career. Set a learning goal with specific benchmarks describing what you want to achieve from the learning activity. Make plans to engage in that learning activity, and follow through on your plans. Assess your progress to see if you have met your learning goal.

2. Interview a culinary professional to find out what she does for lifelong learning. Ask how much time she makes in her schedule for learning and how difficult it is to schedule that time. Ask what the benefit is to her for engaging in lifelong learning activities. Find out what learning activities she recommends for recent college graduates. Compile your research and share it with your class.

3. Write down your professional goals for five, ten, and twenty years from now. List what additional skills and professional development you will need after graduation to reach those goals. List several learning activities that will help you to reach those goals. Share your goals and lists with a teacher to get additional suggestions to help you reach your goals. Record those suggestions as well. Save your lists and refer to them at least once annually. Engage in at least one learning activity from your list each year until you have reached your goals.

4. Interview an instructor at your school. Ask what lifelong learning, if any, she engaged in after college. Ask which learning activities she found to be the most valuable and which the least. Ask what impact lifelong learning has had on her career. Conclude by asking if she could have achieved her current job and stature just on her college degree and work history alone; if the answer is "no," ask her where she believes she would be working instead without lifelong learning. Share your findings with your class.

CONCLUSION

When Do I Reach the Top?

Young culinary school graduates often wish to know how long they need to work before becoming a "master chef." Although a certification with this name does exist, what these students really want to know is "How long before I make it to the top of the industry?" To answer that question is nearly impossible. Not only do different people progress at different speeds up the career ladder, but in today's culinary world there is no defined final rung as one approaches the top of the ladder.

Chefs who grow to become superstars in their local community sometimes wish to compete on a national level. World-famous chefs who run a spectacular restaurant may feel the need to expand beyond a single restaurant and open up a restaurant empire. Some may not feel that they are truly successful until they have published books, developed a product line of food and equipment, and starred in a successful television show. For most successful contemporary chefs, today's achievements are not enough for tomorrow's world. Many of the world's top chefs may not acknowledge that they have reached the top, for they believe that they still have much more to accomplish in their careers. And yet, many culinary professionals consider these best-of-the-best chefs as the pinnacle of the industry.

So how do you know when you have reached the top of the culinary industry? Progress up the career ladder can be found in the small details. One day you may realize that your co-workers come to you every day for advice because they respect your talent. Further down the road you may earn a promotion and everyone around you suddenly starts calling you "chef." Not realizing your own fame after years of hard work in the industry, someday some stranger comes up to you and states that he has always wanted to meet you because he loves your work. If you are fortunate, you will experience these and many other reality shifts as you take small steps toward the top of the career ladder. Hopefully, you will feel a great sense of satisfaction and happiness with each achievement you make in your career; with any luck each one will motivate you to continue to learn, to grow, and to climb even further up the ladder.

A culinary career, like life, is a journey, not a destination. When you enjoy each day and strive to move further down the path of your career, you will be able to look back with joy to see the great distance you have advanced in your journey. Looking for progress daily only turns up frustration as the distance traversed in brief time periods is rarely expansive. You may choose to set goals for yourself, but recognize that each goal is only a stepping stone to the next goal if you wish to approach the top of the industry. Some young chefs become easily frustrated and disappointed that they are not superstars, executive chefs, or business owners in their first few years out of school. They may give up on their quest and stop trying to advance their skills and their careers; they may even leave the culinary arts industry entirely. However, as long as you keep apathy at bay and passion for advancement burning, you will inevitably find that you continue to advance to the top of the field, even when that progress is slow and when the top seems unattainable. If this book has taught you one thing, hopefully it has taught you that investing heavily in your own learning and self-development moves you ahead of others who devote less time and effort to personal growth. Once you have advanced beyond most of those around you, you will find yourself at or near the top of your field.

May your adventures in the culinary field be rewarding. May you easily overcome the obstacles in your way. May you never lose your passion for learning, for advancement, and for excellence. And may your culinary school education lead to a long, successful, and joyful career.

APPENDIX 1

Professional Associations

Below is a list of professional associations of all sorts. Some promote certain products, while others are solely for member education and networking. Some allow individuals (even non-professionals) to become members, while others only have business members. Some represent very specific interests, while others support a very broad spectrum of food-related individuals. The list provides addresses, phone numbers, and Web sites to allow for further research on your part. However, the list is not meant to be comprehensive of all food and hospitality-related associations, which could be an entire book on its own.

This list is merely a small sample of the kinds of organizations out there. A good number of the associations listed below also have foundations for grants and scholarships and some have separate education divisions. Contact information for these foundations and education divisions can typically be located through the Web site of the parent association. If you have an interest in professional associations, you are encouraged to conduct additional research on your own. Each year, more and more associations are created (and some cease to exist). If you do not find the association that meets your needs here, you may be able to find it on the Internet.

American Bakers Association
1300 I Street NW, Suite 700 West
Washington, DC 20005
202-789-0300
www.americanbakers.org

American Culinary Federation
180 Center Place Way
St. Augustine, FL 32095
800-624-9458
www.acfchefs.org

American Dietetic Association
120 South Riverside Plaza,
   Suite 2000
Chicago, IL 60606-6995
800-877-1600
www.eatright.org

American Frozen Food Institute
2000 Corporate Ridge, Suite 1000
McLean, VA 22102
703-821-0770
www.affi.com

American Hotel & Lodging Association
1201 New York Avenue, NW #600
Washington, DC 20005-3931
202-289-3100
www.ahla.com

American Institute of Baking
1213 Bakers Way
P.O. Box 3999
Manhattan, KS 66505-3999
800-633-5137
www.aibonline.org

American Institute of Wine
   and Food
213-37 39th Avenue, Box 216
Bayside, NY 11361
800-274-2493
www.aiwf.org

American Meat Science Association
1111 North Dumlap Avenue
Savoy, IL 61874
217-356-5368
www.meatscience.org

American Personal and Private Chef Association
4572 Delaware Street
San Diego, CA 92116
800-644-8389
www.personalchef.com

American School Food Service Association
700 South Washington Street, Suite 300
Alexandria, VA 22314
703-739-3900
www.asfsa.org

American Society for Healthcare Food Service
  Administrators
455 South Fourth Street, Suite 650
Louisville, KY 40202
800-620-6422
www.ashfsa.org

American Society of Baking
533 1st Street East
Sonoma, CA 95476
707-935-0103
www.asbe.org

American Society for Nutrition
9650 Rockville Pike
Bethesda, MD 20814
301-634-7050
www.nutrition.org

America's Second Harvest
35 E. Wacker Drive, #2000
Chicago, IL 60601
800-771-2303
www.secondharvest.org

Association of Food Journalists
7 Avenida Vista Grande Ste B7 #467
Santa Fe, NM 87508
www.afjonline.com

Black Culinarians Alliance
55 West 116th Street, Suite 234
New York, NY 10026
800-308-8188
www.blackculinarians.com

Bread Bakers Guild of America
3203 Maryland Avenue
North Versailles, PA 15137
412-823-2080
www.bbga.org

Canadian Personal Chef Alliance
1054 Centre Street, Suite 593
Thornhill, Ontario
Canada, L4J 7V2
905-482-2433
www.canadianpersonalchefalliance.ca

Confrérie de la Chaîne des Rôtisseurs (United
  States)
Chaîne House at Fairleigh Dickinson
  University
285 Madison Avenue
Madison, NJ 07940-1099
973-360-9200
www.chaineus.org

Chefs Collaborative
89 South St., lower level
Boston, MA 02111
617-236-5200
www.chefscollaborative.org

Club Managers Association
  of America
1733 King Street
Alexandria, VA 22314
703-739-9500
www.cmaa.org

COPIA: The American Center for Wine,
  Food, and the Arts
500 First Street
Napa, CA 94559
888-512-6742
www.copia.org

Council of Hotel and Restaurant Trainers,
  CHART
P.O. Box 2835
Westfield, NJ 07091
800-463-5918
www.chart.org

Council of Independent Restaurants of
  America/Dine Originals
www.dineoriginals.com
(contacts vary with question category and region)

Cruise Lines International Association, Inc.
910 SE 17th Street, Suite 400
Fort Lauderdale, FL 33316
754-224-2200
www.cruising.org

Foodservice Consultants Society
International
455 South Fourth Street, Suite 650
Louisville, KY 40202
502-583-3783
www.fcsi.org

Foodservice Educators Network
International
20 W Kinzie, Suite 1200
Chicago, IL 60610
312-849-2220
www.feni.org

Green Restaurant Association
89 South St., Suite LL02
Boston, MA 0211
858-452-7378
www.dinegreen.com

Independent Bakers Association
P.O. Box 3731
Washington, DC 20007
202-333-8190
www.mindspring.com/~independentbaker

Institute of Food Technologists
525 W. Van Buren, Suite 1000
Chicago, IL 60607
312-782-8424
www.ift.org

Institute of Hospitality
Trinity Court
34 West Street
Sutton
Surrey
SM1 1SH
+44 (0)20 8661 4901
www.hcima.org.uk

International Association of Culinary
Professionals
455 South Fourth Street, Suite 650
Louisville, KY 40202
800-928-4227
www.iacp.com

International Caterers Association
91 Timberlane Drive
Williamsville, NY 14221
877-422-4221
www.icacater.org

International Council on Hotel, Restaurant, and
Institutional Education
2810 North Parham Road, Suite 230
Richmond, VA 23294
804-346-4800
www.chrie.org

International Culinary Tourism Association
4110 SE Hawthorne Boulevard, Suite 440
Portland, OR 97214
503-750-7200
www.culinarytourism.org

International Foodservice Distributors
Association
201 Park Washington Court
Falls Church, VA 22046
703-532-9400
www.ifdaonline.org

International Food Service Executives
Association
2609 Surfwood Drive
Las Vegas, NV 89128
800-893-5499
www.ifsea.com

International Food Wine and Travel Writers
Association
1142 South Diamond Bar Boulevard #177
Diamond Bar, CA 91765-2203
877-439-8929
www.ifwtwa.org

International Foodservice Manufacturers
Association
Two Prudential Plaza
180 North Stetson Avenue, Suite 4400
Chicago, IL 60601
312-540-4400
www.ifmaworld.com

International Hotel & Restaurant Association
48, Boulevard de Sébastopol
75003 Paris, France
+33 1 44 88 92 20
www.ih-ra.com

International Special Events Society
401 N. Michigan Avenue
Chicago, IL 60611-4267
800-688-4737
www.ises.com

James Beard Foundation
6 W. 18th Street, 10th Floor
New York, NY 10011
212-627-1111
www.jamesbeard.org

Les Dames d'Escoffier International
www.ldei.org
(contact information varies by chapter)

Multicultural Foodservice and Hospitality
  Alliance
P.O. Box 25661
Providence, RI 02905
401-461-6342
www.mfha.net

National Association of Catering Executives
9881 Broken Land Parkway, Suite 101
Columbia, MD 21046
410-290-5410
www.nace.net

National Association for the Specialty Food
  Trade, Inc.
120 Wall Street, 27th Floor
New York, NY 10005
212-482-6440
www.specialtyfood.com

National Ice Carving Association
P.O. Box 3593
Oak Brook, IL 60522-3593
630-871-8431
www.nica.org

National Restaurant Association
1200 17th Street, NW
Washington, DC 20036
800-424-5156
www.restaurant.org

Network of Executive Women
  in Hospitality, Inc.
P.O. Box 322
Shawano, WI 54166
800-593-NEWH
www.newh.org

Oldways Preservation &
  Exchange Trust
266 Beacon Street
Boston, MA 02116

617-421-5500
www.oldwayspt.org

Personal Chefs Network, Inc.
www.personalchefsnetwork.com

Professional Association of Innkeepers
  International
207 White Horse Pike
Haddon Heights, NJ 08035
800-468-7244
www.paii.org

Professional Chef's Association
1207 Hawkeye Court
Fort Collins, CO 80525
970-223-4004
www.professionalchef.com

Research Chefs Association
1100 Johnson Ferry Road,
  Suite 300
Atlanta, GA 30342
404-252-3663
www.culinology.com

Retail Bakers of America
8201 Greensboro Drive, Suite 300
McLean, VA 22102
800-638-0924
www.rbanet.com

Share Our Strength
1730 M Street NW, Suite 700
Washington, DC 20036
800-969-4767
www.strength.org

Slow Food USA
20 Jay Street, Suite 313
Brooklyn, NY 11201
877-SlowFoo(d)
www.slowfoodusa.org

Society for Foodservice Management
455 South Fourth Street, Suite 650
Louisville, KY 40202
502-583-3783
www.sfm-online.org

Southern Foodways Alliance
Center for the Study of Southern Culture
Barnard Observatory

University, MS 38677
662-915-5993
www.southernfoodways.com

United States Personal Chef Association
610 Quantum Road N.E.
Rio Rancho, NM 87124
800-995-2138
www.uspca.com

Women Chefs and Restaurateurs
455 South Fourth Street, Suite 650
Louisville, KY 40202

877-927-7787
www.womenchefs.org

Women's Foodservice Forum
Southpoint Office Center
1650 West 82nd Street, Suite 650
Bloomington, MN 55431
866-368-8008
www.womensfoodservice.forum.com

World Association of Cooks Societies
www.wacs2000.org
(contact information varies by country)

APPENDIX 2

Job Descriptions

Below is a sample of theoretical job descriptions for certain positions commonly held by individuals with culinary school credentials. Although these job descriptions are not taken from a specific company (and thus do not contain elements unique to any one company), they provide the basics common to most individuals with these titles. Salary details are not provided as they vary widely based on region, size of operation, caliber of food, and other factors. For current information on salaries, visit Web sites such as: www.payscale.com, www.cbsalary.com, www.starchefs.com, or www.bls.gov.

This list of job descriptions is not intended to suggest that these are the only jobs culinary school graduates could earn. It is only a small sampling of the many positions that a culinary school graduate could hold. The jobs are listed alphabetically by job title.

JOB TITLE: CHEF DE CUISINE (HOTEL)

Reports To: Executive Chef

Position Summary: The Chef de Cuisine is the highest position in one of the kitchens (banquets or restaurant) and is responsible for all kitchen functions in that kitchen.

Essential Duties:

- Create menu, standardized recipes, and plate presentations for all food served in conjunction with executive chef.
- Oversee food production to monitor proper quality and quantity of food produced.
- Recruit, interview, hire, train, supervise, and evaluate kitchen staff.
- Determine kitchen staffing needs and schedule employees accordingly.
- Oversee/conduct requisition functions for kitchen from purchasing department.
- Maintain proper sanitation in production of all foods by staff.
- Achieve specified food cost, labor cost, and sales targets.
- Participate in marketing and promotional activities.
- Coordinate with the service and/or event staff to meet guest needs.

Common Minimum Qualifications: 5–10 years of kitchen experience, including minimum 3 years as sous chef or other kitchen manager. Food handler's license required. Must have strong culinary, computer, resource management, and leadership skills. Preferred: culinary degree/diploma, apprenticeship, and/or certification.

JOB TITLE: CHEF-INSTRUCTOR (COLLEGE/CULINARY SCHOOL)

Reports To: Department Dean

Position Summary: The Chef-Instructor teaches culinary skills to students in a classroom and/or lab setting.

Essential Duties:

- Create syllabus, lesson plans, and instructional aides for class.
- Submit product requisitions for lab classes.
- Deliver class content to students and facilitate related class discussion/production.
- Monitor production in lab classes to ensure student adherence to sanitation, safety, quality, and other class/school requirements.
- Provide feedback to students to assist in the learning process.
- Create, deliver, and grade student homework, exams, and other assessments.
- Calculate student final grades for the course.
- Advise, tutor, and counsel students.
- Engage in professional development activities.
- Engage in curriculum development.
- Enforce school rules.
- Serve on school committees.
- Attend faculty meetings.

Common Minimum Qualifications: Culinary (or related) degree at least as high in credential as the degree being taught at the college. Minimum 2–5 years experience at a management level in foodservice. Expertise in the subject matter taught, teaching, organizational, and human relations skills. Preferred: industry certification.

JOB TITLE: CHEF-INSTRUCTOR (HIGH SCHOOL)

Reports To: School Principal

Position Summary: The Chef-Instructor teaches culinary skills to students in a classroom and/or lab setting.

Essential Duties:

- Create syllabus, lesson plans, and instructional aides for class.
- Purchases products for lab classes.
- Deliver class content to students and facilitate related class discussion/production.
- Monitor production in lab classes to ensure student adherence to sanitation, safety, quality, and other class/school requirements.
- Provide feedback to students to assist in the learning process.
- Create, deliver, and grade student homework, exams, and other assessments.
- Calculate student final grades for the course.
- Advise, tutor, and counsel students.
- Engage in professional development activities.
- Engage in curriculum development.
- Enforce school rules.
- Serve on school committees.
- Attend faculty meetings.

Common Minimum Qualifications: Culinary (or related) degree and (in some cases) teaching certificate (or similar credential). Minimum 2–5 years culinary industry experience. Expertise in culinary arts, teaching, organizational, and human relations skills. Preferred: industry certification.

JOB TITLE: EXECUTIVE CHEF (CATERER)

Reports To: Owner

Position Summary: The Executive Chef is the highest position in the kitchen and is responsible for all kitchen functions.

Essential Duties:

- Create menu options, standardized recipes, and presentations for all food.
- Oversee food production to monitor proper quality and quantity of food produced.
- Recruit, interview, hire, train, supervise, and evaluate kitchen staff.
- Determine kitchen and event staffing needs and schedule employees accordingly.
- Oversee purchasing, receiving, and inventory functions for kitchen, including selecting purveyors and determining product specifications.
- Oversee purchase and maintenance of kitchen equipment.
- Maintain proper sanitation in production of all foods by staff.
- Determine and achieve specified food cost, labor cost, and sales targets.
- Participate in marketing and promotional activities.
- Coordinate with event staff to meet guest needs.
- Coordinate and oversee delivery of food to event sites.

Common Minimum Qualifications: 5–10 years of kitchen experience, including minimum 3 years as sous chef or other kitchen manager. Food handler's license required. Must have strong culinary, computer, resource management, and leadership skills. Preferred: culinary degree/diploma, apprenticeship, and/or certification.

JOB TITLE: EXECUTIVE CHEF (HOTEL)

Reports To: Food and Beverage Manager

Position Summary: The Executive Chef is the highest position in the kitchen team and is responsible for all foodservice operations in any of the hotel's kitchens.

Essential Duties:

- Oversee/create menus, standardized recipes, and plate presentations for all food served in restaurants, room service, and banquet halls.
- Oversee (through chefs de cuisine) food production to monitor proper quality and quantity of food produced.
- Recruit, interview, hire, train, supervise, and evaluate senior kitchen staff.
- Determine kitchen staffing needs and hire employees accordingly.
- Oversee (in conjunction with purchasing department) purchasing, receiving, and inventory functions for kitchen, including selecting purveyors and determining product specifications.
- Oversee purchase and maintenance of kitchen equipment.
- Maintain proper sanitation in production of all foods by staff.
- Determine and achieve specified food cost, labor cost, and sales targets.
- Participate in marketing and promotional activities.
- Coordinate with the service and event staff to meet guest needs.

Common Minimum Qualifications: 5–10 years of kitchen experience, including minimum 3 years as sous chef or other kitchen manager. Food handler's license required. Must have strong culinary, computer, resource management, and leadership skills. Preferred: culinary degree/diploma, apprenticeship, and/or certification.

JOB TITLE: EXECUTIVE CHEF (RESTAURANT)

Reports To: Owner or General Manager

Position Summary: The Executive Chef is the highest position in the kitchen and is responsible for all kitchen functions.

Essential Duties:

- Create menu, standardized recipes, and plate presentations for all food served.
- Oversee food production to monitor proper quality and quantity of food produced.
- Recruit, interview, hire, train, supervise, and evaluate kitchen staff.
- Determine kitchen staffing needs and schedule employees accordingly.
- Oversee/conduct purchasing, receiving, and inventory functions for kitchen, including selecting purveyors and determining product specifications.
- Oversee purchase and maintenance of kitchen equipment.
- Maintain proper sanitation in production of all foods by staff.
- Determine and achieve specified food cost, labor cost, and sales targets.
- Participate in marketing and promotional activities.
- Coordinate with the service staff to meet guest needs.

Common Minimum Qualifications: 5–10 years of kitchen experience, including minimum 3 years as sous chef or other kitchen manager. Food handler's license required. Must have strong culinary, computer, resource management, and leadership skills. Preferred: culinary degree/diploma, apprenticeship, and/or certification.

JOB TITLE: LINE COOK

Reports To: Sous Chef

Position Summary: The Line Cook is responsible for the production of all food from a single station.

Essential Duties:

- Set up station and prepare all mise en place for the operation of that station.
- Prepare/cook and plate all guest orders from that station according to the given standardized recipes and plate presentations and within the allowable time frame.
- Coordinate with expediter/sous chef and other line cooks to ensure proper timing of food.
- Maintain proper sanitation in food production.
- Maintain kitchen standards for quality and product yield/waste.
- Store all remaining product properly and clean station at shift's end.

Common Minimum Qualifications: Must have strong culinary skills. Preferred: culinary degree/diploma or apprenticeship.

JOB TITLE: PASTRY CHEF (BAKERY)

Reports To: Owner or General Manager

Position Summary: The Pastry Chef is the highest position in the bakery's kitchen and is responsible for all kitchen functions.

Essential Duties:

- Create bakery offerings, standardized recipes, and presentations for all food sold.
- Oversee food production to monitor proper quality and quantity of food produced.

- Recruit, interview, hire, train, supervise, and evaluate kitchen staff.
- Determine kitchen staffing needs and schedule employees accordingly.
- Oversee/conduct purchasing, receiving, and inventory functions for kitchen, including selecting purveyors and determining product specifications.
- Oversee purchase and maintenance of kitchen equipment.
- Maintain proper sanitation in production of all foods by staff.
- Determine and achieve specified food cost, labor cost, and sales targets.
- Participate in marketing and promotional activities.

Common Minimum Qualifications: Minimum 3–5 years of pastry cook experience. Food handler's license required. Must have strong baking/pastry, resource management, and leadership skills. Preferred: culinary/pastry degree/diploma, apprenticeship, and/or certification.

JOB TITLE: PASTRY CHEF (RESTAURANT/HOTEL/ CATERER/CLUB/ETC.)

Reports To: Executive Chef

Position Summary: The Pastry Chef oversees all dessert and bakery production for the operation.

Essential Duties:

- Create dessert menu, standardized recipes, and plate presentations for all desserts served.
- Oversee dessert (and other sweets) and bread production to monitor proper quality and quantity of food produced.
- Design/oversee production of chocolate or sugar sculptures.
- Design/oversee production of specialty cake/dessert requests.
- Train and supervise pastry staff.
- Determine pastry kitchen staffing needs and schedule employees accordingly.
- Oversee requisition functions for pastry kitchen and (in some cases) in conjunction with Executive Chef select purveyors and determine product specifications.
- Maintain proper sanitation in production of all foods by staff.
- Assist Executive Chef in achieving food cost, labor cost, and sales targets.
- Participate in marketing and promotional activities.
- Coordinate with the service staff to meet guest needs.

Common Minimum Qualifications: Minimum 3–5 years of pastry cook experience. Food handler's license required. Must have strong baking/pastry, resource management, and leadership skills. Preferred: culinary/pastry degree/diploma, apprenticeship, and/or certification.

JOB TITLE: PASTRY COOK

Reports To: Pastry Chef

Position Summary: The Pastry Cook is responsible for the production of assigned desserts and/or bread to meet guest needs.

Essential Duties:

- Prepare and bake bread needed for guests.
- Set up station and prepare all mise en place/finished product for the operation of dessert station.
- Prepare and plate all guest dessert orders according to the given standardized recipes and plate presentations and within the allowable time frame.
- Bake and/or decorate any specialty cake (or other dessert) requests.

- Coordinate with expediter/pastry chef and other pastry cooks to ensure proper timing of food.
- Maintain proper sanitation in food production.
- Maintain kitchen standards for quality and product yield/waste.
- Store all remaining product properly and clean station at shift's end.

Common Minimum Qualifications: Must have strong baking/pastry skills. Preferred: pastry degree/diploma or apprenticeship.

JOB TITLE: PERSONAL CHEF

Reports To: Clients

Position Summary: The Personal Chef is the sole kitchen employee for a private family-client but generally has multiple clients.

Essential Duties:

- Interview clients to determine needs.
- Create menu options for clients based on their needs.
- Calculate food costs and determine sales prices; create operating budget.
- Purchase and transport all ingredients to clients home.
- Prepare and store all menu items in client's kitchen with instructions for completion.
- Clean client's kitchen completely at the end of production.
- Maintain sanitation in production of all foods.
- Conduct marketing
- Conduct business administration functions.

Common Minimum Qualifications: Food handler's license required. Must have strong culinary and business management skills. Preferred: culinary degree/diploma, apprenticeship, and/or certification.

JOB TITLE: PREP COOK

Reports To: Sous Chef

Position Summary: The Prep Cook is responsible for the production of mise en place to support line cook station operation.

Essential Duties:

- Prepare mise en place for line cook stations as needed.
- Assist line cook in station setup, operation, and close, when needed.
- Maintain proper sanitation in food production.
- Maintain kitchen standards for quality and product yield/waste.
- Store all prepped product properly and clean station at shift's end.

Common Minimum Qualifications: Preferred: culinary skills.

JOB TITLE: PRIVATE CHEF

Reports To: Client

Position Summary: The Private Chef is the sole kitchen employee for a private family-client and generally has only one client.

Essential Duties:

- Interview clients to determine needs.
- Create menus for clients based on their needs.
- Purchase and transport all ingredients to clients home.
- Prepare, plate, and serve all meals and other foods/beverages to client at requested times.
- Clean client's kitchen completely at the end of production.
- Maintain sanitation in production of all foods.

Common Minimum Qualifications: Food handler's license required. Must have strong culinary skills. Preferred: culinary degree/diploma, apprenticeship, and/or certification.

JOB TITLE: PURCHASING MANAGER

Reports To: Executive Chef and/or Food and Beverage Manager

Position Summary: The Purchasing Manager oversees all purchasing and receiving functions for the operation.

Essential Duties:

- Assist with selection of purveyors.
- Receive bids from purveyors to determine most cost-effective options.
- Place orders based upon requisitions from kitchen and dining room.
- Communicate product specifications to purveyors.
- Receive product to verify product specifications, quality, price, and amount.
- Store products according to proper sanitation guidelines.
- Fill requisitions made by kitchens.

Common Minimum Qualifications: Food handler's license required. Must have strong organizational skills. Preferred: culinary product knowledge.

JOB TITLE: RESEARCH CHEF

Reports To: Corporate Manager or Vice-President of Research and Development

Position Summary: The Research Chef is responsible for the creation of new products for mass production and distribution.

Essential Duties:

- Create ideas for new food products for mass production.
- Collaborate with food scientists to develop the new products and make them easily replicable.
- Assist with development of the production (and in some cases, packing) process for new products.
- Calculate production costs and work to minimize costs while maintaining consistent product quality.
- Conduct focus groups on product and adjust accordingly.

Common Minimum Qualifications: Culinary, food science, or similar degree. Minimum 10 years experience in foodservice, primarily in management. Expertise in culinary product development.

JOB TITLE: SITE CHEF (CATERER)

Reports To: Executive Chef/Event Manager

Position Summary: The Site Chef is the highest food production manager at a catering event and is responsible for the completion and presentation of all event food.

Essential Duties:

- Oversee temporary kitchen setup, operation, and break down at event site.
- Verify proper receipt of prepped food from catering commissary.
- Oversee food completion to monitor proper quality and quantity of food produced.
- Oversee food presentation and service/display.
- Maintain proper sanitation in production of all foods by staff.
- Coordinate with event staff to meet guest needs and to ensure proper timing of service.

Common Minimum Qualifications: 2–3 years of kitchen experience. Food handler's license required. Must have strong culinary, resource management, and leadership skills. Preferred: culinary degree/diploma, apprenticeship, and/or certification.

JOB TITLE: SOUS CHEF (RESTAURANT, HOTEL, CLUB, ETC.)

Reports To: Executive Chef (or Chef de Cuisine)

Position Summary: The Sous Chef is responsible for monitoring the food production of the kitchen and executing all directives from the Executive Chef.

Essential Duties:

- Oversee cooks to ensure compliance with standardized recipes and plate presentations for all food.
- Monitor food production to ensure proper quality and quantity of food produced.
- Train and supervise kitchen staff.
- Maintain proper sanitation in production of all foods by staff.
- Execute Executive Chef's instructions to achieve specified food cost, labor cost, and sales targets.
- Coordinate with the service and/or event staff to meet guest needs.
- Ensure all server orders are filled (if serving as expediter); review each plate leaving kitchen to ensure quality compliance; coordinate timing of food to ensure that all guests in a single party get served at once.

Common Minimum Qualifications: 2–5 years of line cook experience. Food handler's license required. Must have strong culinary, resource management, and leadership skills. Preferred: culinary degree/diploma, apprenticeship, and/or certification.

INDEX